FRIEND? OR FOE?

CITY POLICE is the last word on what a big-city cop is really like!

"... a 'cool' book—low-key, unexcited, shunning rhetoric and dramatic conclusions ... filled with absolutely fascinating detail."
—The New York Times

"AN AUTHENTIC AND UNFLINCHING PORTRAIT OF A MODERN URBAN POLICE FORCE."
—James A. Ahern, former Chief of Police, New Haven, Connecticut, author of "Police in Trouble"

CITY POLICE

Jonathan Rubinstein

BALLANTINE BOOKS • NEW YORK

To the memory of my friend, Bill Morris

Library of Congress Catalog Card Number: 72-96317

ISBN 0-345-28409-7

This edition published by arrangement with Farrar, Straus and Giroux

Manufactured in the United States of America

First Ballantine Books Edition: May 1974
Fourth Printing: February 1979

CONTENTS

PREFACE

This is a study of policemen at work. Despite the attention of countless writers, reporters, and scholars, our understanding of what policemen do and what police work is
remains murky. Policemen have long been an important
source of information about city life and local events, but
they have been exploited mainly for stories of drama, action, and scandal. Prior to the invention of the novel and
the newspaper in the eighteenth century, the ballad writers
who were the major reporters of news initiated the practice
of seeking stories in courtrooms and from constables. This
practice has survived every change in the nature of society
and been adapted to each successive development in public
communication to become a fundamental tradition of urban life. This exploitation of policemen has not been confined to hack writers and police reporters. Daniel Defoe,
Henry Fielding (who was also a police magistrate), Honoré
de Balzac, and Charles Dickens profited greatly from listening to famous policemen of their times telling "war stories."
(Dickens used his connections with the police to take guided
tours of London's and New York's underworlds.) But for
them, too, as for the reporter and the scriptwriter, policemen were adventurers into dark places rather than workers
on the city's streets.[1]

Newspapers and television are filled with stories about
the police, but they tell us little of how they go about

[1] On balladeers and their connections with police reporting, see Helen
M. Hughes, *News and the Human Interest Story* (Chicago, University of
Chicago Press, 1940), pp. 9–10, 136–8, 140ff., 157–8, 166ff.; Philip
Collins, *Dickens and Crime*, 2d. ed. London, Macmillan, 1964), pp.
196ff.; and Philip Stead, *Vidocq: A Biography* (New York, Roy, 1954).
A contemporary account of a novelist's use of a policeman is given by
the author of *The French Connection*, Robin Moore, "Why They Got
Popeye," *New York Magazine* (January 31, 1972).

their work. The police reporter is obliged by the demands of his trade to report the dramatic, the unusual, and the bizarre. Since policemen are his main source of stories, he must be careful to preserve his access to them by not writing anything embarrassing or negative. He gets their names into the paper and curries favor by reporting their version of events. In exchange for "good information" on crimes, scandals, and disasters, the police reporter becomes little more than a messenger who carries the police department's story to the public. Only when a newspaper's directors make a decision to "get" the police is the reporter allowed to write embarrassing and damaging reports. But these exposés always emphasize examples of misconduct and criminality to convey the corrupt character of a particular city administration. While they often serve some public purpose, they also distort the reality of what the police do as much as do the little fantasies which the reporter normally writes.

Like every other kind of work, police work generates demands on the people who do it and encourages them to develop skills and techniques for making the job easier. It may be good or bad work, but it is work, and before any judgments of its moral character or suggestions for reforming it can be made, the work itself must be described. This has not been done. The reporter is always an outsider whose access to the police is assured by his pledge not to reveal what he knows of police work. Scholars rarely have either the time or the inclination to seek close ties with the men they want to study.[2] Instead of studying the work, they report on its organization and administration; instead of describing what the men do, they examine their feelings and values. These may be worthwhile things to do, but they cannot be done properly unless the observer understands the nature of the work whose administration he is examining, and the constraints and contingencies which affect the men who do it.

[2] Two notable exceptions are the pioneering effort to describe police work by William A. Westley, *Violence and the Police* (Cambridge, Mass., M.I.T. Press, 1970), written in 1950 as a Ph.D. dissertation at the University of Chicago; and Egon Bittner, "The Police on Skid-Row: A Study of Peace Keeping," *American Sociological Review*, Vol. XXXII (1967), pp. 699–715.

The lack of any systematic description of police work has enhanced the mystery and speculation which shroud the police. We see them on the streets daily but few of us have any concrete notions about what they are up to. We know they are very important but not exactly in what ways. Their presence makes us uneasy but their absence when they are needed arouses our anger and frustration. We expect the police to prevent crime but city people live in fear for their well-being. We harbor suspicions that policemen are brutal, lazy, stupid, corrupt, and sometimes brave; but since we do not know what they routinely do, it is impossible to make any sound judgments of what we read about them in the press or see in the streets. We generalize from single examples because these are all we have. Since we do not know what policemen do, how they operate, or what they think they are doing, we have no choice but to judge them in terms of our private moralities. Most people think of the police as either the brave and resolute preservers of law and order or as enforcers of private interests who are ruled by personal prejudice and greed; the "thin blue line" holding back the forces of disorder and terror or the "damned cops," "fascists," and "pigs." Whether any of these views accurately reflects what the police are is open to question.[3]

From September 1968 to June 1969 I worked as a police reporter for the Philadelphia *Evening Bulletin*. I had the opportunity to meet many policemen, visit the scenes of numerous crimes and accidents, and participate in the process of giving city people their daily fare of local disaster and tragedy. But almost everything I learned was secondhand, and everything I was told was modified by the careful etiquette that dominates the relationships between the police and the people who report their doings. Therefore, when the possibility arose of making a closer examination of policemen at work, I approached the directors of the Philadelphia

[3]An outstanding example of the view which sees the police as a private force is Paul Chevigny, *Police Power* (New York, Pantheon, 1969). This moving account of some people who claimed to be victims of police misconduct presumes to make general statements about the nature of police work and the character of the men who do it on the basis of indirect evidence. The canons of evidence, which the author so rigorously upholds in the courtroom, are allowed to languish in an eloquent defense of persons he feels are "victims of society."

Police Department with a request for direct access to the patrolmen working "the street."

After a lengthy discussion of my purposes and objectives, I was given permission on the condition that I not report anything I saw to the press and that I not name or directly quote anyone other than from the public record. I added the additional condition that under no circumstances would I report anything I saw to the commissioner, his subordinates, or any other agency. In September 1969 I entered the Philadelphia Police Academy and upon my graduation was allowed to join a patrol unit. Until September 1970 I worked a regular six-day tour followed by two days off in several districts of my personal choice and with a number of special patrol units. From September 1970 until the end of the summer of 1971, I continued to work on the street during weekends and on special occasions with men whom I had come to know particularly well.

Legal complications prevented me from becoming a sworn police officer, although I had fulfilled all the requirements at the academy. But I was permitted to go on the street as an armed observer. Since I worked mostly with uniformed policemen but had to wear plainclothes, I carefully chose some that would give me the appearance of a detective or a superior officer. Many of the men I worked with knew that I was not a policeman (though some believed I was a federal agent or an undercover police operative), but policemen from other units and districts whom we encountered in the course of work did not. Only on a few occasions did my companions inform these men of my identity. On no occasion did any policeman I worked with inform a private citizen of my status in my presence and only once did anyone question whether I was a police officer.

There is no way of judging exactly how my presence affected the manner and actions of my companions. I was keenly aware of my apartness and sought to limit it by locating myself in their midst so that the contingencies of the work would compel them to ignore me or even, in spite of reservations, to count on my being there. I also relied upon the cumulative effect of familiarity to weaken defenses against my presence. Therefore, I never spent less than two months with any unit and was always careful to establish my relationships with the supervisors before going on patrol with the men.

I was permitted to select the men with whom I wanted to ride. I chose mainly those men who worked alone so that I did not have to overcome the stigma of riding in the back seat, which is reserved for prisoners and guests. Riding in the front seat also left open the possibility of being treated as a rookie, using the police radio, and doing the paper work. Before selecting a few men in each unit with whom I worked regularly, I spent time with a large number, acquiring knowledge of their work habits and their relationships with other policemen. In this manner I sought to avoid working with anyone who was excluded from close ties with his own colleagues, a situation which would have guaranteed my distance from the men and their work. There were men who were reluctant to have me along (although none ever refused) and others who were eager for me to join them, but generally I worked only with those men who willingly accepted me as a worker and not just as a passenger. Everywhere I went there were men who granted me their company and introduced me to the police craft by allowing me to share their work.

I have dispensed with the usual scholarly convention of giving the place where I conducted my research a pseudonym, because I believe the question of evidence is crucial in discussing an occupation, such as policing, which is universally practiced but always localistic in character. Since I draw inferences and offer judgments about work and behavior which extend far beyond the city limits of Philadelphia, I think it is important that the reader know the origins of my evidence. All names of persons and streets as well as district and car numbers have been altered to preserve the anonymity of my companions. Only individuals with personal knowledge of the events discussed will recognize when and where they occurred. I have not hesitated to make these changes since they have no bearing on the validity of the evidence presented and aid in the fulfillment of my obligations to those who allowed me to watch them work.

I employed no recording devices and took no notes during working hours but wrote out my observations at the conclusion of each day's work. Unless specifically attributed, every quotation is taken directly from my field notes and is as accurate as my memory and ear allowed. I have not eliminated the profanity in the language because it is an important part of policemen's work talk. I have made no effort to capture the inflections of ethnic speech, although I have on occasion identified people by their race, when I felt this information contributed to an understanding of the issues under discussion.

Since I have openly named the place where I conducted my research, a few comments are in order about the access I was permitted to enjoy in an organization which is reputed by some to be secretive, conspiratorial, and even criminal. Throughout my entire stay in the Philadelphia Police Department I was never denied a single request. Despite a number of incidents in my presence, considerable unrest in the city, and a delicate political situation, no effort was made to restrict my observations or to curtail my work. My only wish was to be left alone as much as possible with the men who do police work and I could not have been given greater freedom or been more generously treated. The point I want to make is that I was granted unrestricted freedom of inquiry by an agency which some people judge to be committed to stifling dissent and diversity of opinion. And if this statement itself sounds like the plea of someone who has been taken in by an institution and speaks in the interests of its public relations, then what follows must serve as the only denial.

ACKNOWLEDGMENTS

It is embarrassing to recall how much help I required in completing this book, but that feeling is mitigated by the recollection of the generosity that so many people showed me. It is a pleasure for me to record my thanks to them here. Since I have not always taken their advice, none of them can in any way be held accountable for anything that I have written.

It is commonplace to thank one's wife last, if earnestly, for her support. In this instance, however, it is not too much to say that without the remarkable goodwill of Naomi Peskin Rubinstein, this book would not have been written. Her dignity and kindness reduced the burdens of doing field work. She listened with much more than patience to many hours of sometimes unpleasant talk without compromising her private vision of how life is to be lived.

A detailed accounting of my obligations to Erving Goffman would require an additional volume. I have acknowledged some of the lesser ones in several footnotes. He introduced me to the idea of ethnography and demonstrated in unique ways some of the techniques of field work. He made me aware of the Chicago school of sociology, in particular the writings of Robert E. Park, Everett C. Hughes, and W. Lloyd Warner. By example and comment, he sought to ease my passage past some of the pitfalls inherent in doing field work. I could not have had a more generous intellectual guide. After doing all of these things, he gave much of his time to a rigorous criticism of the entire first draft. His comments and suggestions have improved almost every page of this book.

The Honorable Frank L. Rizzo, the former Commissioner of Police of the City of Philadelphia, gave me permission to pursue my research as I saw fit, without ever exercising any restraint on my investigations.

Many policemen enriched my understanding of city life by allowing me to accompany them while they did their work. I shall always be grateful to them, and while I cannot publicly thank them individually, I can acknowledge that much of whatever merit this work has is due to their generosity.

Financial support from several institutions made it possible for me to devote all of my time to the completion of this book. An initial grant from the National Institute of Law Enforcement and Criminal Justice (NI-030), a branch of the Law Enforcement Assistance Agency, gave me the freedom to pursue my field work unhindered. I would like to thank Mr. Henry Ruth, the former director of the Institute for the support which he gave me at a time when there was nothing concrete to justify it.

Several additional grants made it possible for me to complete this work. The Center for Urban Ethnography at the University of Pennsylvania supported me while I was writing full time. Its director, John Szwed, is a cherished colleague whose advice and argument have greatly enriched my understanding of urban anthropology. I would also like to thank Lloyd Ohlin and James Vorenberg, directors of the Center for Criminal Justice at the Harvard Law School for providing me with a Russell Sage Fellowship, which allowed me to complete this work. They also permitted me to conduct an informal graduate seminar on policing during the 1972 spring semester at Harvard which was of considerable help to me during the final stages of the writing. Professor Ohlin and the other participants offered me much helpful advice and criticism.

William B. Dickinson, executive editor of the Philadelphia *Evening Bulletin*, provided me with a job when I needed one. During the years I have known him, he has shown me many acts of personal kindness when they counted, and his friendship has meant a great deal to me. Joan Younger Dickinson went far beyond any requirements of friendship when she read all of the initial scribblings I was struggling to turn into a draft. The gentle manner in which she expressed stern and needed criticism was an act of kindness that cannot be fully acknowledged. Howard Darmstadter read the entire manuscript and his scrupulous, reasoned criticisms spared me from suffering some terrible embarrassments.

I would also like to thank my editors, Henry Robbins, Tom Lewis, and Lynn Warshow, for the considerable time and informed care that they gave to improving this book.

There are simply too many other people to thank individually without preparing a lengthy catalogue of my obligations; but I would like to thank the following particularly: Steven Breyer, Edward J. Epstein, Fred Freed, Randy Gallistel, Tom Goffman, Phil Heymann, Russell Leaf; Lynn Nesbit, Dan Rose, John Schrecker, Gino and Nina Gordon Segre, Lionel Tiger, Robert Warshaw, and James Q. Wilson.

Part One

POLICING
THE
CITY

CHAPTER ONE

Origins

The preservation of public order in towns, the protection of property, and the safekeeping of good manners and morals have never been left to chance or to the whims of city people. Long before city police, as we know them, were first established in London in the nineteenth century, townspeople were subjected to the scrutiny either of the military or of local property owners who were obliged to serve terms as watchmen. Their principal concern was to protect the walls and gates which continued to enclose most English and European towns until the sixteenth century, but they also had obligations to police the manners and public behavior of those who lived in the cities.[1] The English constables were charged generally with "maintaining the King's Peace" and "for the better preventing that nothing be done against the Peace any of these officers aforesaid may take (or arrest) suspected persons which walk in the night, and sleepe in the day: or which do haunt any house, where is suspicion of bawdie. . . . Any of these Officers may also arrest such strange persons as do walk abroad in the night."[2] During the day the constables and the watchmen they supervised had the responsibility of enforcing regulations designed to protect the towns from the very real dangers of plague and fire as well as commercial fraud, "in all which, be it matter of corrupting

[1] On the origins of the English police, see W. L. Melville Lee, *A History of Police in England* (London, Methuen, 1901). On the police in London, Donald Rumbelow, *I Spy Blue: The Police and Crime in the City of London* (London, Macmillan, 1971), pp. 25–7.

[2] William Lambard, *The Duties of Constables, Borsholders, Tythingmen . . .* (London, Company of Stationers, 1610), p. 12.

air, water or victuals, stopping, straitening, or indangering of passages, or general deceits, in weights, measures, sizes or counterfeiting wares and things vendible. . . ."[3]

London watchmen were armed with clubs and swords and occasionally they did battle with the gangs of marauding toughs who roamed the darkened streets, but generally they did not patrol their territories in search of suspicious persons. Each city ward appointed its own constables and watchmen and there was no coordination of their efforts. The watchmen wore no uniforms and were distinguished only by the lanterns they carried and their staffs. They stayed at fixed posts, frequently congregating together for comfort and safety. Each citizen was ultimately responsible for his own security and everyone who could afford it lived in a stout house closely guarded by servants, who acted as bodyguards for their masters when they went out of their houses. In the sixteenth century the watchmen were freed of their obligations to maintain a fire watch by the appointment of "bellmen," who walked the streets carrying a "link" (a large torch), calling the time as they tolled their bells, but this did nothing to improve the effectiveness of the "watch and ward" in preventing crimes. The obligation to serve as a watchman or a constable which had been customary since before the Norman invasion was beginning to weaken as the city grew larger and the threat of external attack lessened. More and more property owners sought to evade their service by hiring substitutes to serve for them. Inevitably, the wealthiest withdrew first, and gradually what had been a voluntary service organized by property owners to protect what they had became a paid service employing poor and often aged men.[4]

During the sixteenth and seventeenth centuries, there was no question in the minds of Londoners that they lived in a dangerous place which was ill-protected by their watchmen. The destruction of the city wall and the gates allowed them to give all their attention to the town and its people, but this did not lead to any improvement. The watchmen gen-

[3]Francis Bacon, "The Answers to Questions . . . Touching the Office of Constable," *The Works of Francis Bacon*, Vol. VII, J. Spedding, R. L. Ellis, and D. D. Heath, eds. (London, Longmans, 1858), p. 753.
[4]Rumbelow, pp. 36ff., 84.

erally were considered to be incompetent and cowardly. By the mid-seventeenth century they had acquired the derisive name of "Charlies." It was a common sport of rich young men of the time to taunt and terrorize them, to wreck the watchhouses, and occasionally to murder the watchmen. The large rattles they carried to signal for help were little comfort since they knew their colleagues were not dependable; the watchmen spent a good deal of their time discreetly concealed from the public. Whether people were troubled by these conditions is unclear, but there was no public effort to make any improvements. The city remained dark at night and a regulation requiring householders to place a candle on the street from darkness to midnight during the winter months was not enforced.[5] The well-off continued to live in carefully guarded houses and went about armed. No woman of "quality" went on the street unaccompanied by a servant. As for the poor, who were then as now the principal victims of crimes, nobody cared. This indifference changed with the invention of gin.

Until "geneva," as it was then called, was invented in the seventeenth century by a Dutch chemist, only the rich regularly drank the powerful and expensive brandies which were the only kind of hard liquor available.[6] Most people drank beer, ale, and wine, which could produce drunkenness but hardly had the potency of strong drink. Their near-monopoly on hard liquor may help to explain the attachment of the rich to brawling, fighting, and killing, habits which most people today associate exclusively with the poor. Gin democratized drunkenness and brought new terrors to London and then to all cities. Henry Fielding wrote in his *Enquiry into the Causes of the Late Increase of Robbers* (1751), one of the first (and certainly the best written) essays in criminology,

[5]Walter Besant, *London in the Eighteenth Century* (London, Adam & Charles Black, 1903), pp. 92–3; George Rudé, *Hanoverian London, 1714–1808* (Berkeley, University of California Press, 1971), pp. 134–5.

[6]The distillation of alcohol from grain may have originated in Scotland many centuries before the invention of gin but Scotch whiskey was consumed only locally. It was not introduced into England until the mid-eighteenth century. Berton Roueché, *Alcohol* (New York, Grove Press, 1962), pp. 30–2.

A new kind of drunkenness, unknown to our ancestors, is lately sprung up amongst us, and which if not put a stop to, will infallibly destroy a great part of the inferior people. The drunkenness I here intend is . . . by this Poison called Gin . . . the principal sustenance (if it may be so called) of more than a hundred thousand People in this Metropolis.

The agricultural interests which dominated the House of Commons saw in gin the opportunity to dispose profitably of the grain surpluses which the country produced and every encouragement was given to its manufacture. Within a few decades, London was awash in an orgy of drinking which has probably not been matched in history. By 1725 there were more than seven thousand gin shops in London and drink was sold as a sideline by numerous shopkeepers and peddlers. For a penny anyone could drink all day in any "flash house" and get a straw pallet in a back room to sleep it off. The sale of gin (mainly in London) rose from three and one-half million gallons in 1727 to almost six and one-half million gallons in 1735 and then soared to over eight million in 1743. Public drunkenness became a commonplace sight, and drink-crazed mobs often roamed through the city. The streets of London, never safe, were now filled with people whose behavior was unpredictable and occasionally quite violent. Not surprisingly, the gin craze was accompanied by a great rise in violent crimes and theft.[7]

The government responded to the increase in crime and disorder by improving street lighting, hiring more watchmen, and greatly increasing the severity of punishment for all kinds of crimes. People privately responded by arming themselves with pistols and avoiding the streets at night unless accompanied by a "linkman," a private guard who carried a sword and a large torch to light the way. The rich, who until this time continued to live among the poor, began to move away, stimulating the residential segregation of people

[7]Rudé, p. 91; J. L. & B. Hammond, "Poverty, Crime and Philanthropy," *Johnson's England: An Account of the Life and Manners of His Age*, Vol. I (London, Oxford University Press, 1952), p. 312; M. Dorothy George, *London Life in the Eighteenth Century* (New York, Capricorn Books, 1965, originally published in 1925), pp. 27–42.

by income which dominates most cities today. It was widely recognized that the uncontrolled consumption of gin could not be allowed to continue, and the House of Commons made an effort to eradicate what had come to be seen as an evil which threatened public order. In 1736 a law was passed requiring every gin seller and manufacturer to purchase a license for a fee set so high it was hoped that most gin shops would have to close. To enforce this law, the government offered a reward to every informer who gave information which led to the successful prosecution of an unlicensed retailer or distiller. The law did not stanch the flow of gin, but it did greatly increase the corruption of the constables who had always proven themselves willing to exploit their duties for graft.[8]

The London watchmen had always been responsible for regulating the morals of townspeople, and this had provided some of them with a chance to extort money and accept payoffs. Any person suspected of maintaining a house of ill repute (what is called in contemporary law a "disorderly house") could be lawfully harassed and threatened by the watchmen. Failing a reformation of the owner's manners (or a bribe), the watch was empowered to break open the house, remove all the windows and doors, and make it uninhabitable. These Draconian measures did not discourage prostitution, and in the thirteenth century the city sought to regulate the trade by confining all whores to the "stews of Southwark," the steam baths which were situated across the Thames River from the city. While this measure did not eliminate prostitution, it made it easier for some city magistrates to collect a rake-off for protecting the bathhouses; it also contributed substantially to the establishment of Southwark as a center for criminal activity, which it remained into the nineteenth century.

The watchmen were also responsible for enforcing Sabbath regulations and religious laws, another source of considerable petty cash for them. It was forbidden, for example, to bring meat into London during Lent and watchmen were

[8]George, pp. 33–5; Rudé, pp. 136–7; Patrick Pringle, *Memoirs of a Bow Street Runner by Henry Goddard* (New York, Morrow, n.d.), pp. 34–5.

set at the gates to confiscate the smuggled goods. This meat was then sold and the proceeds dedicated to the support of the city's hospitals and jails. In 1591 the Lord Mayor recommended that the watchmen be allowed to keep half the meat they found in order to stimulate their sense of obligation and to dissuade them from taking bribes.[9]

There had been complaints in the seventeenth century that many constables were employed in the liquor trade, making it impossible for them honestly to enforce the regulations governing taverns and inns. Their involvement in the liquor business increased greatly in the eighteenth century, and the experiment introduced by the Gin Act of 1736 vastly expanded their opportunities for graft. Many constables became coal merchants and vendors of food, which they sold at inflated prices to publicans who could ill afford to alienate them. The law also made betrayal a commonplace occurrence. In many neighborhoods informers were pursued, beaten, and occasionally murdered by enraged mobs, and the constables were either unwilling or unable to protect them. During the seven years the Gin Act was in force, there were almost ten thousand prosecutions for violations of its provisions in London. Despite the enormous enthusiasm of informers, only three licenses under the Gin Act were sold in the city, and there was no reduction in the consumption of gin.[1]

The government wisely abandoned its efforts to eradicate drinking and instead successfully reduced the rate of consumption over a period of several decades by increasing taxation to raise the price of gin and by easing the licensing system. Although the gin craze abated, the fear of crime and the belief that it continued to increase did not. Members of Parliament continued to be accompanied to and from sessions by linkmen, and bulletproof coaches were advertised to thwart the highwaymen who plagued travelers on the roads to the city. In 1776 the Lord Mayor of London was robbed at gunpoint, and within the decade two of England's

[9]Rumbelow, pp. 33–5; Lee, pp. 73f.; David J. Johnson, *Southwark and the City* (London, Oxford University Press, 1969), pp. 64–7.
[1]George, pp. 301, 398; Rumbelow, pp. 48–9, 86; Patrick Pringle, *Hue and Cry* (New York, Morrow, 1955); Patrick Pringle, *The Thief Takers* (London, Methuen, 1958), pp. 104–6.

great nobles, the Duke of York and the Prince of Wales, were mugged as they walked in the city during the day. In the same period, the Great Seal of England was stolen from the house of the Lord Chancellor and melted down for the silver. There was a growing demand for protection, and private societies for the enforcement of the law flourished. Parliament paid rewards to any man who successfully prosecuted a criminal and private "thief-takers" prospered, as did those who were hired by religious organizations. At mid-century, Henry Fielding, who earned his living as a magistrate, proposed that the watch-and-ward system be centralized and constables organized to patrol the streets rather than remaining at their watch boxes. For a brief time he organized a mounted patrol to guard the highways. It languished when he died, but for the first time the idea of a mobile police had been advanced.[2]

In addition to the changes in the character of street life caused by the revolution in drinking, the cities were also the scene of great mob riots. The preservation of order was the responsibility of the constables and the watchmen who were no more able to control the mobs than they were able to catch burglars. Frequently the magistrates had to read the Riot Act and call out the military (garrisoned in all the principal towns), who retained the ultimate responsibility for maintaining the royal peace. The violent tactics of the soldiers encouraged the idea of a non-military force capable of controlling the population, but it did not hasten the arrival of the centralized police. The Gordon Riots of 1780 produced the greatest mob violence in the history of London (and the most brutal military response) but it was not until almost another half century had passed that the police were established. The wealthy citizens who controlled the constables in their wards did not want to relinquish their perquisites to a central authority who might abuse this extension of power to alter the traditional character of English government. The active supporters of the idea of a preventive police, as it was called, urged its creation as the only possible way to

[2]Christopher Hibbert, *The Roots of Evil* (Boston, Little, Brown, 1963), pp. 87–9; Pringle, *Hue and Cry*, pp. 53–6; Rudé, p. 97; Gerald Howson, *Thief-Taker General: The Rise and Fall of Jonathan Wild* (London, Macmillan, 1970) for an introduction to the private prosecution system.

eliminate crime and to reform what was considered a barbaric penal code. Jeremy Bentham, Patrick Colquhoun, and Edwin Chadwick, the principal originators of the idea of a centralized police, along with Fielding, all argued that a police force which constantly patrolled the city would greatly reduce and ultimately eliminate most crime. This would encourage Parliament to treat prisoners in a humane fashion and eliminate the harsh punishments which were imposed for even petty crimes. The police were viewed as a civilizing instrument whose effort and example would make possible more harmonious relations among city people.[3]

The novelty of the preventive police—the New Police, as the Metropolitan Police of London established in 1829 were called—resided in the territorial character of their strategy and organization. For the first time the entire city was to be continuously patrolled by men who were assigned specific territories and whose courses (or beats) were prescribed by their superiors.[4] The experience with the much less ambitious watch and ward had demonstrated clearly that without strict supervision there was no guarantee that the patrolmen, unless they were highly motivated men of great dedication, would actually perform their duties. The founders of the police sought to inspire the men by imposing the principles of military organization and service on what had always been a civilian force.

The Duke of Wellington was then the Prime Minister of England and the British Army was at the height of its fame. It was the foremost model of bureaucratic organization in its time; administrators did not know of any other which could

---

[3]On the reform movement, see Leon Radzinowicz, *A History of English Criminal Law,* Vol. I, *The Movement for Reform* (London, Stevens, 1948); Allan Silver, "The Demand for Order in Civil Society," *The Police: Six Sociological Essays,* David Bordua, ed. (New York, John Wiley, 1967), pp. 1–24.

[4]Hangchow, the capital of the Chinese empire in the thirteenth century and a city of over one million people, had a highly developed police service which regularly patrolled the city. Groups of five soldiers were billeted at intervals of three hundred yards throughout the city and were responsible for enforcing the curfew, maintaining the peace, and aiding the fire service in keeping the watch. Jacques Gernet, *Daily Life in China on the Eve of the Mongol Invasion, 1250–1276* (New York, Macmillan, 1962), pp. 35–6. I am grateful to John Schrecker for pointing this out to me.

produce discipline, strict obedience to orders, and loyalty. But as the first commissioner of the police, Colonel Charles Rowan, discovered on his first day, the policeman is not a soldier. He spent months carefully selecting candidates, then held an inaugural parade-ground ceremony. It was a rainy day and many of the constables arrived bearing umbrellas. Quite a few were unable to stand at attention because they had been celebrating the historic occasion by getting drunk. Rowan's first general regulation forbade any man to carry an umbrella with him on duty; the second forbade drinking. Umbrellas never again posed a serious problem. The military enforced discipline by imposing severe punishments for even minor infractions, but the police could not whip delinquent constables. The only way to punish them was by firing them from the job. In the first years the London police discharged more than one third of the force annually. Rowan became so discouraged that he proposed the recruitment of policemen directly from the ranks of the cavalry regiments, the elite of the military.[5]

Despite the defects of the New Police, their organization and principles quickly attracted attention abroad, mainly in America, where the policing of the towns had closely followed the English pattern. The voluntary character of the watch and ward was entirely absent, because it was no longer an important feature of the English system when the American police were being established, but the watchmen were hired to serve in a specific ward rather than in the town at large. They also guarded the walls and gates and maintained a fire watch. Like their English counterparts, they did not patrol their territories regularly with the purpose of preventing crime and capturing suspects. Although they carried arms, they wore no uniforms and bore no resemblance to the militia. In addition to maintaining the peace, they were also required to police the morals and manners of their neighbors. They were responsible for enforcing liquor laws and controlling the prostitution which was common in most

[5]Belton Cobb, *The First Detectives* (London, Faber & Faber, 1957), pp. 28–58; Charles Reith, *British Police and the Democratic Ideal* (London, Oxford, 1943), pp. 193–5; F. C. Mather, *Public Order in the Age of the Chartists* (Manchester, Manchester University Press, 1959), p. 97.

towns. They, too, were held in low regard by most people, and they were not very successful in rooting out vice or preventing crime. The widespread dissatisfaction with the existing arrangements combined with the admiration of British institutions to produce a rapid introduction of the New Police into America.[6]

Between 1830 and the Civil War, every important American town adopted the territorial organization and strategy of the preventive police. In Boston, New York, Brooklyn, and Philadelphia, the local watch committees were abolished and a central police force established. The distinctions between the day police and the night police which had been imported from England were abolished. Everywhere the men strenuously objected to wearing uniforms. It was argued that a uniform was a kind of livery which demeaned the freedom and equality of those who had to wear it, but these objections were overridden by the argument that the discipline and dignity required of policemen made the uniform a necessity. But Americans also learned that the uniform was not sufficient to assure the proper bearing of the men who wore it. The continuous recurrence of scandal and complaints about his ineffectiveness offer bleak testimony that despite his uniform, a police officer is not a soldier. But people refuse to see him in any other way.[7]

A soldier works in a group whose success is dependent upon the cooperation of its members. He is under the direct supervision of superiors who can punish him if he fails to recognize that his performance is measured by the contribution he makes to the group's work. He is also influenced by the pressure exerted on him directly by his colleagues, his buddies, who are working alongside him. The territorial strategy of policing makes the patrolman a solitary worker

[6]On early American police, see Selden D. Bacon, *The Early Development of American Municipal Police*. Unpublished Ph. D. dissertation, Yale University, 1939; Edwin Powers, *Crime and Punishment in Early Massachusetts, 1620–1692* (Boston, Beacon Press, 1966), pp. 424–9; David H. Flaherty, "Law and the Enforcement of Morals in Early America," *Perspectives in American History*, Vol. V (1971), pp. 203–53.

[7]James F. Richardson, *The New York Police* (New York, Oxford University Press, 1970), Chap. II, 64–5; Roger Lane, *Policing the City: Boston, 1822–1885* (Cambridge, Mass., Harvard University Press, 1967), Chaps. III-IV, 104–5.

who is dependent mainly on his personal skills and judgment. His colleagues offer him support and information, they sometimes come to his aid, but he does not often work with them. The policeman also has an occupational interest in concealing things which he knows from others, even from his closest colleagues. Moreover, the policeman, unlike the soldier, leaves his work and his colleagues behind him at the end of each day and resumes his private life.[8]

The effort to inspire loyalty and a sense of duty in policemen by military discipline has never worked well, although every department uses the initial training period to instill some kind of fear into the recruits and maintains a bulky book of regulations employed to threaten, punish, and dismiss the recalcitrant, the lazy, and the untrustworthy. The failure of this solution should not mask the importance of a problem which plagues every department and inspires tensions between policemen and the people they regulate. A policeman has considerable power and authority. He cannot be paid enough to assure his honesty, loyalty, and bravery. Policemen do not steal because they feel they are underpaid, nor can men be inspired to bravery and high risk simply by offering them a few dollars more.

The preventive strategy of the New Police created severe organizational problems which were greatly complicated by the failure of the new system to achieve the elimination of city crime. Since it was believed that continuous patrol offered the best chance for repressing crime, police administrators have continued to search for ways of making their men more effective and productive. A policeman is obviously most effective at the specific point where he physically locates himself, watching the people around him and being seen by those who might be contemplating criminal acts. He is least effective when he is farthest from the people and places dependent on him for protection. Whether he is walking a beat or riding in a patrol car, the problem remains the same: how can his deterrent power be most effectively employed? Any decision which requires the patrolman to give one part of

[8]Some of the distinctions between the policeman and the soldier are discussed in James Q. Wilson, *Varieties of Police Behavior* (Cambridge, Mass., Harvard University Press, 1968), p. 79.

his territory more attention than others deprives some of the people dependent on him of an equal share of his usefulness. There is no way of knowing exactly whether one form of patrol is more effective than another, and while the police use as a measure of their utility the numbers of arrests they make and the numbers of reported crimes they "clear," there is no proof that this is an accurate way of assessing the performance of policemen. It is not surprising, therefore, that despite the various names given to different police tactics, they continue to rely on the basic strategy initiated by Henry Fielding and Colonel Rowan, requiring each man to patrol his entire area continuously.

In order to make supervision easier, Rowan ordered each man to walk a prescribed route at a specific pace so that his supervisor could know where he was at any time. This was also beneficial to anyone interested in evading the constable's attention and was soon abandoned. But if the men responsible for assuring the correct performance of the patrolmen did not know exactly where they were, how could they properly supervise them? And how could a citizen in need of a policeman find him promptly?

The policeman was required by the nature of his work to be resourceful, eager, and occasionally aggressive, but the isolation imposed on him by the strategy of his employers bred caution and sometimes fear. In order to maintain his morale and assure that he continued to perform his work confidently and effectively, a method had to be found for him to signal his distress to colleagues. Otherwise, the men would huddle together for comfort and security, as had the watchmen. The police were also required to act in a coordinated fashion to put down riots, but how were the men to be assembled if they were scattered throughout the city? These problems of the proper distribution of manpower, supervision, and morale persist despite the continuous exploitation of new developments in communications and transportation during the last 150 years.[9]

[9]In some countries the police have sought to resolve the problems of combining regular service with riot duty by creating special units which are barracked and trained for riot work. While these units are under police command, there is nothing in their training, tactics, or weaponry which distinguishes them from the military. David H. Bayley, *The Police*

When city police were first established, the only way contact could be maintained was in face-to-face meetings or by messengers. In London a special deputy to the commissioner rode on horseback each morning to inspect every station and to confer with the commanders. In Philadelphia and Brooklyn it was customary for the captains to meet every morning with their commissioner before proceeding to their districts. This was the only opportunity they had to discuss events, coordinate policy, and receive orders.[1] If additional men were required in one part of the city, messengers had to be sent to the districts to alert the commanders. Since there was no assurance that the necessary men could be rounded up, most police departments maintained a reserve force which was required to spend its off-duty hours barracked in special dormitories located in the district station houses.

Once the men were dismissed from roll call, their supervisors had no certain way of controlling what they did during their tour of work. The sergeants, who were called roundsmen in Philadelphia and Brooklyn during the early nineteenth century, frequently assigned men "meets," prearranged times and places where the supervisors could visually check on them. The only way a roundsman had of discovering what his men were doing was to follow them around and make inquiries among the people who lived and worked on the beats. If he wanted to watch a man at work, he could, and frequently did, accompany him, but this obliged him to neglect other duties. The men were also isolated from each other, and their only way of attracting attention in moments of distress was by swinging the large rattles which city policemen had been carrying since the sixteenth century.

During the 1850's, the establishment of telegraph networks first linked police headquarters directly with their districts, making unnecessary the daily morning meetings be-

---

and Political Development in India (Princeton, N. J., Princeton University Press, 1969), Chap. I; Philip Stead, The Police of Paris (London, Staples, 1951).

[1]Cobb, pp. 41–2; William E. S. Fales, Brooklyn's Guardians (Brooklyn, n.p., 1887), p. 96; A. O. Sprogle, Philadelphia Police: Past and Present (Philadelphia, n.p., 1887), pp. 73ff.

tween the captains and the commissioner. Reserve platoons continued to be barracked because the department had no way of quickly assembling men who were at home or on the street. Several decades later, a modified telegraph system was invented which linked the patrolman directly to his station. The fire-alarm system that had been introduced in Boston was adapted for police use and the call box became a feature on city street corners. Since it was impractical to teach every man Morse code, the boxes were outfitted with a simple lever which signaled the station that the officer (or whoever pulled the lever) was at his post. A bell system was soon added that enabled the patrolman to tell his district by means of a few simple signals whether he needed an ambulance, a "slow wagon" for routine duties, or a "fast wagon" for emergencies. The wagons and horses were kept at the district stations and did not go on patrol because the telegraph system was only a one-way communication system and had no mobility.[2]

The introduction of the telephone into the call box in 1880 made it a genuine two-way communication system, greatly improving the contact between the patrolmen and their station house and increasing the ability of supervisors to know what the men were doing. A "pulling system" was devised which obliged each man to contact his district every hour. If there were any messages for him, the operations clerk gave him a special signal to open the locked inner box containing the telephone. This double-box system reserved part of the equipment for exclusive police use, leaving the outer part for the public, since people still had no sure way of gaining the quick attention of the police. Local business people were given keys that activated an emergency signal at the station house. A wagon or men from the reserve squad could then be dispatched directly to the area, a system that considerably improved the protection given to merchants and bankers. Private burglar alarms which were first used in the

[2]The information in this paragraph and some of what follows is adapted from V. A. Leonard, *Police Communications Systems* (Berkeley, University of California, 1938), Chap. I. An excellent account of the early use of the police telegraph is in James McCague, *The Second Rebellion: The New York City Draft Riots of 1863* (New York, Dial Press, 1968).

1860's began to be popular and these replaced the less efficient alarm service provided by the corner boxes. But some local business people were allowed to retain keys so they could call the stations for help.[3]

The drawback of the pull system was that it did not allow for any of the contingencies which are part of police work. The patrolman could make unscheduled contact with his station if he could get to the box, but there was no way for the station to make emergency contact with him. A variety of recall systems were devised and built into the call boxes. Horns, colored lights, and bells activated by a signal from the station house were supposed to attract a patrolman to his box for special messages. The horns conflicted with normal traffic sounds, and the lights were very difficult to distinguish during the day. When the systems did function properly, they usually attracted large crowds along with the officer.

The pulling system greatly improved the ability of sergeants to supervise their men, but it did not eliminate the basic problem. It was possible to neutralize the system, and the easily learned tricks were quickly acquired by the men. Like all methods of evasion, the most effective was the simplest. One officer was given the keys to the boxes, and while he walked the district "pulling" on schedule, the others were free to do as they pleased. The transformation from signal boxes to telephone contact required that the collusion be extended to the men inside the station house who worked the phones. But the technology also provided the men with new means of evasion if they could not gain the cooperation of their operators. Because of the prohibitive costs of wiring each box individually, the phones were hooked in series, so that if one were left off the hook, the entire line was interrupted. A squad of men could agree to unhook a phone at the far end of their territory, putting the entire network out of service. Even under normal circumstances, the call boxes required substantial maintenance (they often shorted out in the rain), and this was increased by deliberate sabotage. It was not uncommon for some men to cut the wires or short

[3]David J. Bordua and Albert J. Reiss, Jr., "Command, Control, and Charisma: Reflections on Police Bureaucracy," *American Journal of Sociology*, Vol. LXXII (1966), p. 69.

them out by splashing water on the cables. Frequently the call boxes acted as receivers, picking up radio signals from the local stations that were established in the 1920's. Old-timers recall that some of these boxes were avidly protected from sabotage by local residents and patrolmen who did not have their own radios.

The new communications technology did have beneficial influences on some aspects of police organization. The spread of the call boxes and the widening distribution of telephones enabled the police to abolish reserve platoons. This made it possible to close down the dormitories and kitchens; the station houses built after 1900 were generally much smaller and less elaborate than earlier police stations.

The weaknesses of the new system obliged the supervisors to continue what had already become an acknowledged "game" in police work—finding your men. Some departments sought to aid their sergeants by maximizing the number of "straight beats," which required an officer to walk along a single street for a number of blocks, checking only the alleys on either side. The patrolman's absence from a beat which could be observed by standing in the middle of the street and looking its length was not easy to explain; it was hoped that this would deter men from seeking out their "holes," favored places used for hiding and resting. But these straight beats required hiring additional men for which few cities were willing to pay. Some supervisors informally acknowledged the existence of holes, since this made it easier for them to find someone when he was needed in a hurry. Barber shops were frequently favored as "legitimate" holes because they allowed the patrolmen to sit comfortably and to observe the street. Friendly barbers willingly gave up their keys to regular "beatmen" in exchange for the protection of their property and the little favors which these acts of friendship and solidarity guaranteed. These practices persist in those places where the police continue to walk.[4]

[4]Bruce Smith, Jr., *Police Systems in the United States* (New York, Harper & Row, 1960), pp. 243–4. In New York City, holes are called "coops." Gene Radano, *Walking the Beat* (Cleveland, World, 1968), p. 1. In many neighborhoods barber shops used to be local centers of petty gambling which may have been an inducement to barbers to treat policemen with kindness. William F. Whyte, *Street Corner Society*, 2d. ed. (Chicago, University of Chicago Press, 1955), pp. 135ff.

Sergeants developed methods for discovering unacknowledged hiding places and for surprising their men to discourage unauthorized loafing. A sergeant could order a man to meet him night after night at a specific place. Arriving early, he could watch from a concealed place the direction of the man's approach. Each day he would pick the man up a bit closer to his hole, or if he was skillful and the patrolman incautious, he might follow him. These tactics were well known to experienced men and encouraged them to develop the habit of constantly scanning their entire surroundings as they walked along. It is difficult to follow a policeman even when he is doing his normal duties. The sergeants often used these meets as a warning signal, tacitly informing a man that he was not really getting away with anything. In winter, men who had not been working were loath to allow their sergeant to approach them closely. Some supervisors would put their arm about a man's shoulder in a friendly fashion and "accidentally" touch his tin badge, whose temperature would reveal immediately whether the man had been walking his beat or had just come outside. Some men wore two badges or left their badge outside when they went inside, but this was risky in many neighborhoods.

The call box and the pull system greatly improved the contact between headquarters and the districts, and between the station and the men in the street, but it did not solve the basic problems of supervision, morale, and public service. The sergeants were obliged to continue using tricks and threats to keep their men in line. The patrolman's lot was eased, but his isolation in emergencies persisted. He no longer had to walk prisoners to the station or commandeer a passing carriage if the man was unruly, but his call box offered little solace if he was in personal trouble. Even if he could reach it, there was no guarantee that help would arrive quickly. Since his sense of isolation was one reason why he sought out holes to find relief from the street and an opportunity to chat with colleagues and friends, this inclination would be checked only if the supervisors had a way of monitoring him constantly or of reducing his insecurity.

The call-box system was not very useful to the public. As suggested, some businessmen received extra protection by having keys which allowed them to give alarms or make phone calls when public telephones were still a rarity. But most people had no way of quickly attracting a policeman's attention other than running into the street and yelling. Experiments with open call boxes were quickly abandoned when the number of crank calls overwhelmed the operators and the cost of repairing acts of vandalism became too great for administrators to accept. The needs of the public and the patrolman could be satisfied only when there existed a way of maintaining continuous two-way communication between the public and the police, and the men and their supervisors. The introduction of the patrol car and the development of the wireless radio were heralded as the way to resolve all of the problems created by the territorial strategy of the New Police.

The radio and the patrol car have transformed the relationships between the police and the public, and among policemen, but they have not resolved any of the fundamental questions of administration and supervision. When it was introduced, progressive administrators saw the car as a potential miracle worker. A man cruising in a patrol car could cover his territory with greater frequency than a man on foot, offering increased protection to everyone. When the two-way radio was first successfully used in a patrol car in 1929, it meant that a cruiser could be informed immediately of a call for help, greatly enhancing the chances of capturing suspects and deterring further crime. Some thought this development would finally enable the police to eliminate city crime entirely. The radio cruiser also offered police supervisors a way of knowing where the patrolman was. He could be checked on frequently and without warning. In addition the radio placed the patrolman in continuous contact with his colleagues, putting an end to his isolation and improving his sense of security. Since he was in a car which offered protection from inclement weather and increased his feelings of well-being, he also would be less inclined than a beatman, a foot patrolman, to go off the street. Small wonder then that experts predicted the most spectacular success for the new development while it was still in its infancy. One even suggested that,

with the advent of the radio equipped car a new era has come. . . . Districts of many square miles . . . are now covered by the roving patrol car, fast, efficient, stealthy, having no regular beat to patrol, just as liable to be within 60 feet as 3 miles of the crook plying his trade—the very enigma of this specialized fellow who is coming to realize now that a few moments may bring them down about him like a swarm of bees—this lightning swift "angel of death."[5]

The evident advantages of radio-equipped patrol cars were so great that within a few decades they became the principal means of patrol. In 1930 there were fewer than one thousand patrol cars in service in the United States, and only one city (Detroit) had a police radio system. By 1949 the Federal Communications Commission had licensed five thousand police transmitters, and by 1966 there were more than two hundred thousand in operation. The number of police radio systems is now so large that, in many parts of the country, departments are plagued by overcrowding and interference by signals from nearby systems. Even the relatively few men who still walk beats are now supplied with walkie-talkies that tie them directly into the radio system. Efforts are also being made to develop an inexpensive radio for patrolmen to carry with them when they leave their cars. This will keep them in continuous contact with their dispatcher, further improving their security and the control over their movements. Engineers are also developing radar-operated car-locator systems, which will show on an electrified map the exact location of each patrol car. This will allow the dispatcher to send the nearest available car on any call. Its advocates hope that this additional refinement will increase the efficiency of police response sufficiently to achieve the suppression of crime which was so optimistically predicted when the police were established almost two cen-

[5]This little classic of bureaucratic optimism was expressed by August Vollmer, the leading police reformer of the interwar years in America and a member of the "Wickersham Commission," the National Commission on Law Observance and Enforcement, Report No. 14, *The Police* (Washington, D.C., U.S. Government Printing Office, 1930), pp. 90–8.

The control functions of the radio system are discussed in Albert J. Reiss, Jr., and David J. Bordua, "Environment and Organization: A Perspective on the Police," in Bordua, *The Police*, pp. 48ff.

turies ago. Whatever its impact on the crime rate, however, this new development, like its predecessors, will strengthen the control of supervisors over the movements and doings of their men.[6]

Having found an effective means of placing their services at the disposal of the public, the police set about actively to encourage business. The continuous expansion of the telephone system has made it easier for people to call for a policeman. In recent years large police departments have tied their radio systems directly into the telephone networks and, following the lead of the British and the Belgian police, created emergency numbers which place callers in direct contact with a police dispatcher. These numbers are widely publicized in the press and on television, and are prominently displayed on all patrol cars; pay phones are being adapted to make it easier to call the emergency number from public as well as private places. These efforts have been so successful that they threaten to overturn the traditional conceptions of police work and to undermine the efficiency and purpose of street patrols. Since New York City introduced its emergency number in July 1968, the average number of calls each day to the police has risen from twelve thousand to seventeen thousand, and it is still climbing. In Philadelphia, a city one fourth the size of New York, during a fourteen-hour period of a Friday in June 1971, more than eight thousand emergency calls were received. During peak periods, patrolmen are often unable to handle all of their assignments. They are so busy answering calls that they have no time to patrol their territories. Despite the tremendous increase in the amount of "work" policemen do, the crime rates continue to grow, and harried police administrators are being forced to seek ways of reducing the demand they have encouraged without arousing bitterness and hostility among those people who will be deprived of "free" services. Some departments screen all calls, offering people advice over the telephone, suggesting they seek help from another agency

[6]Figures are taken from the President's Commission on Law Enforcement and Administration of Justice, *Task Force Report: Science and Technology* (Washington, D.C., U.S. Government Printing Office, 1967), pp. 116, 143–56.

or come personally to the station, refusing to send a patrolman unless it is an emergency.[7]

The patrol car and the radio have reduced the policeman's isolation and improved his feeling of security, but they have also deprived him and his supervisors of their privacy. Continuous radio communication not only allows police administrators to mobilize manpower quickly in emergencies and routinely to increase the output of their men, it also has given them for the first time a way of directly supervising what the policemen are doing. Higher officials can listen to the radio whenever they wish, and all radio communication is continuously recorded on tape and kept in storage for three months. This extension of central control has deprived the districts (or precincts, as they are sometimes called) of considerable autonomy and increased the effective control of the department's directors in a fashion that Colonel Rowan would have approved of most heartily.

The territorial strategy of policing made it impossible for any large department to be operated from a single station. From the beginning the district has been the basic unit of police organization. In the nineteenth century the districts frequently had the same boundaries as the wards, which were the basic administrative and political units of city government. Each district was headed by a captain, who often was appointed by local political leaders. Nominally under the direct command of the police chief, many of these captains were virtually independent of their superiors and answered directly to local political bosses. In some cities there were captains who became millionaires as a reward for their role in the non-enforcement of the liquor, gambling, and prostitution laws. The decline of the locally based political machines has allowed the American police to exert greater control over the selection and supervision of their district captains.[8]

Although each district is still commanded by a captain, he is no longer an independent figure. In Philadelphia, for

[7]Figures for New York City, *The New York Times* (March 31, 1970); Philadelphia figure from personal communication.
[8]Sprogle, pp. 73ff., 98ff., 128ff., 144ff., for a description of the early history of police districts in Philadelphia.

example, every district is part of a division commanded by an inspector of police. He is responsible for supervising the policing arrangements of the two or three districts which comprise his division. While the captain directs the district, the policies that guide him and determine the distribution of his manpower are formulated in consultation with the inspector. The inspector is not an independent figure but reports directly to a chief inspector, who is the formal mediator in the chain of command between the men who direct the "line squads," the street police, and the department's administrators.[9]

The decline of local political influence has freed police planners in most cities from restrictions which once prevented them from redrawing district boundaries to reflect changes in population, land use, and patterns of crime. Chicago is the only major American city whose police districts continue to reflect the boundaries of the city's wards. In Philadelphia, planners have been able to make changes which reflect the movement of people and the changes in policing caused by the introduction of the automobile. In recent years the districts have been consolidated, making each one larger than the average district at the turn of the century.[1]

Natural barriers such as parks, rivers, and large commercial streets (such as Broad Street in Philadelphia and Fifth Avenue in New York City) are utilized as district boundaries wherever possible. The boundaries of the "sectors," as they are called in Philadelphia ("posts" in New York and "beats" in London), into which each district is subdivided and which are the territories assigned to patrol-

[9]In Philadelphia there are seven police divisions and twenty-two districts.

[1]Consolidation has also been spurred by declining populations. On early American planning principles, see Lane, pp. 99–101, 172–7. For a summary of the criticism of police districting practices prior to World War II, see Frank Tannenbaum, *Crime and the Community* (New York, Columbia University Press, 1938), pp. 246–8. For a discussion of contemporary planning principles, see G. Douglas Gourley and A. Bristow, *Patrol Administration* (Springfield, C. Thomas, 1969), Chaps. IV–V, and Roy C. McLaren, "Allocation and Distribution of Police Patrol Manpower," *Law Enforcement Science and Technology*, S. A. Yefsky, ed. Vol. I (Washington, D.C., Thompson Book Co., 1967), pp. 599–607.

men, have also been revised to reflect the changes in police tactics. Wherever possible, local business streets are employed as sector boundaries so that these more heavily used places will get the additional protection provided by two men, one from each sector. Both sectors and districts are generally larger than they were when policemen walked and they are frequently altered to adjust to local conditions and problems, but the model which planners use to define their problems and solutions continues to be fundamentally territorial.

Despite the introduction of technology which has greatly improved the policeman's capacity to respond to requests for aid, and increased his mobility and his obligation to heed the commands of his superiors, the basic strategy of city police has not been altered. The number of street supervisors who actually direct patrolmen has been increased, and the radio is used to control their movements. While these changes have reduced the policeman's inclinations to avoid work, they have obviously not made him the fearsome presence who can extinguish crime. The present crime wave that grips the metropolitan areas of the United States is causing cities to improve their street lighting, increase the number of policemen on the streets, and demand more severe punishment for convicted criminals. Privately, people are protecting themselves by deserting the streets, arming themselves, and protecting their homes with a variety of locks and alarm systems that they hope will deter burglars. But the belief persists that there is a police solution to the crime problem. Administrators continue to pore over their maps and schedules looking for ways to get more from what they have and demand an expansion of their personnel every time an increase in the crime rate is announced. How many policemen will be enough to assure the safety of any city? What difference will more policemen make if they continue to do the same things which policemen have been doing for the last century and a half?[2]

[2]On recent efforts to prevent crime by street lighting, see *The Wall Street Journal* (January 6, 1971); *The New York Times* (March 27, 1972); President's Commission on Law Enforcement and Administration of Justice, *Task Force Report: Science and Technology*, pp. 49–51.

CHAPTER TWO

Police Work

The patrolman's conception of his city is different from that of the people he is paid to police. Like all city dwellers he knows the traditional neighborhoods and the nicknames which succeeding generations of people have imposed on their parts of the city in the process of making them their homes. But on his first day at the police academy he is given a city map covered with lines and numbers that do not appear on any street map. His former conception of the city is not erased, but it is gradually embroidered over by these jurisdictional lines of the police districts. As he is gradually introduced to the police craft, these boundaries begin to link up. When he leaves the academy and is initiated into an understanding of what the districts mean in the life of the uniformed police officer, he ceases to see the city as a collection of neighborhoods and begins to see it as a mosaic of linked districts.

There are no painted lines or signs marking the district boundaries, but every policeman (and persons with close connections to the police) knows when he is passing from one district to another. When two officers meet for the first time in a neutral place—at court, the dispensary, a union meeting—they invariably ask two questions of each other before engaging in any conversation: "Where do you work?" and "How much time you got in the business?" The questions are not inspired by simple curiosity but are a policeman's way of placing an unknown colleague. The laconic response "I've been in the Fifty-fifth since I went on the street three years ago" tells the questioner a good deal. He may never have been in the Fifty-fifth district but he knows where it is, what kind of people live in it, and what its reputation is, and these are part of the policeman's knowledge of the city. He is also given an opportunity to discuss mutual acquaintances. The familiar language and the acknowledged legitimacy of the questions reflect a common understanding of what they share. But the substance of these questions also indicates an awareness by the men that what they have in common as policemen is tempered by a man's experience and the place he has acquired it. A policeman may feel himself in possession of special rights anywhere in the city, but he knows that it is in his district that he learns his job and is a policeman.

When the graduating rookies are assigned, the news comes in a brief message on the departmental teletype. The captains' clerks scan the sheets to see if their requests for replacements have been granted, while the rookies are being informed whether their prayers or fears are being confirmed. During their three months' training, they learned informally about the districts from their instructors' stories, from friends and relatives in the department, and from other policemen sent to the academy for additional training. Although in Philadelphia they are barred from working the district in which they live[1] and have been warned not to expect the district of their choice, they hopefully fill out the request forms. Most recruits seek to avoid a district which requires a lot of traveling time from their home. Some worry about being assigned to neighborhoods they do not know or privately fear. A few who claim connections in the department confidently predict a good assignment, but most men wait anxiously, happy at the prospect of leaving the academy, which every recruit comes to despise, but worried about where they are going. As graduation day approaches, rumors intensify, fed by instructors who obligingly pass down what

[1] The residency regulation is one of many rules designed to curb corruption. It was introduced in a number of cities after World War II, but it is gradually being eliminated as police departments seek ways of bringing their patrolmen into closer contact with neighborhood people. The rule was inspired by the belief that the elimination of prior contacts between the policeman and the people of his area would reduce the likelihood of his refusing to take action for personal reasons, accepting money to protect illegal practices which were locally condoned, and refusing to enforce the law impartially. Its effects have been nil.

they learn from their superiors. After the lengthy wait the
disclosure is inevitably anticlimactic. The instructor enters
the room with a yellow sheet of teletype and reads off the
names as they appear on the paper. No one's request has
been satisfied; the class is scattered to districts throughout
the city. Those who had boasted connections gamely claim
they will get a transfer in a few months, others mutter
threats to resign, but most just sit silently. The instructor
listens for a few moments, smiling, and then calls for order.
"Listen, fellas, it ain't as bad as you think. Some of you are
going to tough districts, but that's where you are gonna learn
to be police officers. Some of you are going to farming districts.[2] Well, the girls are friendly and good-looking and they
are good places to study for tests. After a while you can ask
for a transfer to an active district. At least you all have someone going with you. It's good to have a couple of familiar
faces in the district. I remember when I first went to . . ."
but nobody listens any longer. Now the instructor is just
another colleague. Everyone is looking at the large map on
the front wall, studying the outline of his district, trying to
figure out how to get to work and to imagine what the reality
of the abstraction before him is like.

1 · The District

The new policeman usually comes to his district knowing
little about it except by reputation. He has been ordered to
report to the station but not to anyone in particular. Although he is expected, nobody greets him, except possibly
another rookie. He stands about awkwardly, adjusting the
weight of the unfamiliar equipment which tugs at his belt,
fulfilling his first official order by being where he is obliged
to be, while his claim to being there crumbles before silence
and indifference. Other policemen ignore him or he may
wish they did when the grins they cast in his direction are
accompanied by comments about his "nice new suit." When
the sergeant or corporal finally approaches him and officially

[2]Until recently the outlying parts of the city were largely uninhabited
and some people continued to farm the land. Most of it has now been
subdivided and developed, but the population density is low and these
places continue to enjoy good reputations among policemen.

recognizes him, he is taken on a tour of the "district," as the men call their station house.

He is assigned a locker, and after leaving the locker room, the only place in a station where policemen have claims on privacy from the public, he is taken through the roll room, a large rectangular hall with a raised platform at one end which is the formal setting for roll calls, magistrate's hearings (police court), community meetings, and holiday parties. He is shown the lockup, where prisoners are held until being transported "downtown" to the central jail, where they are photographed and fingerprinted. He sees the operations room, where the direct communications with the detective divisions and the central police radio are located, the district records maintained, and the paper work produced by the patrolmen during their work tours is processed.

If the captain is in his office, the rookie is formally introduced, giving the commander a chance to look over a new prospect for his plainclothes detail. If they have common acquaintances, a few friendly words may be exchanged; otherwise the meeting is brief and perfunctory. He is given a work schedule, told which squad he will work with and when to report. Unless he distinguishes himself or gets into trouble, the new policeman is not likely to speak with his captain again.

The captain is a "line officer" who has risen through the ranks and usually has a distinguished record as a street supervisor. But once he takes command of a district, he rarely has direct contact with his patrolmen. He is an executive who devotes his time to listening to the problems and demands of the residents and merchants of the district; he attends meetings and listens to complaints, checks reports submitted to him by his lieutenants and sergeants, and keeps his inspector, who is rarely seen in the district, informed.

The captain personally selects and commands the plainclothes detail, whose sole responsibility is to enforce the city's gambling, liquor, narcotics, and prostitution laws in the district. These five or six men are the only policemen who are directly under the captain's command. Although he selects his own "captain's men," they must be approved by his inspector and the chief inspector in charge of the patrol divisions. This deprives the captain of the possibility of pursuing an independent vice-enforcement policy. Despite their small number, this detail occupies a considerable part of his time. The plainclothesmen are transferred frequently, requiring the captain to be constantly on the lookout for new men. These transfers are necessary because it is difficult to conceal the men's identities from the "vice characters" against whom they operate and to prevent them from accepting the bribes and payoffs which are offered once they become knowledgeable about the local "action." New policemen are favored for plainclothes because they are less inclined to accept graft, but these men usually cannot make arrests of important vice operators. The department tries to control the possibility of corruption without compromising the quality of arrests made by plainclothesmen by mixing young district policemen with experienced "vice cops" who move often from one district to another.

The captain also recommends and implements changes in the distribution of his manpower and patrol procedures. In every district there are locally important commercial streets that receive the additional protection of a foot patrolman who is regularly assigned to the area during business hours. Businessmen's associations and influential merchants are constantly requesting special treatment and favors. The captain can have a man assigned to a meeting or a social event for a day without seeking the approval of his superiors, but any request for a permanent change in the distribution of his manpower must be decided at the highest levels of the department's command. Once the decision has been made to create a new foot beat, for example, the captain has the privilege of choosing the man for the post.

While the captain may know by name many of the men in his command, he generally deals with them through their sergeants and lieutenants. These men are the street supervisors, as he once was, and he will not interfere with their work unless they fail to provide him with the necessary assurance that they are doing their job properly. But the captain is in an anomalous position. He is an administrator who must enforce the regulations that are funneled to him from headquarters, but at the same time he must also seek to protect and encourage his men, who frequently resent what they consider arbitrary and capricious changes in their operating procedures. He balances his obligations by aligning himself with his men, demonstrating to them in their presence that he is a "good guy," and requiring their adherence to changes only after indicating that he is helpless to do otherwise in the face of superior authority.

One afternoon an order was received by teletype requiring the district to provide two policemen to guard a prisoner in a nearby hospital. When the captain was given the order, he stormed out of his office and denounced it before the fifteen or twenty men who were waiting for their roll call. "That dumb cocksucker who made up this order, he's no street cop. They send men out in one-man cars to break up fights between armed gangs and then expect me to assign two healthy men to guard one half-dead son-of-a-bitch," he shouted. The men were very pleased, although they knew that the order would be complied with.

The relationship between the captain and his subordinates requires them to inform him personally of anything that will open the district's work to scrutiny from outside or above. Any formal statement on a policeman's work—whether it be a recommendation for a commendation for outstanding work or a request to "take someone to the front," that is the laying of formal charges for departmental trial—must be reviewed by the captain before being forwarded up the chain of command. The captain must also sign the annual evaluation that the sergeants must make of each man under their command. If a man seeks a transfer, he must first inform his captain before any formal request can be forwarded to divisional headquarters. Most important of all, the captain must personally approve each application for a search warrant after it has been approved by a sergeant and before it is typed for presentation to a judge. Since warrants are used primarily in vice work, this power combined with his direct command of the district plainclothesmen assures the captain of absolute control over all official vice enforcement by the district police.

The captain assumes that his street supervisors will inform him of any occurrence that has a bearing on the appearance of his command. This is the tacit understanding upon which their relationship rests. In exchange for this, he allows the supervisors almost unrestricted control of the squads.

2 • Co-Workers and Colleagues: The Squad

A patrolman identifies himself to other policemen by his district, but his personal affiliation is with his squad. There are often more than two hundred policemen, organized into four squads, assigned to a district, and only some of the veteran supervisors and "old-timers" know most of them. Although all of these squads work the same ground on different shifts, the men are not encouraged to exchange information and knowledge of their working places with each other. The relations among the squads are formally maintained by direct contacts among the supervisors and through the mediation of their captain. Every man has a chance to meet men from other squads when he works overtime, during emergencies, and on special assignments. At each shift change the men going off are obliged to remain by their cars (frequently they do not) until the relief man takes over, providing a few moments' contact each day. Occasionally a man transfers from one squad to another, bringing with him knowledge of ex-colleagues which he offers to his new colleagues, enriching their knowledge about co-workers who are frequently seen, greeted, chatted with, but rarely known in the personal way as are the fifty policemen, the corporal, two sergeants, and the lieutenant who are in their squad.[8]

Every day each district in Philadelphia is policed by three different squads, while the fourth is off. Each squad works a six-day week, followed by two days off. Every week each squad works a different shift, and over a month's time the men have worked "around the clock" on all three shifts. Each district is policed on "daywork" from 8 A.M. to 4 P.M. by one squad, which is relieved on "nightwork," 4 P.M. to midnight, by a second; the last shift of the day is called "last

---

[8] On the differentiation of social and working contacts, see Erving Goffman, "Supportive Interchanges" in his *Relations in Public* (New York, Basic Books, 1971), pp. 69–80, and in his *Stigma* (Englewood Cliffs, N.J., Prentice-Hall, 1963), Chap. II.

out" and is from midnight to 8 A.M. In the regular rotation a squad works daywork and then returns the following week for last out, which is followed by night work.

The district patrolman's working schedule seals him off from other policemen who do not work the same shifts he does and makes it very difficult for him to maintain contacts with people who are not policemen. Not only does he work a different set of hours each week, but he also works a different weekly schedule from the one most people follow. His days off are never the same and he must consult the pocket shift calendar that he always carries with him before he can commit himself to any engagements. He is rarely free on weekends, frequently is working on holidays, and only one week in four does he get home for the evening meal with his family and a chance to go out with his wife.

Throughout the year, on every shift, in all seasons, the patrolman knows he will be working with the same men. It is his squad which helps the rookie learn his job and suffers for his errors. These men exploit his inexperience to lessen their burden as the price for their tolerance, and they decide whether to admit or exclude him from their companionship. None of these things is taught recruits at the police academy, but they are lessons which the policeman remembers throughout his career.

Although his badge has the city's name embossed on it, the patrolman's real employers are his sergeant and lieutenant. They guide him into the nuances of his occupation, teach him his duties, and give him the opportunities to learn his craft. In return for his willingness and commitment to the job, they must protect him from his own mistakes, assume responsibility for his actions if he errs in good faith, and justify his behavior to the captain if the need arises. But if he refuses to do as they desire, they will frequently punish him without permission from above, and if he persists, they will drive him from their midst.

Every squad is divided into two platoons of equal size, about twenty-five men, each directed by a sergeant. The sergeants are of equal rank and are both answerable to their lieutenant, the highest ranking supervisor in the police department, who is in direct contact with the men who actually police the city. Although he is a "white shirt," the squad under his command knows him as a worker who spends his tours of duty riding the street, answering calls when requested by the dispatcher, and intervening at the scene of incidents to control and direct his men. Unlike the captain, he is "there," a crucial distinction in the view of policemen who see their work as a series of moments and actions that cannot be understood unless directly experienced. Until recently, lieutenants were "house supervisors" who were responsible for commanding the station while the sergeants ruled the street. In an effort to increase the efficiency and reliability of the patrolmen, the department increased the number of supervisors by "streeting" the lieutenant and creating a corporal to assume the management of the station house in the absence of the lieutenant.

When the captain is not in the district (he is almost never there on last out and rarely on nightwork), the lieutenant is the ranking officer responsible for all police functions. Though he is now generally on patrol, he is available to receive complaints or organize liaison with people from other units or other city agencies who have business in the district. He tacitly stresses the executive side of his authority by refraining from directly interfering in his sergeants' handling of their men. If he is involved in a serious conflict with a sergeant over control of the squad, he will occasionally interpose himself, a sure signal to everyone to exercise caution. But when there are only momentary disagreements with his sergeants, he is careful not to reveal these before the men. He tries not to create any barriers between himself and the men in his squad. The men are free to speak with him and ask his advice, and he does not hesitate to give them orders directly. But he will not permit any man to ask favors of him which are the sergeants' to dispense. Anyone who seeks to curry the lieutenant's special favor or to evade his sergeant's authority will be rebuffed.

Each platoon is permanently assigned to one of the two "ends"—east or west, upper or lower—into which the district is informally divided. Although the entire squad works the street at the same time, the two platoons do not really work together. In order to avoid stripping the district of police protection at shift changes, the platoons go on the street a half hour apart. Each platoon has its own roll call and the men from one have gone on patrol before their colleagues have assembled. Since they work at the same time, are always available to come to each other's assistance, and constantly meet in the station when they bring in prisoners and paper work, the men come to know each other quite well. New men frequently work both ends before being permanently assigned to one platoon, and every man occasionally works the "other end" when men are absent. The men who work the other end are not just distant co-workers like policemen in other squads, but they are not as close as the members of a man's own platoon.

The apartness of the platoons is sustained by the two sergeants, who carefully avoid intervening in each other's jurisdiction. Inevitably, one sergeant is the more senior man and he may have closer connections with the lieutenant or the captain than his associate, but he is careful not to diminish the authority of his colleague. When one sergeant is absent, the other generally prefers to allow a senior man from the platoon conduct the roll call, although the sergeant is supposed to assume the responsibility. He must act as their supervisor during the tour, but most sergeants are careful to avoid any actions which impinge on their colleagues' arrangements.

Every squad has its own operations-room crew, which serves as the informal bond between the two platoons. The three or four men who work "inside," under the direction of the corporal, are responsible for maintaining the station, guarding prisoners, and keeping the squad's records. Before the communication system was centralized, the operations crew operated the district call-box system; now these men are mainly responsible for processing mountains of paper work. Each day they must prepare the roll-call report, the assignment sheets, equipment records, and overtime pay lists, and send them all downtown. They compile and code all the tickets, summonses, and reports which are submitted during the tour, record all entries in the official district arrest ledgers, and type up the special reports which patrolmen must submit to other units in the department. They also review the constant stream of messages on the teletype, informing the lieutenant and the sergeants of anything relevant to the squad or the district, and keeping the men informed of official gossip.

The operations room is a sanctuary private citizens are rarely allowed to breach. Squad members use it as a place to take a breather or to have a conversation without being interrupted or overheard by the many people who are constantly coming and going in the station. But the room belongs to the crew; it is the territory of men who are barred from working the street and they do not let their colleagues forget it.

The crew is selected by the squad supervisors, who require the captain's approval only for the turnkey, the man in charge of the lockup. Before the central jail was established, these district cellblocks were important places. Prisoners were kept there until magistrates set bail or released them. The turnkey had to be a reliable man because of his daily contact with judges, lawyers, bondsmen, and "fixers." People were often kept in the lockups for days, and there were turnkeys who made money by arranging contact with bail bondsmen, and selling food, cigarettes, and blankets to people who were entirely at their mercy. Much of this has been eliminated and the turnkey is now mainly a custodian.

Crew members are usually selected from among the older men in the squad, with preference being given to those who volunteer, although men are occasionally obliged to accept an inside job if they wish to remain in the squad and the district. A man whose health makes it difficult or even dangerous to work on the street will be allowed to go inside for a rest or to finish out his career. Occasionally a man with a drinking problem will be ordered off the street to spare everyone trouble. A man who "goes bad," whose work causes numerous complaints, will be moved inside for his own well-being and for the protection of the squad. If a man refuses, he is on his way out of the district. Men who are not working well are frequently moved inside to give them a breather and a hint to try harder. Sometimes a man will be brought inside because he is bored with the street and his bosses hope that the change will revive his interest and keep him from seeking a transfer. While the crew performs the necessary administrative functions required by the department, it informally acts as a kind of safety valve for the squad which is utilized to resolve those personnel issues that are considered internal, private matters.[4]

The rookie takes with him to his district a mixture of admiration for, and fear of, his sergeant which has been fed to him at the academy. "Fellas, don't mess around with your sergeant or you'll have a hard road to travel," the instructor said, holding aloft a copy of the departmental Duty Manual. "If he gives you an order to do something you don't like—do it. If you don't, good luck." His attitudes are reinforced by what he sees of his colleagues' attitudes toward their boss; they are also tempered by a recognition that no successful sergeant is a despot. The men must work as he wishes if they expect to get the recognition, favors, and rewards only he can give, but the sergeant must have men who are happy to be working for him if he expects to show the lieutenant and the captain that he is capable and effective.

The sergeant's power is founded on his control over where each man will work his eight-hour tour. Every sector and foot beat has a distinctive reputation which determines its desirability as a place to work. When there were few patrol cars, any assignment to a car was considered a sign of high regard. Now that most men ride, the favored patrolmen are given the choice sectors. The few remaining foot beats are usually on important commercial streets, and these are given to veteran officers who are excused from shift work and are permanently on daywork. On the other two shifts, these beats are usually assigned to rookies whose capacity is not known or not trusted. Since there is nothing much to do but guard the deserted streets and discourage vandals and window breakers, most men do not relish these assignments. Occasionally a sergeant will assign a veteran officer to a regular beat or one that has been .created to deal with an emergency as a warning that he is not performing his job as required. Since everyone understands that these assignments are a form of censure, they provide the sergeant

[4] A lieutenant said of one man who was eager to return to the street, "He was a hell of a street cop, but he just got too hot [short-tempered]." Another man eager to return to the street was obliged to remain inside because his deteriorating eyesight raised doubts about his reliability on the street at night.

with an informal but direct way of communicating his feelings to his men.

Any assignment to a sector car is considered superior to walking a beat—"In winter the cars are nice and warm and the beats are nice and cold"—but only a rookie regards the chance to work a sector car as a sign of the sergeant's trust. If he interprets the opportunity given to him as an indication of his acceptance as an established member of the platoon, he will be set straight quickly by his colleagues. There are men in every squad—rookies, transfers, "oddballs"—who are used to fill in for men who are absent or on vacation. They "bounce" from one car to another and frequently they are "gypsied" to the other end of the district. Although they are in cars, these men have little standing in their platoon.

The sergeant rewards the men he trusts and likes by giving them a permanent sector assignment. A young patrolman who is given his first permanent assignment does not care whether it is considered a "good" sector because he has been around long enough to know that his sergeant is offering him a secure place in the platoon and informing his colleagues that this is a man he trusts. The patrolman assumes a debt to his sergeant in exchange for this trust, which he must willingly honor if he hopes to retain it. If he does not "produce" as expected, and if his relations with the sergeant deteriorate, he will find himself receiving special assignments or even bouncing about. But he can also increase his claims on the sergeant's affections and place himself in a position to get one of the choice sectors or even an assignment to work a patrol wagon (the "meatwagon" or, most commonly, the "wagon").[5]

The most coveted position in the platoon is a permanent assignment to a patrol wagon. Each platoon has several wagons that are always manned by two men each and the sergeant reserves these positions for men he trusts completely. Some men decline because they do not like working the "garbage truck" which obliges them regularly to handle

[5]A sergeant visited a district at the request of his wife to greet her cousin who had just graduated from the police academy. "I told her I can't do much for the kid, but she insisted. If I knew his lieutenant or sergeant, I could get him off the beat and into a car, if he's not shaky. But that's it."

the very ill, the dying, and the dead. The wagons are also used to break in rookies. When a new man comes to the platoon, one of the regular wagon men is temporarily shifted to a patrol car while his partner works with the newcomer, showing him around the district and giving the sergeant an informal appraisal of his character and inclinations. There are men who do not like working with rookies or having partners of any kind and refuse the offer to work in the wagon. This is an assignment which is too important to force on anyone, and if the man is well liked by the sergeant, he will be allowed to choose his own sector. But few patrolmen refuse their sergeant's request.

The wagons are not restricted to patrolling a single sector like a patrol car but have a jurisdiction comprising three or four sectors. Since their primary obligation is to transport the very sick to hospitals and prisoners to the station, the wagon crews are excused from doing a number of jobs that policemen dislike. The police believe that much of their trouble begins immediately after they have made an arrest, and they place great stress on quickly removing prisoners from the scene. (Once a person is arrested, he is a prisoner in the policeman's view.) To assure that wagons are always available for their main work, the wagon crews do not have to perform regular traffic duty or act as school-crossing guards, watchmen, or public-relations officers. The wagons must also transport prisoners from the district station to the central jail, a job which gives the crews opportunities to make contacts in other units in the department. The freedom and responsibility of the wagon crews require the sergeant to select men who are dependable and who will do nothing that reflects poorly on him and his superiors.

The sergeant is reluctant to punish a man by shifting him out of his regular assignment because this disrupts the overall efficiency of his men. If he is displeased, there are several warnings he can use to inform the man or the platoon of his attitude, offering them the opportunity to correct their behavior before he acts. There are numerous departmental regulations that even a very conscientious man will occasionally violate. These are normally overlooked, but if the sergeant is unhappy he will make a comment, carefully avoiding any suggestion that he is contemplating official action, but reminding those who may be taking something for granted of the nature of their relationship and the dimensions of his power. If his concern increases, he will comment directly to the men at roll call and threaten them with some kind of action. "You guys have become too lax. There's too much laying down, and if it keeps up the lieutenant is going to be down on my ass. If you keep it up, I will take memos from every man who is late," a sergeant warned his platoon. He had no intention of doing anything with the memos except throwing them away, but policemen regard anything requiring them to commit statements to paper as a threat. If a man is late and is only reprimanded, it is finished, not recorded anywhere, and soon forgotten; but if he must make an official explanation, there is the possibility that it will be filed in his personal record, permanently registered for others to see any time.

If someone is annoying him, the sergeant will withhold the important little rewards which only he has the power to grant. A man who is out of favor will not be allowed to come to work late or leave a few hours early. If he asks the sergeant for a day off, it will not be granted; this privilege is reserved as an incentive to better performance and as a reward for work well done. The police are given compensatory time off for the official holidays when they are obliged to work and they also accumulate sickleave time. When a patrolman uses holiday time for a day off, he gets paid for the time, but if his sergeant refuses to allow him to use the holiday, the only way he can avoid coming to work without losing the pay is to use some sick time. Any man who calls in sick must be personally visited at home without prior notice by a sergeant from the district where he lives. If his own sergeant does not order the "sick check," the man has a day off with pay. During emergencies and in the summer vacation period, the department cancels the use of holiday time except for genuine family crises, leaving a man no opportunity to get a day off for some private business other than using sick time. A sympathetic sergeant will occasionally let a man off the hook, but any man who does not enjoy a good relationship with his supervisor risks serious punishment for misuse of this regulation.

A man who fails to respond to his sergeant's informal

warnings will begin receiving special assignments that take him away from his regular post. The censure can be strengthened by gypsying the man since everyone knows that no sergeant gives away a man he trusts and depends on to do the platoon's work. If trouble persists, the sergeant may try to trade him to another squad or get him transferred from the district. Although the Duty Manual offers almost un-limited opportunities to bring charges against a man ("If you want to get someone, there is no way he can avoid it," a sergeant said), few supervisors like to resort to formal punishment.

About 3 A.M. a patrolman carried a drunken cab driver into the district. The man was bleeding from a head wound inflicted by a robber who had stolen his taxi to make a get-away. The sergeant looked at the man, shook his head, and walked out of the station without saying a word. The cor-poral said the cab driver was an ex-policeman who had been in the sergeant's platoon. "The sergeant was real good to him," he recalled. "He was real drunk one night and he refused to go home although the sergeant pleaded with him. He wouldn't listen, and when the lieutenant came, he re-fused again. The lieutenant locked him up for drunk driv-ing. He had been to the front once for AOB (alcohol on his breath) which was a favor to him since the sergeant caught him with a broad in the car. They just fired him. Now he's finished."

Although nobody questions a supervisor's right to punish his men (and every policeman can tell stories of some fabled persecutor), he will exhaust every available alterna-tive before exercising his formal authority. For example, the operations room occasionally fills up with men who come in to drop off their reports and hang around to drink a cup of coffee from the pot the crew keeps constantly fresh. The supervisors, even when they are annoyed, rarely tell the men in a direct fashion to get back on the street. It is common to hear a corporal murmur loudly that the "air in this place is getting awfully warm," or if that does not accomplish his purpose, he will tell them to "hit the bricks," carefully avoid-ing directing his remarks at anyone. One day a captain from outside the district was about to enter the operations room when he noticed how many policemen were standing inside. He quickly turned away and walked over to the water fountain, where he took a long drink. Their sergeant, who had been urging the men to move just as the captain arrived, said only, "I think he wants to come in here, but he does not want to embarrass anyone so he is waiting for you to leave."

Even when a man is doing something which his superiors dislike and consider dangerous, they will not compel him to change his ways unless it directly affects his work. A young officer, well liked by his supervisors, who considered him an increasingly important member of the platoon, began drinking in a district bar that enjoyed a somewhat lurid reputation. It had been the hangout of a motorcycle gang which often fought with the police, but a new owner had turned them out and welcomed the appearance of the off-duty policemen as protection against their return. When the gang did come back one afternoon and severely beat the bartender and several patrons with chains, the lieutenant was concerned that in the small war that followed his men might be employed as part-time mercenaries, exchanging their presence (and their guns) for a few cheap drinks.

So, after night-shift roll call, he stopped the man and said, "I saw you the other day in that den of iniquity. I didn't say anything because I didn't want to embarrass you and what you do on your own time is your business. But I don't want you to think that I didn't see you. You know it's not up to me, but I think you and your friends should find some other place to drink. There's gonna be more trouble in there and I don't want to see you get hurt. I know the broads aren't as good, but if you feel like it, drop by the Tavern tonight after work." The younger man listened to the lieutenant politely and thanked him for the unusual and generous invitation, but although he said nothing, they both understood that he was not going to do as suggested. He had been warned, and if there was trouble, he could not claim innocence if he pleaded for protection.

The sergeant's and lieutenant's exercise of their authority is tempered by an understanding of their own dependence on the goodwill and cooperation of their men in maintaining the unity of the platoon and the achievement of its goals. They know they can always get rid of a recalcitrant or dangerous man, but they do not want to antagonize their men, or encourage them to seek transfer. Every time a man leaves, a new man must be broken in, and there is no guarantee that the replacement will be as good as the man who left. They must also worry about the possibility that an angry man will betray them.

Betrayal, "dropping a dime," is the last resort of the persecuted, the ambitious, the threatened, the fearful, and occasionally the honest. Every supervisor who gives a man a break, lets him off without a sick check, allows someone to go home a few hours early without deducting from his pay, accepts "Christmas money," or goes "on the take" must calculate the possibility of being betrayed by his men. He must not make their lot so distasteful that they will do anything to get away from the district, sacrificing the real advantages which derive from working in a place they know well and taking the risks of being branded as a "gink," a spy.

A sergeant watched as a lieutenant got into his car and drove away. "He's a good man, very good, a first-rate lieutenant, but he's getting a real fucking. The word is that some of the men in his squad were going A.W.O.L. when they were being carried as working. He was on the street where he belonged, but without a corporal inside, he let the men make up the attendance sheets. A couple of them were running a bar downtown, and after signing in, they would go and tend bar for a few hours. It's his fault for trusting them, but it's a shame anyway. A thing like that, you know someone dropped a dime on him. And it's not over yet because they fire guys for stuff like that now."

Since every supervisor violates regulations to produce the conditions and circumstances which enable him to get the required work from his men, each must bear in mind the possibility of betrayal. No matter how rare its occurrence, it is both a barrier against petty tyranny and a brake on the capacity of the supervisors to enforce stringent control over their men. They are as much colleagues as they are executives.

3 · Activity

The worth of a man to his platoon does not depend on his success in preventing crimes, arresting suspected felons, or even giving service without complaint or injury. A man may be offered a transfer to a choice unit if he makes a spectacular arrest, but catching bank robbers is not the way to develop a sergeant's friendship. That requires something very different.

It is not uncommon to hear a weary man at the end of a busy summer night, scanning his patrol log, in which he records his official work during the tour, say, "Well, we worked tonight but we didn't get any activity[6] for the sergeant." How can a man who has taken fifteen assignments from the radio dispatcher, patiently listened to complaints, and steered his car through clogged and steamy streets say he has had no activity? His shirt is soaked with sweat and filth, his arms ache from wrestling the heavy steering of a car that quickly ages beyond recognition under constant wear and occasional mistreatment. He is tired from no activity?

"Activity" is the internal product of police work. It is the statistical measure which the sergeant uses to judge the productivity of his men, the lieutenant to assure himself that the sergeant is properly directing his men, the captain to assure his superiors that he is capably administering his district, and the department administrators to assure the public that their taxes are not being squandered.

At the end of each tour, the sergeant signs off his men, examines their patrol logs, and enters in his notebook the activity each man has produced during the tour. There are separate categories for "meters" (parking-meter tickets), "parkers" (illegal parking), and "movers" (motor-vehicle-code violations). Each time a patrolman stops a pedestrian or a person driving a car, he is supposed to file a written report giving details of the person and the circumstances. These "car stops" and "ped stops" are separately

---

[6]See Julius A. Roth, "What is an 'activity'?" *Etc.: A Review of General Semantics*, Vol. XIV (1956), pp. 55-6, for a very useful statement on definitions of activities and non-activities in a tuberculosis hospital.

a two-man car while he is actually riding a "silent car," a vehicle which is reported out of service and has no contact with the radio dispatcher. Officially it is not there. Everyone in the platoon knows about this violation of departmental regulations and it cannot be concealed. It is treated as a collusion among colleagues, a violation required to make their work easier and more successful. It also helps to generate internal loyalty and shows the men that their supervisors are almost as dependent on them as they are on the "bosses."

"Working the meter car" is an easy but not necessarily desirable job. Sometimes the sergeant will give it to a man who has been promised an early dismissal. He will tell him to write a certain number of tickets and allow him to leave when he has finished. With this incentive the man is allowed to determine his own departure time, and the sergeant knows that he will get his tickets. But the assignment is generally given to older men who are no longer interested in doing police work or to rookies the sergeant wants to keep out of the way. Because of its menial character, this job can also be given to an officer as a signal of displeasure, especially if the sergeant knows him to be a man who is interested in trying to make vice arrests.

Individual statistics remain in the districts, and only the totals are forwarded to divisional headquarters. There is no competition among platoons for leadership in activity because of the differences in the territorial character of the areas they police. The number of parking meters varies from area to area, and parking violations are treated differently in business and residential sections. One platoon, working in a largely commercial area, wrote 1,717 movers, 759 parkers, and 994 meters in a year. In the same period the other platoon in the squad wrote only 559 movers and 310 meters, but 785 parkers. They had far fewer meters to check and more disputes over parking because of the residential character of their territory.

The department uses the production of car and ped stops to measure the patrolman's commitment to the prevention and suppression of crime in his sector. Whenever there is an increase in the weekly totals of crimes reported, the men are urged, but not ordered, to be more "aggressive" on patrol and to "increase the number and quality of vehicle and pedestrian stops" they make. This attitude is motivated by the belief that the more actively a man is involved in scanning the people and cars about him, the more likely he is to detect and prevent crime. These car and ped stop reports are also used to provide the department with information about cars and people at specific places and times, facts that may be of aid to other units investigating matters unknown to the patrolman making the report. Whether they are actually of any value has never been demonstrated, but since their introduction (about 1955), they have provided the department with another way of influencing the amount of work each patrolman does.

Individual officers may aggressively seek out opportunities to make felony arrests, but there are no production pressures linked to the arrest rates of squads or patrolmen, except those men who belong to anticrime patrol units. The department is anxious to increase its "clearance rate," the percentage of reported crimes solved by an arrest, and it is believed that aggressive patrol and rapid response to calls are the best ways to accomplish this. In the past, efforts to achieve higher rates of arrest have encouraged patrolmen to make false arrests and to suppress reports of crimes.[9]

A sergeant cannot order his men to go out and make felony arrests without also encouraging them to commit illegal acts. All he can do is tell them to make more stops, although there is no measurable link between the number of stops by a platoon and their success in arresting felons. For example, nobody knows how to evaluate the importance of the 2,626 car stops and 2,575 ped stops made in 1970 by one platoon working a predominantly commercial and industrial area, or the 2,184 car stops and 3,110 ped stops made by the squad's other platoon. There is no way of arguing that these were sufficient, too many, or not enough to assure the "proper" protection of the people and property of the district

[9]At the turn of the century in London, commanders in high-crime districts were paid a "charge allowance," a bonus for felony arrests which exceeded an informal quota. In order to assure their bonuses, many commanders pressured their men to make false arrests and to add charges. G. Reynolds and A. Judge, *The Night the Police Went on Strike* (London, Weidenfeld–Nicholson, 1969), pp. 25–7.

during the time that squad was working. It is not known how many unrecorded stops these men made, since frequently policemen do not bother to "make paper" if they are not under pressure or if they know the person they stop, but there is no way of evaluating what loss may be incurred by the police and society when any information is allowed to go unrecorded.[1]

Individual patrolmen may produce significantly larger quantities of activity than their colleagues without arousing hostility. Policemen are not piece-rate workers who are paid a bonus for each ticket they write over a minimum number. If one officer meticulously writes up each ped stop he makes, it has no effect on a senior colleague who may write up only a third of the people he interrogates and so give the appearance of doing less work. Even if a squad goes ahead of its previous rate of ticket-writing and creates a higher requirement for the following year, the obligation of each patrolman is not increased by very much and the bulk of the additional work will be carried by the men who work the meter car, those with the lowest status in the group. Patrolmen are much more concerned about efforts by their superiors to increase their work load or to introduce "reforms" into their work. Since the statistical measures used to evaluate their work have no demonstrable effect on the performance of those duties for which they are principally hired —the preservation of order and the protection of life and property—the patrolmen have the means of embarrassing their bosses and exerting significant counterpressure. For example, if the men are ordered to increase their ticket output, they can exceed their orders by so wide a margin as to assure an outcry from outraged citizens who find their cars ticketed for violations they did not know existed. On the other hand, when ordered to do something which they disapprove, the men can temporarily refuse to do any ticket writing. No police official can say publicly that his men are too zealous and should disregard violations which they discover. Nor can he effectively counter arguments that the

---

[1] An effort to establish the value of information is made by M. A. P. Willmer, *Crime and Information Theory* (Edinburg, Edinburgh University Press, 1970).

men are spending too large a part of their time doing things which fail to increase the security and well-being of the general public. The power of patrolmen to embarrass their superiors without violating their formal obligations enables them to restrict their productivity within the limits they find "normal" and attainable and acts as a brake on those administrators who want to make them more "efficient."[2]

Arrest quotas are rigidly enforced for vice arrests, however, and continuous competition among platoons and individual officers is encouraged by threats and rewards to assure production. Every platoon must exceed its annual total by at least one arrest each year. Regardless of their success in fulfilling other departmental goals, any failure to produce the necessary vice arrests means trouble for the captain, the lieutenants, the sergeants, and all the men in the district who have assignments they want to keep. The kind of vice activity varies from district to district but the arrests are made principally for numbers,[3] dice games, card playing, horse-betting parlors, prostitution, illegal manufacture and

---

[2]The restriction of production is a well-known phenomenon in industrial settings where workers are paid piece-rate bonuses. See the very useful studies by Donald Roy, "Quota Restriction and Goldbricking in a Machine Shop," *American Journal of Sociology*, Vol. LVII (1951/52), pp. 427–42; "Work Satisfaction and Social Reward in Quota Achievement: An Analysis of Piecework Incentive," *American Sociological Review*, Vol. XVIII (1953), pp. 507–14; and "Efficiency and 'the Fix': Informal Intergroup Relations in a Piecework Machine Shop," *American Journal of Sociology*, Vol. LX (1954/55), pp. 255–66.

In one New York City precinct a new commander established a quota of fifty tickets a month for his foot patrolmen "to get these people back in the habit of working." His men responded by raising their production from 147 parking tickets on a Friday to 1,154 on Monday and 1,294 on Tuesday. Their efforts produced the desired result: the inspector called off his "reform" effort, *The New York Times* (January 20, 1972). Chicago police recently went on a ticket-writing spree in support of their demand for collective bargaining and other changes. In some districts commanders confiscated ticket books and threatened punishment to halt the flood of tickets, *The New York Times* (October 1, 1972).

[3]Numbers is the principal form of urban gambling. It is called policy in New York and has many other names, such as lottery and nigger pool. The best study of numbers is Gustav Carlson, "Numbers Gambling: A Study of a Culture Complex." (Unpublished Ph.D. dissertation, University of Michigan, 1940.)

sale of alcohol, the sale of alcohol to minors, or the sale and possession of illegal drugs.

Vice enforcement, particularly of gambling, has always caused severe problems for all big-city police departments. Often, gambling has been protected by politically powerful people and the police have been discouraged from pursuing enforcement. This attitude has been aided by the offer of payoffs and bribes to officers. Every department has been touched by scandals and revelations of payoffs for protecting gambling. Many different approaches have been tried to limit the inclinations of some policemen to accept graft from gamblers; in Philadelphia a policy of decentralization is pursued. Instead of concentrating antigambling efforts in one or two specialized units, a competitive situation has been created. It is hoped that this will make men fearful of offering protection to anyone since they cannot know when another unit will intervene and possibly expose them. The district platoons must compete with the captain's men and also with special squads under the direction of the commissioner's office. Each platoon has its own quota, although one successful platoon will frequently "carry" another for several months. Although no distinctions are formally made in the kinds of vice arrests computed, the most important are for gambling. An increase in the number of narcotics arrests, for example, is not an acceptable substitute for the required volume of number pinches.[4]

Everyone in the squad seeks to make a contribution to increasing vice activity. Even the operations crew takes a hand when the opportunity arises, to "create a pinch," as one corporal said. Every arrest must be entered in the district arrest book, and vice arrests are recorded in bright-colored inks, allowing anyone to see at a glance the number of pinches made in a day. When policemen from a special unit bring their prisoners into the district for processing, the operations crew must handle their paper work and record the arrest. If any kind of vice violation is involved, the men are sounded out about the possibility of allowing some of the

[4]On gambling enforcement see Bruce Smith, Jr., *Police Systems in the United States*, 2d ed. (New York, Harper & Row, 1960), pp. 237–8, 258. In New York City a centralized gambling policy has been followed and the uniformed men have not been responsible for making arrests.

district men to go on the pinch. This is never done with the
captain's men or a downtown squad, since they are in direct
competition with the district and they are not supposed to
know anything about each other's work. But patrolmen who
work in crime-suppression units are often willing to trade a
narcotics arrest, for example, with a district man who has
made a "gun pinch," or failing anything worthy of trade,
they may allow the corporal to add a name along with their
own as a way of encouraging good relations with the district
personnel. Once there is agreement, the corporal simply
writes in the name of one or two men from the platoon
that works the end where the arrest occurred; they are then
formally credited with an arrest and their platoon gets a vice
pinch. The men do not appear in court or participate in any
way in the legal process initiated by the arrest. The corporal's action is entirely an internal matter, affecting only the
norms established by the department to measure the work of
its employees. The corporal sees his effort as a harmless but
useful act which aids the interests of his closest associates.

There is absolutely no doubt in the mind of the district
patrolman about how seriously vice arrests, particularly for
gambling, are regarded by his superiors. He may not know
what other value they have, since the more experience he
acquires in making vice arrests, the clearer it becomes to
him that gambling is not deterred by them; he does understand that the department wants a lot of them.

During one nightwork roll call, the sergeant requested two
men to come forward to receive letters of commendation
from the department for their part in the arrest of some men
who were burglarizing a warehouse. He congratulated them
warmly, and as they returned to their places in line, he continued, grinning, "Of course, none of this police work counts
for much. Only vice pinches count." The men laughed in
appreciation and wondered whether they were behind in
their obligations.

Each week every district captain is required to submit a
report detailing all vice investigations made by his command.
These reports are forwarded by the divisional inspectors to
headquarters so department administrators can keep abreast
of all vice enforcement in the city. Any falling off from the
previous year's totals is immediately noticed and pressure is

applied directly to the captains. If the lag persists, the inspector will increase the pressure by formally warning all district supervisors that he is personally watching their performance and that he will supersede their captains' power unless there is improvement. One memo from an inspector to a district's squads read in part: "The 89th district is behind eight arrests for illegal lottery and if there is no improvement in the results of the uniformed men, changes will be positively made." Every man was put on notice that his job was in jeopardy unless he produced.

There is a constant demand for vice activity, but when the captain or inspector threatens intervention, the supervisors openly pressure their men by warning of a general reshuffle of assignments. The sergeant speaks to the men individually and warns them collectively at roll call. No opportunity is ignored to remind them that he wants a pinch. When a sergeant calls after a wagon crew heading out the door to begin their tour, "Watch out you don't lose your cushion," they know his smile hides a sincere admonition.

Captains seldom address their men at roll call, but one afternoon following the serious injury of an officer, a captain came to express his solidarity with the injured man's colleagues. When he had finished his little speech, the sergeant stepped forward and said, "While he is here I will mention vice to you. He says that he would like a number pinch, but he will take a bottle, and if not, narcotics. But he wants a vice pinch. He also wants meters. I don't know when you are going to do this, maybe between shootings, but he *will* have a vice pinch." The men smiled silently until the captain laughed, then they burst into a roar.

Rookies and younger officers often impress their sergeants by the activity they generate, but the sergeant knows that eagerness and devotion are of little value in locating a number writer or a speakeasy. This requires skill, knowledge, information, and inclinations which develop only with experience. Even among the veteran members of any platoon, there are only a few who, working closely with their sergeant and lieutenant, produce the flow of information and the arrests which meet their collective requirements. These veterans are rewarded with their choice of sector or a seat in a wagon. They are the men who consistently receive the highest evaluations on their annual performance ratings. As one lieutenant said, "You can be a good guy, a great bull-shitter, keep your car clean, make a lot of arrests, but without vice you'll never get an outstanding from me."

A man is capable of producing vice information only after he has been in a district for some time. During the time that he accumulates his experience and knowledge, he also develops contacts and interests in other areas of the department. He knows people, once his colleagues, who have advanced to higher rank and can offer him positions under their command. The men whom sergeants and captains wish most to retain are the ones who are most capable of getting a transfer. Frequently they are content to remain where they are, because their value stems from their unique personal knowledge and connections, which will quickly atrophy when they leave; and their supervisors are willing to go to considerable lengths to keep them happy and encourage them to remain where they are. They are granted freedom in their work and relief from numerous petty obligations, a freedom younger men, who frequently make more arrests and produce the bulk of the platoon's activity, do not have. Activity demands are part of an informal apprenticeship accepted by younger men because they know they cannot make the vice arrests necessary to maintain the platoon's stability and coherence. And without these, they have no assurance that the men who are teaching them how to be policemen will be around to complete the training.

4 · Roll Calls

Roll call is a remnant of the decaying military tradition used to discipline the police. When a platoon assembles for roll call, the men are rarely called to order but assemble themselves as their sergeant mounts the platform. There are no claims to a specific place in the rows of eight that line up before the sergeant as the men await the daily attendance call and the issuing of orders and instructions. The policeman does not realize how informal the procedure really is until after he has left the academy, where he was subjected to daily roll calls for twelve weeks, his instructors forcing him to do push-ups and penalty work for not having the proper haircut or the correct shine on his shoes. His recollections of these silly exercises, which contrast so sharply with the reality of his daily life in the district, only deepen his contempt for the training he was given, causing him frequently to disregard many of the more important things he was taught.

"Let's see your tin," the instructor ordered, beginning the final week of training, with another mock roll call. The three rows of men stood stiffly in the cold morning air, tugging out their wallets as he shuffled down the front line. Several men had forgotten their badges and another had neglected to cover his with the black band required to honor an officer murdered the week before. The instructor ordered them to submit written explanations of their failure to comply with official orders and canceled their lunch period. "From today you will carry all required equipment and we will have full inspections at all roll calls just like in the districts."

At the afternoon roll call he smiled as the men struggled to hold their gear together without breaking ranks. "Fellas, it's not required but get a heavy rubber band and secure your flashlight, notebook, street guide, and ticket book together or you'll be making a racket at every roll call." He then casually walked through the lines looking at their whistles. "Get a plastic one because those nice shiny ones freeze in winter and will rip up your lips when you go on traffic post." He inspected ball-point pens, wristwatches, clean white handkerchiefs sealed in plastic for emergency first-aid use, change for the telephone (a dime was passed surreptitiously down the line for use by those who did not have one), and a brass key used to open traffic signal control boxes for manual operation. Blue riot helmets lined the ground before the rookies. They shifted awkwardly to show the instructor their handcuffs, slung over belts. They jammed nightsticks into their armpits so their hands would be free to pull out black-jacks from back pockets. Although they had no guns or holsters (these are not issued until graduation day), they were obliged to simulate them on the command of "draw pistols," even jiggling their "gun" to show the instructor that it was loaded.

Equipment checks are rarely held at district roll calls, although policemen know they can be revived at any time as a warning to a faltering platoon or to punish a recalcitrant man. The equipment they carry are the tools of the police trade; it is assumed by most supervisors that the men will come to work with their gear in working condition. After a shooting or an accident, supervisors may conduct gun checks, urging their men to clean their weapons and periodically change the ammunition. Most policemen do not think their colleagues take proper care of their weapons; the department has instituted a program that requires every patrolman to requalify at the pistol range annually. The instructors take this opportunity to inspect and clean the guns, which are, after all, public property.

Formal inspections are held only when there are visitors to the station. Policemen do not like surprises, and there are rarely unannounced visits from higher commanders to a platoon roll call. When an inspector is planning to come to the district to address the men, there is usually ample warning from sympathetic colleagues at divisional headquarters. The captain always informs his lieutenant of any impending visit. "John, the inspector is going to address the men at roll call today. Will you see that they behave themselves accordingly?" The patrolmen know that no one will protect them, regardless of their position in the platoon, if they give cause for embarrassment during these visits. Their response is governed by the visitor's reputation. If he is considered a "ballbuster, the kind that makes you show a dime," they will carefully assemble all the required equipment, borrowing from the operations crew, who do not stand roll call, to replace whatever is missing. If the man is "all right," they will simply take care that their appearance offers no cause for comment.

Only the captain, whose office is near the roll room, attends roll call without prior notice, but when he does, it is usually to comment on some special circumstance and not to check equipment or appearance. It is common to see a captain, obliged to cross the room during a roll call, make certain by the quickness of his movement and an occasional joking remark that nobody will interpret his appearance as ginking or harassment.

The sergeant does not have to resort to discipline and equipment checks to maintain order and attentiveness among his men. He is not a military leader; he is a foreman whose men are scattered over many city blocks. His men rarely work in his direct sight and he needs their goodwill, just as they need his protection and advice to get the job done properly. An understanding of their mutual obligations is sufficient to keep even the most rambunctious in line. Nobody speaks out without permission or interrupts him while he is talking. Any man who is allowed to first-name the sergeant in private is careful to address him formally at roll call. Even someone who disdains his sergeant will refrain from open acts of contempt, except in rare moments of rage or whimsy. But a supervisor who is disliked, especially one whose claims on his men are slight or disintegrating, will be treated contemptuously. Calculated violations of normal conduct, which are insufficient to disrupt the routine and warrant formal punishment, are expressions of opinion rather than rebellion, and they inform the sergeant of his standing. On some occasions these messages can be brutal.

A vacationing sergeant was replaced without warning by a sergeant who had once commanded the squad's other platoon. He had been relieved when the men refused to produce for him. Prior to his departure, several of his men had been transferred to the platoon he was now temporarily commanding. They were displeased and he knew it. "I have a few rules as you know which will be obeyed while I am here. I do not like minutemen. Roll call is on the dot—don't be late. I also have a lot of equipment to carry and I expect you to do the same. Where are your helmets? All of you get them, including the Italian contingent in the back row, and keep them with you at roll call." Silently the men broke ranks, and when they reassembled, one man who had left his helmet visor behind walked from the line to retrieve it while the sergeant was talking. Before returning, he took a long drag from a cigarette he had left burning in an ashtray, staring directly at the sergeant. As he entered the line, the others turned to him and smiled their approval. That was just the beginning.

The next day everyone came prepared for a full-scale inspection. Their equipment was neatly piled up, waiting for the sergeant, who had to content himself with ordering several men to get haircuts. As he passed down the line, each man turned toward him silently, grinning broadly, while the men ahead openly talked to each other. At no time did anyone write down any of his instructions since they had no intention of doing any work for him. On the last day of the shift, at the end of roll call, he ordered a pistol check. Staring directly ahead, the men unholstered their revolvers and, keeping their fingers carefully away from the triggers, pointed them toward the ceiling, while a voice from the back row said quietly, without a hint of menace, "Watch out, Sarge." There were no more inspections.

Roll calls are used by the sergeant to inform his men of their common and mutual obligations as well as to keep them abreast of any departmental news of importance to them. The captain's clerk and the operations crew sift the continual flow of messages from headquarters that are transmitted over the teletype, culling announcements of schedule changes and alterations in administrative procedures to read out at roll call. The sergeant also uses the opportunity to give his men information from official departmental sources and unnamed informers about possible crimes in their end of the district during the tour. If activity is down, he will exhort them all, but only rarely will a sergeant single out an individual for any criticism. Everything that the men are told at roll call is considered general knowledge, intended to help them do their work more efficiently.

The department regularly compiles information regarding criminal activity in the city and the district which is distributed to the men before they go on the street. Every few days a list of stolen auto-license plates, a "hot sheet," is issued for the patrolman's reference to cars that attract his attention on patrol. It is also a source of inspiration for officers who play the numbers. There are lists of serial numbers from reportedly stolen appliances which the men can use, although they rarely have the opportunity, to check against any they find during their tour. The department also prepares information sheets detailing recent trends and techniques in street crime, illustrated descriptions of burglary tools the men may not know, and photographs of people being sought for questioning or arrest.

Each week the men are given a crime bulletin prepared by the divisional staff describing the frequency of reported street crime, burglary, robbery, purse snatching, car theft, assault, noting the sectors which are most active. The rates are compared with the same week in the previous year, and any increases are accompanied by requests to step up car and ped stops. The distribution of these aids is rarely accompanied by any other comment from the sergeant. He knows his men personally, who among them is working hard, who is not; what are their capabilities for the job. Offering them helpful hints will only increase their exasperation with him, not their effectiveness. If he urges or demands that they make arrests, he knows that some of them will ignore the law and the truth to improve their performance. Any hint of complaint from above, which is rare, is angrily rebuffed by the patrolmen, who defend their record by arguing that they are prevented from doing "real police work" (catching criminals) by the heavy load of public services required of them by the men who now criticize their record. When the pressure is strong, the sergeant urges his men to increase their activity, but he does not ask them to make arrests.

Because everyone to whom the patrolman has some obligation is competing for his attention, there is a constant stream of requests, which are read out at roll call. They are not of equal importance and the sergeant has techniques that indicate to the men their relative importance. For example, persons seeking the return of some cherished property, a car or a pet, occasionally offer a monetary reward, prompting him to mention the request rather than simply tacking it on the district bulletin board. More frequently, requests are routed through the captain's office and their announcement is prefaced by saying, "The captain is interested . . ."; this tells the men to pay attention.

If there is a complaint coupled to a request, the sergeant will stress his own concern that the matter be rectified. He does not criticize anyone personally at roll call but simply informs the platoon that they are on notice from him to do their job as he wants it done. "There's been a complaint to the captain that the illegally parked cars on Atlantic Street are not being tagged because the ward committeeman's office is on that street," a sergeant said to his platoon. "That's bullshit. The reason is someone is not doing his job. The captain and I want those cars tagged, and if there is another complaint, I will personally call the sector car and write them myself."

The sergeant may have a personal interest in seeing that a request is fulfilled, and he does not hesitate to let the men know that he considers their careful consideration a courtesy to himself. The wise sergeant does not make a habit of making numerous requests of his men, using up credits which he has accumulated by judicious favors, but his men do not object when he occasionally asks something of them. "There's a woman living on High Street who has been getting threats from her neighbors. Keep an eye on the house when you ride by. She has been helpful to the police in the past," the sergeant said, with a smile. "She was the girl friend of someone who used to be in this squad—so she was helpful." The men smiled as they wrote the address in the notebooks, which they use to record messages and personal information.

Most of the sergeant's remarks are perfunctory warnings designed to keep the men informed of problems in the district that do not require direct action. He mentions playgrounds that have been the scenes of fights and places where special events such as dances or block parties are occurring. This informs them of circumstances that may produce trouble and gives them some idea of what to expect if they receive a call to one of these locations.

Periodically, after complaints from local merchants and residents accumulate, he urges the men to move juveniles off corners where they habitually congregate. These requests are not treated too seriously since most men understand that boys on corners are part of the landscape and driving them off is like the tide washing the shore: it is an endless cycle. But if there has been unusual trouble or if something occurs which is seen as a challenge to the police, the sergeant will make demands that his men treat as a command. "Those deprived children broke every light on Hicks Street last night and made it through an alley before I could catch them. I don't want you to fool with them any longer. I don't want any more ped stops. If they are hanging on the corner tonight, scoop 'em up and bring them in. I mean it, call for a wagon and we'll put 'em on the books and let them have a hearing. Make their parents come after them."

When there is reliable information about a possible problem in the district, the men will be informed, usually without mentioning the source. If, for example, there is a rumor of a holdup, the sergeant will order the sector car and the wagon to check the premises each half hour. If he does not consider the information to be accurate, he will mention it only in passing, covering himself against the possibility that it will turn out to be correct, without giving his men any specific instructions. The man on the sector is then free to treat the information as he sees fit.

The sergeant also uses the roll call to warn his men of any circumstances and conditions in the district which can affect their well-being and his reputation. Since the roll call is the only time when the platoon is assembled as a unit, he uses the occasion to tell them anything which requires general cooperation to avoid embarrassment. These warnings also free him of any obligation to protect anyone who ignores them. "Inspector Blood is riding the district tonight and I expect everyone to answer immediately when radio calls you. If anyone has come to sleep tonight—you know who I mean— you better go off sick right now."

Occasionally, the warnings are graver and consequently more circumspect. The sergeant does not tell the men where his information comes from, nor do they allow themselves to display any curiosity about the warnings. They just listen. "There is a funny wagon with fake door panels parked on the corner of the 1800 block of Vale Street. Don't hang around there, and if you get a job in the area do it right, do it quick, and get out. And don't stare at that wagon when you go by it. Remember, you are strictly on your own out there." Everyone in the platoon understands that the "funny wagon" is a blind for a hidden camera used by the department's internal inspection unit, the ginks, to conduct secret investigations of complaints against policemen. They are what every police officer fears most, even the scrupulously honest. Nobody can know for certain why the wagon is there, but if anyone in the platoon has "something going" in that area he will stay away. Men who are innocent are warned to avoid committing any blunders which might involve them in something they know nothing about. Everyone in the platoon who is doing anything against regulations has been put on notice: the man who intends to slip off for a few drinks, the fellow who is planning to visit the apartment of a woman he knows, the man who is thinking he could use a few dollars. Those who plan to do nothing but the job for which they are paid are made nervous and insecure.

Everyone in the room stares directly ahead while each man tries to figure out who is being investigated. Nobody doubts the truthfulness of the sergeant's warning because his men know that he has no reason to make them fearful. He does not have to resort to subterfuge to make them work; he can simply order them to stay away from any place he does not want them to go. The warning also reminds each man of the limits of collegial intimacy, recalling how little each man knows of what the others are doing on their sectors after they leave the station.

There are things of considerable importance that are never discussed at roll call. The supervisors are constantly getting information about gambling and other vice operations which they do not disclose to the platoons. Although vice arrests are the most consistently demanded work of the platoon, no sergeant seeks to increase the men's effectiveness by encouraging general discussions of vice conditions or exchanges of information about vice characters. Every district is required to maintain a "vice book" containing the photographs and police records of all known characters operating in the area. Departmental regulations require that every man examine the book at least once a year, and the lieutenant is obliged to remind his platoon at roll call and have the men sign a departmental memorandum which acknowledges their compliance with the regulation. "You all know what this is," the lieutenant told the assembled platoon, holding aloft the thick vice book. "You all know where it is and I urge you to go and look at it once in a while." The men laughed. The book is kept in the captain's office, available to any man who requests it. Most men do so rarely. The supervisors distribute their information privately to individual platoon members who enjoy their special trust. The only cooperative aspect of vice enforcement in a platoon is the common understanding of everyone not to ask anyone about what he is doing, where he gets his information, or how it is acquired.

Rookies and new men are told only what is absolutely necessary to maintain the unity of the platoon. Everything the men are told at these daily gatherings is considered public information. Much of the platoon's most important work is never discussed, nor are the men encouraged to discuss among themselves any aspects of the problems they encounter on their sectors. They know that the warnings, the information, and the exhortations given them daily by their sergeant are meant to aid their performance and not to create additional burdens for them. Their attentiveness to his requests and commands strongly affects the chances of each man to advance, to get himself off his feet and into a car, and then into a sector which he can call his own eight hours a day. As he advances, the patrolmen learns gradually how much there is to know that is not discussed at roll call. The more of an insider he becomes, the more closely must he adhere to his sergeant, because he is also learning that nothing is permanent. The sergeant affirms this every day by reading out the assignments each man will work. Even men who have worked the same car for years are told anew each day where they will work. This is a little reminder that nobody is in permanent possession of anything, and only their commitment to the unity of the platoon preserves what they already have and keeps open the promise of additional reward and advancement.

5 · Going to Work

At the academy, recruits are introduced to the lore of shift work by instructors who have been relieved, often unwillingly, of the burdens of working around the clock and are now on "steady daywork." There are constant warnings about the dangers to the stomach caused by irregular eating habits, accompanied by opinions of the shifts and how to prepare for them. "Four to twelve is great for working, lots of action, but it's hell on your life. You feel like you're always working or getting ready to go to work. No time for yourself." "Daywork is all bullshit but you get to meet some nice people and make a lot of contacts." "I won't kid you fellas, last out is rough. I tried everything but I could never go to sleep in the morning when I got home. And then maybe you got to go to court. Man, when the sun comes up, it's murder. You just have to drink a lot of coffee and keep shaking your head. But it's part of the job." When he arrives in the district, the rookie knows that each shift has different characteristics; he has only the vaguest appreciation of what they are.

A policeman who understands what he is likely to be doing when he goes to work knows that he has little control over what he may be called on to do. Many claim this unpredictability is a virtue of the trade, an important reason why they prefer police work to other labor. "You never really know what you'll get next in this business, but you can bet it's always something different." However different one "job" may be from the next, he does have some general assumptions about the *kinds* of work he actually must do. He knows, for example, that he must always be ready to give first aid. On any day he may be asked to place himself in danger, consider a suggestion that he discredit his office for personal gain, or perform a solicited service which, while not a requirement of his work, he may consider a fulfillment of his nature. It is a condition of his trade, which all who actively pursue it must acknowledge, that while these may be "part of the job," he cannot know from moment to moment what demand will arise.[5]

While the rookie is learning to adjust his body and his life to the wrenching rhythms of shift work, he is acquiring an understanding of what the department and his sergeant expect of him and an understanding of the people he is paid to police. He is learning about the changing obligations of his work which accompany the progress of the clock and of the seasons, and he is also developing a set of expectations about what he will be doing during his tour that enables him to impose a limit on the uncertainties inherent in his work. As he stands at roll call day after day, listening to his sergeant

[5]The police are not unique in claiming unpredictability as a virtue of their work; cab drivers, salesmen, and newspapermen make similar boasts. These occupations share three things in common: they deal with a public which cannot be screened prior to contact; the work is performed in an open framework, not on an assembly line or in an office where work routines are patterned; and they have low status with the majority of the public.

issue orders, demands, and requests, he begins to formulate concretely his conceptions of the shifts.

Each shift has some compulsory obligations that must be met regardless of other demands. On daywork half the tour is spent directing rush-hour traffic and guarding school crossings. There are other obligations. Shopkeepers and merchants who want protection from robbery and larceny can ask the department for a "store log," which the sector officer must sign, requiring him to visit the place regularly. Logs are also placed inside all banks and subway toll booths. The sector patrolman and the wagon covering the area must sign these every day and the sergeant must sign the bank logs; the subway logs must be signed on all shifts. If the sergeant discovers unsigned logs or receives a complaint, he will order his men to "get your logs," threatening them with the specter of a headquarters investigation. Daywork is also the primary time for getting meters and parkers, and any pressure on a platoon to improve their production occurs on daywork.

While these obligations consume a large part of each daywork tour, they are subordinate to the continuous pressure for vice arrests. Number writing, the predominant form of urban gambling, is almost exclusively a morning activity. The local "writers" usually finish the day's work by early afternoon; thus most gambling arrests must be made on daywork. Anyone in the platoon who wants to advance himself is trying to obtain some kind of information he can use for a pinch or to give the sergeant as evidence of his effort. In poor neighborhoods, especially in the slums where poor blacks, Puerto Ricans, and Southern white migrants live, speakeasies are common, usually informal affairs operating in someone's parlor. Although they are more numerous on the weekends, Sunday daywork being the most common time for raids, every officer is alert for signs of a "speak" as he patrols and chats with people on his sector.

Because the platoon has so many formal obligations on daywork, the sergeant normally restricts himself to reminding the men of these rather than encouraging them to be alert for other things that commonly occur on daywork. The men know that bank robberies are almost exclusively a daytime event, but if the sergeant urges them to do any more than sign the logs, he will be encouraging them to spend their time on the main business streets when he wants them to be looking for vice and promptly answering the radio calls they are constantly receiving. Similarly, house burglaries are a common daytime occurrence, especially in neighborhoods where a large proportion of the women go out to work, but he rarely mentions this because he knows his men will be alert for housebreakers if they have time to patrol.

The night shift is generally considered the action tour since the men have fewer formal obligations during a time when most people are neither working nor sleeping. Some men will have a traffic post for the homeward rush hour. Others may spend the few hours of the tour before sundown "making statistics" by getting some meters. But the sergeant requests meters only if the platoon is considerably behind, because he believes the night shift is when they "earn their money" and he does not want to burden his men with work that can be done another time. He will urge them to pick up their activity by making car and ped stops; to check for juvenile curfew violators in an effort to cut down car thefts and burglaries, common crimes of night associated by the police with young men. The twilight hours are the likeliest time for street muggings and purse snatches, but he mentions this only if there has been some unusual increase in the district. Holdups too, primarily of bars and liquor stores, are common at night, but special mention will be made of these only if the sergeant has some information. The regular sector men know the places they have to keep an eye on. Also, the night shift brings the heaviest demand for service and the sergeant knows his men will spend a large part of their tour answering radio calls.

The men evaluate the days of the week differentially, profiling them as they do the shifts. Some days are likely to be more active and others have a high probability of being quiet. On daywork, the weekend is most appreciated because many of the formal duties are eliminated, and Sunday, which is considered the quietest tour of all, usually produces only bizarre crimes, the delayed result of weekend celebrations or the eruption of some smoldering kinship connection. The nightwork shift, especially in summer, is viewed as hard work all the time, but in other seasons city policemen believe it is primarily the weekends, which for them begin on Thursday afternoon and end early Sunday morning, that produce most of their action. City police associate much crime with heavy drinking and payday; they believe that the availability of large amounts of cash encourages some people to go drinking and others to rob.

Except for weekend nights, last out is usually a quiet shift. After the bars close, there is little action on the street. Since violations of the closing laws are a vice pinch, some men watch the bars and clubs on their sector closely. The sergeant encourages his men to increase their activity on this shift since the demands on their time are relatively small, and this is the best way he has for combating the professional car thieves and burglars, who prefer to work during these hours. The department also takes advantage of the low demand on the patrolmen's time to order surveys for abandoned cars, potholes in the streets, and defective traffic signals.

Some men enjoy last out because there is relatively less to do and there are few supervisors on the street. Most men feel that "the night is made for loving and sleeping," although there is some disagreement over where these things are best done. Last out produces the highest rate of absenteeism: a man who does not feel like working is most likely to stay put when he has to leave for work at 11 P.M. It is also very difficult to sick-check a man on this shift. His sergeant must have a compelling reason for believing he will not be at home before asking another sergeant to awaken a household after midnight. But a man who makes a habit of not appearing for last out is inviting his sergeant to look into his bag of tricks for informal ways of torturing him.

Unless a sergeant exerts very firm and unrelenting control, there is a considerable likelihood that some men will slip off into holes and others will disappear on private visits. It is not easy even for the conscientious to remain alert throughout the night, and men frequently stop at the station for a cup of coffee and a chat. When the sun begins to rise, the desire to sleep is very strong, and many men pull their cars up and just sit rather than continue to patrol and risk accidents. There are supervisors who allow their men to "go down" and others who continue to employ the tricks and harassments that supervisors have always used to compel their men to toe the mark. A sergeant who suspects someone is sleeping will ask the radio dispatcher to call a man for a meet every hour, day after day, and he will continue to do it until he has convinced the man of his intention to keep him honest. Patrolmen who refuse to sleep often speak contemptuously of their colleagues who do, but every policeman understands the desire to do it, and the obligation to work last out is an important source of the feelings of solidarity that policemen share.[6]

New men often utilize the freedom of last out to explore their district and sector. They nose their cars through back streets, learning which alleys are wide enough for a car and how to travel most directly from one place to another. They are laying the foundations of their territorial knowledge, one of the things which distinguish policemen from most other users of the city streets. They are under no formal pressure to do these things, and many do not, but those who enjoy their work do not need any encouragement to explore.

The policeman's expectations of particular tours and times often fail to materialize, but the belief in the generalizations which are used to characterize them is not shaken. Variations may be ascribed to meteorological or even astrological conditions which are shrugged off as special cases not affecting the validity of the belief. It is sustained by the policeman's need to have firm expectations about his work, although he knows that uncertainty and contingency are two of its fundamental characteristics. He knows that the activity demands made on him have little bearing on his ability to "fight crime," but he also knows that these demands impose clear, defined obligations on him that can be satisfied. These give him a considerable security because he knows that if he produces, he will gain the support and protection of his sergeant. Like any other worker, he seeks the esteem of colleagues and the rewards produced by good work.

[6]Sleeping on the night shift is common in industry also. See Melville Dalton, *Men Who Manage* (New York, Wiley, 1959), p. 80; and in other branches of public service, Erving Goffman, *Asylums* (New York, Anchor, 1961), p. 204. Nightwork also produces solidarity in other occupational groups, such as musicians and railroad workers who have little in common with policemen. Edward Gross, *Work and Society* (New York, Crowell, 1958), p. 230.

CHAPTER THREE

Communications

The power of the police department to control the city, its capacity to serve the people who want its services, and its ability to regulate the work that policemen do have been considerably extended by the development of radio communications. In emergencies, manpower can be mobilized quickly and concentrated anywhere in the city; in a personal crisis, a wagon can be dispatched promptly to bring a seriously ill or injured person to a hospital. The patrolman is obliged to adhere to the commands and promptings of the dispatcher who gives him his assignments and shares with the man's sergeant and lieutenant a responsibility for supervising his performance. The autonomy of the districts has been ruptured by the radio and every policeman is now obliged to work under the scrutiny of unseen persons.

In a small department, the radio network consists of a single channel and the supervisors can easily listen to all of the traffic. However, it is impossible to follow closely what is going on by listening to the multichannel system that coordinates the work of a big-city police force. Although all the broadcasting is done from one large room, there is a separate radio channel for each police division which is operated from its own console.[1] In addition to the seven divisional channels or "bands" which are broadcasting simultaneously, there are other bands serving detectives, special units with no

---

[1]There are several alternative broadcasting centers to ensure the continuous operation of the radio in case a disaster or sabotage destroyed the central communications room.

fixed territorial obligations, and a city-wide band used to coordinate operations involving several divisions or different units. Each police car is equipped to receive its own 'divisional band and the city-wide channel called "J-Band."

Each console operates autonomously, but they can all be coordinated with one another by an intercom system that allows the dispatchers to speak to each other without broadcasting. This enables them to ask questions of each other and to transfer information from one division to another. Any important call involving a serious crime in progress or an emergency which may affect more than one district can be broadcast over the entire network from any console by depressing a special key that cuts a divisional band into the entire network. Since every message of importance is broadcast over J-Band, this is the one usually listened to by the department's directors and anyone else who has no special interest in the routine messages that dominate the traffic on the divisional bands. The dispatchers on J-Band work constantly with the knowledge that at any moment the most important officials in the city may be listening to them. They are also responsible for handling all dispatching during emergencies, from a traffic jam on an expressway to a riot. These men enjoy the highest status in the radio room and an invitation to move from a divisional console to J-Band is considered a privilege.[2]

Since it is impossible to listen to all radio calls, the department must resort to threats to assure the proper performance of the dispatchers and the patrolmen. All calls made to the dispatchers through the emergency telephone number are automatically taped, and all live radio transmissions are continuously recorded. These tapes are kept in locked storage for three months before being erased and used over again. This allows the internal-security division and any other in-

---

[2]There are many kinds of radio systems in operation throughout the country and the specific technology of each affects the character of the relationships among the men using them. But I believe the fundamental issues are similar to those described in this chapter. On the general role of communications in large, complex organizations, see Chester I. Barnard, *The Functions of the Executive* (Cambridge, Mass., Harvard University Press, 1938), pp. 89–91, 175–81.

vestigators to listen to every message that has a bearing on matters under review. Every dispatcher knows that his performance can be checked at any time and that everything he says on the air or over the telephone is part of his official record.

The recruits are told at the academy that they are expected to behave like gentlemen on the radio. They are not to interrupt when others are speaking unless there is a genuine emergency, and they are never to use foul or abusive language. They are fed horror stories by their instructors which graphically illustrate the dangers caused by malicious misuse of the radio.

"I remember one time," the instructor said, "a cop is down on the ground and gettin' his ass kicked pretty good. He's fighting off these guys, and he's got one hand in the car grabbing his phone. He's trying to call for help while these guys are workin' him over. While he's giving his location, some asshole, I can't even call him a policeman, screams over the radio, 'Chicken Man, Chicken Man, he's everywhere, he's everywhere.' The dispatcher could make out only the street but not the block, and it took the cars a couple of extra minutes to find the officer. In that time he could have been stomped to death."

The department no longer allows patrolmen to preserve the anonymity of their voices, a practice that tacitly encouraged some misuse of the radio. Every recruit is required to give the department a special recording of his voice, which is transcribed by a process called Voiceprint. The instructors assure the men that the technique is as accurate as fingerprinting and enables a technician to compare the print with a tape recording of a live transmission and make a positive identification. The men are warned that anyone discovered violating departmental regulations governing the use of the radio will be summarily fired and prosecuted for any violations of the federal statutes that regulate the use of the public airwaves. The instructor tries to calm the recruits' objections but points out to them that they have no choice. "Fellas, I promise you that this will not be used for any purpose other than protecting you and the radio. If you don't fuck around, you got nothing to worry about. Anyway, it's in the Duty Manual. This is a direct order from the commissioner. If you refuse you are out. That's it."[3]

This measure has eliminated much misuse of the radio. At one time it was common to hear abusive remarks such as "chicken man" after an officer called for assistance, or obscene epithets directed at public figures or other members of the department. An angry policeman can no longer say anything without risking discovery. The only way he can safely vent his anger is by disrupting the technology. He can keep his transmitter button depressed, introducing static and noise into his channel and making it difficult to hear. He can make it even worse by driving with his receiver trailing out of the window. This produces a powerful noise which makes broadcasting almost impossible. Such occurrences are rare, and although the department seeks to suppress them, they are much less worrisome than careless remarks that can be heard by anyone who is listening to the police radio.

While radio communication has extended the authority and control of the department's administrators, it has also created an unprecedented opportunity for outsiders to monitor police activity. Anyone can buy a cheap receiver and tune in to the police frequency. In some cities there are clubs whose membership is devoted to listening to police and fire calls. Many professional burglars and car thieves carry receivers to diminish the chances of unanticipated interruptions while they are at work. Unfriendly politicians and "protest groups" listen to the radio to gather unfavorable information to use against the police. Reporters listen for leads to stories, as do wreck-chasing lawyers, doctors, and tow-truck operators in search of business.

It is forbidden by city ordinance to possess an unlicensed receiver, but this is hardly a bar to anyone who is seriously interested in following the doings of the police. To prevent unauthorized listening, the police are spending considerable amounts of money to install sophisticated radio-scrambling equipment in all their cars. This prevents a normal receiver from picking up any messages in an intelligible form. Un-

---

[3]When the system was introduced into Philadelphia, one officer refused to be printed and resigned. To my knowledge no policeman has been prosecuted. Voiceprint has recently been ruled as admissible evidence in some state courts. *The Wall Street Journal* (March 13, 1972).

fortunately for the police, this equipment requires a great deal of maintenance and must be changed frequently to prevent anyone from discovering the wiring patterns used to scramble the messages. Also, anti-scrambling equipment is becoming available at prices even poor protest groups can afford.

The need to prevent embarrassing disclosures has forced the police to avoid exercising fully the control the radio gives them. It is necessary to compromise with the dispatchers and the patrolmen in order to encourage their cooperation in preventing the occurrence of anything that might cause harm to all of them. Every patrolman learns a set of adaptive techniques which allows him to preserve some private time and to inform his dispatchers of situations that he does not want to discuss openly. The sergeants and lieutenants cooperate in this practice because they have the same interests as their men. While many of these techniques are used to keep information away from prying outsiders, they are also used to protect the squads against intervention by officials from outside the district. The dispatchers avoid mentioning certain things on the air and use private telephone lines to inform the districts of matters considered too sensitive for public disclosure.

The department's administrators, all of whom have been patrolmen, understand what is going on, and they allow it as an adjustment necessary for the overall success of their policies. There is continuous conflict between the effort to supervise the men closely and the need to allow them to escape from control. Informal measures have been developed to limit the degree of both freedom and regulation. It is a principal obligation of the dispatchers to mediate these conflicts, although naturally this is not anywhere recorded as one of their duties. Dispatching is their formal function; refereeing their informal work. Success at both is required.

1 · Dispatchers

Each console has a crew of policemen and "civilians" who are responsible for answering the telephones, dispatching the calls, and maintaining the records used to regulate the work of the patrolman. The console crew works the regular shift system and every crew serves around the clock with the same squads. The number of people assigned to each console varies with the amount of work it has to do, but there are a minimum of three people working at any time. Since nobody can broadcast continuously for eight hours, there are at least two people who take turns dispatching, while the others handle the phones and do the paper work. There are some women dispatchers (mostly Spanish-speaking), although patrolmen contend that they and others who do not have street experience are not reliable in an emergency.

The dispatcher's major responsibilities are to interpret incoming calls and to dispatch assignments to the cars on his network. When one of the phones at a console rings, the "phone man" makes out a card containing the address of the caller and the nature of the complaint. The card is handed to the dispatcher, who sits before a lighted panel marked with the numbers of all the cars and wagons assigned to his division and a detailed map with district and sector boundaries clearly marked. He punches the card on a time clock and assigns the "job" to a car. He then files the card in a slot above the lighted panel reserved for that particular car and flips a switch, turning off the light under the car's number on the panel. When the officer reports back to the dispatcher that he has completed the assignment, the card is again time-punched and the light turned on.[4]

Any call made to the police on the emergency number is automatically routed directly to the console that serves the area from which the call was made. The system is designed to receive an unlimited number of calls without giving a busy signal. Every console has a minimum of eight phone circuits; they are never all in use. If all the circuits in use are busy when a phone call arrives, the call is automatically placed in a holding circuit until the phone man is able to answer. The men are under instructions to answer every call by the fourth

[4]Many of these functions have been computerized in some advanced radio systems. For example, New York City has a system called SPRINT that allows a dispatcher to tell the computer where a call is coming from and he receives a response telling him the sector of occurrence, and the nearest cross streets and hospitals, and the call numbers of the cars which service the area. This is flashed on a screen directly in front of the dispatcher and he need only read out the information after contacting an available car. See *The New York Times* (October 2, 1969).

ring and at one time there was an over-ring desk which automatically took over all calls after four rings. Some departmental administrators used to check up on the efficiency of the phone men by occasionally dialing and counting the number of rings before their call was answered, but budget pressure eliminated the over-ring desk, and the standard of efficiency set for the radio crews cannot be maintained. During peak demand hours, over-rings are common as there are simply not enough men available to answer all the calls. There is no way of knowing how many of these calls go unanswered because people get tired of waiting and hang up. In June 1971 there were 22,000 over-rings.

The phone man has an obligation to receive the phone message as quickly and accurately as he can. Most of these people are experienced policemen whose informal knowledge of interviewing is the basis for applying the few formal techniques taught to them. It is assumed that many people who call the police are under stress and will not behave normally. The phone man is not only required to be courteous, he must also take command of the conversation and extract the necessary information rather than waiting for it to be volunteered. Each time he answers the phone, the man is obliged to identify himself before listening to the "complainant" describe the reason for the call. After he has an idea of what the problem is, he gets the caller's address. He does not usually ask the person's name, but if he is not rushed and it is offered, he will take it. If the caller is reporting a "crime in progress," the phone man must keep him on the line while he tries to obtain a physical description of the suspects, the manner and direction of their departure, and whether they are armed.

The phone man and the dispatcher are not allowed to decide whether a car should be dispatched. Many calls are made to obtain information, and if the phone man can satisfy the caller or direct him to another agency, he is permitted to do it. But if the caller insists on having a police car come to him, the phone man must accede. If he has any suspicion about the call, he may inform the dispatcher, who will advise caution when he assigns the job, or he may go directly to the lieutenant in charge of the radio room and request him to make a decision. There is no way of knowing how often the phone men exercise discretion in violation of their obligations and refuse to send cars, but the department does not want to give them a formal right which can be easily abused to reduce the work load of colleagues, or to satisfy some personal whim.[5]

The dispatcher's relationship to the patrolman's work has been exploited to increase the department's control over the district men. At the beginning of each tour of duty, the district operations crew delivers by phone (followed later by a hand-delivered copy) a record of the officers assigned to each car, wagon, and foot beat, and a report on the status of any cars and wagons not in operation. The dispatcher keeps a copy of this "pulling sheet" for his own use during the tour and submits the originals to a staff officer, who assembles a report on the manpower and equipment working throughout the city on that tour. Copies are forwarded to the department's records division for payroll and equipment-maintenance control. These pulling sheets make it more difficult for district supervisors and operations room crews to give someone free time, helping to control a once widespread abuse. These sheets also force the districts to adhere to a departmental policy requiring that all available vehicles be used, even if all the cars must be manned by a single officer. The only way to evade this order is for the district to disable cars or falsify departmental records. Both things occur but

[5]Radio calls have been used to lure policemen into traps. Ron Porambo, No Cause for Indictment (New York, Holt, Rinehart & Winston, 1971), p. 132. Many requests are still phoned directly to the districts. The operations man who takes the call occasionally tells the person to use the emergency number; more often the request is taken and then he calls the console and asks the dispatcher to send a car; sometimes the calls are ignored. There are also occasionally crank callers who plague every console. The police are generally on very good terms with the telephone company and use their services to trace these people and prosecute them.

In 1969, in Philadelphia, there were 1,575,113 calls received through the emergency number. In 1970 there were 1,611,311 calls and in the first six months of 1971, 881,461. In Detroit, where a different procedure is used, 1,027,000 were handled in 1968; 370,000 (36 percent) were resolved by the Police Complaint Operator without sending a patrol car to the scene. In the same year, New York, working with a similar system, handled 5,200,000 calls, 40 percent without dispatching an officer. T. M. Bercal, "Calls for Police Assistance," American Behavioral Scientist, Vol. XIII (1970), pp. 681–91.

are done only with careful consideration and in a special circumstance.

Each time he gives a job to an officer, the dispatcher writes a district control number on one corner of his assignment card. At the end of each tour, the patrolman turns in to his sergeant all of his reports. These are written on a triplicate form called a "48" (the form number) that every patrolman carries with him. There must be a 48 for every job assigned. In the radio room the assignment cards are processed during the following tour by the incoming console crew, who prepare a numerically ordered list of the "DC numbers" for each district, then give the list over the phone to the "48 man" in the district operations crew. He has two obligations. The 48 man uses his list as a guide to see whether any of the required reports are missing. If he discovers that an officer has failed to file a report, which happens frequently, he leaves a memo for the man's corporal to obtain the delinquent report on the following tour. At the same time, the 48 man gives each report a job classification code number. This coding system enables the department's administrators to analyze the kinds of crime reported each day and the different kinds of work that the patrolmen do. The copies of the 48 are then coded and distributed within the department. One copy remains in the district files and is retained for two years. A second copy is forwarded to the reports and control division, where the codes are checked and analyzed. This unit also receives from the broadcasting center a list of the assignments given on each tour in every district. This is used to check any errors, omissions, and collusions between the patrolmen, the operations crew, and their radio dispatchers. A third copy of the 48 is for the patrolman to keep in his own files, to prepare himself to testify in court or for reference. If he wants to keep a report, he tears off his copy before turning his paper work over to his sergeant at the end of the tour. Most of the reports are without significance and are thrown away.

The dispatcher has a direct influence on how each man does his work. Since each work card is time-punched at the beginning and end of a job, there is a formal record of how long the assigned man took to perform the work. These times are used by the research and planning division to analyze the work patterns of the men. More importantly, they serve to remind the men that they are being clocked and watched even when they are out of their cars. There are no formal limits for the completion of any kind of assignment but no patrolman is likely to remain "out of service" for more than half an hour without informing his dispatcher that he is still working on the assigned job.

In addition, any time a man leaves his car for any reason, he is supposed to inform the dispatcher. Men frequently leave their cars for a few moments without telling the dispatcher because they do not have the time or intend to be away only briefly. Although this regulation is designed to protect the patrolman as much as it is to control his movements, the dispatcher knows that each man must be allowed some latitude to exercise his private judgment while patrolling.

All communication is by numbers, combinations of the district number followed by the sector number to which the car is assigned. When the dispatcher calls a car number and no reply is received, he is supposed to file a report on the delinquent officer. Few men deliberately "blow a call," however; the dispatcher normally gives them the benefit of the doubt. He will call a car several times at intervals of up to a minute, if it is not an emergency assignment, before giving the job to another car. Sometimes a man will leave his car briefly and ask a colleague to cover for him. If his number is called, the covering car will respond and ask for the assignment. This is usually granted without question.

If a man has blown a call, his friends (if he has some) usually set out to look for him, because it is always possible that a car's radio has failed without the officer knowing it. Some dispatchers who are not on good terms with the units they serve stringently enforce this regulation and the men on their channel must exercise considerable caution. On the other hand, many officers are on close terms with dispatchers and they know that if they do not answer on the first call, they will not be called again. The dispatcher's reluctance to enforce this regulation can be overruled by a sergeant or a lieutenant intent on making an example of someone. If they ask the dispatcher to continue calling a car that does not answer, he will not refuse their request. Normally a dispatcher will not make out a delinquent report on a car until fifteen minutes have passed, more than enough time for the man's friends to locate him and advise him of the call.

The dispatcher's reluctance to enforce his supervisory role is limited by the knowledge that his performance may be monitored. Also, his sympathy for the patrolman is limited, since every man on the street knows the rules and can take the simple precautions necessary to avoid trouble. If a man neglects these, he must accept the consequences. He must give his lieutenant a written explanation of his failure to answer a call. The lieutenant must file a report with the captain, who in turn must answer the queries of the inspector who heads the radio division. If there is no legitimate excuse for the man's negligence, he can be taken to the front; or if his superiors are willing to protect him, he may be punished informally in a way that reminds him not to do anything which requires the sergeant or the lieutenant to write reports to the captain. He may be given "shit details" or refused any requests for time off until he demonstrates that he has learned his lesson.

The dispatcher has an undisputed right to assign jobs to patrol cars. Most assignments are distributed according to territorial responsibility, but if the sector car is out of service for any reason, the dispatcher usually gives the job to the nearest sector car showing "available" on his board. He cannot know exactly where the car is and normally he does not ask. No assignment may be directly refused, and even if the man is a long way from where he must go, he cannot say anything to the dispatcher. A colleague who feels that he can more easily take the job can offer his service, but it is up to the dispatcher to decide.

Even if a man wants to refuse an assignment for personal reasons, he may not explain to the dispatcher. This might be embarrassing and invariably takes up a lot of time. One of the dispatcher's obligations is to eliminate excessive talking and to maximize the available free air time for those who need his attention. The demand for air time is low much of the day, but the dispatchers must maintain a consistent discipline that will allow the most efficient use of the channel during peak hours. If a man is allowed to talk at length on Sunday morning, the dispatcher will have a difficult time enforcing the necessary control on Friday night.

In order to meet the demands of the dispatchers and the needs of the patrolmen, an informal convention has evolved which allows the patrolman to signal his disinclinations to the dispatcher without directly refusing an order. Usually he claims an involvement in some matter that does not require prior permission from the dispatcher, such as issuing a ticket or making a stop. The dispatcher understands what is being asked of him and is allowed to make the final decision. If the man is ordered to take the job he cannot refuse, although what he actually does after he accepts is up to him and his sergeant.

One afternoon a dispatcher gave out a job to a patrolman who was evidently disturbed by the order. Without thinking, he said, "I know the people who live there. Could you send another car?" There was a brief silence while the surprised dispatcher considered his reply. But the officer recovered himself and, realizing his breach of radio etiquette, sought to redress the situation he had created. He came back on the air and formally addressed the dispatcher as if his initial response to the assignment had never occurred. "Car 656 to radio. Could you please send another car to that location. I am issuing a TVR (traffic ticket)." The relieved dispatcher accepted his request and the matter was quickly forgotten.

The dispatcher usually accedes to these requests because he knows they are not evasions inspired by laziness. If the call was an emergency, there would be no time for discussion and anything else the patrolman might be doing would not take precedence over the job. These special requests can occur only on "routine" assignments, which allow a man to be free of the radio for as long as half an hour. Anyone wanting to loaf would be happy to take the routine job and steal a little time at both ends of the assignment. A refusal, therefore, means that the man either has a personal reason for not wanting to go to a particular place, or is engaged in doing something, perhaps a vice surveillance, that he does not want to make public. If he were actually writing a ticket, for example, he could accept the routine job and easily arrive in time after finishing with the driver he had stopped.

The dispatcher's control over his channel is absolute. Since only one person may speak over the channel at any time, the dispatcher must himself direct the entire flow of talk. Although everyone on the channel can hear what is being said over the air, each person may speak directly only with his dispatcher. Patrolmen are not permitted to talk to each other. Even the sergeant and lieutenant may not speak directly with their men on the air but must issue instructions through the dispatcher. Only the highest officials of the department can violate this rule, and they are also the only persons who may ignore the regulation that forbids the use of personal names on the air. But other than the commissioner and several of his closest commanders, no one may ignore the dispatcher's control of his channel.

The dispatcher does not hesitate to order men to stay off the air while he is broadcasting or taking a message. His demands at these moments are curt and direct. Interruptions are allowed only in emergency situations, which must be clearly marked to assure their recognition. If a patrolman is in personal trouble, all he must do to bring the entire channel to a standstill is to call "assist," then give his location. An "assist officer" call has absolute priority over all other air traffic, and the dispatcher will not resume broadcasting until he has acknowledgment that others know exactly where the officer is and are on their way to his aid. If the officer has an emergency not involving his personal safety, he will say, "Car 5269, emergency," which is a cue that will clear the air of all routine traffic. If a patrolman has someone who is badly injured or if he discovers a fire, for example, he will use this cue to assure his message the priority treatment it requires.

If a dispatcher suspects a man is having difficulties which he is reluctant to admit, he does not hesitate to interrogate him. He listens to the voices of the men on his channel; many of them become quite familiar to him. He knows their normal radio voices, and if he suspects a note of tension or a hint of special exertion, he will ask if everything is all right. Some patrolmen are unwilling to call assists or even to ask the dispatcher to "send me a couple of cars," despite the constant urging of their supervisors, who constantly remind them not to be ashamed to use their radios and ask for help. If he is not satisfied with what he hears, the dispatcher can initiate an assist or order another car to go to the officer's location. If the dispatcher calls the assist, it is the only time he will allow the patrolman to contradict him. A request for cancellation will be granted, although by that time other cars are on their way and will continue regardless of what additional orders they receive.[6]

During a hot, humid summer night, a Thursday, there was a call of a "gang fight and a shooting" in an area which had been the scene of several shootings and a murder during the previous few days. A number of cars were mobilized to go into the area, investigate the call, and break up any fight that was going on. The radio was silent while the cars sped quickly into the area, but the silence was soon broken by a faint voice giving a car number and asking the dispatcher to send his sergeant to an intersection. It is another unspoken rule of radio conduct that when a man asks for his sergeant to come to him, it means he has a serious problem. Simple respect for rank requires that he ask the dispatcher if his sergeant is available when he wants to discuss something. The dispatcher will ask the sergeant, who has the option to affirm or deny the request, and then give a location where the patrolman can meet the sergeant. When a man asks his sergeant to come to him, something has occurred that he cannot leave or discuss over the air.

The dispatcher, troubled by the sound of the officer's voice, immediately asked the man whether he was having any "difficulty." There was no response. The sergeant announced that he was on his way, and another car said the man was not at the location he had given the dispatcher. Every car in the platoon was now mobilized in search of the officer, streaking back and forth through the area with their emergency lights flashing. The dispatcher ordered all cars off the air as he quietly and patiently called for the missing car by its number. After the tenth repetition, the officer's voice was heard correcting his location and asking for help. The district cars rushed to the intersection and found the officer pinned behind the wheel of his wrecked car. He had been driven off the road as he entered the intersection and his car smashed into

---

[6]Each assist-officer call is investigated and the circumstances of the event established. A police officer does not want a record that indicates he called for help when it was not warranted. Occasionally men call one in the panic of a moment and then try to call it off.

the wall of a building. The car was surrounded by a crowd of more than two hundred people, some of whom were taunting the painfully injured man.

Patrolmen are extremely reluctant to criticize one another's work directly, but dispatchers, who are also patrolmen, do not hesitate to correct errors and order adjustments. These must be accepted without protest by everyone on the channel. For example, the police use a standard holdup memorandum form, which lists in a set order the prescribed questions an officer must ask a witness when he arrives at the scene of a robbery. When he has finished the interview, he tells the dispatcher that he has a "holdup memo," giving him priority over routine messages. The dispatcher uses a blank form and the officer simply reads the answers off in the established order. When the dispatcher has copied down all the available information, he rings a warning bell, which precedes all priority messages, and announces "flash information" before broadcasting to the entire network. The signal and the announcement are meant to give the patrolmen a moment to get pencils and turn their attention to the radio.

Not uncommonly, officers are so anxious to deliver the information that they do not properly control their voices, or they read so quickly that the dispatcher cannot follow them. This defeats the purpose of the procedure, which is designed to minimize the time between the commission of a serious crime and the mobilization of cars in search of the fleeing suspects. The dispatchers take charge and order the man to speak more softly or to slow down. Usually a simple command is sufficient to assure the adjustment. On one occasion a young officer twice failed to heed the dispatcher's commands. The delays had destroyed the potential usefulness of the information, but the dispatcher was now concerned with giving the man some badly needed instruction. Quietly and firmly he ordered the patrolman to stop reading and to give him the answer to each question as the dispatcher read them from the printed card. The officer had no choice but to comply. When they were finished, the patrolman's sergeant requested the dispatcher to send the man to him.

Departmental procedures require that every holdup announced on the air be followed by a memo. Sometimes there are delays in arriving at the scene, or the available information is so scant that it is not worth broadcasting. But there must be a memo since a radio-room supervisor keeps a list of all major crime calls and checks the memos for time delays. Any unusual time delays must be explained in writing. In order to meet this obligation, dispatchers often take useless memos over the telephone rather than waste air time or embarrass someone for no reason. But in this case the dispatcher had decided to teach the officer a lesson in radio courtesy since he is personally responsible for explaining the delay. Undoubtedly the sergeant emphasized the lessons to be learned at their meeting.

The dispatcher is outranked by the sergeant and lieutenant but they, too, must heed his commands. They are obliged to respond to all crime calls in their areas, and the dispatcher is required to broadcast their numbers to remind them when he dispatches a crime call. The dispatcher also has the authority to order cars to stay away from certain places without consulting the street supervisors. During busy periods, the dispatchers are authorized to return cars to service after specific intervals without reference to the men who supervise street work. The sergeants know that these orders come from higher authority and they cannot protest.

The dispatcher and the sergeant are both careful to avoid the possibility of conflict that exists between them. The dispatcher invariably responds to any questions or requests with a "sir," even if he is privately on a first-name basis with the man. The lieutenant is always called "commander." A dispatcher rarely relaxes the formal address he uses when speaking with either the sergeant or the lieutenant. Many dispatchers decline to exercise their authority and politely ask the sergeant to decide things that are actually their responsibility. For example, when an incident has attracted several cars, the dispatcher is supposed to make the formal assignment and order the extra cars to go back "in service." Rather than deciding himself, the dispatcher asks the sergeant which car should remain; and he gives the appropriate orders only after getting the answer. The dispatcher is careful to avoid undercutting the sergeant's and the lieutenant's authority on the street, while using his power to aid their supervision. The street supervisors see the dispatcher as their ally, a man who gives them the courtesy and respect due their rank.[7]

The dispatcher only infrequently has to invoke the considerable authority at his disposal to win the active cooperation of the patrolmen. Their dependence on him is too great to risk his antagonism; if he is not an active ally, their entire working situation becomes dangerously unpredictable. The dispatcher can harass and embarrass a platoon by continually demanding accounts of every minute the men are working. But possibly even more important than what he can do to them are the things he may refuse to do for them. He has numerous little favors he can grant a man that will ease the burdens of the tour. For instance, the patrolman can go to "lunch" (policemen refer to all their meal breaks as lunch, regardless of the hour) only with the dispatcher's permission. If the dispatcher wants a man to remain in service, he simply tells him that he cannot go. The men are not supposed to eat together and the dispatcher is responsible for seeing they do not gather. A sympathetic dispatcher will allow several men to share their lunchtime by permitting one man to give a location where the dispatcher knows the police do not eat. An experienced dispatcher knows by the locality alone what restaurants and important stores are in its vicinity, and he will know where the officer is actually going. He has the telephone numbers for many of these places and occasionally will phone a policeman if he needs to reach him quickly. But an unsympathetic dispatcher does not have to allow this favor to the men under his supervision.

Each man is allowed twenty minutes to eat; his car is automatically returned to service without the man announcing his return to work. Most patrolmen assume they will be given an additional ten minutes' grace, permitting them to have a real respite from the constant chatter of the radio and the monotonous rhythms of working in the car. The dispatcher does not have to grant anyone this little civility and is risking censure by doing it.

Some men try to exploit their right to obey calls of nature

[7]On conflicts arising from subordinates giving orders to superordinates see William F. Whyte, *Human Relations in the Restaurant Industry* (New York, McGraw-Hill, 1948), Chap. V.

to make free time for themselves. For example, a man who wants to go to lunch during a period when it is forbidden by department regulations (as during school recess periods, when many men have crossing-guard duty) will tell the dispatcher to "take me out on a personal." A "personal," by its nature, cannot have a set time limit, but a strict dispatcher can keep a close account of the number of personals a man takes and put pressure on him if the officer's sergeant has not already told him to stop abusing a right that can be restricted at any time. The dispatcher who does not get cooperation in this matter may file a memorandum with his superiors to cover himself, forcing the squad's lieutenant to explain the patrolman's behavior. Excessive exploitation of this right is rare because it is such a transparent ploy, but an unfriendly dispatcher can make it impossible to use, even for a quick cup of coffee and a smoke.

The policeman is also dependent on his dispatcher to protect him from the errors he commits unwittingly. When a man wants to speak over his phone, he must depress the transmitter button located in the handle. A tiny red light goes on when the button has opened the channel, but the light does not always work properly. Occasionally, the button will stick after the man is finished transmitting and the light will not indicate that his channel is still open. When a man has a "hung carrier," anything he says in the vicinity of his radio will be broadcast over the channel. Naturally, this impedes broadcasting, but it can also be very embarrassing. An alert dispatcher recalls the numbers of the cars which most recently contacted him and their location at the time. He usually sends other cars quickly to locate the man and to correct the situation, but if he is on bad terms with the squad or personally dislikes the man involved, he can allow events to take their course.

The patrolman is also dependent on the dispatchers for protection from the occasional indiscretions committed in moments of exhaustion or agitation. Each transmission is quickly followed by the next, so that unless particular attention is given to a remark, it will soon pass and be forgotten. There is no training for these moments, but they give evidence of a dispatcher's character to the men who depend upon him.

One night, an officer was describing a suspect who had escaped his custody. He was out of breath and racing through his report wildly, finally losing control of his temper. "The nigger prick is cut on the head because I jacked him good," he said. The dispatcher immediately cut him off and began to rebroadcast the description, concluding with the words, "The suspect may have a laceration on the back of his head inflicted by the officer in pursuit."

The men are under strict orders not to make any personal comments on the air, and they rarely do. During the dreary hours of last out, when it is a struggle for many to remain awake, some men silently beg the dispatcher to give them a job that will keep them going. One night a dispatcher called for a wagon to return to an address it had just left and pick up a person who required transportation. The wagon had been to the location several times during the night and did not answer immediately. A sector car called in its number, and the officer said in a tired voice, "I'll take the shanty-Irish bitch." While every man on the channel smiled or laughed, sharing in the confines of his car the speaker's exasperation and exhaustion, the dispatcher said with only the slightest hint of laughter in his voice, "O.K., Car 5915, thank you. The wagon can resume patrol." At that hour of the morning there were probably no listeners other than policemen; the police reporters who listen to the divisional bands around the clock are either sleeping or deeply engrossed in a card game. If the dispatcher had not chosen to ignore the slip, he could have caused trouble for the officer, but he let it pass and it disappeared into the air, quickly forgotten.

2 · Work Signals

The patrolman's working time is consumed by many conflicting interests and pressures. He is on the lookout for activity, talking to people for information, scanning passers-by for signs of suspicion. Some of his time is spent completing formal obligations, signing store logs, directing traffic, more of it with administrative duties, making out reports, checking the records of suspects, speaking with detectives; but the majority of his patrol time is spent responding to calls from the dispatcher. The dispatcher initiates most of the patrolman's work. A study of a middle-sized police department in California revealed that less than 20 percent of the work done by the patrolmen was self-initiated. This work took up less than 10 percent of their patrol time. The rest of their work was directly assigned by the dispatchers or involved administrative duties.[8]

What the dispatcher tells a man when he gives him an assignment is all the patrolman knows about what he will find until he actually arrives. The dispatcher must tell him everything relevant to the job in the most economical way, to avoid wasting air time. He must also try to get the entire message across in one attempt, since repetitions slow the patrolman's response time and tie up the radio channel. The instructions must be unambiguous and in plain English. Some police departments have used numerical codes to designate specific assignments, but they have not been very successful. Each patrolman is required to learn a set of code numbers which he translates into assignments when he hears them. This method has the advantage of confusing eavesdroppers, but it also causes confusion and misunderstandings between dispatchers and policemen. There is a possibility for error at both ends of the wire, particularly when the men are under stress. It is also not certain that coded signals actually save air time, the principal reason for using them. In Philadelphia they are rarely used now.[9]

The patrolman must have faith in the skill and experience of the dispatcher because what this unseen person relates to him establishes his initial expectations and the manner of his response to the assignment. When he has received the message, he never asks the dispatcher if there is anything else he should know; he assumes that he has been told every bit of

[8] J. A. Webster, "Police Task and Time Study," *The Journal of Criminal Law, Criminology, and Police Science*, Vol. LXI (1970), pp. 94–6.

[9] On the problems of human error in communication systems, see George A. Miller, *The Psychology of Communication* (Baltimore, Penguin Books, 1969), pp. 14ff., 45ff. The few codes still used in Philadelphia are employed irregularly. Policemen are called 369 and a dispatcher may tell a man to "meet the officer" on "meet the 369," each digit pronounced separately. A report of a possible dead person, without regard for the manner of dying, is a 5292.

relevant information. The first thing the dispatcher usually tells him is the address. He is rarely given a name, since this is information that can be obtained by the officer from the complainant, or if the call is an emergency, a wounded person or a robbery in progress, the name is irrelevant. If the dispatcher suspects for any reason that the call might possibly involve violence or the presence of weapons, these facts will be explicitly mentioned and caution urged. Any assignment suggesting the prospect of difficulty or danger obliges the dispatcher to ask the patrolman whether he is "two-man" or "solo." If the officer is working alone, the dispatcher will order another car to accompany him.

The specific assignments are transmitted to the patrolman with the aid of key words and phrases that are familiar to all policemen. These have been developed by the police over a long period of time, beginning with the introduction of the call box into police service. They differ from city to city, but they are part of every policeman's intimate craft knowledge, and he uses them in private conversation as well as when he is testifying in court. These key words derive from legal terms and phrases which the police learn from the penal codes, the only formal literature of the police trade, and also from local cultural traditions. They reduce human conduct to those essentials of interest to the man who must go to work and deal with them. When a patrolman hears the dispatcher say "corner loungers" or "disturbance house," he has a very clear idea of what to expect when he arrives. These words are not formally taught to the recruits at the police academy, although the instructors use them constantly; it is presumed that the words will be learned quickly by observation and association. The dispatchers have no formal list of assignment phrases; they simply apply their knowledge to the complaints they hear on the phones and translate them into familiar trade phrases.

If the dispatcher does not give an accurate description of the assignment, the policeman may unwittingly approach the job without proper regard for his own safety and for the needs of his prospective clients. Errors are not infrequent and these can cause embarrassment and danger, even on routine assignments. One morning a patrolman was given a call to aid a boy with a cut. The dispatcher said, "Hospital case. Boy with a bleeding arm." The patrolman set out immediately for the address, making his way through the mid-morning traffic. Since the dispatcher had not said it was an emergency, which is part of his obligation, the officer did not use his flashing lights or siren to speed his arrival. As he parked his car, the boy and his mother were already at the curb. The mother, holding a towel on the boy's arm, and her daughter, who came out of the house, berated the officer with a stream of invective, accusing him and all other policemen of being lazy, cruel, and indifferent to human suffering. She threatened to call his captain and expose some scandalous doings involving several policemen and young women from the neighborhood. He and his partner ignored her with some difficulty as they helped the boy into the car. The mother continued to yell all the way to the hospital. The patrolman was somewhat embarrassed because the cut was serious and he could have gotten to the boy more quickly if he had known it was an emergency.

In this instance, the policeman did not blame his dispatcher for the error. He knew the man personally and considered him to be absolutely reliable at his job. He did not presume that the dispatcher had or had not made an error, but he was willing to allow him the benefit of the doubt. He had no way of knowing whether the man who took the call had interpreted the information correctly, or whether the person who had called the police had accurately described the boy's condition. There are dispatchers whose performance arouses hostility and even fear among the men on the street. Some dispatchers speak too quickly or have poor radio voices; some make numerous dispatching errors or cannot recall past assignments they have given out. The patrolmen do not hesitate to ask their lieutenant to request a change; they urge him to pool his efforts with the other lieutenants in the division to have the man removed. They do not make any direct comments to the dispatcher, although they may convey their dissatisfaction with his performance by asking him to repeat messages needlessly. A bad dispatcher has as much power as a good one and he is not someone a patrolman can afford to antagonize.

When a patrolman arrives at the scene of his assignment, he gives the people an opportunity to reaffirm or deny their request for his presence. If it is not an emergency call, he asks whether anyone has called the police; if he is told no, he will usually terminate the encounter without any further questioning. Until he has been personally connected to the people he is serving, he remains somewhat detached from the proceedings. He is not angered by the frequency with which calls turn out to be "unfounded"; he accepts this as part of his working life. He knows that some people call just to have the police appear, or to give someone in their neighborhood or household a warning, or to express intent to take more serious action if the problem they are not prepared to discuss with the patrolman persists. There are some people in every district who call the police with great frequency, and the patrolmen inform the dispatchers through their sergeant to ignore any calls from certain addresses. This must be done informally since it is a violation of department regulations.

While he is not necessarily committed to doing anything once he has taken a job, the policeman is alert to any indications which imply reasons for his being there. An officer was called to a house to settle a family dispute. When he arrived, all was quiet. The elderly lady who answered the door said they had not called, but he was welcome to come inside. She and her sister appeared quite nervous, glancing at their brother, who was sitting quietly in an easy chair. They insisted again they had not called. The officer believed something was wrong but he had no reason to act. As he was leaving, he asked the lady who had admitted him whether she had need of the police. She hesitated before saying no. Instead of leaving directly, the officer stood by the door and listened. When he heard a loud thud from within, he knocked on the door and entered immediately. The women were cowering in a corner and a table was overturned in the dining room; near where the brother sat were two loaded revolvers on the floor. The officer picked them up. The sisters pleaded with him to take the guns but not arrest their senile brother. They admitted calling the police when they found the guns, then denied it after their brother threatened to hurt them. The man had no permit for the guns and the officer confiscated them. He acceded to the pleas of the elderly ladies and left their brother with them. If he had not been warned of a disturbance and the women had not acted curiously at the door, he would not have entered the house. But his decision to go inside was a measure of his initial suspicion, deepened by the behavior of the residents.

In the majority of his assignments, the patrolman is not even told the exact nature of the problem. The most common call he receives is a "meet complainant." He is not told anything but the address. When he receives this call, he knows the assignment does not involve any emergency and will probably require him to make a judgment about whether a crime has been committed. People frequently call the dispatcher and report, for example, that their daughter is missing or that their car has been stolen. The dispatcher has no way of knowing whether he has been told the truth and must leave that determination to the investigating officer. There is no purpose in mentioning the specific complaint since it will all be repeated by the complainant when the officer arrives at the scene. This signal is also used to give an officer an assignment that involves a complex personal tale that the dispatcher cannot recount over the air or was unable to understand in the initial telling. He does not want to label it as a family disturbance and imply the possibility of violence, so he simply uses the most general terms available to him.

"Hospital case" is the second most common call given to the patrolman. The dispatcher usually does not know the nature of the problem; even if he does, he will not mention any specifics unless it is a maternity case or some other kind of emergency. If he knows the person to be aided cannot walk, he must assign a two-man team with a stretcher. These cases are handled by wagons, all of which are equipped with hinged stretchers for carrying persons down narrow staircases in a sitting position. If the dispatcher knows the person is bleeding, he mentions this to hurry the officer along, not to allow him to take any special precautions. There are none, and getting dirty is one of the fundamental obligations of being a policeman. If the dispatcher knows the person is suffering from a dangerous communicable disease, such as tuberculosis, he will tell the officer to CRD (contact radio division on the telephone). He then explains on the phone the procedure the officer must follow to protect himself from exposure to the disease.

There are two additional calls that are linked to the paramedical role of the district policeman. The first is a "sick assist," a call to aid someone who is bedridden or too frail to go to the bathroom alone. Sometimes an old person will fall out of bed. If his aging companions are too weak to lift him off the floor, the police are called to help put the person back in bed. On one occasion, a sick assist occupied a patrolman and his partner for almost four hours on a New Year's Eve. They arrived at a dreary apartment building to find a terrified old woman in fear for her aged husband's life. Their electricity had gone out and the refrigerator containing his medicine was getting warm. The patrolmen found the basement locked and they were unable to get to the fuse box. The landlord could not be reached; his babysitter said he was at a party. They scavenged some wire and extension cord from the apartment and returned to their station to pick up some more, in order to run a line from the refrigerator into a hallway where they had located a live socket. When the refrigerator was working again, they bid the couple good night and returned to work.

Unless he is told the hospital case or the sick assist is an emergency, the patrolman will not rush to arrive because if he has an accident on the way, he has no legitimate excuse to offer in his defense. But he knows that most of these calls are "founded" and he does not allow himself to be distracted. If he is on his way to meet a complainant and sees anything suspicious, he will stop to investigate and may even make a car stop or issue a ticket if he needs the activity; but on a paramedical run, he does not look for work and he does not see any.

The other paramedical call is a "check the well-being of the occupants." A dispatcher will not give out this call unless he is told something concrete to arouse his suspicions. If he has any doubts about the merits of the caller's case, he will give the patrolman a meet complainant. Therefore, when this call is dispatched, the patrolman presumes the basis for concern is quite real and he is not surprised to find his sergeant arriving with him. People often call the police to complain that they have not seen a friend for a while; this is not sufficient to cause the dispatcher to treat their concern with gravity. If someone calls with a complaint of a bad smell coming from an apartment, however, that is sufficient for the dispatcher. Every policeman knows the stench of death; the recruits are given a tour of the city's morgue and are required to pass through the "smell room," where the decayed bodies are kept. It is an unmistakable and unforgettable odor. If an officer smells death, he immediately calls his supervisor, who must make the decision whether to force entry into a private place without a warrant or suspicion of felony. Most patrolmen frankly admit their distaste for this work and some refuse to enter an apartment filled with the odors and insects produced by a week-old corpse. In summertime, these bodies ripen quickly. Frequently they cannot be picked up, but must be shoveled into rubber bags and then frozen before an autopsy can be performed. The patrolmen are not equipped to handle this work, and they depend on their sergeant to exaggerate the amount of decay, if necessary, to get the morgue to dispatch a crew.

The police are obliged to perform certain functions for the fire department, which are promptly attended to, although they are not emergencies. In recent years, firehouses have been the targets of burglars and vandals; the tradition of leaving the firehouse door open as the engines roar away has been abandoned. In many areas a police car is assigned to guard the station even though the doors have been locked. When an officer is told to "cover the firehouse," he knows he is required to do nothing but park his car in front of the station until the engines return. He does not delay his arrival except for the most important emergency calls, because the firemen, as municipal workers, are given extra consideration by policemen. Also, if anything should happen at the station in his absence, the officer knows he will be required to explain his failure to people who know all the excuses.

The police must keep a record of all false alarms. These violations of city ordinances are called "special assignments." The assigned man must hurry to the scene because he is obliged to get the number of the fire wagon that responded to the call, the commanding fire officer's name, and the alarm-box number. If he dawdles, he is obliged either to make up the information or go to the fire station. This requires him to do extra work, which he does not willingly do; therefore, he drives quickly to avoid the need. When there is a real fire, at least one car is assigned to the scene to direct traffic, control the spectators, and make an official report. The officer is told by the dispatcher whether it is a "local," reported by phone, or a "box," reported by an alarm. This tells him how many pieces of equipment are at the scene. Each additional alarm sends more equipment, and the police department has formal rules governing the number of patrolmen and supervisors who must be assigned with each alarm. The dispatcher is responsible for reminding the appropriate supervisors of their obligations. The men know a large fire attracts higher officials, but the radio reminds them by announcing that outsiders are arriving. This gives every man ample warning to be on his best behavior.

The police are municipal employees who must concern themselves with street conditions to protect the people's welfare and spare the city civil suits for injuries and damages. Calls to "investigate a dangerous highway condition" or a "defective traffic signal," "to check for an abandoned car," and to turn off an "open hydrant" are generally assumed to be legitimate since the dispatcher would have given the officer a meet complainant if he questioned the call. He is rarely given any information other than the location, and it is from this that the officer must decide how he will respond. If it is an important intersection, he knows any delay that allows a problem to develop will cause complaints and possibly even the captain's intervention. Sergeants and lieutenants assume, until proven wrong, that their men know how to make the proper judgments in these matters. If a man shows poor sense in something so elementary, they are not likely to trust him with anything more important. Few men fail to respond to these calls, but unless the location suggests something important to the officer, he will not hurry his arrival. These are the kinds of assignment he uses to make some free time; if he is not carefully supervised by his sergeant, he might use the cover provided by these jobs to take an extra lunch break.

Sometimes there are numerous calls about the same problem. The dispatcher does not mention this when he gives out the job. If the calls continue, he will return to the air and tell the assigned patrolman there are additional complaints. The man is being told to get on with his work and stop dawdling. He usually responds by telling the dispatcher that he is just arriving at the location. If this is not the truth, the patrolman increases his speed so he will arrive before anyone can check on him.

District men must get parkers, but when they are given a call for "illegal parking," they rarely hasten to the location even if they are under pressure from their sergeant. Most of these calls are the consequences of disputes among neighbors, or between garage owners and local residents, who must compete for parking spaces. If the officer is told that it is a "clean sweep," meaning he is to tag every car on the block, he assumes it is a business dispute. Few men are in any hurry to land themselves in the middle of what they presume will be a big argument. Since they do not have to report their actions to the dispatcher, they take their time.

A more serious call requiring a direct response is an "auto accident." The dispatcher tells the patrolman whether it is an "auto–auto," an "auto–ped," or a "hit-and-run," and whether there are any reported injuries. If there are people in need of aid, he goes directly to the assignment; otherwise he is in no hurry to arrive. A patrolman who drives past the scene of an accident which does not seem to have caused any injuries is often likely to continue on his way. In both instances, the man's behavior is caused by his dislike for the acrimonious disputes that accompany many accidents and the elaborate reports he is required to prepare for the department's accident-investigation unit and the insurance companies. Any man who is out of service when another car is assigned an auto accident on his sector and goes on the air to take the job is given considerable (if unspoken) credit for solidarity and reliability. Even when a man knows he cannot avoid handling the assignment, he will take his time in the usually vain hope that the people will have left before his arrival.

During a sultry Saturday afternoon, a patrolman took a call for an auto accident. When he was within sight of the crash, which he saw was minor, although it blocked a side street, an emergency call for "man with a shotgun" was issued. He was only several blocks from the announced location, and without hesitation he swung his car around and headed for the emergency call. After a fruitless chase over several blocks, involving many patrolmen and the search of several abandoned buildings, in one of which the officer fell through a rotten floor, injuring an arm slightly and getting himself covered with filth, he returned to his car. He was driving toward the scene of the accident when he heard his sergeant ask the dispatcher to send a car to that location and clear up the traffic jam that was developing. "Oh, come on, Sarge, don't fuck me now," the man muttered as he picked up his transmitter. He told the dispatcher he had been delayed by the shotgun call but was just arriving at the accident and would handle the assignment. He considered his sergeant's action an unwarranted sanction, in view of his commitment to the job attested to by the state of his uniform. But the sergeant was concerned that the traffic jam might erupt into a battle among the increasingly angry motorists, and the patrolman had violated department regulations by not going directly to his assignment. The sergeant felt himself entirely justified in pressuring the man, whose whereabouts he did not know. Later in the day, the patrolman met the sergeant at a local hospital while he was getting cleaned up and sought to explain his absence, without revealing the annoyance he still harbored.

There are frequent calls involving juveniles and teenagers that the policeman accepts as routine assignments unless they are amplified by an accompanying commentary. The most common of these calls is for a "disorderly crowd" or corner loungers. The sector patrolman usually knows from the location who he will find, and if he is quite familiar with the area, he may even know who made the call. The swiftness of his response is determined by the officer's knowledge, the importance of the corner in the sector, and his previous experiences there. Generally he is not in any hurry to arrive, hoping that the group will have moved along before he reaches the scene. Similarly, when he gets a call to "investigate juveniles walking," or even to "investigate a person acting suspiciously," he does not rush because he does not expect to find anything worthy of haste.

But if any of these calls contain an explicit possibility of conflict, violence, or vandalism, his response is very different. A call of a "gang fight," of "males carrying guns," "males breaking into a building," or even a "fight on the highway" brings a multiple-car response and rapid reaction. Many of these calls are never heard in some districts. In others they are almost a daily occurrence and even more frequent in summertime; this does not lessen the speed of the patrolman's reaction. Location also plays a role in the experienced officer's response to these calls because he "knows" there are places in his district where such things do not normally occur. He will investigate promptly, but he will not risk injury by rushing in. If the location is one he knows as a place where these things do go on, he goes to the scene as quickly as possible.

There are naturally some men who do not rush in on any calls, always driving in a leisurely manner, hoping that time will do all their work; some others, usually rookies, drive too quickly everywhere, even to lunch. One officer was given a call of males breaking into house. Instead of driving quickly to the address, he moved ahead slowly, commenting that the street was a little alley with many abandoned houses on it. He did not know whether the particular house was abandoned, but he had written off the entire street as a place of little consequence. When he arrived, he watched passively as several young boys leaped out of the side of the abandoned shell. He grinned. "You can't keep those little pricks out of them houses. Even if you whipped their ass, they'd be back tomorrow. These places are natural playgrounds for them." He told the dispatcher the call was unfounded.

A similar call, in another part of the same district, elicited an entirely different response from the young patrolman who took the job. When he heard the address, he mentioned it was on a street where he had had a run-in with a local motorcycle club. He assumed some of its members might be involved in this call and he treated it as an emergency, using his lights and siren. He was disturbed to find only an abandoned building with a few little children playing in it. He unfounded the call.

Any report of fighting brings a direct response. If it is accompanied by a claim that weapons are involved, the officer's approach to the scene is rapid and alert. Disturbance-house calls are commonplace in poor and working-class areas of the city, and the police do not rush headlong to answer them; but if one is accompanied by a claim of "man with a gun," the call is treated as an emergency. This is particularly note-worthy because many patrolmen who work these areas believe that poor women have learned they will get faster action from the police by claiming someone has a gun or a knife. This does not deter the speed of the men's response. Disturbance calls to public places generally receive a more rapid response than calls to private places, but any call which suggests violent conflict is treated as real and promptly investigated.

A call reporting a felony, such as "robbery in progress," "burglary in progress," "rape," "report of gunshots," or "report of purse snatch," elicits an emergency response from the patrolmen in the area. These calls are always prefaced by the alarm bell, which alerts the men to listen carefully and also to prepare themselves for the exertion which quickly follows. The information on these jobs is announced first, then a specific car is assigned to handle the paper work. This is done to minimize the amount of time required to get the men into action since the police believe their best chance of capturing felons is at the scene of their crimes. Any car in the area may go on these calls, even cars which have other assignments, although a car which is on a hospital case is forbidden to do anything else. All felony calls are repeated on J-Band to allow any police car that happens to be in the vicinity of a reported crime to take part in the mobilization. Occasionally men mobilize for these calls without informing the dispatcher if they feel he will order them not to go in. Since policemen take their greatest risks answering these calls, the dispatcher usually accompanies them with a reminder to use their lights and siren while driving and to drive carefully. They are also told to turn their sirens off as they approach the scene in order not to alert the criminals of their arrival.[1]

A sergeant is required to respond to every emergency call in his area, and the dispatcher reminds him on every occasion. The appearance of the sergeant on these calls is one reason why the response of most patrolmen is quick on all felony calls, but even without their sergeant, the men are anxious to show their commitment to the risks and dangers

[1]Throughout the day, the dispatchers read off reminders and "quips" to the policemen about how they should act, when they are allowed to use their guns, and how to drive properly.

they all must share. Patrolmen take careful notice of who comes in on emergency calls, which men tend to be first most often, who does not show up at all, and which men seem to arrive just a little bit late. There are few district policemen who can stand being labeled a "traffic cop," an insult which implies that a man has no stomach for risk-taking. The recognition that colleagues consider someone a coward is usually sufficient to drive a man out of the district, and any man who wishes to stay must learn to accept the risks of fast driving and dark alleys.

There are relatively few calls reporting the sale or use of drugs in public places, but these generally elicit a very quick response. One reason for this is that any drug arrest counts as a vice pinch, and younger policemen who have no sources of information are unable to make any vice activity except by pinching a junkie off a street corner. Glue-sniffing is widely practiced among young teenagers in some neighborhoods and there are men who specialize in pinching "huffers." Calls involving glue-sniffing frequently come out as a disorderly crowd, but the astute man knows his corners as well as a trout fisherman knows the pools of his favorite stream. When he hears the call for disorderly crowd, he just listens for the location and decides whether it is a possible vice arrest.

"Open property" is a call similar to a burglary call, although the police respond quite differently to each of them. An open property is a report that a building or house has been discovered with a window or door ajar. While these calls are almost always legitimate, more often than not they turn out to be a nuisance. The person who called did see an open window but failed to inquire whether the people of the house were at home. Few police officers regard this call as a signal to rush anywhere, while the men almost always drive quickly on burglary calls which are frequently unfounded. Burglary calls imply that a crime is in progress and that there are people on the premises, while an open property leaves entirely unclear whether a crime is in progress, whether it has already been committed, or if there is any crime at all.

People who are "cop-wise" are aware of the characteristic responses of the police. Occasionally this knowledge is used to draw policemen away from areas where a robbery or burglary is going to be attempted. A false robbery call will be planted in the hope that the police will respond in force and strip the target area of coverage. The police seek to counteract this by obliging supervisors to order all cars at a robbery scene back into service, except for the one or two cars needed to guard the "crime scene" and interview the victims. The dispatchers are also under instructions to assist the supervisors by ordering cars outside the immediate area to remain on the perimeter. The police also have plans that require cars to go to preassigned locations on a given signal, establishing a network of informal roadblocks covering possible getaway routes.

There are neighborhoods, mainly poor, where the police response to assist-officer calls is well known to the residents. The police believe this knowledge is used against them. Following a conflict between police and local residents, it is common to hear a number of assist calls. Many of these are made in good faith, but some are malicious, called in by people who hope that the speeding police cars will get into accidents. The dispatchers seek to limit these risks by announcing whether the call has come from a "civilian by phone," a "civilian by police radio," or "police by radio." A call from any non-police source is treated more circumspectly than calls from police officers, although they are all answered. It is the responsibility of the first car at the scene of an assist call to verify it and to notify the other cars to continue to the scene or slow down. Men who arrive first are given no public rewards nor are they thanked ostentatiously, but their colleagues do not forget them or fail to credit their action.

A policeman has no way of judging the validity of a call prior to his arrival at the scene. His response to a call cannot be taken as a measure of his belief in its truth but rather as a measure of what he sees as being necessary to do his work successfully *if* the call is correct. People who want to make a report to the police or ask advice are not likely to disappear if the officer is a few minutes delayed in arriving. If they are gone when he gets there, he feels they did not really need his help. But crimes are acts which take only a few moments and speed is the only thing the officer has to improve his chances of success.

3 · Obligations and Collusions

A squad that works with a cooperative radio crew can make arrangements that are mutually beneficial and protect both from embarrassments. Many squad members exploit any opportunity to develop personal and informal connections with their radio men. Because a detailed geographical knowledge of an area is crucial to a dispatcher's success, these men are often selected from the district that their console serves. Therefore, it is common for a prior relationship to exist between a dispatcher and some of the men on his channel. The operations-room men must speak with the console crew frequently each day; these phone calls provide a routine contact, which is easily exploited to develop personal connections. Also, each day one squad member is assigned to hand-deliver the pulling sheets and the attendance and equipment lists, giving him a chance to get to know the dispatcher and to perform little kindnesses for the crew.

Each console operates autonomously and the crews have closer contacts with the men on their channel than they do with the other radio crews, although they are separated from each other by only a few yards of carpeted floor. The console works according to a rhythm established by the people who live and work in the area it serves. When one console is not busy, its neighbor may be overloaded. Also, the district men are so insistent in their offers to do favors that each crew is more effectively tied to the men they see only occasionally than to those they see six out of every eight days. The veteran men in the operations room, and some of the older squad members, know exactly how each person on the console likes his coffee and what kinds of doughnuts and cake they favor. Since the police rarely have to buy coffee, the district men keep their radio crews swimming in it.

A patrolman occasionally asks his corporal to give him a "mail run," the transferring of records from the district to headquarters, "a job downtown," or "a call for coffee," if he wants to get out of the district for a little while. There are opportunities for these on every tour and they are granted to those men who are in good standing with their sergeant. If the radio crew wants coffee, the corporal tells them which car to call and the dispatcher gives the man a "report" call that directs him into the station, where he is given his assignment verbally. These trips give a man an opportunity to establish friendly contacts with the radio crew. Even when they go downtown on other business, patrolmen frequently stop at the radio room for a chat. The wagon crews, who regularly make trips to headquarters, are familiar figures around the communications center. Occasionally a man who stops by will help out a burdened crew by taking a few phone calls. Some men are even allowed to test their voices by dispatching some assignments during slack periods. Once the connections between a squad and its radio crew are established, there is little modesty on either side. If the radio men want coffee and have not received an offer, they do not hesitate to call one of their squads and place an order.

Each squad also seeks to assure the goodwill of its radio men by giving them Christmas money. It is a common practice in the department for the men who work the street to share their Christmas gratuities with those who are not in a position to earn their own. A collection is made for the operations-room crew and another is taken for those who work the radio. Each man contributes a dollar or two, which imposes no burden on him, but each radio crew collects from two or three squads. It adds up to a nice bonus at the end of the year. Most men contribute willingly, but sergeants and lieutenants consider the matter sufficiently important to compel the recalcitrant to cooperate.

It was a cold, rainy Sunday evening and the radio was very quiet, or "dead," as patrolmen say. A sergeant had just delivered his squad's Christmas gift to the radio room, and he was explaining to the dispatcher the plan he wanted to use to demonstrate their error in judgment to two men who had declined to put up a few dollars. The sergeant proposed that they invent an assignment and have the dispatcher tell the two men, who were partners, that they had blown the call. The dispatcher laughed and then prepared the necessary paper work. The sergeant returned to his car where, with the aid of another officer, he faked a conversation over the air between himself and the dispatcher. After assigning the fake job to another car, the sergeant, with a cloth over his microphone, pretending to be the dispatcher, ordered the innocent delinquents, who had been listening to the entire conversation, "to contact radio immediately." The sergeant drove around, waiting for his men to finish talking with the real dispatcher and then call him for a meeting. The dispatcher would tell them they had missed an assignment and that he was filing a memo on them. The sergeant knew they would call him.

When the call came, he told the dispatcher that the men would have to wait awhile, as he was busy at the moment. The men told the dispatcher that it was urgent, and the sergeant, stifling his laughter, acceded to their plea. When the car arrived, the sergeant composed his face and got out of his car to meet the approaching men, who saluted him smartly. "Sarge, the dispatcher said I missed a call. I don't know how. We chased a couple of kids around a school, but that's the only time we were out of the car together. I can't figure it out. I'm out there doin' the job and they give us this chickenshit," one of the men said. The sergeant suggested he calm down and write out a memo explaining exactly what they had done, cautioning him not to "put any bullshit in it." He said that he could promise them nothing, but he would go down to the radio room and see what he could do. The men were upset and confused, but as they were about to go back to their car, the sergeant said to them, "You see, if you guys treated them right, you wouldn't get involved in anything." They looked at him wordlessly, surrendered, and reached for their wallets. With his arms draped over their shoulders, the sergeant accompanied his team to their car.

A friendly radio crew can perform many favors and grant numerous requests to make the patrolman's day easier and his squad more secure, but it takes much more than free coffee and a few dollars at Christmas to assure cooperation. Every patrolman must use his radio properly and try not to embarrass his dispatcher in any way. He must not make unintended revelations, or violate the informal conventions which have been established. This is not easy, and it can be a painful process, because the things the patrolman must know cannot be taught to him at the police academy. They are mainly informal and some of them are illegal; there is no way to include them in the teaching plan.

Recruits are given no instruction in the use of the radio; each rookie must teach himself by listening and watching his colleagues. Working a wagon and walking a beat give him an opportunity to adjust to the irregular, unending flow of talk, but when he gets into a car he must also learn to drive and listen to the radio simultaneously. While he is learning, it is in the best interests of his squad that he know as little as possible about what the men are doing because he will inevitably make blunders and cause problems. The rookie knows that his skill in handling the radio is an important measure of his capacity to do the job, but he will inevitably stumble until he learns the conventions that govern the radio. Nobody tells him what to do, but his colleagues point out his errors and the dispatchers willingly, and usually gently, correct him.

A patrolman must learn to avoid any appearance of incompetence or inadequacy if he hopes to maintain the respect of his colleagues. Every man must go to considerable lengths to cover up any weakness or error that might reflect poorly on his competence. First, and most importantly, a man must record his assignment accurately when the dispatcher gives it to him. In order to minimize repeats, the dispatcher usually calls the car number and waits for a response before proceeding with his message, but when they are very busy, dispatchers sometimes try to save time by giving the assignment without waiting for confirmation. In these circumstances, if a man asks for a repeat, there will be no comment; a second-repeat request will raise doubts about a man's competence (and possibly his sobriety). Only rarely does an officer ask for a second repeat, and it is always accompanied by a formal apology or a comment on the poor reception in his car. The quality of reception does vary in different parts of the city, and there are even a few dead spots, where no reception is possible. These conditions also provide useful cover on occasions.

If an officer gets only part of his assignment, he will usually go to the street named and wait for someone to approach his car. (If he got nothing, he will look for a colleague and ask him if he got the assignment.) If nobody approaches the car, he can ask the dispatcher to give him a repeat on the house number, saying that nobody seems to be at home. If it is a minor call, he may simply tell the dispatcher that the call was unfounded.

One afternoon, a sergeant was asked to meet a wagon crew he knew was serving a warrant for numbers. He rode over to the street but did not know the house number. He saw the wagon parked at the curb, but rather than ask the dispatcher to repeat the location, he knocked on several doors before one of the men looked out a front window and beckoned to him.

On another occasion, a sergeant gave a dispatcher an assignment for one of his men. A few moments after the man was told what to do by the dispatcher, he came back on the air and asked the dispatcher if he would arrange a meet with his sergeant for him. The sergeant went on the air and told the dispatcher to inform the man that he was on his way. "That dummy, I bet he forgot the address," the sergeant muttered, as he drove across the district to deliver it personally. The man apologized to him; it was the only reason for the meeting. The sergeant, who could have repeated the address over the air, at the expense of the man, laughed it off.

Rookies and men who have been newly transferred into a district are frequently unfamiliar with the streets they patrol. Except in a dire-emergency, no patrolman will ask over the radio where a street is or where some place is located. On emergency calls the confused and the ignorant frequently will wait until they see the flashing lights of a colleague's car and use them as a guide to the assignment. These men are not reluctant to ask a colleague personally where a street is, nor will they hesitate to ask someone walking down the street or driving by; it is taboo to ask the dispatcher.

Patrol cars rarely run out of gas, but it happens occasionally. Each station has its own pump, and the cars are normally fueled at the beginning of each tour. A full tank of gas will keep a car going for one day of normal driving, so that only one man has to gas each car every day. Most patrolmen do not like to gas their cars regularly, and when they find they are left with an almost empty tank for a few days running, they will tell the turnkey, who also runs the gas pump, to fill it only halfway, forcing a man on another shift to fill it again. Sometimes a man forgets to check the gauge, or discovers too late that it is broken, and finds himself immobilized. If he is near a gas station, he will buy enough to get back to the station, where he can fill up. If he is not, he will wait patiently for a colleague to pass or ask the dispatcher to send him a car.

The dispatcher knows that a man who wants to speak with a colleague can cruise around until he spots him, without informing the dispatcher and his other colleagues that he has something to discuss. He can also wait until the car he wants goes on the air, then meet the officer at the location he is heading for. When he asks for a car to meet him, he must have a specific reason. The dispatcher knows the men are reluctant to discuss any problem they have, but since he has a responsibility for their well-being, he always asks them if they have some difficulty. The patrolman knows he must respond politely to this inquiry, without revealing anything that will reflect poorly on his own competence. Since he has no right to ask others to leave their sectors to meet him, he will usually claim a technical failure, such as not being able to start his car; this excuses him from personal responsibility and informs the dispatcher that the matter is not serious. The dispatcher may, for form's sake, ask the officer if his car has jumper cables; since he knows the answer will be affirmative, he usually does not bother. Cars do break down and sometimes fail to start. Then the patrolman does not hesitate to inform the dispatcher that he needs aid; he will not ask for a specific car to meet him.

Each man is obliged to avoid remarks that raise doubts about a colleague's competence. If any are made, the affected man must refrain from compounding the initial error by offering corrective statements over the air. One summer, on the daywork shift, a sergeant informed his platoon that an order had been issued requiring each car to carry a hydrant wrench, used for opening and closing the valves of fire hydrants. He explained that any car that reported to radio that it could not close a hydrant because the officer had no wrench would oblige the officer's sergeant to file a memorandum with the captain, explaining why the car was allowed to go on patrol without the proper equipment. He told his men that if their cars had no wrench, they were to tell the dispatcher that their wrench did not fit the kind of socket on the hydrant they were assigned to close. Two hours later, the sergeant's confidence that his men had understood him was broken when he heard one of his rookies tell the dispatcher that he could not accept a hydrant assignment since he had no wrench. After swearing for about thirty seconds, the sergeant asked the dispatcher to tell the man to remain at his location, as his sergeant wished to speak to him.

On another occasion, two officers responded to a burglary call. It was a very busy tour, and they were the only men at the scene. After carefully examining the doors and windows, assuring themselves that the building was secure, they informed the dispatcher the call was unfounded and that he could put them back into service. A few moments later another car came on the air, and the young officer announced that he had a suspect on the burglary call that had just been unfounded. The two patrolmen were livid. "That fuckin' rookie prick. Making me look like a cunt. All he's got is a lot of bullshit, but at least he should have called me for a meet." The angry patrolman did not reach for his transmitter. Instead, his sergeant came on the air and asked the patrolman with the suspect to await his arrival. A few minutes later, the sergeant returned to the air and said the suspect was being taken in on a matter that had nothing to do with the burglary. The officer shook his head, grateful to his sergeant for protecting him, but still angered by the stupidity of his colleague.

An officer was holding a man suspected of burglarizing an automobile. He asked a rookie who had joined him to watch the suspect while the officer talked with the car owner, who had just arrived. The young patrolman decided to be helpful, while he was alone with the suspect. Using the other officer's car number, he asked the dispatcher to send a wagon. He assumed the prisoner was going to be arrested and there was no point in wasting time. Meanwhile, the car owner had decided not to press charges, since nothing had been taken. When the patrolman was told that the rookie had called a wagon, he became angry. After cursing the young man, he asked him to take the prisoner into the district, since the man was not going to be charged. He declined, increasing the older man's anger. The veteran still did not ask the dispatcher to cancel the wagon. This would have involved him in explaining to the dispatcher and his sergeant. He waited for the wagon and let the crew take the man to the district, where the officer released him and drove him back to the place where he had been arrested.

"Car 5314 to radio. I have an open property at 274 Bond Street." Before the dispatcher could ask another car to join 5314 on his investigation, several cars had responded. The men knew that 5314 was manned by a rookie who was working alone ("single-o" or solo). Searching an open building at night is difficult enough for experienced men working in pairs. A lonely rookie needed company. A veteran officer pulled up at the location and without moving from behind the wheel of his car, observed the building and the young patrolman, who was standing with his flashlight on and the safety latch of his holster unsnapped. "What ya got, Jimmy?" the man asked, although he had heard the young man say it was an open property. "An open property, Henry," he said, with some anticipation, trying to conceal his annoyance with the man, who had still not moved from his seat. Two other cars arrived. "Uh, Jim, uh, what happened to all the windows on the second floor?" The young man's eyes traveled up the beam of his flashlight to scan the double row of blackened window frames covered over with tin sheeting. It was an abandoned building, closed up by the city. The door had probably been broken open by some neighborhood kids or a local wino. Anyway, it was not a place patrolmen had any interest in searching. Wordlessly he clicked off his flashlight and latched up his holster. He asked the older officer if he would tell the dispatcher to cancel the call. Henry smiled and told him not to worry about it. He did not tease him, although a few of the men were laughing in a restrained way. "Just don't worry about it, Jimmy, my man. You write up the 48 and turn it in. They'll change it inside. Now, you take a few minutes before going back in service, while Ruby and me get us some coffee."

Even more dramatic errors, whose consequences cannot be foreseen, are handled internally by a platoon whenever possible, rather than embarrass one of their own. A quiet Sunday morning was broken suddenly by the call of a young officer who claimed to have several armed men trapped in a car. From all over the district, cars went speeding to his support. Within moments, it was clear the patrolman had misstated the case. Someone had stopped him as he was patrolling and said that a young woman was being held in a car by two armed men. Before investigating, he had called for some help. He had not seen the men or any guns. When he had arrived at the car, the woman claimed she had been raped at gunpoint and her attackers had fled.

The woman was not their problem; whether she had been raped was a matter for the detectives to determine, and although one of the men knew her to be a local prostitute, he made no comment. But since the call was very serious, the men knew that the dispatcher was waiting to be informed and that roving supervisors heading for the scene had to be deterred. So a veteran officer got on the radio and told the dispatcher that the suspects had fled and there was no flash information immediately available. The injured woman was being taken to the hospital for treatment, and when released, she would be handed over to the detectives. Having established that there was no need for more personnel at the scene, he then told the dispatcher he would give him additional information over the telephone. This was, of course, a signal to the dispatcher that there had been some kind of confusion, not to be treated too seriously. Meanwhile, the dispatcher had sufficent information to protect the men if any "big bosses" called the console to find out what had happened.

Each patrolman is responsible for assuming his share of the platoon's assigned work, and no more. A man does not have to be aggressive or make a lot of arrests to obtain the favor of his colleagues; he must do his own work and not evade the routine service jobs, the "bullshit calls," which most patrolmen dislike but come to accept as part of the work. Some men do not like to answer service calls or look for vice; they usually become very unhappy in the districts and try to get themselves transferred into some kind of special unit that concentrates on crime suppression. But while a man is in the

POLICING THE CITY 111

district, he must share the work everyone is called on to perform.

Once an officer accepts a job from a dispatcher, he has no obligation to the radio until he returns himself to service. During very busy periods, dispatchers may be ordered by divisional inspectors to put all cars back in service after a specific time, without waiting for the men to call in. This is clearly announced over the air, and the men are warned they must come back into service or have a very good reason for remaining out beyond the allowed time. A sergeant or lieutenant who wants to compel his men to work harder, or who is seeking to impress his superiors, can ask the dispatcher to check continually on the status of cars out of service. These orders interrupt any arrangements that may exist between a dispatcher and some patrolmen, but this is an infrequently used technique. Any sergeant who persisted in supervising his men in such a manner would soon notice a decline in the platoon's activity.

In order to avoid the constant domination of the radio, to spare himself the possibility of getting another job, to take a moment to catch up on his paper work, or simply to rest or loaf, a man will not immediately put himself back in service when he has completed his assignment. If two cars are out on the same job, it is understood that the man who is "handling the job," that is, writing the paper work, is responsible for going back in service. All the other cars on the assignment will not return until he has announced he is ready to go to work. Men who do not know each other well, particularly when they are working with rookies, will specifically confirm that their colleague understands the rule. Supervisors do not object to their men taking these few minutes if they are in their cars and listening to the radio. It is expected that if a man hears a job in his sector being given to another car, he will take it. It is commonplace to hear a man tell the dispatcher to put him back in service after hearing a job being given out. "5511, you can put me back and I'll take 1821 Stone. It's on me." The dispatcher is not obliged to give him the assignment, even though it is in his sector, but he usually does. The officer who has been relieved usually expresses his thanks formally, but indirectly, by acknowledging to the dispatcher his reception of the message and saying "thank you," one of the very few occasions when policemen publicly acknowledge the support given by a colleague.

A man may offer to take a job that is not on his sector if he feels the assigned car has to come a long way or if he happens to be in the area. If no cars are available for a job, the dispatchers are under standing orders to pass the job along to any car available in an adjoining district. Very few, if any, squads are eager to have men from outside their district come into their territory for any reason except an assist, and any car that is available, but not owning up, will usually come on the air to take the job before a car from outside the district is assigned.

There are times when the dispatcher cannot raise any cars for an assignment. There may be several cars in service simply not answering. If he cannot raise a specific car, the dispatcher will ask if there are any cars or wagons in the district available for an assignment. If he cannot raise a car, he has the option of calling a car from outside the district or giving the job to a sergeant. Few sergeants will allow a car to come from outside, preferring to pitch in and work themselves. They are not required to take assignments since the department wants them to be supervisors and not workers, but most sergeants willingly take an occasional assignment when they know their men are busy. While the sergeant is prepared to do the work, his acceptance is a signal to any free patrolman sitting in his car to ask the dispatcher for his sergeant's assignment. A platoon that does not want to antagonize its sergeant will not allow him to take many radio calls. Courtesy and common sense compel them. The sergeant listens to the radio, he knows how many jobs are being given out, and he also knows how much activity his men are producing. He is the best judge of whether they are working or not. If they are not, and he is, he is not going to let them forget it.

A confident supervisor who relaxes his vigilance over his men always risks embarrassment from unanticipated events which can strain the adjustments and collusions normally concealing errors and laxness. If a single man is found delinquent, there is not likely to be much discredit cast on the unit or its directors, but if the collective negligence of a platoon or squad is established, the supervisors are held directly responsible. At the least, they are held up for ridicule by their friends and enemies throughout the department who quickly hear of the trouble. Even worse, they can be disciplined or transferred. There are few worse things that can happen to a district sergeant or lieutenant than to be transferred from a post he enjoys. Even if he is moved to a "good district," it will take him some time to become re-established, to know the men under him and the captain above.

Shortly before 8 A.M., a deputy commissioner, stopped on his way to work by an unattended traffic jam, asked the J-Band dispatcher to have the district lieutenant meet him at his car. Overnight, the water department had dug up part of a major street without informing the police, and a real jam-up was building. Prior to the commissioner's arrival, the sergeant had noticed the traffic slowing down and attributed it to some double-parked demolition trucks. He had moved them out of the traffic lanes, allowing the cars to move more quickly toward the blockage point, which was in the other end of the district. The other sergeant was off that day.

The lieutenant was not on the street, but the dispatcher sought to cover for him. He told the commissioner the lieutenant was not available, but when the commissioner, familiar with all the routine subterfuges, challenged him by asking what assignment the lieutenant had, his nerve failed. It was one thing to cover for a colleague, but to tell a lie to a commissioner, especially one that could be exposed, was beyond any obligation owed by one officer to another. He admitted that the lieutenant was not on assignment. The commissioner asked for several cars from the traffic squad to come to the scene and for the lieutenant in a neighboring district to contact him on J-Band.

The divisional dispatcher was unable to raise any cars, although the sergeant answered that he was on his way. The sergeant switched his radio to J-Band to listen to the conversation between the commissioner and the lieutenant, and learned about the hole dug by the water department. Since department orders forbid anyone to switch channels without explicit permission, the sergeant could say nothing and offically knew nothing. He rousted a few men out of coffee shops on his way, but when he arrived, the commissioner had departed. He and the men set to work sorting out the traffic, while his lieutenant went on the air to repair his connections with the dispatcher. He asked whether there had been any calls for him, since he had been obliged to leave his car to check on a suspicious person. While he was recording his official cover story, the district corporal was calling the neighboring district to suggest to his colleague that his lieutenant stay on their side of the line. He did.

Although the problem was quickly settled, the squad was exposed to ridicule throughout the division and among higher commanders everywhere in the city. The district captain had heard the messages on the radio as he was driving in to work, although willing tongues would have informed him immediately, especially since he would have to discuss the matter with his inspector. The sergeant, who was involved in organizing a departmental fraternal occasion, was kidded throughout the morning as he spoke with men from other parts of the city. Some of them had heard the commissioner on the city-wide band and others had been told about the snafu. The captain sought to protect his men by blaming the entire matter on the water department. The commissioner was mollified because the problem did not recur, and for the remainder of the shift his passage through the district was speeded by the work of many patrolmen. Every traffic regulation was enforced to the letter, and the sergeants and their lieutenant personally supervised the men during the rush hour.

The lieutenant was one who rarely addressed his men at roll calls, but the following morning he spoke to the negligent platoon. "If you guys don't know how to get your coffee without going out of service, or telling radio you're taking a personal, then you are going to get hurt. I don't lay on your ass and neither does the sergeant, because we know that you are doing the job when it counts. But I don't want to hear radio calling for cars at eight in the morning with nobody answering up. If I do, there's going to be trouble."

Although dispatchers perform many supervisory functions, sergeants and lieutenants are still responsible for assuring the men's adherence to their fundamental obligations. They rarely see their men at work, because of the territorial character of police work, but by listening to the radio carefully, every supervisor is able to learn a great deal about each man's inclinations, skills, and character. Just by listening to the radio, a sergeant can know whether a man is willingly handling his assignments, helping out colleagues on busy sectors who have additional work to perform, and participating in the emergency crime calls, which require several cars to operate in support of each other. What a sergeant hears on the radio, in combination with the amount of activity a man brings him at the end of each tour, gives him a way of accurately assessing how the man is meeting his established obligations.

The radio also offers the sergeant a number of ways to bring pressure on a man whose performance is lagging and who does not respond to private requests for improvement. He may ask a dispatcher to keep calling for a car when it does not answer for a job. If the man is out of service, he can ask the dispatcher how long the man has been out, continuing this practice each time the man remains off the air a moment longer than his sergeant thinks is warranted. The sergeant may periodically ask the dispatcher to order the man to meet the sergeant, often several times during each tour. The sergeant will utilize these occasions to scan the man's patrol log carefully, sign it, and renew his demands for more work. Supervisors seldom use these tactics; often when they are employed, it is only for a day or two, because most men take these warnings at face value and conform. But if a sergeant wants to get rid of someone by encouraging him to seek a transfer, these techniques offer forms of inescapable harassment only the strongest wills can endure for any length of time. The patrolman who is subjected to them must conform to his superior's demands, risk severe punishment, or move on.

A supervisor can also use the radio to enforce working standards if he is dissatisfied with the performance of the men under his direction. This occurs infrequently, since most platoons quickly establish understandings between the men and their bosses, but new supervisors who feel their men are not responding properly have a powerful prod at their disposal when they use their radio astutely.

A patrolman was given a call to meet a complainant at a local bar. It was a routine assignment. "That fuckin' junkie bar. Some broad probably got slapped in the face. We'll just finish our coffee and then go on over," he said. After acknowledging the call he leaned back and continued to sip his coffee. When he was finished, he threw the cup and lid out of the window and put the idling car into gear. As he drove toward the bar, his lieutenant came on the air and reported there had been a larceny at the bar. "Shit. That new lieutenant is a bastard. I guess we better make it over there." When he arrived, his lieutenant had already departed. The barmaid said that two men (yes, she knew who they were, but not their names; yes, they were junkies) had stolen a March of Dimes box from the bar and run out. Her description of the men she admitted knowing was very vague. "You think she don't know who took the money? Shit. She just wants a cop in here to make them think she's gonna put some heat on them if they try any more of that silly shit with her. She ain't gonna get 'em caught. If it wasn't for that lieutenant going on the air, you know we'd deep six this one. The detectives are gonna dump it anyway. Well, we better go look for them anyway." The officer went to three other bars in the area, asking each bartender if he had seen the two men. They had not. He also asked each one if his lieutenant had been there. He had. Smiling, he asked if the lieutenant had taken a drink and was disappointed when told he had not. "Well, I'm just checking up on him the way he checks up on me." The lieutenant did not say a word to anyone in the platoon about the incident, but everyone listening on the radio got the message.

It is impossible for any man to escape supervision if his sergeant utilizes the power the radio has given him. In a brief time, each man learns to recognize the radio voices of his platoon colleagues. He may not know the voices of some of the men on the other end of his district, and he will recognize only a very few voices of men from other districts on the channel, but every voice in his own platoon is immediately known. When one man covers for another by using the other's number, it is a collusion within the platoon permitted only with the sergeant's sanction. He can forbid this, if he wants to, over the radio, without revealing himself to anyone but his platoon and the dispatcher.

In one platoon, there was a wagon crew that had particularly close connections with its dispatcher. Whenever the wagon went downtown, the crew stopped in for a chat and brought coffee. One of the men was considering a transfer to the radio division and liked to answer the phones and do some dispatching when he got a chance. The wagon crew was closely linked to their sergeant, who did not usually object to their taking a few minutes off now and then.

One night, when it was particularly busy, the dispatcher stopped broadcasting and was replaced by the clear voice of the wagon man. After a few minutes, the sergeant came on the air. "66A to radio. Do you have 6601 wagon available?" The driver of 6601 replied, "No, sir, we have him out of service at the detention center." "Thank you, Radio." Everyone in the platoon, except possibly the new men, understood the sergeant was giving his wagon crew a direct order and were not surprised when the regular dispatcher came back on the air immediately. A few minutes later, the wagon was on the air, announcing its return to work. Anyone listening who did not know the voice of the wagon man could not have had any idea that this innocent transmission had an entirely different purpose from the one conveyed by the question the sergeant had asked.

The supervisors on the street are not inclined to employ their powers fully unless they believe someone is consistently shirking his obligations. If a man employs all the well-known techniques to make a bit of time, to avoid a job or two, or even loaf for several days, he will not be censured. But if he persists, obliging others to carry him, he will not be allowed to continue. Everyone on the street knows the routines, and if the sergeant does not act, the man's colleagues will be angered, because they know they are being forced to do the work for which he is being paid. Platoon morale cannot be maintained over a period of time if everyone is not pulling his own weight.

The easiest direct evasion requires no formal cover. Many jobs turn out to be unfounded, crank calls, or calls by people who want a police car to come to their house, without their acknowledging to the people in the house or on the street that they have called. The officer can simply refrain from telling the dispatcher the call is unfounded, taking the time he would use for the assignment for his own purposes. There are some assignments that can be used to consume a lot of time and men who want to avoid working will try to get these. Transportation assignments and hospital cases, for example, are usually easy work, and cannot be timed, because often the officer has to take the person outside of the district. If the sergeant knows a man is a loafer, he will tell the dispatcher to give the assignment to another man. He will also forbid the operations crew to give the man any mail runs, or other jobs that allow him to take free time.

Technical failures are also employed to evade work. A man can sabotage his car, flatten the tires, neglect to check the oil and transmission fluid, or even crack it up in a faked accident. These acts are infrequently employed, and only by men who are indifferent to their sergeant's wrath and want to leave the district, and possibly the job. The use of technical failure to avoid work obliges the man to tell a lie to his sergeant; it is also an affront to the sergeant's competence, suggesting that the man believes his superior to be sufficiently stupid not to know what is going on. Any doubts in the sergeant's mind about a man's truthfulness will quickly undermine their relationship, because a police sergeant requires loyal behavior as a condition of cooperation more than most types of supervisors. Such a lie can work once, but any recurrence will invite the most careful attention from a man's superiors.

A man who does not drive a sector car regularly cannot be held responsible for its maintenance, but policemen who do not want to avoid work listen carefully to their car engines before they go on patrol. Any possible malfunctions are reported to the sergeant before they leave the station, freeing them from any suspicion of inventing a problem that may occur later.

There is an analogous deception, sometimes used by lazy men, involving the recovery of stolen cars. When an officer discovers a stolen car, he must either disable it or remain by the car until it can be driven into the station. Most cars can be disabled by removing the distributor cap, but sometimes an officer will claim a particular model cannot be crippled or that he is unable to open the hood. The dispatcher must accept the man's word, but the sergeant does not. If he wishes to protect the man, he can announce he is going to investigate and then not bother going. This collusion is iron-clad, unless one of the roving commanders sent out from headquarters happens to drop around.

The patrolman can also claim a malfunction in his radio to cover any failure to acknowledge a call. The radios do require a considerable amount of servicing, and it is an important responsibility of the dispatchers to detect any indication of malfunction and send the car to the repair shop before the radio can go out of order while the patrolman is working. But if a man misses a call, he frequently will ask the dispatcher, "How do you read me?" It is possible that the car was in a dead spot; the dispatcher has no way of knowing. The failure of technology implicit in the question is allowed to stand, but if it is repeated often, the patrolman will find himself having a conversation with his sergeant, who will explain the facts of life in a very direct fashion.

It is only the naïve or stupid man who thinks he can put something over on his colleagues and superiors. Every moment the men are allowed to take is granted to them informally, with the best wishes of the department and their sergeant. The collusions the men employ provide them all with the necessary cover to protect themselves from unknown ears. Revelations of laxness are almost always the consequence of some incompetence. The punishments that follow are as much payment for failures to maintain cover as they are for violations of department regulations.

The sergeant allows his men time because he considers it necessary to maintain their cooperative spirit for work, and the work cannot be accomplished without willing workers. He knows his men demand absolute privacy when they are in quest of vice information or conducting surveillances; this means nothing can be said over the air that reveals what they are doing. He also knows the men are obliged to work to the rhythms established by the dispatchers. There are days when they have few radio calls and others when they are driving back and forth taking one job after another. If a man occasionally avoids work, he also goes to the aid of colleagues on days when they are not feeling well or are slowed by heat and fatigue.

A squad that cooperates with its radio crew, and does not cheat, is aided to make time. When it is not too busy, a man who has some private business is allowed to go out of service over the telephone. Unless the man is well known to the radio crew, the call will be made for him by the corporal, or another inside man, to assure the dispatcher that it is not some greenhorn trying to take liberties. A sergeant or a lieutenant who wants to do some work which he prefers not to broadcast publicly can make the necessary arrangements over the telephone that links the operations room with the console. The proper cards are filled out and the man involved is officially "covered." Similar arrangements are made for vehicles put out of service. Sometimes a car will be carried as working while its assignments are being taken by another car. The radio man, who knows what is happening, carefully avoids calling the car that has taken the assignments. The dispatcher does not have to do any of these things to protect a squad or to ease their burdens, but he does them because the men are his colleagues and friends.[2]

An amiable dispatcher can also provide useful information that aids the sergeant is protecting the autonomy of his unit. For instance, the department assigns roving captains to work different divisions each week, authorizing them to go in on all important calls and to take command of any situation they feel warrants their attention. The district squads have no way of evading these men, whose right to supervise must be acknowledged. The dispatchers know which captains will be working on their channel and can inform the operations crew prior to roll calls. The men are then informed by their sergeant whether the man assigned is an "all-right guy" or someone "you have to watch out for."

Similarly, if the radio receives requests for aid which are recognized as possibly troublesome for the squad, the as-

---

[2] The telephone lines between the districts and the consoles were not covered by tape recorders when my field work was in progress. Since then all phone lines into the radio room have been "tapped." This presumably has necessitated additional adjustments at both ends of the line.

signment will be delivered over the phone before it is put on the air. Sometimes they are not aired at all. One night, a lieutenant was asked to report immediately. When he arrived, the corporal told him radio had received a call from a local hospital reporting a bomb threat. Any bomb-scare call requires the implementation of an elaborate and precise department policy, mobilizing special units from outside the district, cordoning off areas, evacuating the hospital, and searching its floors room by room. The dispatcher told the lieutenant that the call came from the hospital administrator, who said it was probably a hoax connected with a current labor dispute, but she had felt obliged to report it.

The lieutenant proceeded directly to the hospital, determined to avoid a bomb alert. He conferred with the administrator, convincing her that a search of the hospital was unnecessary and impractical. He offered protection against any disturbance in exchange for forgetting the bomb threat, still not officially a police matter, and she agreed. He then conferred with the detective assigned to cover the labor dispute, thereby assuring himself that any report the detective submitted would coincide with the report the lieutenant was going to file with his captain. Then he telephoned the dispatcher and told him to forget the matter unless there were additional calls. If the call had gone on the air, the entire night would have been spent searching the hospital. Fortunately, in this case there was no bomb.

The granting of favors and the establishment of collusive arrangements are greatly appreciated by the district men, but the favors are far less significant to the district squads than the aid the dispatcher gives them in meeting their vice-enforcement obligations. Any outsider who seeks to learn anything about illegal gambling in the city by listening to the police radio will be very disappointed. There is never a report of serious gambling put out over the air. If there is a complaint about a few men having a dice game on a sidewalk, the dispatcher does not hesitate to give out a call for "gambling on the highway," but an avid listener will grow hoary and deaf before he hears any call regarding a number writer or a horse parlor. There are calls about disturbances in taprooms, particularly around closing time, that may involve liquor violations. A Sunday-morning call to pick up "a DK on the highway" may cause a flurry of activity because the astute patrolman knows a Sunday drunk is a solid indicator of a speak and that is a good vice pinch, but there is never a report of an actual speakeasy or an after-hours place over the radio. There are phone calls to the radio complaining about gambling and illegal drinking, but they are never put out over the air. If the district corporal is a well-established person who has been around for a long time, the message might be given directly to him; usually the dispatcher will tell the street supervisor to report, then give him the information over the telephone.

The private and secret character of vice enforcement is maintained absolutely. Every possibility of disclosure or embarrassment that might cause the men trouble, and bring police officials from other units of the department into the district, is controlled by this silence. Also, squad members are able to learn little about the vice work of their colleagues. When a man goes on a vice investigation, he will frequently give the dispatcher a false location in order to keep nosy colleagues from coming around. The only time a patrolman tells the dispatcher precisely where he is going on a job involving gambling is when he is serving a warrant. Then he wants everything to be administratively and legally complete. The warrant is a public document and the man has no reason to hide his actions.

Some dispatchers are willing even to violate the law and the Constitution to help their friends make a vice pinch. It is possible to use a false radio call to make what appears on the surface to be a legal entrance to a private place. The call must be for a serious violation, which will make plausible the patrolman's emergency response and allow him to justify the extraordinary action he is about to take. If he has information on some gambling activity in a house but does not have time to get a warrant, or cannot justify one, illegal entry is his only hope of not losing the pinch. The false call used must be for something which will justify looking inside drawers and cupboards. If the dispatcher gives out a call that reports a man has been seen dragging a woman into a house the officer may "take the door," but he cannot legally defend looking inside the oven for her. "Report of gunshots," however, is particularly well suited in this connection, because

the search for a gun allows the officer to look just about anywhere. After the arrangement is made, or after the policeman makes a phone call to the dispatcher, often anonymously, he sits around the corner and waits for the call to go on
the air and be tape-recorded. When his legal needs are satis-
factorily met, he can then rush in under the cover of duty
and obligation.

The radio has made hard workers out of patrolmen, but it
has not brought them under the complete domination of their
superiors. Putting men in police cars has not changed policemen from what they have always been, solitary workers patrolling their territory. The autonomy of the districts has been
ended, but the squads preserve considerable privacy and freedom to conduct their work without fear of damaging disclosures and unanticipated interventions from outside the
district or, even worse, from outside the department. The
need for the absolute cooperation of the men in doing their
work, and keeping prying outsiders (and some insiders) in the
dark, has compelled administrators to allow adjustments and
collusions between the men on the street and their dispatchers.
These arrangements, in turn, encourage some men to do
blatantly illegal things, which are not sanctioned but cannot be prevented. The administrative dilemmas created by
the territorial strategy for policing the city are probably insoluble, but they are made more difficult to deal with by the
department's need to deny that there are any. Meanwhile, the
directors of the police rightly point with pride to the great
increase in the amount of work their men do since the time
the car and the radio were introduced into police service. On
the other hand, they cannot demonstrate that the car and
radio have made the city a safer place or have improved
the general well-being of city people.

Part Two

POLICING
PEOPLE

On his first day as a policeman a rookie may capture an armed felon, be cracked on the head with a rock, be offered sexual favors, free food, or money; he may be confronted by a naked woman, screaming hysterically, or a belligerent drunk who outweighs him by fifty pounds; or if he begins on last out, he may spend the entire tour trying to fight off the desire to sleep. He has no control over what he will learn first, and when he will learn it, because he has no control over what he must do. Regardless of what occurs, he is obliged to be immediately what he has chosen to become, although his colleagues know he has only the vaguest appreciation of what that is. The department has told him he is expected to "prevent crime, protect life and property, arrest law violators, assist the public, preserve the public peace, regulate public conduct and control and expedite the flow of vehicular traffic."[1] He does not know whether he can do any of these things, and the only way he can find out is by being what he is officially—a policeman. He acquires bits and pieces of knowledge, information, and experience which he alone can put together to make himself independent, effective, and valuable to his colleagues. While he is learning to do his work, he is also defining for himself the nature of his place on the street, discovering the contradictions inherent in his position as a guardian of the "public" peace and the ambiguities of being a regulator of people's conduct.

[1] Philadelphia Police Department Training Division, *Police Practices Training Manual,* Vol. 6, Pamphlet 5, "Police Patrol" (Philadelphia, Police Department mimeo, undated and unpaged).

CHAPTER FOUR

Territorial Knowledge
and Street Work

Before the policeman can do any work easily, he must know where he is. The framework of a patrolman's geographical knowledge is established by the extent of his territorial jurisdiction. He usually carries with him on patrol a sector map of his district, or cuts his district out of a detailed road map and tapes it to the back of a clipboard. He has no need to know about places beyond the district's limits. The first thing he learns about his district, after the location of the station house, is its boundaries. His knowledge of what lies beyond them is limited and his curiosity restricted. If he is assigned to work a border sector, he may get to know several of the men who work opposite him; he may even share lunch with them occasionally. Otherwise, contacts across district lines are limited to chance encounters at local hospitals and occasional exchanges when the men come to each other's aid on assists. Even if a man regularly drives into a neighboring district to use a hospital or to speak with his divisional detectives, who may be headquartered there, he does not linger or take much notice of the places he passes. His attitude is reinforced by the responses of district men to the sight of patrol cars parked in places where they do not belong. The patrolman is approached directly and asked bluntly what he is doing, and if his explanations are not satisfactory, he will be told to move off, and even threatened with exposure, since no man has a right to leave his district without the permission of his sergeant or his dispatcher.

The new man's knowledge of district geography is knitted together from disconnected bits of information. He is constantly moved from one assignment to the next, each day seeing new faces and places. His only reference point is the station house, and he orients all his information around this one fixed point. He learns the names and directions of the major commercial streets in the district; he does not view them as arteries that link together different parts of the city but as strips of territory whose locations are defined by their relationship to the station. As his familiarity with the district increases, the centrality of the station in his geographical conception declines, and the major arteries in the district become linked as he learns to travel the choice routes from one part to another.

The distinction between the two ends of the district has little meaning to him at first because he is frequently working all over the district. As he becomes established in his platoon, his knowledge of its streets and places becomes substantially greater than his knowledge of the rest of the district, and he is reluctant to go to the other end. It is not a boundary he cannot cross, but his inclinations to do so are dampened by his limited knowledge of the area. Every time he crosses that line he feels like a rookie again, unless he is going somewhere on a main street or to an important public building everyone knows.

One day a sergeant was obliged to supervise his squad's two platoons. He remained with his own men except when he was ordered or specifically requested by someone on the other end; although he was a fifteen-year veteran with three years in the district, he had considerable difficulty locating places there. On one call, he had to go to a street only four blocks from the station. It ran off a major road he used regularly; although he had driven past it hundreds of times, he did not know its name. He was not embarrassed and passed off his failing by noting, "None of these places are on me and I don't come here often."

The anxiety caused by doing new work is greatly increased by the patrolman's constant confusion about where he is. Almost every day he works a different area and sees new faces. If he is working on a wagon, he frequently has to ask his partner where they are before he can give the dispatcher their location. If he has an emergency and there is no time to ask, they are both in trouble. Many neighborhoods have been stripped of their street signs, a by-product of juvenile exuberance, gang warfare, and malicious vandalism, and if he does not know the street names or recognize them by landmarks, he is lost. When this happens to him a few times, he needs no additional spur to learn his geography. Directional signs, too, have been torn away, or worse, turned around, and he must learn the direction of one-way streets without reference to any external aids. A constant fear of embarrassment and failure, combined with his inability to do anything which impresses his sergeant, often forces an aggressive new policeman unwittingly to take unusual risks in answering emergency calls. Being "first in" is the only way he knows to establish himself.

He organizes his knowledge of district geography around prominent public places pointed out to him by senior men during the first weeks, when he works on a wagon or rides a sector car. Whenever he passes a school, playground, bus depot, or municipal building, he notes its location. He also quickly learns the locations of all the fire stations and hospitals in his district. These will be very important to him because they are the only public buildings, except his station, where the patrolman exercises private claims. When he wants to make a phone call, wash up, or just relax, these are the places to which he usually goes. A patrolman learns to go into any public place with confidence, but these special places acquire a private dimension for him. His uniform alone is sufficient to guarantee him certain privileges there, but he uses these as a named person rather than as a man with a badge number. When he is given a report call, the patrolman usually drives to a firehouse or a hospital to make his phone call. He does this not simply to save a dime or consume time but also to take advantage of the opportunity to relax momentarily among people who treat him in a personal manner without making constant demands on his time and service.

While he knows all the hospitals in his district, contacts with them are determined by the working relationship between the officer and the institution. In one district there were six hospitals. Two were small, private clinics with no emergency facilities. The sector men went in only when they received a call, and although they knew a few nurses who worked there, they had no personal connections with the hospital staffs. A third was a children's hospital that was seldom used for cases taken by the police; however, it had an excellent canteen, making it an attractive stopping place on last out. The men had unrestricted access to the canteen, which was situated so that its use required no formal contacts with hospital personnel. While many patrolmen went there for coffee, they did not stop to use the phone or to chat. A fourth hospital was run by an order of Catholic nuns. Although it had an emergency facility, it was used sparingly. "There's no policy. Most of the men are Catholic and don't like to bring our niggers, pigshitters [Irish lower class], and dogpatchers [Southern migrants] there because they want to spare the sisters the filthy talk, the carrying-on, and all the cuttin' and sewin'. It ain't fair but that's how most of the men feel and that's why we don't use it much. If it's real serious, why, nobody hesitates to come here," a lieutenant explained. The majority of all emergencies were taken to the two large public hospitals located at either end of the district. It was to these hospitals that the men went when they wanted to report, to wash up after a particularly onerous job, or simply to chat with the staffs.

The patrolman's need to secure quickly a sound knowledge of district geography is complicated by his additional need to cope with the special conditions created by driving a vividly marked police car. When he first works with older men, he gets little opportunity to drive, except on last out. Usually he acts as "recorder," handling the radio, maintaining the patrol log, helping out with the paper work, because veterans are very reluctant to trust the wheel to men whose skill and temperament are unknown and untested. But the constant juggling of assignments gives each new man frequent opportunities to discover what it is like to drive a patrol car.

Until he learns to compensate for the unusual responses of most drivers to the presence of police cars, the patrolman's ability to scan the area he is passing through is restricted, because he must give considerable attention to avoiding accidents. In normal city-driving situations, many motorists are reluctant to pass a police car, regardless of its speed and the specific conditions. When stopped at a light, most drivers will wait for the police car to move first. Even when they have the right of way and stopping may be hazardous, many drivers will not move until the police car goes. If the patrolman is not alert, he may be slowly cruising along a street with a growing line of fuming drivers trailing behind. He must learn to pull over and allow cars to pass, and to be careful about how quickly he stops.

He must also learn to do illegal things with his car. At the academy the recruits are told to obey all traffic laws and signals except in emergency situations; caution is constantly urged upon them. At the same time, they are told to respond quickly to crime calls and calls for aid. There is an unresolvable conflict between the department's desire to have its men drive carefully and prevent accidents (as well as inflating maintenance costs) and its tactical decision to use the car's speed and mobility to suppress crime. Nobody suggests to the recruits that there are times when it is right and proper to do something illegal with their cars; they are quickly shown on the street.

A sudden snow squall on a wintry morning rapidly turned the streets to ice and the radio was filled with a rash of accident calls. A young officer, cruising very slowly along a major road, was just able to stop in time to avoid two cars that had collided ahead of him. He pulled his car in front of the wreck and beckoned to the two drivers to approach him. He invited them to share the warmth of his patrol car while they exchanged papers, and he filled out the accident report and the ticket he was going to give one man for following too closely. A rookie gets his activity wherever he can! As he started writing, another patrol car pulled up. The officer had heard the rookie tell the dispatcher he was going out of service with an auto accident. He looked at the men in the car and slowly shook his head. He took the rookie's radio-phone and, identifying himself with the younger man's call number, asked the dispatcher to send a salt truck to the area. After he signed off, he said to the rookie in the presence of the two motorists, "Don't you know anything, boy? First of all, get these cars out of the street. You're cutting it down to one lane. There's a traffic jam back to the light already and it's getting longer. We don't want the sergeant coming over here."

"Whaddya mean, off the street?" the young man asked.

"Hey, dummy, put them on the sidewalk." The rookie looked at his mentor, shrugged, and then, in his best voice, ordered the two drivers to bring their cars up on the pavement behind his own. The old-timer nodded and urged the young man not to bother him any more; he was going to breakfast. A few moments later the sergeant drove by and, noticing the three cars out of the way, smiled, gave the thumbs-up sign, and continued on his way.

The new man spends as much time as he can learning how to patrol in a car. Despite the differences between cruising and walking, the fundamental technique of patrol observation used by men in cars is the same as that used by men on foot. Although the intense use of the streets for car parking makes patrolling as difficult as street cleaning, the patrolman tries to drive in the curb lane, moving very slowly in order to scan the sidewalk and building line. When policemen walked they were under orders to proceed in a specific manner. "The patrolman shall pace his beat in a military manner along the route designated . . ." one manual ordered, "ordinarily following the curb line continuously." The men were instructed to stay on the outer part of the sidewalk to make them more visible to people in need of their aid, to allow their sergeants to see them, and also to give themselves a good view of the street. At night they were obliged to not "too conspicuously follow the curb line, but . . . occasionally cut through alleys, yards. . . ."[1]

The policeman restricts his patrol during daywork to the main streets of his area. He does not venture into the small side streets and alleys where there are fewer people about. At night, especially on last out, he begins to work the back roads. He learns to use the powerful spotlight, fitted for operation from inside the car, to examine doorways and windows without leaving his car. He gets out of his car to "hand-check" places that appear suspicious or that he cannot see

[1]*Patrolman's Manual* (Philadelphia, Bureau of Police, 1913), paras. 31, 35.

well, but as his experience increases, he is less likely to do so. Foot patrolmen still have specific handchecks assigned on their beats, but these are being abolished because they consume a great deal of time and rarely reveal any breaks.[2]

The basic patrol technique is dictated by the restrictions on vision imposed by the physical environment, which also conditions the public movements of people. Buildings are obviously fixed objects that people must walk in front of, between, around, or through. Traffic is channeled along streets, sidewalks, and alleys. Many of these alleys connect to pathways, which parallel numerous streets. These pathways and alleys cannot be easily seen, although they are as much a part of the public way as the more heavily used streets and sidewalks they link together. Intersections are the most important places in the city because the convergence of multiple streams of traffic makes them the most intensively used points on any street. The open space provided by four streets and four sidewalks coming together also offers the maximum possibility of seeing what is going on in an area. This combination of intense use and free vision quickly encourages the patrolman's special attention. Before the policeman knows what he is looking for, before he realizes that intersections are the scene of many accidents and traffic violations, and the boundary markers of the "gang boys" who "hang on the corners," he begins to glance into the cross streets he passes. When he approaches an intersection, he slows his car, even if he has a green light, and scans it intently. Nobody tells him to do this and he was not instructed at the academy to do it; he just picks it up naturally or sees his colleagues doing it. This alertness gradually becomes automatic, and he relaxes the habit only on emergency calls. Even when he is going on routine assignments, such as a meet complainant, he checks out each intersection he passes on his way to the job. This technical habit is a continuation of the same practice used by foot patrolmen when they made their rounds. A

[2]A recent observer of some Scottish patrolmen has written, "On night duty . . . he has a series of turns to do. . . . On these turns there are particular doors . . . which he is required to check; he tries the handle or pulls the padlock and shines his torch along the edge of the door to see if it has been tampered with." Michael Banton, *The Policeman in the Community* (New York, Basic Books, 1964), p. 40.

patrolman who walked a beat in Los Angeles during the 1920's recalls his own practice: "Turning east on Ninth Street, I followed the old custom of walking on the outer edge of the sidewalk, and looking sharply to the right and left at each intersection."[3]

Intersections also provide the new man with another way of fixing the fragments of geography in his mind. He identifies places by their relationship to the station, and then in reference to the major public buildings he locates. Soon he recognizes a few key intersections and acquires some knowledge about their supposed character. Initially he is almost wholly dependent on what he is told. If he is alert, some of the locations and names the sergeant warns the men about at roll calls cease to be abstractions. He begins to accumulate a stock of opinions and attitudes about specific places in the district. Before roll call, he listens to the men talk about their recent experiences (when they allow him into a circle of conversation); when he is assigned to work with an older man, he frequently is given lectures about the habits of the people he is policing. Soon he is making judgments about places, referring to one corner as a "bad spot," or a street as a "good place," without distinguishing whether he knows this from personal experience, advice from another officer, or comments at roll call.

The distinctions are not important to him because the references are not moral judgments reflecting on the character of the person expressing them; they are the comments of working men assessing the places they police. As his time in the district increases, he will "name" more and more places, adding the judgment of his personal experience to the stock he inherits. He, in turn, will pass along names to succeeding generations of policemen, treating them, not as his own, but

[3]Jess Kimbrough, *Defender of the Angels* (New York, Macmillan, 1969), p. 52. This glancing also has a defensive, protective character which was important when policemen walked. As one Denver, Colorado, patrolman recounts: "You look both ways before going across an alley. You always hesitate a minute before going across an alley. You walk toward the outside of the sidewalk." "A Quiet Strip: Officer Schalbrack's Story," as told to Edward Rose and Anthony Gorman, Bureau of Sociological Research, Report 26 (Boulder, University of Colorado: September 1965), p. 9.

as a product of his craft, part of the knowledge of anyone who is "street-wise."

The naming, which begins on the first day, is a way for the confused man to fix in his mind the many strange places he sees all at once. One patrolman recalls walking out to his beat in Harlem on his first day, in the company of an older officer, shortly after the First World War. He writes:

I was assigned Post No. 12, a single block. . . . Kid [he said], the lieutenant tossed you the hot one. . . . We call it San Juan Hill. . . . Kid, you got a lot to learn. San Juan Hill is a battlefield. There were two murders there last month. That is where they break cops . . . especially rookies.[4]

1 · Sector Geography and Public Perceptions

A district is too large for any man to know in a detailed way. After he has learned the major streets, intersections, and public places, he has difficulty extending his knowledge is a systematic manner. Once he is given a sector, he has a restricted territory he can master. As one man commented, "You work a steady car, you know when you come to work where you're gonna be. You learn it cold, you know what you got to do and where you got to go. I worked this sector so long that my wife wakes me up by calling my car number. It started as a joke, you know, but it worked, and she does it all the time now."

It requires time and concentration, but by applying himself to this relatively small area, he gradually memorizes his sector. He learns the names and directions of the streets, and he knows each intersection by its buildings. His knowledge of the streets is dictated by his concern to achieve maximum mobility with his car. In emergency situations, especially chases, an adept patrolman sometimes likes to go the wrong way on a one-way street because he knows most people, even desperate ones fleeing the police, will rarely break this basic traffic rule. Thus he has a chance to drive right into

[4]Robert McAllister, *The Kind of Guy I Am* (New York, McGraw-Hill, 1957), p. 61.

their path of escape. For the same reason he pays careful attention to the little connecting streets and alleys. He examines, in time, every open place to see whether he can push his car through it. He carefully checks empty lots and fields to see whether he can safely drive his car over them. He is also constantly monitoring the streets and making route changes required by construction work.

One sector was cut in half by a set of railroad tracks, which could be crossed easily at one street. A construction project closed off this route and the sector officer had to find another, or make a five-block detour to reach the other side. One night, he parked his car and carefully examined the ground on both sides of the track to see whether he could drive his car along the uneven ground to another crossway about a hundred yards down the tracks. When he was satisfied that there was no other way to go, he eased his car slowly along the experimental route. After he had made the trip several times from both directions, and was satisfied that it could be safely managed with care, he called for a meet with his sergeant to inform him. Since the blocked route was used by other patrolmen to answer emergency calls, it was important that this information be distributed to his colleagues.

The patrolman treats most of his geographical knowledge as private information to be used to increase his own effectiveness. He does not share it because he does not think others have any reason to know about his sector. One night, there was a call of "juveniles breaking into a store." As soon as he heard the location, the patrolman put his car in gear and moved off quickly. Instead of taking a right turn at the approaching intersection, he braked suddenly and jumped the car over the sidewalk into what appeared to be an empty lot filled with rubble. Moving steadily along a path he obviously knew, he crossed the lot and nosed the car into an alley that was hidden by the shadows of adjoining buildings. He drove quickly down the narrow alley for two blocks and braked to a stop beside the store being burglarized. The young thieves were probably less surprised than the patrolman's colleagues, who arrived several moments later to find the handcuffed burglars sitting quietly on the curb. When the patrolman's exuberant partner began to explain their success, his mentor interrupted and told him to move their car, as it was blocking the street.

One afternoon, there was a call of males breaking into a house. The sector man listened to the address and commented that it was near the corner. Before arriving, he cautioned his partner to be ready to do some running, as he was going to leave the car at the corner. The one-way street was too narrow for quick driving, and there would be cars coming from the other direction. He drove up on the sidewalk, and after pulling out the keys, he ran toward the house as two other cars made their way down the little street. Seeing nothing unusual at the front, he headed directly into an alley beside the house which connected with a pathway that paralleled the street. As he reached the rear of the house, he was able to grab a boy who was desperately trying to clamber over a high wooden fence while his associates were escaping by running along the pathway to another alley, which connected to a different street. Their progress could be followed by the growing chorus of barking dogs penned into the back yards by owners who hoped they would discourage housebreakers. The officers who neglected the alley, or chose to go through the house, arrived too late to pursue the others.

The patrolman's territorial knowledge of his sector is dictated largely by what he needs to know for the effective use of his car. Alleyways too narrow to drive through are rarely patrolled. Since he is not worried about wearing out the car, he is willing to drive any place that will not crack an axle or scrape a door. When he finds he cannot get his car into a place, he loses interest. Very few men make any effort to examine systematically the many passageways and alleys that can be navigated only on foot. If a patrolman is in pursuit on foot, he does not hesitate to go into these places, but he rarely takes the time to examine them for breaks in the fences, branches, concealed passageways, or dead ends. He even acknowledges the tactical superiority of teenagers, whose skill in exploiting local topography frequently allows them to escape capture. Even his frustration and momentary anger do not encourage him to examine these partially hidden places with the meticulous care he gives to areas where his car can go.

When patrolmen walked beats, their familiarity with these alleyways and passages must have been much greater. In the early part of this century, population densities were much higher in the central cities than they are today and the prevalence of tenement housing made these local passageways important. Today the patrolman does not go into them because he does not view them as public ways requiring regular policing. Every time he does enter them, he comes out covered with the evidence that they are abandoned. His shoes are covered with dog filth and their soles are cut by the broken bottles crushed under his feet. He continues to pursue people into alleys, but he never gives them the routine attention he pays to places which he sees as having a public character.

The patrolman's knowledge of the buildings in his sector is determined by his obligations. Over a period of time he comes to know every business place in his sector. He visits regularly only those having store logs that require his signature and those run by people he considers personally friendly to him. In areas where street crime is high, many small businesses have a store log. The patrolman usually gets to know well the dry cleaners, grocery stores, liquor stores, and check-cashing agencies[5] on his sector; their proprietors usually are very happy to see him. Places without store logs are not visited routinely, but the sector man knows the owner of every gas station and garage in his area. He has so many calls to these places for one thing or another that he cannot avoid getting to know the people who work in them.

He also knows all the restaurants and diners, although he does not regularly go into them. He usually has one or two places where he eats during each shift, or if his sector has none, he eats in an adjoining sector. Larger businesses that are not open to public traffic, factories, warehouses, wholesale

[5]Check-cashing agencies are quasi-banks that have developed in poor neighborhoods where many people who receive checks have no banks to cash them or checking accounts to pay bills. These agencies sell money orders and collect utility rents for substantial fees. The less scrupulous owners also buy stolen checks (mainly from drug users) at substantial discounts.

houses, are not visited regularly. On his normal patrol, he is reluctant to stop anywhere that is not a public place. He has no reason to go into a factory without a call, and unless he has some specific business, he would rather avoid the awkward moments that inevitably attend his arrival when the manager or foreman who does not know him carefully and politely asks what he wants. Calls to these places are frequently exploited to develop personal connections with their employees and managers, especially if they sell things he might want to buy, but he still does not visit them in a routine fashion as he does the local coffee shop or the auto-parts store.

He also knows the name, location, and proprietor of each taproom, bar, and private drinking club in his sector. These places are so often the setting for his work that he would quickly come to know them, even if they were not also linked to his interest in vice activity and money, if he has an inclination to "take." The department forbids a patrolman to enter a bar without his sergeant, unless it is an emergency; this does not inhibit anyone from knowing these locally important places, although it may curb the inclinations of some men to drink on duty. Every bar has a reputation the officer uses in evaluating calls to them. Most of the bars and taprooms in cities are located on or near intersections, and they frequently serve as convenient place markers, the key feature used by the policeman to identify a corner. When a patrolman refers to a certain corner as being bad, he often means the bar on it, which might be a weekend "blood pit."

His knowledge of the private places on his sector is dependent on the demands made for his service, the calls he receives, and the requests put to him in person. He does not casually knock on people's doors to introduce himself, nor does he stop them on the street just to say hello. If people approach him, he talks with them, but they rarely invite him to their house, and if they did he would be reluctant to go.

There are, however, in every sector places and properties, once private, whose character has been altered. Although the policeman knows these are frequently used for criminal purposes, he all but ignores their existence unless given a specific call. He treats them as if they continued to be privately held, even though he knows most of them are not.

A • ABANDONED CARS

In recent years calls to remove "abandoned cars" have greatly increased. These are cars left by their owners as beyond repair, or stolen cars not reported to the police. On streets where they are uncommon, the patrolman quickly notices when one appears. If he does not, local residents call the police emergency number to point it out to him. If the car is intact, that is, if it has no broken windows, the tires are still on it, and it has a license plate he can check, he will inquire if it has been reported stolen and, if not, will write it up as abandoned. He turns in his report, which is then forwarded to another unit responsible for carting it off to the junkyard.[6]

The abandonment process is very quick. Cars abandoned intact do not remain whole for long. The tires are taken, engine parts removed, every useful part stripped off by those persons, including some policemen, who have need of them. The hulks are burned by neighborhood children or local residents protesting the city's failure to remove them quickly. One morning an officer took a call for an auto accident and, when he arrived, found an almost new car sitting on the sidewalk with its nose embedded in the crumbling wall of an abandoned building. There was nobody about, but the officer was certain it was not abandoned. He wrote a ticket for illegal parking and left it on the vehicle, assuming the owner would come back and claim so valuable a piece of property. Several hours later he drove by and noticed that the tires were gone, and he stopped to look more closely. He discovered the radio was missing, along with many engine parts, including the fuel pump. After checking again to make sure it was not stolen, he wrote it up as an abandoned car.

Most policemen do not object to people abandoning cars as long as they do it in places where such actions are seen as normal. One afternoon, an officer answered a call to investi-

---

[6] In New York City in 1960 it is reported that there were 2,500 abandoned cars towed away by the police. In 1965 there were 21,943 and in 1970, 72,961, The New York Times (January 24, 1971). In Philadelphia, it is reported, in 1960 there were 834 cars removed; in 1965, 12,341; and in 1970, 23,499, Philadelphia Inquirer (January 31, 1971).

gate a report of several abandoned cars. While he was looking them over, a man came out of a house and said to the patrolman that one of the cars belonged to him. The officer mentioned that he should move it since there was a $500 fine for willfully abandoning cars on public streets. He assured the officer that he was fixing it up and would drive it off the street as soon as it was repaired. After taking down the information on the vehicles, the officer bade the man a good afternoon and slowly pulled away. As he drove off, he told his partner to look at the man in the rear-view mirror. He removed the battery from a car, took it into his house, and then returned for the license plate. The patrolman erased the license number of the car from his patrol report and reported it abandoned, along with the others. One more abandoned car on a street already littered with them did not make any difference to the officer and he saw no reason to give a man a summons requiring him to pay a fine he could never afford.

Once the patrolman has decided that a car is abandoned, he ignores it. Although he knows that many of them are being used, he does not see them as features of a public place but as garbage. In some neighborhoods people live in them during the summer. They are used as storage places for contraband, "drops" for illicit sales, hiding places for the pursued, as well as toys for the little children of the neighborhood. But he does not stop and look inside them, ask anyone whether he has seen people fooling around them, or do anything else that might be evidence that he has even seen them unless he is specifically directed to the car by a call or the actions of a person he has seen on the street.

One afternoon a patrolman took a call for an abandoned car and was told by the dispatcher that the order "came from your captain," a command suggesting that he handle the assignment promptly and thoroughly. From the address he recognized that the car was parked behind a neighborhood health center operated by the city and that this was what had interested the captain. The car was on a narrow street filled with abandoned hulks, but there was only one at the rear entrance of the center. After taking the license tag off the car, he examined the inside and found several sets of "works," needles used by heroin addicts, and a couple of pocketbooks. Obviously the car was a storage place for street thieves, who concealed incriminating evidence before continuing on their way. He did not bother to look at any of the other cars, and after turning in his 48 at the captain's office, he took the pocketbooks to the detective division, where those with identification would be returned to their owners. If the call had not come from the captain, the officer would not have looked inside the car, and if there had not been a call, he would not even have taken notice because this was a street where cars were abandoned regularly.

B · ABANDONED BUILDINGS

The patrolman has a similar reaction to the buildings he sees on his daily rounds. When he finds a burglary in a house or a business place he knows to be occupied, he takes considerable care to guard the scene, secure the break if he can, and contact the owners. The operations room keeps a register with the home phone numbers of all local businessmen, and the corporal is required to contact them whenever there is any problem. Departmental regulations require that any open property that cannot be secured must be guarded by a policeman until the owner or resident can be contacted. He offers the people advice on how to secure their places better and is generally solicitous of their care. But as soon as a place appears to be abandoned, his treatment of it changes dramatically.

Every building in the city is connected to a network of citywide systems that provide the services most people take for granted. A building stands on its own foundation but is linked to every other place in the city by water, gas, electricity, and sewage systems. The maintenance of a living place (whatever its style or use) requires a constant investment of human energy. When this involvement breaks down or ceases, disintegration begins and proceeds quickly. At this point the police alter their view of what they are seeing.

Two officers took a call of males breaking into a house. They had to go a considerable distance, negotiating heavy afternoon traffic, but they arrived quickly. From the outside the building appeared normal. The front door was locked, and when they went to the alley at the side, passage was barred by a locked iron gate, whose elegant, rusting filigree communicated another age. At the end of the alley they saw two boys streaking out of the house and over a fence. A woman came out of the adjoining house, said she had called, and offered the patrolmen the use of her house as a way of getting to the rear of the building. She told them that the woman who lived in the house had died recently and that her children were going to sell it. She said it was a beautiful house but neighborhood youths were always breaking in; she feared they would burn it down. The men listened attentively to her. Her house was poorly furnished but immaculate. Her care and concern were evident everywhere and the patrolmen attended her words carefully.

Climbing a rickety fence, they found the back door open and a scene of reckless vandalism inside. The floor of every room was strewn with pieces of furniture, clothing, and bedding. The building had been ransacked but it was basically intact. The older officer looked about—he did not go past the second floor—and said, "Let's go, it's abandoned." He noticed that the electricity still functioned and that water flowed from the taps. He returned next door and called the water department and the utility companies to come and shut off service. He did not want the property to be flooded or burned down, causing him additional work. He asked the woman, who continued her tale of the depredations wreaked by the nightly invasion of neighborhood youths, for a hammer and some nails. When she was unable to find any nails, he thanked her and said, "It don't matter." He wrote up a 48, making the call unfounded and declaring the building abandoned.

Unfounding calls is one of the ways policemen have of reducing the amount of paper work they are obliged to do and also curbing the rate of reported crime. When a patrolman tells his dispatcher that a job is unfounded, he is claiming that his investigation has not substantiated the initial claim of the person who called for a police officer. Frequently this is the case, but often enough it is not. If a police officer takes a call to investigate a prowler but finds nobody at the scene, he can claim that he has found nothing. He is not saying that it was a false report, only that he found nothing when he investigated. But the judicious use of the same claim provides the policeman with a lie sparing himself and his co-workers a great deal of what they see as needless effort. For example, if the patrolman who investigated the call of males breaking into a house had acknowledged sighting juveniles in the building, he would have had to file a burglary report with the divisional detectives. A detective would have been obliged to go to the scene and conduct an investigation. Since nobody lived in the house, the detective bureau would not have sent anyone, producing instead a false report. If someone was living in the house or was in any way responsible for it, the officer could not ignore the incident; but since the house was abandoned, he knew that a failure to conduct an investigation would not be protested by anyone. His actions were not prompted by laziness, since a proper handling of the matter would have taken him from the street for an hour, filling out paper work and talking to the detectives. His action was prompted by his understanding of what the detectives and his own superiors wanted him to do and was sustained by his perception of this course as reasonable; but it was still illegal.

Two officers took a call of males breaking into a house and hurried to the location. Outside they found a group of children, who told them that "he" had gone. The door stood open and an odor of excrement wafted toward them. As they entered, they found a place that appeared still to be lived in: furniture in place, windows secure; but the floors were littered with food and excrement, and the bathtub had been converted into a latrine. A boy stood in the doorway, watching the policemen, and said that "the pigs" had moved away but returned occasionally to claim some more of their possessions. "He," the reported prowler, was a child of the family that had once lived there who often returned to stay overnight. The policemen went through the house, opening drawers and taking bottles of pills. They used their sticks to turn out the contents of drawers and closets, leaving them where they fell. They did not even bother to close the drawers or closet doors. They left the front door as they had found it.

Several wagons and cars, on another occasion, responded to a call of "males in a building." When they arrived, they found a solid brick building that appeared to be occupied. The first floor was locked, but on the second they found seven men and women sprawled on mattresses and couches in a narrow room. The stove burners and the oven were turned on to give off heat, and the floor was covered with roaches and insects enjoying the warmth. Rat poison was liberally doused everywhere, giving off a very powerful odor. The people did not react to the presence of the policemen, who stood about looking at them. "They're why I don't wear my uniform home," one young patrolman murmured. On the third floor they found an elderly lady sitting in a wheelchair with a suitcase at her feet. She had called the police. She was waiting for her son to pick her up and move her to a rest home. Her furniture and belongings had been moved out during the day. She was sitting quietly and looking at the place she had lived in for forty years. While several officers carried her downstairs, the others roused the slumbering group, prodding them with their sticks. When it was determined that only one of them was under the influence of something other than wine from the empty bottles which were strewn about, they were allowed to remain, except the one fellow, who was taken into custody. As they prepared to leave, the elderly woman's son arrived and took her away. The policemen walked out without bothering to close the front door. A ground-floor window flew up and a woman stuck her head out. "Fuckin' cops. Why don't you close the door? What kinda way is that to treat people? Ain't got no manners, damned motherfuckers." The window slammed down; the policemen shrugged and walked to their cars with the stench of abandonment in their nostrils.

When the city formally condemns a building or claims it for redevelopment, its utilities are turned off and the windows and doors are boarded and tinned to prevent people from entering. Many of these buildings are in usable condition, but it does not take long for the pipe thieves to get in and cut out the plumbing and wiring, emasculating the building and disconnecting it from the city. The patrolman knows these buildings are in use, for he constantly sees evidence, but he rarely looks into them unless he gets a report of someone being inside or actually sees someone going in. Although he knows the buildings are used as "shooting galleries" by drug addicts, settings for rapes, as well as private places for making love, gang hideouts, drops for contraband and incriminating evidence, he does not examine these places on his route. Street kids have an intimate knowledge of them; they know which ones offer escape routes to different directions and use them artfully to evade the police. The patrolman is interested in all of these uses, but it does not encourage him to study systematically the buildings on his sector. They are no longer buildings in the formal sense. They are like the alleys the patrolman does not go into because he does not see them as being either public or private places; regular examination would benefit neither the people of the neighborhood nor himself. His primary interest is to know and control the public spaces used by the people he polices.[7]

2 · Territorial Discretion and Public Privacy

When a patrolman is permanently assigned to a sector, mutually acknowledged obligations are assumed by everyone in the platoon. An assigned sector's boundaries quickly become barriers that colleagues cross only for specific purposes acceptable to the regular patrolman. They enter his sector freely, handle radio assignments without qualms, and occasionally take action if they see something amiss, but they can-

---

[7]In response to a call of a "purse snatching in progress," several partolmen chased a youth into an apparently abandoned building where, in addition to arresting the suspect, they found more than one hundred handbags, the result of many months of robbery. The bags were collected and turned over to the detectives for examination, but the sector patrolman did not bother to go into the building again to see whether it was still being used as a hiding place for escaping muggers. Their failure to examine empty buildings is not a result of its being a new obligation or one that is not clearly defined, as the following indicates. "The patrolman must pay particular attention to unoccupied and temporarily vacant houses, diligently protecting them against damage and theft." *Patrolman's Manual*, para. 38.

not poach. Any unassigned sector is treated as free territory by platoon members, who may look for activity there and develop informants and contacts without permission. But an assigned sector is the preserve of its regular patrolman, who must also acknowledge the rights of his colleagues by seeking his activity only in his sector or on free ground. Any jobs that are "on him," emanating from his territory, must be taken by the sector man if he is available. These rules are understood and accepted by every man aspiring to a secure place in his platoon.[8]

A veteran patrolman develops a studied inattentiveness when he is out of his own sector. At the beginning of each tour, he does not look for activity until he gets to his own work place. He scans the people, checks intersections, listens to what the radio offers, but only an emergency call or the sighting of some serious disturbance—a fight in the street —causes him to act. He notices things that he might look into if they were on him but passes them up. Even if he is under pressure for activity, he does not allow the conventions to break down. If a street is a sector boundary, he will write meter tickets on one side but ignore the other side. If he is covering an adjoining sector for an absent regular, he has the right to take activity, but he is careful not to do anything that might reflect on the quality of his colleague's policing. If he discovers that there are some broken parking meters, he will not report them. If someone approaches him and complains about an abandoned car, which has lain unattended for weeks, he will do nothing officially, no matter what he says to the complainant. There are two exceptions to this

[8]A sector is a territory in the sense that it is a clearly defined physical space, not in an ethological sense. The policeman has no permanent, exclusive, or final claims to it, since each sector is assigned to four different men and his claims may be revoked at any time. His claims are jurisdictional in that they flow from assigned rights, but his exercise of these rights involves him in the protection of ground as well as the protection of rights over the ground. In other words the policeman's claims have both territorial and jurisdictional characteristics, and the use of either term in the restricted sense in which it is usually employed implies an incomplete description of the policeman's role. For a discussion of the distinctions between territory and jurisdiction, see Erving Goffman, "The Territories of the Self," in *Relations in Public*, pp. 28–35, and Philip D. Roos, "Jurisdiction: An Ecological Concept," *Human Relations*, Vol. XXI (1968), pp. 75–83.

rule. Any car parked in a dangerous manner or any obstruction likely to cause an accident is noticed by a passing patrolman, and if he sees anybody about, he will stop and make them repair the situation. He will not issue a ticket unless he feels obliged to support his request with the force of law, nor will he claim any kind of activity for his trouble. Among colleagues this is viewed as "helping out." He is not impinging on his colleague's work because no official record is made, and he may have spared him an unnecessary assignment. Also, if he is assigned a job by the dispatcher, he must accept it, even if it involves taking activity.

When the dispatcher orders another car to handle a job on an assigned sector, the regular man will check it if he hears the call. He does not necessarily question his colleague's obligation to handle the work, but he wants to know what is going on. He does not need to conceal his curiosity since he has a right to know what is being done in his sector. On the contrary, if he shows no interest, his colleagues begin to think that he does not care if they do work in his territory, and the more ambitious will encroach if he does not resist them. His defense of the sector lines is informal, but it is also ceaseless.

While on another assignment, a patrolman heard the dispatcher give an illegal-parking assignment to a wagon on a block in his sector. When he finished his own job, he remained out of service and drove over to the wagon's location. When he got out of his car, the wagon driver approached him and apologized for writing the tickets, but added he had no choice since the dispatcher had informed him that the complaint had come directly from the mayor's office. The patrolman nodded. He patted the wagon man on the shoulder and told him to forget it.

The territorial discretion practiced by the district men obliges the patrolman to develop a specialized orientation to his own sector in order to exploit it more intensively and efficiently. The particularized knowledge he has of people which he develops by answering calls, making stops, and watching the public while he cruises is utilized to help him understand the uses of different areas in his sector. He has places where he gets certain kinds of activity: corners that are trouble spots, where junkies are found, where narcotics are sold; corners where "he has to move them or they will walk all over you," where he must lock his car when he gets out; corners where he has no problems and he can relax and do some paper work. He also has places where he can hide his car if he is inclined, and other places where he never stops without a call from the dispatcher.

He develops notions about what is the "normal"[9] character of behavior in different parts of his sector which he uses in deciding how to handle his assignments. His views are strongly affected by the formidable zoning power of the city government, which can transform the character of an area in a few years. He is also affected by the habits and customs of the people who work, live, play, drive, and walk on the streets he patrols. Whatever judgments he makes of the people, even if he holds them in low regard, he does not fail to account for the ways in which they use their places (or the places allowed them) on his tour. Behavior tolerated in one place is disallowed in another because it violates his notions of what is right in that place. These judgments are overruled only by specific commands from the radio dispatcher or the patrolman's sergeant, who has a right to intervene in his work at any time.

The residential streets of poor and working-class neighborhoods are used differently from the same kinds of streets in middle-class settlements. Children ignore the distinctions so carefully nurtured in penal codes and city ordinances between public and private use. They learn from their families to use the streets as extensions of their private spaces. Since their elders casually use the sidewalks and stoops before their houses to sit, sunbathe, cook dinner, make love and sometimes war, and watch others doing these things, it is not surprising that their children should extend this attitude into the streets on which they live. Even adults occasionally use the streets for private purposes. It is not uncommon in summer to see people draped over the hoods of cars, reclining in

---

[9]For a discussion of "normal," see David Sudnow, "Normal Crimes: Sociological Features of the Penal Code in a Public Defender Office," *Social Problems*, Vol. XII (1965), pp. 255–76.

unused space out of the way of others, taking the sun. The experienced patrolman does not tell them to get off or even ask whose car they are using unless he gets a call. It is part of the local landscape and he sees nothing wrong in their behavior, regardless of how he personally characterizes the people. But if he sees the same thing on a street whose character he views as having other purposes, his attitude is very different.

The police are organized to control the streets and the successful patrolman is an informal specialist in street use. He combines his knowledge of local behavior with his conceptions of how the public streets are used to analyze and perform many of his routine obligations. He informally rationalizes his search for activity and minimizes, in his own terms, the need for conflict with the people by constantly evaluating the character of the ground he patrols and its uses.

A • DAMAGED CAR STOPS

A basic form of activity required of a patrolman is a damaged car stop, used by the department's accident-investigation unit to trace cars involved in hit-and-run accidents. The officer is supposed to file a report on any car he sees with fresh damage to the front end or the side, noting the license number, the make and color of the car, as well as the time and location of the sighting. Since he must look at both the front and rear ends of the car, an inexperienced man either makes these reports from sightings of parked cars or from cars he has ordered to stop. He does not want to make a car stop, but he has no other way of obtaining the information he needs, so he must do something other than he intended to fulfill what is a very routine obligation. The experienced patrolman has little regard for this work and is willing to give it only minimal effort. He knows that car stops are rarely pleasant, and he does not lightly undertake the risks that always attend them. He uses his territorial knowledge and observation to get his activity without causing any unnecessary discontent among the people he is policing.

At a quiet time during daywork, he parks his car at a

heavily used intersection. Although he would like to use a commercial intersection where the traffic is heaviest, he cannot, because of the large volume of passing pedestrians. The public often assumes (and the patrolman always assumes the public assumes) that a policeman sitting in a parked car in plain view is not working, and the officer prefers not to give people a chance to think that way about him; he also does not want to be bothered while he is doing his work. Parked at the curb in the direction the traffic is flowing, he uses his side mirror to scan the oncoming traffic. When he sees a car with the appropriate damage, he notes the make and color, and then, as it passes, he takes down the tag number. The driver has no idea he is being observed and that a police report about him is being prepared. In a short while the patrolman has the activity for the sergeant, and he has not exerted himself in any way.

B • MOVING VIOLATIONS

The patrolman is not under pressure to write as many tickets for moving violations as possible but he is expected to write some regularly. In almost every squad there is one man who develops a reputation as a traffic cop who turns in large numbers of movers, but his zeal is not an embarrassment or an annoyance to less productive colleagues. If it were, they would make him stop. His actions are usually attributed to a lack of interest or courage for "real police work" and he is allowed to go his own way. Patrolmen have little regard for this kind of work because movers are so easy to get and frequently the people they stop may argue or fight. But each man must write some every month. Movers also can be used to produce fake activity. When a patrolman writes a mover, he can also make up a car stop, giving him credit in two categories for the same action. Many patrolmen disdain this practice, but there is hardly a man who has not utilized it occasionally to please his sergeant.

While cruising, the patrolman frequently sees driving violations. Often he does not stop the offender because he has more important things to do, the car is too difficult to reach, or he does not care. If someone suddenly pulls out from a curb, causing him to swerve, or hits him, he will stop and almost certainly write a ticket. If he does not stop, he cannot blame the other driver for the accident or any complaint made against him. Unless he is in a selective-enforcement area, where he is expected to write some tickets and show his superiors that he is doing what they feel is necessary to protect the lives and well-being of the citizenry, he may simply warn the driver. If he needs to write a ticket he will, but when he is looking for movers, he does not depend on this incidental activity.[1]

Most movers are written for violations at intersections. This is due partly to the patrolman's technique for easing his work and partly to people's inclinations to commit infractions of the numerous rules that govern traffic at intersections. When the patrolman needs a mover, he sets up a trap without formally concealing himself. He chooses an intersection where violations are common, in an area sufficiently built up so that he can park close to the corner without being seen by oncoming traffic. Usually he selects a corner with a traffic light or a stop sign, near a school or a factory. He favors these places because they have pedestrian crossings but are heavily used for only a few hours each day. Impatient drivers often choose to run lights or to "walk" stop signs, slowing down but never quite coming to a full stop, when they do not see anyone coming, and the policeman is ready for them.

When he goes to these locations, the patrolman is committed to getting some activity. Occasionally he parks his car at one of these places while taking a breather, sipping a container of coffee (an experienced man keeps his container lid on the dashboard until he is finished), or catching up on some paper work, allowing himself the chance to get a mover while the going is slow. If he is under pressure for activity, he may go directly to this spot when he leaves the station. There are many occasions when a motorist can talk

---

[1] If he is angry and for any reason cannot stop the motorist, the patrolman can "submarine" a driver. If he has the license-plate number, he can trace the name and address of the owner and send him a ticket, which must be approved by his supervisor. This is seldom done because the patrolman cannot know who was driving the car and the tickets are usually thrown out in traffic court. But the officer may force the person to spend a day in court.

a policeman out of a ticket. Often the patrolman is not committed to writing a ticket but is satisfied to give the person a warning. In these moments he is greatly affected by the demeanor of the motorist, who the patrolman sees as one who has committed a "crime," but a crime that he takes so lightly that he is willing to forgo sanction. But when he is working his ticketing ground, it is almost impossible to dissuade him. At these moments he is not concerned with protecting the public, improving the image of his department, or even making some money if he is dishonest; his foremost concern is with satisfying hs sergeant's demands. He is not going to tell anyone this, but it is his primary reason for being there in the first place. If the person is belligerent, the officer may increase the sanction by issuing a ticket for reckless driving, which is a more serious violation that requires a personal court appearance; but even if the motorist is well mannered, he will get a summons.

C • PARKING VIOLATIONS

The patrolman is required to give tickets for parking violations, but his opportunities so far exceed his obligations that he has great freedom in deciding whom and when to ticket. He sees ticketing either as a personal sanction against someone whose behavior has warranted punishment (under the absolute cover of law) or as an impersonal action necessary to maintain what the patrolman views as the rightful nature of a particular place. Ticketing is not seen as a solution to a problem or even as a source of revenue (unlike meter tickets, which are viewed explicitly as a sanction designed to assure the effectiveness of meters as a source of revenue). The policeman knows that there are too few spaces bargained for by too many car owners. But he is not interested in solving the parking problem. He is concerned only to maintain what he sees as the legitimate nature of particular places, to prevent accidents that can be ascribed to parking hazards he has allowed to occur, and to allow the unimpeded flow of traffic, whose interruption will cause additional work and provoke the intervention of his sergeant or some higher official.

Conflict over the use of public streets for car parking is

endemic in cities. While this conflict preceded the automobile —the directing of carriage traffic was an important part of police work in the nineteenth century—it has become critical with the mass production of the automobile. Most policemen detest any obligation linked to the regulation of traffic because it causes them so much trouble in return for very little sympathy and the only rewards it offers are illegal. From the moment he arrives at the police academy, the recruit is warned to expect trouble over parking tickets. He is told that people will be angry at him, fight him, threaten to "get" his job, and generally make life miserable for him. This comes as no surprise to the recruits, who are eager to discuss run-ins they have had with policemen who have treated them unfairly, demeaned them with foul language, even arrested them. The instructors allow that these things happen and urge them not to take ticketing seriously. "Look, fellas, this is a hell of a city to park in. Unless there is a meter violation, or the street is blocked, or there's a complaint to the district, don't write 'em," the traffic instructor informally urged his students.

The rookie is quickly familiarized with ticket writing, since it is one of the first jobs he is given when he comes to the district. He is frequently assigned to do nothing but write meters and parkers after receiving explicit instructions from the sergeant. He learns how easy it is, and he also learns that his own freedom to write or not to write parkers is restricted only by his sergeant, who may or may not tell him why he cannot write parking tickets in one place, or why the place he was not supposed to write them a week before is now to be carefully scrutinized. When he gets his own sector, he is told explicitly (if he does not already know) whether there are places that are not to be tagged. "It ain't right. I don't give a fuck if the people park on the sidewalks, but it ain't right if I have to give tickets on Smith Street and I don't give them over here. You know, I'd like to kick my beloved sergeant's teeth in," a man said, as he drove along a row of illegally parked cars. While a patrolman may not wish to accede to these arrangements, or refuses to accept any rewards that might flow from them, he has little choice, unless he is willing to give up his sector and probably his position in the platoon.

The city also puts pressure on the police to issue tickets in certain places, to keep intersections open for buses, and to protect public property. Cruising through a thinly populated commercial area, an officer cursed when he saw a car parked beside a sign forbidding parking at any time on that side of the street. "Shit, I hate this. I mean I got to ticket this guy because the city is bitching. When they park here, trucks making the turn have to go up on the sidewalk and they break the sewer inlet cover. City's put three in since last year. So now I got to write 'em because if another one gets broken, it's my ass. You watch, as soon as I get out there, the guy will show up. That's why I write my tickets in the car, so I don't have to stand around for people to see me." While he was putting the ticket under the windshield wiper, the driver came out and showed him the note he had taped to the window, informing anyone interested that he intended to return after making a delivery. The patrolman shook his head and told him he could not tear the ticket up but that in the future he should put his sign near his license plate since that's where a policeman looks. The man was angry but not nasty, and the patrolman told him to go to court and protest the ticket. He even promised to write an explanation on the back of the court copy of the ticket which would assure its cancellation. "What did I say. It's a bitch. He was O.K., but some people are unbelievable. Nineteen years in this district and nobody would believe some of the battles I've had with people. Even fought a cop once. Now that poor bastard has to waste a friggin' day in court or spend six bucks."

When the patrolman is given a radio call to ticket illegally parked cars, he is free to make his own decisions if the place is not covered by some formal arrangements. Often these complaints come from irate neighbors or from persons who are involved in a dispute with their fellow workers. They call anonymously in the hope that the police will mete out a punishment, which they can enjoy without being disclosed as the culprit. "Look at that. All those cars parked on the sidewalk. Nothing wrong with this, is there? They ain't blocking the street and nobody walks here. Fuck it, I ain't writing them," the sector man said, surveying a row of parked cars beside a factory. But before he departed, he went into the factory to ask the manager if he had called. When he was told that nobody in authority had requested the police, the officer thanked him and left.

A patrolman was given an illegal-parking call, and as soon as he heard the address, he said that he probably would not write a ticket. "We'll just go on over there and make sure nobody is blocking the corner." In two blocks there were thirty-eight illegally parked cars. "Right, nobody doing nuthin' wrong here," he said with a quick grin. "Some of these porkies [Puerto Ricans] get to hate their neighbors and then they call us to punish them. Not me." Several days later the officer got another call in the same neighborhood. As he pulled up, a woman came out of a house and pointed at three trucks parked near her house. "He did it on purpose. He knows I keep this space for my son's car. If we don't park it in front of the house, someone will steal it." He explained to her that she did not have a legal right to the space and that everybody could park wherever they wanted if it was not forbidden by law. She nodded, took the officer by the arm, led him around the trucks, and pointed to a sign that forbade parking beyond the end of her house. He nodded and wrote two tickets, while she watched him place them on the windshields of the offending vehicles.

As he was about to drive off, the owner of the trucks arrived; they knew each other well and exchanged friendly greetings. The owner claimed the woman was a "nut"; he had left the trucks there only until he got his yard cleared out. "Does she think I'm gonna leave my trucks on the street overnight? The protection I get from guys like you, they won't be here in the morning," he said with a laugh. The patrolman laughed with him and said, "What are you yellin' about, you ain't gonna pay those tickets anyway," and they both laughed. Before he left, the patrolman asked the owner about some new tires he needed for his car and they agreed on a price. "Naw, he ain't gonna pay. He ain't paying me but he's got someone in traffic court. So what the hell. The old lady is happy and she's got her point. He don't give a shit and I got my snow tires."

An officer took a call on a narrow street that was not wide enough to park a car. As he entered the street, he saw two cars on the sidewalk beside a NO PARKING sign. A woman was sitting on a stoop with a young baby, staring at the patrol car as it rolled toward her. "Good morning. Do you know anything about these cars?"

"Ya. One's mine and the other belongs to my son. My husband put 'em up on the sidewalk before he went to bed. He's gonna move 'em when he gets up later on."

"O.K. But if he doesn't, I'm gonna tag 'em, because they are blocking the front door of those two houses across the street and the sign is very clear."

"Ya, I can see. He'll move 'em, sonny," she said, after taking a drink from the beer bottle she held in her free hand. The officer did not return to the street again that day, but the next morning as he drove past the street he recalled the incident. He braked his car, backed up, and looked down the street to see the two cars parked in exactly the same place. "Fuck her, that shanty-Irish bitch," he muttered, as he swung his car into the narrow way. As he pulled up, the woman from the day before appeared. He neither gave nor received any sign of recognition. When he had finished tagging the cars, he drove off without a word or a glance. But he was not angry; he could have given two tickets to each car—one for illegal parking and another for parking on the sidewalk.

Later in the day there was a call to investigate an auto accident. When the two patrolmen arrived at the narrow back street, it was evident that the call had been made by an irate neighbor protesting the blocking of the street by a rented truck, which someone was using to move his belongings; there was no accident. The driver maneuvered the patrol car around the truck and parked it on the sidewalk. The officers walked back to the truck, and the driver asked to speak with the head of the house. A woman went quickly into the house but for several minutes nobody appeared. The patrolmen were becoming impatient as they stood in the street, watching the neighbors come out of their houses and stare at them. One of the people in the group said loud enough for all to hear, "Oh, boy, those cops are mad now. They'll give it to them Spanish." Finally the head of the household came out under a load of clothing, which he dropped into the truck. He was about to return to the house when one officer called out to him. "What you want?" "Is that your car parked on the sidewalk in front of the truck?" he asked coldly.

"Ya."

"Good. Let me see your truck-leasing agreement and let me have your driver's license and owner's card." What had begun as a simple investigation, which would have ended in a polite request to move the truck, had been converted into an entirely different matter.

The man handed the patrolman his papers and said, "Go ahead and give me a ticket. I don't give a damn. I don't pay them. You know State Representative Morales. I work for him. He pretty big guy around here, take care of me, and we take care of you two." The patrolman turned without saying a word and walked to his car. "I'll give that mother-fucker a ticket. I'll give him three for his truck and a couple for his car. He'll fix 'em. When I get finished writing on the back of these tickets, he'll need the fuckin' governor to get them fixed." He wrote an illegal parking, a parking on the sidewalk, and an obstructing a garage ticket on the truck, and on the man's car he wrote two additional tickets. "Take your stick," he said to his partner, who already had it in hand as they returned to the waiting man and handed him the five tickets and his papers. Not a word was spoken, and the neighbors, whose expectations of a good fight were enhanced by the appearance of the sticks, were only slightly mollified by the stack of tickets they saw handed over.

In commercial areas where there is no consistent departmental or district policy, the patrolman tends to grant the merchants what they want. Patrolmen and merchants occasionally get into personal disputes, and the ticketing power of the individual officer can be used to great effect. One patrolman always gave parking tickets to a woman who ran a small diner after she refused to buy a chance for a charity raffle he was selling. Another beatman used his discretion to force some businessmen to release him from unwanted obligations. This man's regular beat was extended two blocks by the department at the request of the businessmen's association. He was unable to get the order changed even after he appealed to his captain. He did not want to give up his post and retaliated by giving parking tickets and enforcing city ordinances governing littering and the use of public sidewalks for displaying merchandise in the blocks that were added to his patrol. After a few weeks the businessmen demanded his replacement, while the people in his regular beat area defended him. Finally, the business people asked that the extension be canceled and the patrolman resumed his old beat. The sector car in the area was ordered to give more attention to the business people who had sought a beatman for their personal protection.

He will write meter tickets but refrain from writing parkers unless they pose a hazard. Even when he is going to write one he can be dissuaded from doing so if the driver appears before he has begun to write it. But once he has begun writing, he will continue, because with "no fix" tickets he simply cannot rip one up and throw it away. Each book of twenty-five is numbered, and when he takes it from the corporal, he must sign for it. He has to account for every ticket, and the only way he can void one is to file a series of special memos explaining his reasons along with the voided summons. He is rarely willing to do this, especially since he can always write a mitigating explanation on the back of the court copy asking that the fine be voided.

One afternoon an officer was given a call for illegal parking in a commercial area well off his sector. He was fairly new in the district, and it took him awhile to find the address. When he arrived he saw a car parked in an obviously dangerous and illegal manner at the corner of a small street. He took out his ticket book and wrote it up. As he was placing the ticket on the car, a man came out of a store on the corner. He approached and asked whether the officer had come in answer to his call. When the patrolman said that he had, the man replied that the car that had been bothering him had already left and he hoped the patrolman was not going to tag his car. "Hey, I'm sorry, pal, but it's already written."

"I expected Officer Reno, he's usually on 6515 car. I'd appreciate it, Officer, if next time you would stop in before you write them up." The patrolman was slightly confused.

On one hand he felt he had done the right thing because it was a radio assignment that had to be treated seriously. He also felt that if the storekeeper was so familiar with the police he could have called the operations room and asked them for a car without putting anything on the air. On the other hand, he was relatively new in the platoon and did not want to disturb any private arrangements he did not know about between the storekeeper and the regular patrolman. He said politely and frankly, "Mister, how would it look if I went into every store before I wrote up a ticket and asked if it was all right? What would people think I was doing? What would you think I was doing?" The man shrugged his shoulders and smiled. "You're right, son. O.K., forget it. Listen, stop in sometime if I can help you with something." He patted the patrolman on the shoulder and returned to his business.

The most troublesome parking disputes arise between garage owners and private residents. The garages require space to park their cars, angering the residents, who feel they are deprived of the right to use their streets. These disputes are endemic, and the patrolman knows immediately from the location of a call whether it is a garage. The problems are insoluble since the interests of the parties are absolutely opposed. Occasionally the garage owners counterattack when a neighbor parks in front of their shop door in violation of a city ordinance; but most of the calls are from neighbors. The law also forbids the garage owners to display for sale cars on the street, to block the sidewalk, to repair cars on the public pavement, or to park cars which are not in operating condition on a public street. When the situation gets badly out of hand, the police enforce all of these regulations and compel the owner to clear the street. They rarely ticket and then only when they get no cooperation. A patrolman will warn a garage owner numerous times, arrange little compromises, and only then, if he gets no compliance from the owner, will he begin writing. He does not think of his actions as leading to any solution; he knows the calls will begin again, and he will have to start the process of accommodation anew. This continues as long as the personal relations between the officer and the owner do not sour. It also depends to a degree on the attitude of the sergeant, who listens to the captain in these matters. Since these disputes lead the policeman and the businessman into considerable contact, a personal relationship develops which can either reduce friction or create an animus that has nothing to do with disputes over illegal parking. But the owner knows that unless he has some kind of local political influence, he is dependent on the police, whose control over the streets is absolute. If they will allow him to continue operating, he is willing to take tickets occasionally as part of his operating costs and allow the police to show the neighborhood people that their interests, too, are not being neglected.

D • STREET CORNERS

During the warm months of the year, especially after the schools close, the streets and pavements of the city's residential neighborhoods are heavily used. In many areas people live out of doors much of the time. In places where they have no yards or porches, it is common to see families set out beach chairs and portable grills to prepare picnics on the pavements. Young people fill the streets with games and play. Older youths hang on the corners, talking, scanning, planning, and plotting, as policemen driving past often say. It is common in some neighborhoods to see groups of children or teenagers using a street as a stage for practicing coordinated dancing, "drilling," as black youths call it. It is not uncommon in some areas to arrive at a street in the darkest hours of the early morning to find it ablaze with light. Floodlights have been set up, cloths spread on the sidewalk, and engine parts carefully laid out. With music playing, a little beer being passed about, the neighborhood men are working on their cars. The patrolman is familiar with these scenes, and while he notes them, he does not stop unless he is curious and certainly does not try to curb these activities.

But the intensive use of the streets does produce conditions that interest him greatly. The patrolman is empowered by the common law, penal code, and city ordinance to clear street corners even if there has been no formal complaint. His is the duty to evaluate and judge street behavior. Even if he had no right to move corner loungers, he would be kept sufficiently busy by the number of disorderly-crowd calls he gets during the summer months. How he handles a group of people on a street corner depends a good deal on their response to him, his knowledge of their habits, and the orders he has received at roll call. But even prior to seeing them, he makes some judgment about what he will do. There are corners where he ignores people massed together, and others where he will move just one or two people who seem peaceful and quiet. These are not random decisions, nor are they simply the product of personal animus toward individuals or groups.

"Disorderly crowds are the worst. Where are ya gonna move the kids? I tell 'em to get off the corner because some old bag doesn't like them hangin' around. Or maybe they're bouncing a ball off her wall. They move but they come back, because they don't have no place to go. If they give you some shit, maybe you lock 'em up. Can't smack 'em so much any more. But it don't do no good, they'll be back on the corner tomorrow. That's why nobody hurries on these calls. If it's a fight on the highway or a disturbance, you know you got something, but these are just a lot of bullshit," a patrolman said.

Cruising down a major street in his sector, a patrolman commented on the children gathered on the corners. "See those little girls, fourteen, maybe fifteen. I know 'em all but I don't move 'em. Some of the younger cops do, but not me. There are no complaints. You know what they're doing? Hustlin' their ass. Old guys in the bars start 'em off, give 'em half a buck to get their rocks off, and then next year they start sellin' it. It's terrible, sure, but if I push 'em off the corner, they're just gonna go in the back door of the bars and then there will be real trouble. If there's no complaint, I let 'em stay." A few blocks farther he pulled up at a corner where three boys were standing. Without moving from the car, he yelled, "Move it," and watched while they shuffled off. "The guys hangin' here panhandle and steal from the women who use the supermarket. If I don't move 'em, there will be a call soon." As he drove along he passed a group of eight or ten teenagers standing at another intersection. "They're probably talkin' about where they can steal some glue to huff for the weekend, but they don't do none of their shit here, so I leave 'em," he commented.

Once he has named a place, this opinion assumes precedence in determining what is going on there. He cares less about who is there than where they are. He does not make evaluations of the people at each corner every time he cruises past, but makes assumptions about them based on his conception of the place. These can be altered by personal knowledge of some of the people he sees, but if he does not know them (which is more often the case), his response is determined by his ideas about the place.

On one sector there was an abandoned intersection that had acquired a reputation for muggings and robberies. Three corners were empty lots and the fourth was occupied by a collection of abandoned houses. At this corner there were a bus stop and a liquor store. These services assured the corner of continual pedestrian traffic. Since nobody lived on the intersection, there were never any complaints to the police about the activities of the boys who used the stoops of the abandoned houses for their gathering place.

A local teenage gang known as the Dirty Dozen, instantly identifiable by their immaculate dress and spotless white caps, had appropriated the corner. Every patrolman who passed— even men who were not assigned to the sector—always looked to see whether the steps were occupied. During the day there was no inclination to stop, although the sector patrolman knew one or two of them personally. But at night the police altered their attitudes toward this group. The sector patrolman kept tabs on how many boys were sitting on the corner, and he kept checking each time he passed. If the number decreased, he patrolled the area carefully, assuming that some of them had gone off to make a "hit." Occasionally he stopped and just stared at them for a while. If there had been a mugging, he would run them off, if they were around, although he knew they would return the next day. Sometimes he would call another car and search them all.

The patrolman and his colleagues did not conceal their dislike and contempt for these boys, whom they considered robbers and muggers. On the other hand they were not a territorial gang interested in fighting turf wars, and they were seldom found with any weapons other than pocket knives. If the patrolman had news of impending gang fighting, he would warn them to stay off the street. He did not deny them the corner, because he saw it as an open space not belonging to anyone. He and his colleagues had urged the closing of the liquor store and the transfer of the bus stop, but when these requests were refused, he felt that there was nothing more that he could do. He continued to check the boys out, letting them know they were watched, but whenever he saw them elsewhere—sitting on the steps of their houses in the adjoining block—he ignored them.[2]

The patrolman views residency as the most powerful mark of legitimacy. Unless he has a specific call, he never moves people off the stoops of private houses in the middle of a block. He assumes they have a right to be there, and if there were objections, he knows the dispatcher will give him a call. He frequently sees children on the small intersections in the interior of his sector. He stops and tells them to move, and if they object to being moved away from the places where they live, he allows them to stay. "We live here," has a powerful effect on the patrolman's attitude toward these people. If there has been a complaint about the juveniles on one of these corners, he will ask each one where he lives and arbitrarily send those who do not live near the corner back toward their own houses. Even if the boys or girls live only a block or two away, he will tell them, "Go back over where you live," as if he were referring to some distant place.

Corner lounging poses an acute problem for the policeman in areas where teenage gang fighting is common. The patrolman understand that the gangs have territorial interests, but he is not interested in honoring any of their claims or giving them official sanction. Their boundary lines rarely coincide with sector lines; often there are several in one sector, creating the conditions for continual conflict in his area. Also, his own jurisdictional interests are diametrically opposed to the actions which gang members take to protect their "turfs." Any effort to control the streets by force is seen by the pa-

---

[2]See Gerald D. Suttles, *The Social Order of the Slums* (Chicago, University of Chicago Press, 1968), pp. 73–83.

trolman as a direct challenge to his authority and he resists it with all his power. The department has a specialized gang-control unit which monitors the actions of the most aggressive street gangs, and the patrolman has few personal connections with gang members. He may know a few of the boys, but most are hostile faces on the corner. Their informal competition for what each regards as rightfully his bars close contacts and leaves the patrolman only one course to follow. If he sees a group assembling, he will order them to move, rather than risk the development of a skirmish. If the crowd is sufficiently large to require an additional car or two, he and his colleagues will arbitrarily break it up into small groups and send them in different directions. He does not know what impact his actions have on their inclinations to fight, nor does he care. He knows that he personally cannot prevent them from fighting if they want to, but he can remind them constantly that they do not own the ground. If they resist his demand, he is prepared to use whatever force is necessary to protect what he sees as his fundamental "rights" to the street. For the patrolman the street is everything; if he loses that, he has surrendered his reason for being what he is.

Most disorderly crowds are handled by the patrolman without leaving his car. When he gets a call he knows there has been a complaint, and the speed of his response is determined by his conception of the place and the frequency of complaints about the place. When he arrives he usually tells the groups to move along without getting out of his car. This is not laziness but his way of indicating to all that he does not take the matter seriously; if they comply with his wishes, there will be no trouble. He does not ask their names or make out any ped stops unless there has been a curfew violation. If they do not move, he may speed them along with a few choice remarks, or he may open the door of his car to indicate his increasing involvement in assuring their compliance. During a tour, any return calls to a corner are treated as a continuation of the initial job, and the patrolman begins his work at a higher level of involvement. The second time, if there is no open hostility displayed toward him, he will only threaten them with the "net." If there is a third call, there are no discussions upon his arrival and he will ask the dispatcher to send a wagon. A good dispatcher recalls the repetition of assignments, and if it is a busy time, he will offer the patrolman a wagon when he gives him a "return" call.

The patrolman sees arrest in these situations as a sanction against the parents of the teenagers. They must come to the station to secure the release of their children, and the patrolman hopes the inconvenience will encourage them to punish their children. When this happens at the station house, he openly applauds any beatings that are administered. But the patrolman does not think that arrests will keep the youths off the corners. He just "scoops 'em up" when his patience has been exhausted and he feels they are challenging him. Since he can more or less choose when he is going to arrest them, these occasions also offer him an opportunity to make some extra money. He knows the same groups will be out night after night; if he chooses the right day, he can get his court hearing on his day off, assuring him of some overtime pay. A patrolman sat in his car one evening pondering whether he should take a corner. "Tomorrow night we lock them up. Yup," he said, looking at his pocket shift calendar, "that will give us four hours' overtime."

These calls also provide the patrolman with an occasional opportunity to acquire beer for his platoon. No policeman has to worry very much about buying beer at a good price, but most sector men like to confiscate beer, which they can put in the operations-room refrigerator. It is a little kindness the corporal appreciates; a form of activity that makes a good impression and is recalled when the corporal makes up the overtime sheets or needs a man to go downtown. The patrolman knows certain places on his sector where teenagers do their drinking, and if he gets a disorderly-crowd call in the vicinity of any of these places, he responds quickly in the hope of finding beer. He knows the youths are on the lookout for him because as a working-class person he recalls the times when he had his own beer confiscated by the police. If he sees a juvenile buying beer, he may stop him and try to make a vice pinch; otherwise he closes in quickly to "get the goods" before they are consumed. He sees his actions as part of a competition with the teenagers, who are constantly causing him trouble, doing acts of vandalism, committing petty thefts, stealing cars, and burglarizing stores. Actually what he is doing is stealing their beer, although he would be outraged by the characterization and reject it angrily; it is just a rent he collects.

"There goes one, up the steps to the freight yard," an officer commented to his partner, who was driving. "Beer patrol. If you saw them, they saw us, so let's go," his partner said, quickly parking the car and heading for the steps. They raced to the top and into the tall grass that fringed the railroad trestle at the edge of the freightyard. Their quick arrival cut off the escape route of the last youth, who was concealing a case of beer in the grass. "O.K., boy, where is it?" There was no reply, and while one patrolman stood close guard over the teenager, his partner went into the grass and returned in a few moments with a large carton. "Very nice, iced too. We thank you." The young man said nothing. "I ain't gonna lock you up. What's your name?" "Murphy." "Well, Murphy, while we got you here, I think we should have a little talk. I been meaning to talk with you boys and this is a good time. There's been a lot of trouble in the freight yard recently, stealing, people throwing rocks off the bridge at cars. I want you to do me a favor. Tell your friends there's gonna be some trouble if it keeps up. I don't know about those cops across the line in the Thirtieth, but we're gonna whip your ass if it don't stop."

"It ain't us. We just drink beer up here. It's that group on Fish Street. They're all huffers, they get goofy and do all that shit. Not us."

"Is that so?" the officer said. "O.K., I believe that, but listen, tell your friends anyway, because we ain't kidding. It's getting to be summer and we got a lot of work to do, so fuck-around time is past. Next time it's for keeps, my friend. Now beat it, and thanks for the beer."

E • OPEN HYDRANTS

Another commonplace concern of the patrolman, strongly affected by his conception of place, is the turning off of open fire hydrants. The opening of hydrants is almost exclusively a summertime occurrence. People do not violate the ordinances regulating the use of hydrants for malicious purposes as do those who ring false fire alarms. People do not turn them on in the winter when the water might freeze and cause hazardous driving; they turn them on when they are hot and sticky with city dirt and want to cool off.

Hydrants are public property; that is, they are owned by the city. The excessive number of them in some of our older cities is the long-forgotten consequence of graft and the hustling politicians whose portraits adorn our city halls. They are operated by turning a hexagonal nut in the top of the hydrant with a special wrench. When fully open, each hydrant will gush about a thousand gallons per minute, producing a powerful stream of water. With the use of simple tools—a board or a discarded tire—it is possible to convert the flow into a geyser, a fountain, or other streams to meet the needs of children. They do not care that the hydrants belong to the city and that opening them, except in case of fire, is forbidden by city ordinance.

When the hydrants in an area are fully opened, the water pressure to homes, factories, and hospitals disappears. People above the first floor can get no water. If there is an outbreak of fire, the hydrants must be shut off before the hoses can get sufficient pressure to put out the flames. In recent years some cities have sought to meet the demands of the people and the needs of the fire department by issuing sprinklers that attach to the hydrants and allow a controlled flow of water. Unfortunately for the city, these sprinklers let the water flow only at the rate of twenty gallons a minute. You can get wet but there is no possibility of creating a gusher, flooding the street for a swim, or washing down a passing car. So the children unscrew them where they can or just break them off.

The patrolman fully understands the motives for turning on hydrants. He knows that disputes over hydrants have led to riots in some cities and are a constant source of controversy between the people and the police. He has been urged to be tactful in dealing with "open hydrants." At the academy an instructor said, "The people are hot and angry. Nobody has given them a pool, and then you come along and turn off the one they are making. If you aren't careful you'll end up wearing your wrench." The patrolman is reluctant to turn off hydrants for many reasons, but one officer put it succinctly, as he was getting out of his car to stop a flood in a teeming street: "Well, here's how to become the instant bad guy."[3]

There are also occupational considerations that discourage the policeman from turning off hydrants: it is hard work. One or two a day does not matter, but if a man has to turn off fifteen or twenty in a steaming afternoon, in addition to his other work, his back muscles tighten and become stiff. The hydrant wrench each patrol car carries weighs about five pounds. The officer must make about ten turns with the wrench to get the nut tight enough so that only another wrench will open it. Some people buy wrenches or steal them from police cars, but a length of pipe also can be used to open a loosened nut.

Moreover, every time a patrolman closes a hydrant, he risks getting wet. The water spills over the curbing and splashes around; sometimes he must step into a flood to get close to the nut. The wrench is only a little over a foot in length, making it difficult to avoid getting at least his shoes and pant cuffs wet. But that is, as they say, part of the job, and what is the point of complaining? To whom? To the people who are being deprived of the opportunity to cool themselves? To the hospitals and the fire department?

Several days each summer the complaints from hospitals and factories become so intense that the divisional inspectors order the dispatcher to issue a general call to turn off all open hydrants without waiting for a complaint. When this order is received, the patrolman usually responds by turning off those hydrants he comes across. He will not go out of his way to turn one off, and he does not go looking for one. In some districts the sergeant will assign a "hydrant car" to the task, and one man will be obliged to spend the day doing nothing else. Since the patrolman spends most of his time on daywork cruising the main streets of his sector, it means that he is informally making a decision to ignore the hydrants on the private residential streets unless he receives a specific call.

There is no unanimity in any neighborhood about leaving hydrants flowing. Frequently they flood streets whose inlets have been clogged with soda bottles and refuse. The water

[3]An account of one hydrant riot is in Mike Royko, *Boss: Richard Daley of Chicago* (New York, Dutton, 1971), pp. 149–50.

spills into cellars, and if it is allowed to run, it eventually cuts away the road surface. It is common in some areas of the city for streets to collapse or to be undermined by the constant flow of water. These problems keep the patrolman well supplied with specific requests and opportunities to get wet.

When he receives an open-hydrant call, the patrolman responds because he expects to find the complainant waiting for him. He considers many of these complaints justified and honors them without hesitation. A gusher makes it difficult for cars to pass; a store owner is prevented from doing business because customers are required almost to swim to his front door. But there are calls he considers unjustified, and if there is nobody about to urge him on, he will leave the hydrant open.

A patrolman pulled into a nearly deserted street to find a few children splashing by a hydrant. Although the water was not bothering anyone, it was running down the street to join other streams, which were flooding a large intersection. He looked at the children and then put his car in reverse, backing out of the street. "What the fuck. If them niggers want to splash in that filth, that's their business," he said, as the children cheered wildly when they saw the car going.

If there has been no complaint, the patrolman can choose to turn the hydrant off in accordance with the law or ignore it in accordance with his own feelings. The only hydrants he consistently closes without a call are those which pose a traffic hazard, impede a merchant's business, or are flooding an intersection. Usually he does so because he is anticipating a call and sees his action as preventive work, which saves him from having to return to the place in a few minutes. Almost invariably this means that he will turn off only those hydrants located on important local streets and on corners.

When he sees a hydrant that he is contemplating closing, he usually approaches slowly while making his decision. The children at the hydrant are acutely aware of his approach but rarely acknowledge his presence until he actually stops the car or goes on past, causing them to break into delighted shouting. But if he stops, they will rush up, pleading vainly with him not to close it down. He has no way of softening their disappointment. If he refuses to leave it open, they plead for a chance to turn it off, while others rush into the stream to get a final moment's enjoyment from the water. If he allows the children to remain, they will splatter him with water, so he chases them back, which brings him no rewards. He is also reluctant to let them turn the wrench because he has heard too often of little children scooting down the street with a wrench in hand, chased by an embarrassed policeman. If he does let one help, he invariably warns him of what will happen if he tries to run off with the wrench.

The policeman's knowledge of his working place accumulates gradually. The more he knows about it, the stronger are his ties to the place and his desire to remain there. If he must move from one district to another, it will not take him as long the second time to learn what he has so painfully accumulated initially, but he will have to suffer the discomfort and insecurity that befall every policeman who must work an unfamiliar territory. Since so much of what a policeman is required to do is dependent on his knowledge of places for its proper doing, he has a real occupational interest in remaining where he is. This inclination and interest are exploited by every successful street supervisor to keep his men in line.

The patrolman, however, knows that the department wants him to be an effective and efficient worker. Any man who works on unfamiliar ground is a potential embarrassment to his bosses. A patrolman who individually restricts his activity to protest his situation is easily exposed to the wrath of his sergeant, but if the man is moved to an area he does not know, he can legitimately claim that his lack of knowledge is hampering his capacity to do the work. Therefore, the department has an interest in keeping the patrolman happy and also in keeping him where he is. The interests of both the supervisors and the patrolmen are clear, and either can threaten and undermine the other at any time. The basis for a fruitful compromise, beneficial to both, is provided by the nature of the work and the organization of its doing. These informal compromises, which are made in hundreds of ways daily, in every district, help the department carry on without disruptions, internal upheavals, and unpleasant revelations.

CHAPTER FIVE

People and Information

The patrolman's knowledge of the people he polices develops far more slowly than his knowledge of their places. He goes home after work, takes off his uniform (if he wears it to and from work), and lives a life apart from his clients. He understands that people do not like to be stopped by a policeman for a little chat. If a new policeman thinks otherwise, he is quickly informed. People ask him for directions, to make change, about a place to eat, but they rarely approach him with information about a bank robbery. An old lady, laden with bundles and stricken with shortness of breath, does not hesitate to ask him to stop a cab, other taxis having ignored her outstretched hand. The driver halts immediately, even affably promising the officer to help her with her packages when she arrives at her destination. The officer muses that perhaps she will return the favor sometime by giving aid to a policeman in distress, but he knows that he will probably never see her again. They do not know each other; he will not recognize her in a week.[1]

1 · Personal Knowledge and Street Work

The first persons the patrolman meets in his district are the station-house regulars. A police station is a public place, and people are continually coming and going, for information, attention, and shelter. In every district there are a few people, mostly alcoholics, who establish a tenuous legitimacy in the

[1] Erving Goffman, *Behavior in Public Places* (New York, Free Press, 1963), p. 124.

station by their regular appearance and their willingness to be useful. Their position is entirely dependent upon the attitude of the supervisors; they attach themselves only to squads that allow them access to the operations room, and they frequently stay away when their favorite group is not working. Occasionally one will be adopted by the station and protected by the captain. At one station a man was allowed to live in the basement in exchange for janitorial service. He was an admitted alcoholic, but the captain's clerk maintained a bank account for him, paying him a weekly allowance from his social-security check that did not allow his drinking to interfere with his working. The only protection these hangers-on have from occasional harassment and intimidation is the strength of their relationship with the operations crew and their own capacity to absorb humiliation without resistance.[2]

One man had been in a district for five years, outlasting several captains and numerous supervisors. Although some lieutenants had barred him from the operations room, he now had free access and was allowed to "supervise" the teletype machine. He carefully addressed all of the supervisors by their rank, although he first-named a few of the patrolmen who were kind to him. He, of course, was first-named by everyone. Like many of the "characters" who hang around police stations, he had accumulated pieces of the police uniform which he wore every day—a badge, shirt, hat, and a pair of inspector's eagles. One afternoon he walked into the station in a sullen rage because the night before he had been "locked up" by a lieutenant in another squad who had stripped him of his "uniform." "His" lieutenant got it all back for him.

New patrolmen see these people walking around the district; they are the first persons who are recognized and "known" by name, reputation, and habits. The young patrolmen occasionally stop to chat with them, even buying them lunch in the vain hope of making an exchange for some vice

[2]The lodging of people in station houses probably goes back to the time when the American police maintained dormitories and soup kitchens for drunks who could not find their way home or had none to find. Lane, pp. 190–5.

information. While supervisors occasionally give their characters a little money for any information they provide, the protection their authority guarantees ensures that any useful information will go to a sergeant and not to a patrolman.

The new patrolman is introduced to a number of persons in the district by the men he works with. He meets the waitresses and countermen who work in the places where they eat lunch and pick up their coffee. He also is introduced informally to the nurses and orderlies who staff the emergency wards of the hospitals which the men use as places for washing up. These are people he sees almost daily, who share with him some of the burdens of serving the public and working unusual hours. Some of them may become his intimates, all of them are almost colleagues. He also meets a number of the local businessmen when he is working on the wagons. Some of them are personally introduced but most are not. For many young policemen, these are their first contacts with people outside of their own ethnic groups. They meet Jews, Italians, Greeks, and Poles who are locally important persons, and with the aid of their colleagues something is learned of these persons' reputations. A new man is told circumspectly that one "is good to a cop" and another "likes to see a cop" while a third is "no good." At first the man is told no more. He is escorted to the fringes of the "wholesale world," but any further penetration is dependent on his colleagues' evaluation of him.

He also comes to know about the "cop buffs," the women who actively pursue social contacts with the district men. Unlike the nurses and waitresses whom the police contact initially in the course of their work, these women usually have no occupational connection with the patrolman. The new man hears their names mentioned by other policemen, and occasionally an older officer will point one out to him on the street and even introduce him. But usually he meets them casually; they approach his car to strike up a conversation or ask him to take them for a ride. At squad parties, which are held in the holiday season, the buffs are often the star attractions. On warm nights they can be seen wandering the streets of their neighborhoods at all hours. Whatever comfort they seek from knowing policemen is private and obscure. They are not prostitutes or "hustlers" looking to buy protection with sexual favors; they want to be friends. They are known to most district policemen by nicknames that celebrate reputed qualities or places where they circulate. "The Fang," "Whitelips," "Susquehanna Rose"—the mere mention raises grins on men's faces, even those men who have nothing to do with them. They have no real names, at least not for the men they chase. While an officer may have a private relationship with a woman who lives in his district, the buffs are treated as collective property. Colleagues openly exchange information about their reputed skills. The return of a buff who has been absent for some time is reported to every squad member with remarkable speed and economy; it is one of the few kinds of information policemen share with each other. Some patrolmen taunt their colleagues about being seen with buffs and they often seek to catch each other in compromising situations. Any effort to hide a relationship with a buff is a challenge no patrolman's colleagues will let pass.[3]

The patrolman's chance to know people well comes only with his assignment to a sector. He is provided with a geographical framework and a set of obligations which allow him to see regularly a number of persons who live and work on the sector. When he is signing store logs on daywork, he chats with the shop clerks and discovers what is going on inside these places. He begins to meet the attendants and owners of the gas stations and garages on his sector. Even if they do not have logs, the calls he gets to their places to settle local parking disputes assure that he will get to know these men. He discovers gradually that there are businesses in his sector whose owners do not care to see him, and even if he is

---

[3] The interest of the police in cultivating contacts with local women is not new. An anonymous observer of the London police commented shortly after they were organized: "Housebreakers employ themselves in courting the servant girls; by which means they frequently obtain admittance to the house. . . . I am in hopes that this practice will not be so available to them in the future, as I daily observe our police all over the town engaged in these amours which must render the fair damsels of the broom somewhat less eager for chance paramours. It is therefore much to the credit [of the police] that they have selected so many fine tempting young men for service." *Fraser's Magazine* (London, November 1832), pp. 463–4, cited in J. J. Tobias, *Crime and Industrial Society in the 19th Century* (New York, Schocken, 1967), p. 123.

obliged to go to them daily, his visits are brief and per-functory. Any bank in a sector must be visited every morning on daywork, but the patrolman rarely stops to chat with any of the employees.

He quickly meets the owners and bartenders of all the clubs and taprooms in his sector. Frequently, when a man is newly assigned to a sector, his sergeant will personally intro-duce him to some of these men.

A call came out of "fight in a taproom," and the regular sector man said to his rookie partner that he had been mean-ing to stop in as the place had a new owner. There was no sign of disturbance as the patrol car parked, but the officer looked inside through a window before entering. They did not wait for their sergeant. All was quiet. The black owner of the modest establishment came toward them and offered his hand first to the older black policeman and then to his white com-panion, who stood slightly behind. The man said that some-one had thrown a rock at a window, causing a break, and that was why he had called. The black policeman told him that nobody could gain entrance through the break but sug-gested that he board it up temporarily.

The bar was almost empty and the part in which they were standing was deserted. The owner asked if they were the regular men on the sector car, and when this was affirmed, he smiled and offered them a drink. The black officer, who did all of the talking, thanked him for the kind offer but said he never drank on duty. He added, however, that he would take a rain check, and the owner's face, which had fallen, bright-ened considerably. He urged both men to return. "I don't want anyone to think I'm prejudiced," he said, and they all laughed. When they left, the younger officer said that the man seemed pretty nice. His mentor nodded and then said, "Don't trust any of them. Offering you a drink in uniform. Don't even know you. He must think we're some kind of jerks. But I'll go back and sample his whiskey prices."

The patrolman has a license to go into any public place, but he is reluctant to go where he is not welcome unless he is on a call. But there are some businesses whose owners can-not afford to antagonize the police because their existence depends on them. In addition to bars, pawn shops, poolrooms, dance halls, and secondhand stores all require licenses, granted by the district police, to continue operating. Many of them deal in stolen property, occasionally without intending to, and its discovery on the premises could be very embarrassing. Whatever the personal feelings of these business people toward the police generally and the sector man in particular, they cannot afford to be frosty. But the patrolman is sensitive about giving the impression to anyone that he is looking for a favor or that he is looking around without a legitimate reason. And if someone does not like him, he does not go into his business place.

One evening a platoon was informed that the captain's men had received information of a holdup planned for a neighborhood grocery store. The men were urged to check the place frequently during the night. The patrolman in whose sector the store was located headed there directly after he left the station. He said that he wanted to find out whether the information had come from the owner or from a secret source. The veteran black patrolman commented that he rarely went into the place "since the Jews sold out" because the new owner, a young black man whom he admired for his dedication and success, "don't much like me."

The patrolman walked into the store and noted the look of surprise on the owner's face. He came over and the black policeman asked him for a pack of cigarettes. The officer said that he didn't have any tickets to sell, but the owner only grunted while he made change. The two men stood silently, and the patrolman said the store was looking pretty nice. He then asked if the owner was having any problems. His comments and questions brought no direct reply, merely grunts, and the icy exchange was interrupted by the appearance of another customer. The officer shrugged and, as he walked out, said to his partner, "Fuck him. We used to get along O.K., then one night his brother got drunked up and started acting up. He knocked down a cop, Bob Jones, you know him. I popped him with my jack, just a tap to put him out, you know, so he wouldn't get hurt. I even had him handcuffed before Bob got on his feet. Good thing, too, because Bob was gonna kill him. Since then he ain't been too friendly.

Fuck him. Anyway, he don't know nothing about the rumor, so it ain't on me."

The patrolman wanted to find out whether the storekeeper had gone around him to appeal to the captain. This would have reflected poorly on his relationships with the local business people and required him to give an explanation informally to his sergeant. But since the owner did not appear to know anything, he dismissed it as another rumor dredged up by the captain's men to show their boss that they were working. The policeman did not return to the store again that evening or at any other time during the night shift.

The patrolman also begins to recognize, and then to know, some of the people who frequent the streets he patrols. The size of sectors varies from place to place, but in the densely settled parts of the city they are rarely larger than five square blocks. Even if a man is not particularly alert and attentive, he cannot fail to see and recognize some of the people who regularly use the streets he patrols. Young children are the easiest to meet, and they often seek to establish relationships with him without waiting for an invitation. When a police car pulls up on a street, it is often the occasion for a race to reach the car first. Even if he does not encourage their attention, he usually allows them to crowd about the car, lean on it (which he does not allow other people to do unless he knows them quite well), listen to the radio, and ask him questions. He does not object when they call him "cop" or ask how many people he has killed.[4]

Unless silenced by older children, these youngsters are willing to speak freely with the police, and a patrolman who is inclined can learn a great deal about the people of a neighborhood by chatting with little kids. Most do not. If he has a school crossing, many faces become familiar to him, although he does not know the names of most of the children he sees

[4]Many black people use the word "cop" as a standard form of address to policemen, and this is recognized and accepted by many men. They respond without rancor when an adult calls after them, "Hey, Cop," or "Mr. Cop," although in white neighborhoods it is uncommon for any person to use the term "cop" when addressing or speaking to a policeman unless he is angry or is personally connected to the man with whom he is speaking.

and rarely says any more than a perfunctory hello. Those he does come to know frequently first-name him and look forward to the occasions when he makes an appearance in their neighborhood, providing them with an opportunity to show off their relationship to him.

One patrolman, who was not reluctant to express his contempt for the black people he was obliged to police, was moved by the plight of the poor children he saw each day while he stood at his school crossing. One wintry morning he arrived at work with a large package. His colleagues taunted him, claiming they had never seen a policeman come to work with a package, although they often saw them go home laden down. He rebuffed their queries and refused to be drawn into discussing what he was doing. When he got to his school crossing, he stopped some of the little children as they passed and distributed to them the clothing his own children had outgrown. He said nothing about what he had done, nor did he show any particular interest in talking with the children.[5]

People who use the street for their work cannot fail to know the patrolman on a sector, and he usually allows them to operate if they do not violate the established informal rules. Some of these people are "legitimate," such as cab drivers, truckers who work a regular route, and delivery men, who get little favors from him that ease their work. Others are "illegitimate," but he frequently treats them in the same way unless specifically ordered to do otherwise.

"There's my old whore," a veteran officer commented, pointing out a woman standing in the shadows of a building on a well-traveled main street. "I thought she was gone for

[5]Youngsters do provide incidental information and services to the police occasionally. A man will ask a little boy about a girl he has seen, or to go into a store and buy him a newspaper. A retired policeman recalled his own relationships with the police in New York City prior to World War I this way: "I became a buff for the ninth squad . . . twelve men who worked from four in the afternoon until midnight. . . . They were on fixed posts with no time off . . . A good buff was a godsend . . . My job was to be an errand boy, rush them their raincoats . . . bring them warmer clothes . . . sneak them sandwiches and coffee . . . and lay chickie [keep watch] for the sergeant while they consumed them." McAllister, p. 45.

good. She's been here for ten years now. A junkie. She's a wreck now but she still gets some action. Even from the white guys who drive through." He got out of the car and exchanged greetings with her. They first-named each other, and as he walked back to the car, she called after him, "Stay cool, baby."

"When she came here she was some good-lookin' spade. She worked the bars then, the plainclothesmen pinched her a lot and knocked her over plenty, too.[6] We had lots of whores then, she's about the last. If I catch her with junk I'd pinch her, but she wouldn't carry. I get information from her sometimes, but she don't know much any more. So long as she don't trick on the street or in the alleys, I don't care what she does. That's how I operate."

On the same street, a major city artery, several blocks were used at night by homosexuals, dressed in drag, selling themselves as female whores to passing motorists. The men working the area knew them by sight and name. "We don't bust 'em much. You can take 'em any time, but they are a good source of information. If guys want to come up here and fuck 'em—white guys, too, don't kid yourself—that's their business. If they get rolled, they don't deserve no better." The sector man and the wagon crew, as well as the lieutenant and sergeant, frequently stopped and chatted with them, calling them by their female names. "If we picked 'em up, they'd only be back here tomorrow. Only way to get rid of them is to lock 'em up or fuck 'em up. But they ain't so bad except when they get to fighting among themselves. They are treacherous with a knife when they get jealous," one patrolman commented. He and his colleagues viewed them as sources of entertainment and information. Since a uniformed man cannot make a prostitution arrest—he must testify in court that he has been solicited and no judge would believe that a prostitute had knowingly solicited a policeman—and

---

[6]"Unfortunate females are often cruelly oppressed and laid under contribution, for permission to infringe the very laws, which it is the duty of these nocturnal guardians of the Police to put in execution." Patrick Colquhoun, *A Treatise on the Police of the Metropolis,* 6th ed. (London, Mawman, 1806), p. 413. Some policemen have been collecting one form of rent or another from prostitutes for a very long time.

the city does not now condone the harassment of homo-sexuals, the patrolmen do not have any interest in keeping them off the street. If they misbehave or commit crimes on the street, the men are obliged to take action, but as long as their behavior on the street gives no cause for indignation they can be left alone and used when needed.

Since the police control the street, those who use it reg-ularly must accept their relationships with policemen as they develop. One morning a woman came into the station house with her four-year-old daughter. She was very upset but man-aged to explain to the sergeant that a man had made her little girl "do something" to him. The sergeant listened calmly to this claim since he had heard similar stories many times be-fore, but he became very angry when the girl described the man to him. From the description he knew whom she was re-ferring to and was willing to believe her story. He called for his lieutenant, and after conferring, they agreed that nothing should go out over the air. A wagon was detailed to spend the tour looking for the suspect, after dropping the mother and daughter at the hospital. The lieutenant and sergeant also told other squad members informally to be on the lookout for him. Several hours later the wagon crew found the man drinking in a bar that he frequented.

Any squad member who wished was allowed to beat the suspect from the ankles to the armpits with his stick. Men came in off the street to participate in the beating and then returned to patrol. Before he was taken downtown, the sus-pect had been severely battered, although he had no broken bones. At no time did he utter a complaint, ask for mercy, or curse the police. Without a murmur he absorbed a brutal beating, which caused him to foul himself and drew the ad-miring comments of several men who admitted he could "really take it."

Nothing more was heard of the matter for several weeks, until one afternoon the lieutenant saw the man coming out of a local barroom. He parked at the curb and just stared at him. After a momentary hesitation, the man approached the patrol car and greeted the lieutenant. Without replying direct-ly, the lieutenant asked him what he was doing on the street. He said that he had gotten a lawyer and an agreement had been made to release him on psychiatric probation. "I heard you got a lawyer. What's all that about?"

"Don't worry, Lieutenant, I ain't makin' no complaints to nobody. I ain't one of those peace freaks or niggers. I got just what I deserved. I want to thank you, Lieutenant, for helping me to straighten out." When asked where he was living, he said that he had moved back in with his wife. "When my girl friend died, I got fucked up, but I sold the house she left me and moved in with my wife." She was standing in the doorway of the bar and came forward when beckoned. He introduced her to the lieutenant and the patrolman in the car. He said he had reopened his exterminating business and offered to do any work that the lieutenant needed done free of charge. The lieutenant watched him walk back into the bar and said, "Ain't he something? You ever see anybody who had more reason to make a complaint about police brutality? Those cops were really mad. They all got little kids. And now he's out here again. We'll get him. He won't stop. Next time I hope it's not my squad who finds him."

Most of what a patrolman knows about the people he polices is learned with their active cooperation. Aside from businessmen, service personnel, and street workers, he has met most of the people he knows personally because they have called for his assistance. This is particularly true in poor neighborhoods where the police take people to the hospital, settle disputes, take reports on thefts and robberies, and are asked to answer questions about income tax welfare benefits— almost anything imaginable. If he gets no calls, he is much less likely to know the people who live in the houses he drives past daily. "It's a funny thing," a patrolman commented, while going on a meet complainant. "I've been on this sector for two years and this is the first call I've had on this block. Here and the next block, these people take care of their homes and themselves. You come through here and didn't know better, you'd think it was white people living here. No disturbances, no knifings, no garbage in the streets. I don't know anyone. But down on Harvard Street, I must know every one of them motherfuckers."

Working the same sector regularly, the patrolman develops a collection of impressions and facts about the people he deals with. These are what he uses in evaluating them. Frequently he sees people he must stop because he has previously arrested them for violations which he believes they will continue to commit. Often he just notes their passing, but they do not pass unnoticed. It is common for people to go by him without any hint of recognition, although both parties are keenly aware of each other's presence. "There goes our defendant," an officer mumbled, as a man who had been captured in a factory two days earlier walked past.

"She looks peaceful, don't she? Locked her up two years ago for shootin' her old man. Told me she killed another dude in North Carolina. She don't look rough but she is. She was O.K., though, didn't give me no trouble. A real lady," he said, as a woman crossed in front of a patrol car stopped at a traffic light.

"There's our junkie. Let's see where he's going. Shit, he seen us." The man had looked directly at the officer without a flicker of recognition. "He knows me all right. He won't ever forget me," the patrolman said.

These recognitions are not always covert. If he has arrested persons who were cooperative, an almost friendly relationship can develop. "Hey, beautiful, if you weren't a boy I'd give you a kiss," a patrolman yelled to a long-haired truck driver. The fellow looked down from the cab with a big grin, replying, "Jack, if you weren't a cop I'd sell you something." They were both laughing as the truck drove off. "A motorcycle thief. A real good burglar, but he don't work around here. I wonder if he had anything in there. Anyway, I know where to find him when I want him." Another time an officer stopped three boys in a car to ask about their mother's health. As they were about to leave, he asked the driver whether he had stolen any good cars recently. No reply, just a big grin. "They are a bad bunch. I went to school with their mother, but they are no good. They'd strip your car faster than you zip your fly up."

Most of the people he comes into contact with are not known to the patrolman. Unless someone has required his services several times or caused him any kind of difficulty, he is not likely to recall his face or the circumstances of their encounter.[7] He recognizes, for example, but does not know (either by name or by character) most of the youngsters he drives off the corners. He sees this as an impersonal action—he is clearing the corner, not moving the people. If he has to get out of his car and chase them or lock them up, he is sure to recall this experience when he encounters them again. Some patrolmen maintain lists of the juveniles who live in their areas that are used to invent ped stops when activity is needed. "You take out your list and just write a few 48's. If someone checks 'em, you're in the clear because it's a real name. Use a fake name and address and you could catch some shit."[8]

The patrolman's knowledge of people develops haphazardly. He is constantly recording bits of information about people he meets which he uses in making judgments about them if he encounters them again. He remembers places where he has had trouble or where trusted colleagues have met resistance. These recollections can affect his attitudes toward the people he meets even before his arrival at the scene. Pulling into a block on a meet-complainant call, an officer said to his partner, "Isn't this where you and Bob got jumped by those Irish gypsies?" When his guess was affirmed, he replied that "there won't be any bullshit from them tonight." While he knew little of the difficulties and nothing about the people who had been involved except their ethnic origin

[7]"On the average day we talk to and contact perhaps a hundred to a hundred and fifty people on that street. And of that 150 . . . how many are likely to have been persons that you recognize? Two-thirds . . . I know them by names and by actions. And I know exactly what to expect of them. What makes you know the name of a person? Oh perhaps writing it on an arrest report a half dozen times. The one thing I would be sure to remember is whether that man were likely to be involved in a crime of violence." This is a statement from a patrolman who worked for more than a decade on Skid Row in Denver, "A Quiet Strip: Officer Schalbrack's Story," p. 39.

[8]A study of police attitudes toward the ghettos in a number of cities found "that among the policemen interviewed, thirty-one per cent reported that they did not even know one important youth or teenage leader in their precincts well enough to speak with whenever they saw him." W. Eugene Groves and Peter H. Rossi, "Police Perception of a Hostile Ghetto," *American Behavioral Scientist,* Vol. XIII (1970), p. 741. This situation is not restricted to the ghetto.

(which he presumed from the neighborhood), the fact that some policemen had had a battle on the block made everybody who lived on it suspect.

Policemen constantly use derogatory slang in referring to people's ethnicity. The department takes a strong line against its use in public, but in private the restrictions cannot be enforced. A measure of the degree to which black policemen have become established in the department is the infrequency of the use of the term "nigger" by a white officer in the presence of a black policeman. At one time this was commonplace, and men recall incidents where white policemen would curse a black supervisor directly, or black prisoners in the presence of Negro supervisors, without rebuke or fear of rebuke. This can no longer happen. It is, however, common to hear black persons use this epithet against other blacks in the presence of the police and against black policemen when they are angry. Only rarely do black policemen use the term in the presence of white officers. Policemen of any ethnic strain are reluctant to use common slurs on their own coethnics in the presence of other policemen of different origins, although it is done when the person is regarded as morally inferior. The ethnic tensions that exist in all police departments, between the Irish and Italians for example, are controlled and regulated somewhat by an almost continuous banter among colleagues over their ethnicity, and the telling and exchange of ethnic and racial jokes.

People whom the patrolman knows and personally dislikes can acquire legitimacy in his eyes if they are identified within the established order of the place he polices. In a white working-class neighborhood there lived a man who wore his long hair tied back with a red ribbon. He was a factory worker who had a steady job and shared a house, which he owned, with several men in the neighborhood where he had been born. He also spent a good deal of time in a local bar with a group of male friends. He was an avowed homosexual, but he was well liked by his neighbors, who had known him most of his life. During the summer months when the neighborhood people spend a good deal of time on the streets, the patrolman would occasionally stop and chat with the fellow. They had friendly contacts, and the sector man said there had never been any trouble with him. "He's a faggot, no question, but the neighbors like him, he lives his own life, and he don't bother nobody. So why should I fuck with him?"

In a different sector in the same area a house had been rented by several young men who wore their hair very long and rode ornate motorcycles. Their neighbors constantly complained about the loud noise they made with their bikes and music. They adopted the local custom of sitting on the front stoop in warm weather, with music coming out of their open front door. Neighborhood children dropped in frequently, and there were complaints of drugs. The sector man said he had stopped them a few times, given out some tickets for driving motorcycles without wearing safety helmets, but had since given it up as he now knew who they were. "What for? If they got drugs, they ain't carrying them dressed like that. They know I don't stop 'em, but if they go off the sector like that or into the Thirty-fifth, every cop will stop 'em," he said.

One night there was a complaint of a "loud party"; the patrolman knew from the address what the problem was. He and his partner parked at the end of the narrow street and walked toward the people who were milling about while others sat in beach chairs. One patrolman tucked his stick under his arm and talked to an irate neighbor, who was threatening to kill "them," while the sector officer spoke with the boys. "We ain't doing anything they ain't doing. Just sittin' out and playin' music. You gonna lock us up?" The patrolman looked at him for a moment, glanced at the others sitting on the steps and inside the open doorway to the house, took a deep breath, and then said, "Get the bike off the street and onto the sidewalk. You can't block the street. Do me a favor and turn down the music. I'll get them to turn down theirs. Stay away from them. Try and hold down the noise with the bikes. You know what that guy's like. He ain't kiddin'! He will cap you one night, boy."

The knowledgeable patrolman adjusts his responses to people he knows to be troublesome or difficult. There are people who are chronic callers, people who see things in the dark. They are "decent" people, established in their neighborhoods, not drifters or persons who have no identity within his territory, so he allows them to make demands upon him. Two patrolmen took a call to "investigate a burglary." When they arrived, they saw a woman standing in front of the building. One officer whispered to his younger partner as they were approaching, "She's been to the farm. If she called it's bullshit, but don't insult her no matter what she says. Let me handle it." The woman told them that she was watching the building for the owners and had heard a noise. The patrolman told her they would check it out. Although the building was secure, they carefully and elaborately checked the windows and doors. The woman followed them around the building. "Just ignore her," the older man cautioned. "I don't want to make a trip to the clinic with her." When they were finished, they returned to their car and departed without speaking; she watched them drive away.

While many of his decisions about situations are based on his reading of the setting in which they occur, the policeman is also strongly influenced by his personal knowledge of the people involved. One afternoon an officer paused to aid a special patrol unit that had made a car stop; he also wanted to see what they were doing on his sector. He stood by without saying a word. The driver of the car admitted to the officers that he had borrowed it from a friend without taking the registration or his license. The sector man knew the driver personally but he did not intervene. "It's not my job," he mumbled. The car was not listed as stolen, but the interrogating officers decided to take the boy to the district station, where they could conduct a more thorough investigation. He appealed to the patrolman to accompany him to the friend's house, where he could get the registration. The officer shrugged and the boy was taken to the station. Since he was known to the sector man, he was allowed to ride in the patrol car rather than be handcuffed and taken in a wagon.

On the way to the district the patrolman said, "He didn't steal that car. I know his grandfather will kick the shit out of him when he gets home and the kid is scared to death of him. But these fuckin' cops are pinch crazy." Inside the station the boy was allowed to call his friend, who came to the station with the registration. The arresting officers, who had no personal knowledge of the boy, had acted in a professionally proper manner. The district man, however, would have settled the business right on the street and not given the boy a ticket for driving without his license.[9]

Often a patrolman will informally settle involvements with persons he does not know personally. This can occur even if he is contemptuous of them. It may happen because the patrolman does not feel arrest is warranted and the person has done nothing to anger him. Perhaps the officer feels that arrest is not as severe a punishment as the person will receive informally. Also, the policeman may feel that an arrest will cost him more time and effort than is justified by the circumstance. While his actions are frequently taken as evidence that the policeman is a "good guy," his decisions do not necessarily have any relationship to his assessment of the persons involved or his own personal character. On another occasion he might treat the same person in a similar situation quite differently.

One night two patrolmen answered a call of male in a house. In the basement of a darkened building they found a black teenager clutching a hatchet and cowering in the corner. They had searched the main part of the house first and, before descending into the basement, had noted a flickering candle go out. They entered the basement with guns drawn. Upstairs they had seen that the newly renovated house, which was still unoccupied, had been vandalized. The floors had

[9]A New York journalist recounts his experience with a policeman in his Lower East Side Manhattan neighborhood shortly after World War I. He was riding in a car which had been stolen by some other boys when they were spotted by the officer. "Nearing Grand Street, Joey, who could not have had much driving experience, slammed on the brakes to keep from hitting a horse drawn wagon. . . . The stop was so noisy that the cop on the beat came up. He looked in the car and at me, particularly. He knew me because my father used to give him sheets and pillow cases at Christmas and towels at Easter. He knew the other youths in the car also.

" 'Whose car is this?' he asked Joey.

" 'Mine.'

" 'Let's see the ownership,' the cop said. 'Baloney! You stole the car. Open the door and come outta there.'

"I was first out. . . . The cop, George, took his club and slapped me hard across the behind and shouted, 'Get the f— outta here, ya little bastard, before I tell your father.' " Arnold Beichman, "What Do You Do with a Fifteen-Year-Old Mugger?" *New York Magazine* (June 7, 1971).

been chopped up with a hatchet and some windows had been broken. The boy claimed he had run into the building when some other fellows had chased him. His hands and clothing were not dirty. The patrolman also recognized him as someone they had stopped earlier in the afternoon running from the scene of a gang fight. He had been polite and cooperative without any display of nervousness or anger. They had believed him when he said he was not a gang member, and they tended to believe him now when he claimed he had not used the hatchet on the floor, but they were going to book him anyway. The house was a wreck and they would let their sergeant decide what to do.

When they left the house, they were greeted by a mountainous woman with white hair and eyebrows. Her eyes blazed at the boy as she asked, "What my grandson do, officers?" When they explained the situation, the woman exploded and smacked the boy across the face with her fist. He reeled back against the car and cowered without saying a word. She asked the patrolmen to release him in her care, as she would like to punish him personally. "I think he'd be safer locked up, Grandma," one of the officers said. "He's yours." The patrolmen stood in the street along with some of the neighbors, watching the woman drive the boy down the street, smacking him with his belt buckle, which she had stripped from him. "I guess that call was unfounded," the patrolman said to his partner.

Two patrolmen took a meet complainant on a hot, steamy Saturday night. For them it was a relief from more than four hours of continual involvement in emergency calls for gang fighting, holdups, fast driving, the smell of burning brake linings, and the continuous whine of their siren, which makes almost every other sound inaudible. It was one of those days when every minute seemed to bring another ringing of the dispatcher's alarm bell and the announcement of some new horror. They had already seen a three-year-old girl with the back of her skull blown open by a rifle shell.

When the car arrived, a black woman rose from a stoop and approached. She held a baby in one arm and was swaying slightly from the effects of the liquor she had obviously been drinking. "Oh great," the driver muttered to his partner. They got out of the car and listened to her complaint. She said that her husband, "a fuckin' junkie," was not living with her but came around to steal her property. He had been by earlier and she was fearful that he was hiding upstairs. She wanted the police to search her house and, if he was there, to make him stay away from her. The officers followed her into the house and insisted that she precede them up the stairs and accompany them on their search. "We ain't takin' any complaints from this deuce that we stole her money," one man muttered. The husband was not there. When they went downstairs, they found him sitting on the front stairs. The patrolmen told him that his wife wanted him to stay away and he should honor her request or they would take him in. He was quiet and polite; he was stoned out of his mind.

A short while later the patrolmen took a return call to the address. There was no doubt in their mind what was going on. The woman was yelling hysterically when they arrived. Her husband had come back and hit her with a plate, she claimed, and then run off. "If we don't lock his ass up, we'll be back here all night long," one man commented. As they got back into their car, the driver spotted him standing at the corner, talking to another man. They got out of the car and approached him. He waited for them. "Look, my man, this is the way it is. Either you act like a good nigger or a bad nigger, and you get treated accordingly. If you don't stay away, you're locked up. Do you understand? Now, if you walk off right now and don't turn around, you can go. O.K.?" The man nodded and started walking as the patrolmen returned to their car. The woman said nothing. As they started to drive away, they noted the man standing in a doorway. "Oh, fuck this, he's going." They stopped and quickly approached him. He was frisked and cuffed without a word being said and placed in the rear of their car.

The man's wife came running up to the car. "He's got my money in his pocket. I want the money before he goes in." She reached into the car, grabbing at the man and swearing loudly. "Lady, if he's got your money, you can get it at the station. I don't know if he's your husband." "No, I don't want to wait. He won't have no fuckin' money on him when he gets to the station." "Lady, get the fuck away from this car before I whip your ass." The angry men drove less than a block when a call came out for males with a shotgun in a neighboring street. The man in the back muttered his displeasure and rolled onto the floor as the driver raced to investigate. As they entered the block, they spotted three boys walking abreast. The car pulled alongside and the driver asked the recorder, "Whaddya think?" "Let's take 'em." In a moment they were out of their car, guns drawn, and the three boys were stopped. Other cars arrived. A woman leaned out of a window and yelled, "That's them, they're the ones." They had no weapons on them but the sergeant arriving at the scene ordered they be taken off the street and investigated at the station house.

The patrolmen returned to their car, which had been left in the middle of the street, its doors wide open. Their prisoner was still on the floor. They hauled him back onto the seat and drove toward their station.

It was 9 P.M. This was the last day of their shift. If they arrested the man, one of them would have to appear in court the next morning, a duty that was not part of their holiday plans. Alternatively they could have "DK'd" him, locked him up informally as a drunk and have him released after four hours. But they still had to go into the station and process him. He had given them no trouble personally, had not done anything to them directly. "Whaddya think?" the driver asked his partner. "Fuck it, cut him loose." He nodded and headed the car for a deserted street that paralleled a railroad track, about six blocks from where they had picked him up.

When the officers turned to talk to the man, they found him cowering on the floor, his eyes filled with tears, a look of terror on his face. Had he been beaten by policemen? Rolled? "Look, my man," the driver said, ignoring what he saw in the man's face, "if we cut you loose, will you stay the fuck away from the house? If you don't and if we have to come back there, I will personally whip your motherfuckin' ass off. Now beat it." The recorder opened the door and hauled the man out, removing the handcuffs that still bound his wrists behind his back. The men drove to the end of the block and turned their car around. As they approached the man, he was still standing, dazed or confused. The driver said to his partner, "Give the poor prick a cigarette to get him going." They stopped and the man cringed, possibly thinking the police had changed their minds. When he saw the cigarette being handed to him, he said, "Thanks, man," took the light silently, and was left alone before he could say anything he might have on his mind.

There are many persons the patrolman recognizes and even knows well whom he does not believe and whose requests, no matter how politely made, will not be directly honored.[1] "Bums," "winos," "deadbeats" are common in many neighborhoods and are not restricted to skid-row areas of the city. If they are in their "normal" places, the sector patrolman does not bother them, although he fells unrestricted in his freedom to approach and question them. They rarely object when he does so, as years of experience have taught them that acquiescence is frequently the price of their freedom. They do not belong anywhere, and the patrolman treats them as if they were part of the public scene they inhabit; he checks them as he does a complaint about a broken traffic light. Even when he sees them at unusual hours, he will not take special notice so long as they are where he expects them to be. "The winos are sittin' out early—a sure sign of summer. Countin' their blessings and seein' who made it through the winter," a patrolman noted, as he cruised slowly down the otherwise deserted streets at sunrise.

The winos are treated informally, as a group of persons apart from the others who live and work in the neighborhood. They are not segregated, but they may be handled in different ways than other persons. Their actions are rarely a cause for concern. When they get very drunk or act up, the patrolman may lock them up. If they become incontinent in the wagon, they may be beaten and certainly compelled to clean up their own mess. ("Hey, Bo, you shit in my wagon this time, you are gonna eat it.") If they claim someone has robbed them, the patrolman rarely reports it. When they die or are killed, the officer does not care. They have no privacy; the patrolman feels free to enter their hotel rooms or apartments without knocking, something he rarely does anywhere

---

[1] On the influence moral judgments have on the treatment of clients in other trades and professions, see Julius A. Roth, "Some Contingencies of the Moral Evaluation and Control of Clientele: The Case of the Hospital Emergency Service," *American Journal of Sociology*, Vol. 77 (1972), pp. 839–56.

else. Some patrolmen treat them harshly, steal their money; others are considerate; but every patrolman sees them as persons set apart—outcasts who do not live like other human beings with established residences, private property, and purposeful lives. The patrolman, however, is their guardian, no matter how reluctantly he performs this service, because nobody else cares to pick them out of the gutters when they fall or seeks to find ways to keep them from being there at all.[2]

The experienced and knowledgeable officer believes everything and nothing about them. The only thing that interests him about them is disorder. Whether he locks them up or not makes no difference. Driving past a bar one night, a patrolman was hailed by a woman. He pulled up and was joined by the sergeant and a wagon. The woman turned immediately to the sergeant and said, "You gotta get Jack out of the bar. He's actin' up plenty, climbing the walls." The officers looked inside and saw the man sitting with his back to the wall, quietly huddled over a beer. The sergeant looked at her and said, "He looks pretty calm to me." She protested that he was terrible before they arrived. The bartender came out and said, "He's all right. No trouble at all." The sergeant turned and told him to be quiet and go back to his business. He said to the woman, "Old Jack must have a few bucks tonight. You want him so you can roll him." She stared at the sergeant and said with dignity, "He's the father of my child. I wouldn't do that." "You wouldn't? I know he's the father of your nitwit, and I know that you and your boy friend over there were gonna roll him. Now get the hell outta here before I lock you the fuck up." Without a word she walked away in the company of a man who had stood back throughout the exchange. The sergeant turned to the bartender, who had remained in

[2]See the revealing account of police behavior on Skid Row in Egon Bittner, "The Police on Skid Row: A Study of Peace Keeping," *American Sociological Review,* Vol. XXXII (1967), pp. 699ff. In a survey of 101 habituals on Seattle's Skid Row, it was reported that 23 percent claimed they had been rolled by the police on the street; 6 percent claimed they made a "voluntary payoff" in exchange for their freedom; more claimed they were rolled in jail by the turnkeys. While many of the informants said they had been beaten, insulted, and mortified, almost half said they had never been verbally insulted by a patrolman, and more than half claimed they had not been beaten or kicked. James P. Spradley, *You Owe Yourself a Drunk* (Boston, Little, Brown, 1970), pp. 140ff., 146–8, 281–91.

the doorway, "You get the hell back in there. I knew he was acting up, but when you come out here I knew he must have some dough or you wouldn't be fightin' to keep him in." The bartender laughed and said, "Come on, Sarge, business is tough." Jack still sat stiffly over his beer, awaiting his fate. The sergeant leaned in the door and said, "Take it easy, Jack," and the police left.

The patrolman is frequently hailed on the street and asked for aid by persons he does not know at all; then he must assess the validity of what he is asked to do, as he has nothing else to work with. Some of these requests are accepted without question. Any bus or trolley driver who wants to put someone off his vehicle need only clang his bell or blow his horn to get instant attention from a passing car. Rarely will the officer even ask him what the problem is. If the driver has a problem it is legitimate, and the officer will use his power to eject the offender. But the patrolman will not be so quick to act if the driver wants someone arrested. Usually it is only a case of removing a drunk from the bus, and the officer will not lock him up unless there is a disturbance on the street. Then it has become a personal matter for the patrolman to settle.

Public-service employees generally are accorded cordial treatment by the policeman out of regard for their position. A man from a utility company or a city employee is assumed to be telling the truth in any dispute that does not require the officer to do something he will have to justify on paper. If his mere presence will resolve the problem, he is willing to give aid. Cab drivers, too, are given similar treatment because they are seen as legitimate street users who share many of the same burdens as the police.

Claims are often accepted by the patrolman from people he knows, not because he likes or trusts them, but because their claims are put forward in the context from which these persons derive their legitimacy. A news vendor who claims that two boys were trying to steal his money is believed if he is at his newsstand, while similar claims with the same lack of proof in a bar or a movie theater will be treated with skepticism. The patrolman treats as legitimate any claim made by a businessman in his place of business. Any complaint of a disturbance in a hospital is treated as serious by the officer, who will even take risks to answer the call, because he believes, even without any evidence, that his colleagues are being attacked. But if a hospital employee he knew well approached him with some story about a fight in a bar, he would not react with the same unqualified trust and commitment. The person might be believed simply because the policeman knows him, but this alone would not guarantee him special treatment.

People the officer considers legitimate are granted consideration, but if they make requests that he considers out of bounds, he will not hestitate to refuse.

One morning a patrolman standing at a school crossing was approached by the principal, who told him that he was having a problem with the man who ran the candy store across the street. He had asked the man to stop selling after a certain time so that the children would get to class promptly. The man had refused to comply, and the children continued to straggle into school late. The patrolman had never met the principal before and did not know if he was the principal. But he went directly to the store, chased the children out, and told the man that if he continued to flout the principal's request, he would find his business closed down.

A few weeks later the same patrolman flatly refused to honor a request from the principal, whom he now knew personally. He and his partner took a call to the principal's office and were told that one of the kitchen helpers had gone "crazy" and he wanted her removed before the children had lunch. Since the lunch hour was near, he wanted her out immediately. The three of them went to the lunchroom and found the woman talking loudly to herself while she continued preparations for serving the meal. One patrolman asked her if she would like to go home and rest, but she politely refused, saying she would leave only when she had finished her work. The patrolman discussed the matter with her for a few minutes and then told the principal that they could remove her only with force and they were not prepared to do that. The principal became agitated, and one patrolman said he would call their sergeant while the other offered the principal his stick. The gesture was not appreciated. He walked out while the patrolmen continued to speak with the woman. A few minutes later the principal returned and told the woman that the head dietician was on the phone waiting to speak to her. When her supervisor ordered her to go home, she complied. She went to her locker after hanging up the phone, got her hat and coat, and walked out in the company of the officers.

A patrolman was stopped on the street by an elderly woman who said she was looking for her daughter. The woman said she had found a house where her daughter might be and wanted the officer to come with her to check it out. He explained it was not possible, since he could not just go into people's houses. The woman said her daughter had been missing for three days. He asked her how old her daughter was, and when she replied, forty-two, the patrolman said not very politely, "Lady, anybody over eighteen is not lost. If I broke into your house, you'd be callin' the NAACP and the Black Panthers, but now you want me to break into somebody else's place. Well, it's illegal. Now, please take your arm off my car so I can go back to work."

Anyone approaching a patrolman's car who is drunk, disheveled, or dirty is not likely to be granted a request. Children are rarely believed unless they are in the presence of an adult who will vouch for them. Two patrolmen were approached by a boy who claimed that his bike had been stolen by two other boys. He received a scowl and a suggestion that he keep traveling. The same officers, approached by an even younger boy in the company of his father, who reported he had been robbed, accepted the complaint without question and asked them to get into the car. They cruised the area, and when the boy pointed to two fellows sitting on a stoop, the officers quickly arrested them and took them into the station for investigation. If the boy had not been accompanied by his father, his claim would have been discounted, unless he bore physical marks which might give credence to his claims. While the patrolman may discount the claims of children (and of drunks) as a way of avoiding work without sanction, it is also true that they are simply less "believable."

A patrolman was flagged down by a young girl who claimed that a neighbor had beaten her and called her a "trollop." The young patrolman, trying to look serious, asked her what that meant. She said she did not know but was sure it was not nice. He replied that he thought she was pretty nice but his pass only made her angrier, and she demanded he do something. He was about to leave when the girl's mother approached and substantiated her claim. He parked his car and accompanied them to the home of the accused.

These judgments cut across racial and class lines. In every part of the city, patrolmen are making judgments daily, based on their notions of local legitimacy. These are unavoidable because each man must make quick decisions without help from his sergeant. Often the requests require immediate action to prevent the escape of persons accused of serious crimes. Any officer may begin his career by accepting as truth whatever he is told, but his experiences quickly encourage caution. Even after he has developed cues and techniques for assessing the validity of claims made upon him, he will be conned into exertions and dangers. Each time this happens, his suspicion of things he is told deepens and the circle of people he is likely to believe shrinks.

Two officers were looking for a runaway girl in a neighborhood pool hall. As they came out, a well-dressed man hurriedly approached and said that his nephew had just threatened to kill him with a sawed-off shotgun. One patrolman gave the dispatcher a description of the boy and, with the man in the back of their car, they commenced a search. The man yelled, "There he goes," the car came to a sudden halt, and the patrolmen began chasing the fleeing youth. He was cornered in a dark alley and ordered to put up his hands. When the trio returned to the car, the boy's mother arrived. She falsely accused the patrolmen of beating her son, causing murmurs in the crowd of people that was gathering. The officers were getting nervous and told her of the charges made by the boy's uncle. They told her and the uncle, who had already started arguing, to come to the station. When they arrived, the mother and uncle were continuing their now bitter fight. One patrolman took the boy aside and asked him if the man was really his uncle. The youngster began to cry, admitted threatening the man, who was not a relative, but vehemently denied he had a gun. The patrolman asked the man if he had actually seen a shotgun and was told that it was pretty dark and he might have been mistaken.

The patrolman, resisting the impulse to beat the man, returned to the boy, promising to release him if he would keep away from his "uncle." He turned back to the man and muttered a threat after him as he walked out of the station. "I believed that bastard. When I saw the kid in the alley, he had his hands in his coat. I would have shot him if he hadn't come up with his hands. That would have been wonderful. Oh, I hate these fuckin' people."

If these events are not frequent occurrences, it is due partly to the patrolman's reluctance to believe what he is told. What many may regard as cynicism, callous disregard, or indifference are also qualities that can be traced to an occupational need to disregard claims. Since the patrolman must spend so much of his time dealing with people he does not personally know, and even known persons who lie to him, he must rely on his knowledge of places and personal character to assess what he is being told. It is one thing to listen to complaints, but when a policeman is being complained to, it is because someone wants him to *do* something. That is quite another matter.

2 · Private Information

"See that guy? If I knew what he does about the people here I'd be the best cop in the district. I been here twelve years and I don't know what he knows. And I know more than most. Goin' in their houses every day, seein' what kinda mail they get, checks and stuff," a patrolman mused, watching a mailman making his deliveries.

The only formal incentive to collect information is the advancement in his platoon that "vice activity" assures the patrolman. Anything else he learns about the nature of his territory and the habits of its people is a private matter reflecting his personal involvement in his work. There is no pressure on him to know anything. He is not asked to share what he knows with anyone else, nor does he confer formally with the men from other squads who also police his sector. Each of them acquires information independently. When a man finishes his tour of duty each day, nobody asks him if he learned anything of value to the department or to the squad that follows his onto the street. He may share something he has learned with another patrolman or a detective in exchange for a favor. The police, like many of the people from whom they get information, use it as an exchange commodity to pay debts among themselves and encourage preferential treatment. But this is not a systematic activity, and if a patrolman's sergeant finds out that he is giving information to men outside their platoon, the man risks punishment and retaliation. The only information the patrolman is required to share with the department is what is known by the people he arrests who are turned over to the detectives for interrogation prior to booking. But this is a by-product of his work; the information he obtains directly is his own.

The children on the streets are the most fertile source of information about the geography and the street behavior in a sector, but the patrolman makes little effort to exploit them. When he has a specific problem—looking for some youths drinking beer, pursuing someone down an alley, trying to find out about a person seen committing a burglary—he does not hesitate to question the children standing about. They are willing to talk to him and display very little solidarity with their peers. Frequently they offer him information which he ignores because he does not care about the problem. Many local fires are caused by juvenile arsonists, and it is common to see little children being shooed away by the patrolman whom they are trying to inform. He does not want to know about the fire, he is just watching the crowd. It is not his problem. But if he arrests a juvenile for some crime, he will listen carefully to any offered information on other criminal activity. He is willing to credit their veracity in situations where he is extorting information from them, but not otherwise.

Children are also willing to tell him things about their neighborhoods which he would otherwise not know, but often they have to force this information on him. He does not stop to ask the children to help him out but accepts the information in the context of a working situation where he sees it as having specific connections to the job at hand. If it has a longer-term value, that is incidental.

Two patrolmen were investigating a call of males in a building and could not find a way into the place. As they were checking, a boy approached and showed them a concealed door leading to the basement which he said "they all use." He offered to show them what went on inside, leading them through a building that had been converted into a clubhouse, a shooting gallery for addicts, and a love nest. The officers did not ask him who used the place or whether there were any other places in the neighborhood being similarly used. They had been past the place hundreds of times without knowing how extensively it had been exploited by neighborhood youths. Without their voluntary informant, the patrolmen would have remained in the dark.

Several officers were searching a railroad trestle on a males-with-rifles call in an unsuccessful effort to locate the boys, who they thought were trapped. There were police at both ends, and the officers could not figure out how the boys had eluded capture. Several teenagers—about fifteen years old—were watching the police conduct their fruitless search and, when the officers were about to leave, approached. "They didn't have no guns," one said. "They were just up there huffin'. They always huff up in the yard." In response to several questions, the children willingly conducted the patrolmen on a tour of the freight yard, showing them where the boys hid merchandise stolen from the boxcars, when and where they hid while glue-sniffing, and, finally, how they got on and off the trestle. "Nuthin' to it," one boy exclaimed, eager to display his expertise. He shimmied up the twenty-foot iron support column, using the bolts as foot rests. After he had shown them how easy it was to slide up through the railroad ties to the top, he quickly climbed down the other side. The patrolmen just shook their heads as the boy said, "Everybody around here can do it. Even she can," nodding to the girl standing nearby. The policemen did not share this information with anyone, but incorporated it into their personal conception of the area and used it to make a number of arrests during the summer.

The patrolman's disinclination to exploit children for information is all the more curious when it is understood how limited are his other voluntary sources. In high-crime areas adults are willing to call the police in moments of extreme danger or if their anonymity can be assured, but they are very reluctant to do anything that will disclose them as informers. Some patrolmen are angered by this attitude, but most sector men accept the fact that people fear reprisal. The patrolman knows he cannot protect anyone all of the time, and their fear is seen as a legitimate reason for keeping quiet.

Two patrolmen went to the house of a woman whose windows had been broken by a gang of teenagers, but she refused to identify them. She wanted the police to corie, which would put an end to the attack, but she did not want to be marked as a person receiving special treatment. Anyone might have called them. When one officer offered to accompany her to the local grocery store after she mentioned that she had no food in the house, she looked dumfounded and quickly refused. The patrolman was angry, until his partner explained that if she were seen on the street with the police, people would identify her as someone who sought the protection of the police. He said this could provoke attacks on her, unless the officer wanted to move in and protect her around the clock.

Frequently people who willingly call the police simply deny their participation if they are required to reveal themselves as the source of information. Two patrolmen were investigating a disturbance. A man standing on the street said he had seen three men go inside a taproom after pushing some construction equipment into an excavation. The patrolmen walked to the bar and looked inside. There was only one threesome, and they were ordered outside and taken to where the man was standing. They were followed by several men from the bar. As the group approached, the man said, "What are you comin' to me for? I didn't see nuthin'." The patrolmen smiled, shook their heads, and allowed the three men to go.

In moments of agitation, people often give the patrolman information which they would normally withhold and conceal. The experienced sector man is used to being informed in this way, and he allows people to yell and shout at each other in his presence. His first inclination is to put a stop to any possible violence, but he learns to be in no great hurry to quiet them when he is in a position to listen. These situations occur frequently in disturbance-house calls, when people are agitated and begin accusing each other of being number writers, speakeasy operators, or junkies. "He's just a fuckin' junkie. I'm so tired of his stealin' all my stuff. Get him outta here. I've been . . ." The woman was cut off in mid-sentence. "Is he carrying?" the patrolman asked. "No. He shot up before you came. I came back and found my radio gone and he was shootin' up. Get him outta here, please." The patrolman turned to his partner and said, "There's no point in taking him now. He's noddin' out. Take a good look at him and we'll stop him on the street when we see him."

The patrolman is approached on the street by people who offer him information that they hope will increase their own security and well-being. People come to him with tales of abandoned houses being used, juveniles breaking into stores, or burglaries they have seen committed. His interest in any of this is very limited, unless it is specific information about a person or a place that is being used at certain times. General information has little value to him since he cannot do anything with it. The department is not interested, and it does not help him to make an arrest. He cannot sit and watch a place, and unless he knows when people are going to be there, the information is useless. So he passes it off.

Businessmen, storekeepers, cabdriver, and hospital personnel are good sources of casual information for the patrolman. They occasionally are interested in telling him things about what is going on. Frequently this information is exchanged for personal attention. In a poor black area of the city, where cabs were scarce, an informal and illegal taxi service was organized. There were regular stops, unmarked but well known to local people. The police allowed it to operate because the drivers gave them "tips." These sources are irregular, as people must be careful about whom they tell and how they convey the information. For example, one drugstore had been held up so many times the police decided to put men inside the store to wait for the robbers to strike again. In six months' time the place was robbed four more times, each time a few hours after the police had left their stakeout. Presumably one of the employees or a policeman was informing the bandits, who timed their holdup so as to evade the trap.[3]

The alert and skillful patrolman supplements his knowledge without aid from others by exploiting the opportunities his work provides. In areas where speakeasies are common, for instance, he casually scrutinizes liquor bottles for tax stamps. This is something he learns to do, and those who do not are dismissed as not "vice-wise." Two rookies answered a disturbance-house call that was quickly settled. The people of the house had not called and were anxious for them to leave. The patrolmen had been admitted because there was too much noise for the occupants to deny that something was amiss. It was Sunday morning and they could not claim they were just having a party. Ten or fifteen bottles were on a table, but the patrolmen did not take much notice of them. As they left, one officer noticed that a person who had been inside and had asked to leave had just gone back into the house. One patrolman said to the other, "Did you see all those bottles?" The other nodded, the light of recognition in his eyes. He said they had just blown a speak. They knocked on the door again, but it was not reopened. They had three alternatives: to call their sergeant, to break down the door illegally, or to leave without mentioning their error. They left.

There was a call of "shooting and a hospital case" at a bar; the lieutenant drove quickly to get there. When he arrived, he was pleased to see several cars already at the scene. The call was unfounded, and he stood on the sidewalk looking at

---

[3]On businessmen and the police in relation to criminal information, see Albert M. Reiss, Jr., *Studies in Crime and Law Enforcement in Major Metropolitan Areas,* Vol. I (Research Study of the President's Commission on Law Enforcement and Criminal Justice, Washington, D. C., 1967), Sec. 2, pp. 10ff. Much of this information is channeled directly to detectives and other units bypassing the district men and even the captain.

the people. When the sergeant arrived, he called him over and said, "Do you see all the juveniles in there? I want you to hit this place later."

Two patrolmen took a call to "investigate an open property." They arrived at a well-maintained house, the front door of which stood open. A man approached and said that he had called. He lived across the street and knew the owner was not at home during the day. He noticed the open door, rang the bell, and then called the police when he received no answer. The three men entered. It was empty, the thieves having left in a hurry from the appearance of the living room. There were several appliances, a record player, and three television sets sitting in the middle of the floor, waiting to be moved. "Either he scared 'em off or they found somethin' else they wanted more," the older officer said, while he was checking the bathroom window through which the burglars had come. "I've never been here in all the years in the district," he said, as he began to look around. "Talk to that old man and see what you can find out." A few moments later the officer called down from the second floor, "Hey, Ruby, come up here a minute."

The upstairs had been ransacked: drawers pulled out, books thrown on the floor, and cabinets overturned. "Lookin' for cash. That's all them junkies want." He pointed to the bed and peeled back the mattress to reveal two fully loaded pistols. "They found money and stopped lookin'. These are worth thirty or forty apiece. They'd a taken 'em for sure if they'd seen 'em." The .25 and .32 automatics were in holsters, and the patrolman commented, "Maybe he owns three. Anyway, he sleeps prepared." He rolled the mattress back in place, leaving the guns where they were. He did not take their serial numbers, unless he had done that before calling his partner.

After questioning the friendly neighbor about the owner, the patrolmen continued to look around the house, and then locked it. They asked the neighbor to tell the owner to call when he came home, since only he could inform them of what had been taken. "I wonder what that dude looks like," the older officer mused. "I'm gonna make a point of meetin' him. Three TV's in his house." He did not intend to tell anyone what he had found. He had violated department regulations by investigating the house without calling his sergeant, but with fifteen years in the business, he was beyond these technicalities. Anyway, if he had called, he might not have learned so much.

Later in the day the owner came into the district to report the burglary. The patrolmen were called in to take the information. He thanked them for coming to his house and said that $125 in cash and some jewelry had been stolen. When he was leaving, one officer said, with his friendly smile, "I'll be seein' you around." Later he commented, "It could have been a lot more. Around here you don't want people to know how much money you got in your house. You might get broken into again real soon. Next time I see him on the street, I think I'm gonna make me an illegal car stop." He chuckled.

The experienced patrolman does not expect to learn the things he is interested in voluntarily. He gradually learns about other methods of obtaining information from watching colleagues, and he must decide whether he will use them. Most illegal activity in any area is carried on discreetly. The illicit activities an inexperienced or new man learns about are usually operated under some kind of informal (and illegal) police protection and are therefore of no value to him. Most of the people who have information are not interested in giving it to the police, and when they are, they are usually in a position to give it to someone with more influence than a patrolman. Even on his own sector, there are people with good information whom he cannot really exploit. Bartenders, pool-hall owners, and anyone whose business is linked to the police licensing power gives his information to a sergeant or lieutenant, unless the sector man is known to be closely linked to his supervisors. This restricts the opportunities available to the patrolman who wants to make vice activity and advance his career.

His steadiest source of information is what he collects as rent for allowing people to operate without arresting them. "Prostitutes and faggots are good. If you treat 'em right, they will give you what you want. They don't want to get locked up, and you can trade that off for information. If you rap 'em around," a very skilled patrolman said, "the way some guys used to, or lock 'em up, you don't get nothing." At a lunch counter another officer said, looking at the waitress who was getting his order, "She thinks I don't know she's hustlin' the truck drivers. She'll find out tomorrow. I don't care if she makes a few bucks on her back, but she is gonna tell me what I want to know." People who are arrested often try to get better treatment in exchange for information. Inexperienced patrolmen are willing to "cut someone some slack," but they often do not know how to go about it and frequently are unwittingly introduced to the ins and outs by people who are a lot more cop-wise than they are.

Two officers answered a call of "male breaking into an auto." The dispatcher gave a good description of the suspect, and when they arrived, the recorder spotted him immediately, partly concealed by a car. When they stopped, the man came forward with his arms spread out, to show he was not armed. "Did you want to talk to me?" he said. The patrolman had not seen him do anything, and they had no reason to hold him. He said that he had not broken into any cars, but a woman leaned out of a window and said, "That's him, the junkie motherfucker." He had not been accused by anyone whose property had been disturbed and therefore could not be charged with any offense. The patrolman asked him what he was doing, and he said he was a pool hustler. When he told them where he lived, he was asked, "What are you doin' here, my man, so far from your place?" It was several blocks away.

"I was goin' to my girl friend's to pick up some money, but she wasn't home."

"How many bags a day you usin'?"

"Honest, I ain't shootin' no more."

"Let's see your arms. Take off your coat."

"Sure I got tracks, but I ain't usin' no more. Don't lock me up. I don't want to go in. I got no money, nobody to take care of me. I'll get all fucked up inside." His hands shook and there were tears in his eyes. The patrolmen had no reason to hold the man, and they were on the verge of releasing him when he said, "If you treat me good, I'll give you good information on some pushers."

They put him in the car and took him to the district. They knew little about narcotics and needed someone who could corroborate what he told them. They got the corporal to call another man in off the street.

The three patrolmen and the informant stood in a tight circle, while other policemen came and went. Nobody stopped to chat or lingered in their vicinity. Even the lieutenant, who had come into the station, walked past without acknowledging their existence. The informant, displaying his experience, asked, "What area ya interested in? I don't want to give you nuthin' you don't care about."

"Just give us everything below Beacon Avenue," one officer commanded.

"Hey, man, I don't know any of their names or nothin'. Just where they push the stuff." He mentioned several places, bars and hotels, where heroin was sold. The third officer said, "Come on, pal, get it up. Everybody knows those places." They stared at each other for a moment, and then the informant mentioned a place where heroin was being bagged and an apartment where a man driving a Cadillac "with a phone in it is droppin' twenty bundles [fifty bags to a bundle] twice a week. Look, I don't know no more. I give you good information. They'd kill me, man. That's all I know. What's gonna happen to me?" The patrolmen exchanged glances, and after the third man nodded, the older of the arresting officers said, "I pronounce you guilty and sentence you to six months' probation. Go on, beat it." He said nothing, turned on his heels, and walked quickly from the station.

The information was obtained on the last tour of daywork. When the squad returned to work, it would be last out, a bad time for narcotics raids, since most heroin is sold by early evening. This meant that the patrolmen could not use their information for at least ten days, when they would be going on the four-to-twelve shift. Although they knew that narcotics information is notoriously short-lived, because operators keep shifting around to evade capture, the men had no intention of sharing what they had learned, just as they had no interest in obtaining information about places outside their district. The arresting patrolmen told the third officer that they didn't want anything to be done with the information until they went on the nightwork shift. "I don't want the sergeant to know about this until we're ready to get warrants. He's got to know then, but not before," one man said, and the third patrolman replied, "Oh, come on, he wouldn't fuck with narcotics." "Oh yeah? I don't want him to know nuthin'." They agreed.

The men had another problem that had to be resolved before they could use their information. After agreeing not to do anything for the next ten days, they had to decide how to bring the patrolmen who worked the sectors which they were going to raid into their operation. "The way they're pushin' for vice, they wouldn't care if we made one in another district," one quipped, "but we still can't go tearing up another guy's sector."

The patrolmen said nothing until they were ready to apply for their warrants. "I think he's O.K., but there's no point in telling a guy too much or too soon. This guy don't understand that I was on that sector before he come to the district. He don't own it yet," the man said. But when he made application for the warrants, he had to tell the sector man. While cruising one night, he saw the man drive by and hailed him over. The patrolman mentioned that he was going to hit a place with a warrant and wanted him to come along. He did not mention the address. The man asked where it was and, after he was told, said that he would like to know if there were more. "The reason I'm askin' is I don't want to duplicate the work. There's a couple of places I'm lookin' into and I don't want them ruined on me," he said. The first officer replied, "I seen you in the project yesterday. Don't worry, the things I'm lookin' at ain't in there." He had lied and had no idea if the other man knew or would find out. The previous day he had been ordered by the lieutenant not to request a warrant on an apartment in the project because one had just been approved. A few hours prior to their conversation, the sector man and the lieutenant, along with a wagon crew, had made a successful raid and the patrolman who had once "owned" the sector wanted to conceal his disappointment. But he let the man know when he got his warrants and shared the credit with him for the arrests that were made.

The district patrolman is not loath occasionally to pay money for vice information if he finds it necessary. One Sunday morning a sergeant watched an elderly black man stumble in the street. He halted his car and watched the man regain his feet, then called him to the car. "Hey, pop, where did you make your load?" The man grinned and offered to give the sergeant a speak if he would put up the money for a bottle. The sergeant smiled affably and called for his favorite wagon crew. When they arrived, he drove the man to the location mentioned. He gave him enough money to buy two bottles, one for evidence and one for drinking, and told him to come out soon after he had made the purchase. The old man asked the sergeant not to let on that he knew him. "If that bitch knows I ratted, she'll get me killed. No shit, you gotta treat me rough. I'll put up a stink, too." The sergeant laughed and agreed. He watched the man go around the corner and knock on a door.

The police waited, sitting in a side street but not concealed. The wagon was parked so that the driver could observe anyone coming from the house. When the man stumbled out about a half hour later, the wagon crew grabbed him. The sergeant took him, and the two officers knocked on the door and went directly in without waiting. A few minutes later they came out with a woman. She looked at the old man, who was jumping up and down, shouting at the sergeant and calling him names. The wagon men handcuffed the woman and put her into the wagon. Then they smacked the old man across the face and handcuffed him. The woman was arrested for illegal sales. In the station the sergeant put a false name down on the arrest book for the informer. "When they call him for court, they won't find him. It will be dismissed, but we got our vice pinch. Anyway, they would kill him if he testified." The old man was quickly released and allowed to take one bottle with him. He thanked the sergeant and the wagon crew for holding up their end of the bargain and offered to come by any time they had the price of a bottle and give them another speak.

The interest of the police in vice crime, particularly gambling and drinking, as well as prostitution, must be satisfied by information supplied to them by their own under-cover agents or by informers. Even in neighborhoods where some people oppose drinking and gambling, they are loath to inform the police because they fear reprisal and banishment by their neighbors. The police know this better than anyone else and they pursue their information covertly. Most uni-formed men who make vice arrests achieve their successes by luck, when they stumble on something in the course of looking into an unrelated matter, or by getting occasional information from someone who has access to the action. Some men who have been in a district for a few years come to recognize and know people who are involved in the rackets. They have seen colleagues bring in persons charged with writing numbers; they know which bars and clubs are associated with gambling activities. Whenever they see one of these people around during daywork, they make an effort to follow him. "Well, well, there goes my old friend," a patrolman chirped, as he spotted an ancient car, driven by an elderly man, pulling out ahead. "Take down his plate number and we'll check it out later. I think we will just take a little ride and see where he goes this morning."

Men who have any experience with vice work are alert to the appearance of any new people on the streets during the morning hours. "I just don't know that old guy. The one going into the restaurant. I don't know where he lives yet, but the way he keeps floating around, he's gotta be a writer. He turned up a couple of weeks ago and I only see him on daywork. I don't know anybody who knows him yet, but I'll get him," the patrolman said.

The vice-wise policeman is constantly on the alert for any behavior that may indicate gambling. Nothing is too innocent to be overlooked and checked out. "Oh ho, what do we have here? Don't turn around when I pull up at the corner. Did you see those two guys talkin' on your side when we went by? Did you see how they moved together when they spotted the car? You stay here while I go into the store. Watch where they go and we'll check 'em out." When the sergeant re-turned with his newspaper, he was told which building the men entered and noted the address as they drove past. The police car did not slow down, nor did the men look at the buildings as they drove past, but they calculated the address by counting the number of houses to the corner. When they were off the block, the sergeant asked the dispatcher to send a wagon crew to meet with him. He gave these reliable men the address of the suspected house and told them to make inquiries about who lived in it.

Not all informers are paid, although many of them are. Sometimes the police will use their station-house characters, paying them by the pinch for the information they provide. In some districts there are people who give the police information because they genuinely support what they believe the police are doing. "You know, Jack's father lives in the district and he gives us good information. That's why he ain't going on this raid. The old man lives around the corner and it could be embarrassing if his son took the door." Occasionally, local pensioners who sit around their neighborhoods all day give the police information. Some of these people may be number writers who are trying to protect themselves by clearing their areas of junkies and others who threaten their own businesses. There are also paid informers, "rats," who are treated on a stringently commercial basis. They are not protected and they get paid for what they produce.[4]

An officer was cruising an area looking for a man. "There he is, my chief rat." The man was called to the police car, but the officer did not get out. The man said hello and then asked for his money. "You'll get paid when I get the right information. You gave me the wrong address. I can't hit her where she works. It's a fuckin' church. Get me her home address and I'll see you later in the day."

If the policeman is seriously interested in maintaining his informant, he is stringently careful about when he meets

[4]In common law an informer was eligible for protection and payments, which were scaled according to the crimes on which he gave his information. The legal status of the informer was not revoked in England until 1951. On the role of informers in the history of the law, see Hibbert, pp. 91ff.; and Radzinowicz, Vol. II, pp. 138–67. A very useful account of an informer system used by narcotics detectives in an American police force is in Jerome H. Skolnick, *Justice Without Trial* (New York, Wiley, 1967), pp. 112–38.

him and where he acknowledges recognition. One night after work several officers were having a few drinks in a district bar that they frequented. A man known to them walked in but passed by without any recognition. He stopped at the other end of the bar, where he met several people. The policemen did not comment on his arrival. After a few hours the bar had mostly emptied and the bartender was introducing the remaining customers to each other, indicating to all that the three men at the far end were police officers. They all shook hands with the man who had been at the other end. "Nice to meet you, Lieutenant," he said. He was the lieutenant's rat and nothing was done to threaten his role.

Some patrolmen never develop any interest or skill in vice work. It is almost impossible for a white officer, for example, working in a black area, to develop sources of information that are not rooted in some form of compulsion. Many men do not have the stomach for this kind of work, and even when they stumble across a speakeasy, they will let it pass if it is small and informal. Others who do develop skills feel obliged to limit their activities because they know that their connections to the local people can be damaged if they press their vice work vigorously. Ethnic connections frequently create links for an astute policeman to exploit, but he must be cautious. In some residential areas a patrolman who has worked the same place for a long time may decline to make any vice arrests. "Look at Norton," a sergeant said. "He's the best vice man in the platoon, in the squad, but he won't lock anybody up on his sector. He told me when I took over that it was embarrassing for him and that people would stop talking to him. So we made a deal. He gets me the information and the wagon makes the pinch. But he offered to make a grab on another sector for someone else."

Although it cannot be known exactly, it is reasonable to ask how much information is denied the patrolman about criminal matters in areas where vice activity is widespread because of people's reluctance to call policemen into their homes. No matter what he is called for, the patrolman is always keeping an eye out for an illegal bottle or a number slip, or listening for some loose talk about a game or a party.

Since vice is usually found in the same places where street crime is most common and the demand for police services greatest, it is interesting to speculate whether the patrolman does not lose more than he is able to squeeze out.

The patrolman's sector is not exclusively his, but what he learns on it is his own. His colleagues—the wagon men and other patrolmen—cannot come into his sector for any reason without informing him, unless they want to risk his wrath. But others may penetrate his territory regularly without prior consultation. His sergeant and lieutenant do not have to tell him what they are doing, and an astute sector man often spends some of his time trying to find out what his superiors are doing in his sector. Plainclothesmen, headquarters units, and detectives may operate without his knowledge. There are also two wagon crews and two other patrolmen who work his territory each day besides himself, and he knows little of their activity. They may tell him some things, and he can learn more from people who live and work in the sector, but these men have no obligation to tell him anything. Less frequently, but with great discretion, his sector is visited by agents from the district attorney's office, state police agents, military policemen seeking deserters, F.B.I. agents, federal treasury, narcotics, and alcohol agents; insurance investigators and private detectives, too, operate without his knowledge. He has no control over any of these men, but he is usually not concerned about what they are doing unless he is involved in some kind of illicit or illegal actions. But his own colleagues do interest him and he does have a measure of control over them. He fortifies his control by denying them the information he accumulates and sharing it with them only when he feels it is to his benefit.

Much of what he knows is not of any particular interest to them, since they do not work his area, but the other men who do work the same area do not get much information from him. His sergeant and lieutenant may share some information with other squad supervisors when they are pressed by their captain, but this is infrequent. It is only in very rare circumstances that the department makes any effort to get the men who know more than anybody about what is going on in the streets to share their knowledge with each other.

It was two days after a patrolman had been murdered in the district. A rookie had been gunned down by three young men as he stepped from his car to speak with them. His gun had been found snapped in its holster. Detectives from homicide had come to daywork roll call to speak with the men. They looked tired, probably because they had been up most of the night. One man said, "Fellas, you know why we're here. We need information. We ain't askin' any questions. If you saw anything that night, anything at all, put it on a 48 and send it to us. If you were some place you shouldn'ta been, we don't care. You don't have to sign it, just send it downtown. Anything you can do will help. You know some people, you got sources of information. Squeeze 'em. We need it. It's for all of us. It could be any one of us next time."

Each man is obliged to learn his own territory and acquire the informal notions of public behavior he uses to evaluate what he sees about him. He gets no systematic help from anyone. How many more people would he know on his sector if he pooled his information with the other men who work his territory? How much time and how many errors might he be spared if he were cooperatively introduced into the lore of his area? Most of the people he sees on his sector are not known to him personally. He is obliged to rely on his notions of local behavior and of the legitimate use of public places and on the behavioral cues people give him when they come into his presence in making judgments of what they are doing.

Because he cannot know a good deal of what is going on, and since much of what is going on people do not want him to know, he is frequently obliged to rely on suspicion to guide him into actions. This will probably always be so, but it is far from clear that it is not possible to improve his personal knowledge. If he is obliged to do certain kinds of work, he will certainly have to continue using the techniques that the police have always employed to get information from unwilling participants. But these practices are not going to encourage any group of people to support actively, not simply decline to oppose, the men they are told to depend on to protect them from violence and depradations, the men who are supposed to shield us all from ourselves in our most violent and disordered moments.

The longer a patrolman is in a district, the more he knows about its people and their lives. His sources of information increase, as does his knowledge of how to exploit them for activity as well as for personal gain. A patrolman needs a solid knowledge of geography and people to do his work with confidence. The more he knows about the manners and habits of the people he polices, the less likely is he to become involved in misunderstandings and fights which arise from a misreading of what he sees. The more people he comes to know, however, the more likely he is to develop private and even intimate connections with some of them. This involves the police in an insoluble dilemma.

If the experienced patrolman is not allowed to remain where he is, the private stock of information and knowledge he accumulates will be dissipated. But if he remains in a district for many years, his inclinations to ignore many illegal things may increase. His personal involvements with some people may influence him to ignore their violations of the law. He may exploit his knowledge of gambling and illegal drinking to cash in on some of the easy money that is around and being collected by some plainclothesmen and, he suspects, by men even higher up in the organization. But even if he is not corrupted, he may become lazy and difficult to control. The more he knows about vice, the more valuable he becomes to his sergeant and lieutenant; if he provides them with activity, they will not supervise him too closely or demand of him the work they require of others. He can exploit his position to increase his personal freedom. At the same time, this relationship provides a model of success to younger patrolmen that undercuts the department's efforts to promote "professional" goals and attitudes in its men. The men who work the street see clearly who gets rewarded informally and for what. The department does not approve of this situation, but it has not changed much in the last century and a half.

CHAPTER SIX

Suspicions

"What do you see?" the lieutenant asked.

"Just the usual bunch of dirtyneckers in the playground, nothin' else."

"Look again, boy," he said, getting out of the car. They walked toward the corner, carefully scanning the people in the area. There had been fighting between white youths who lived in the neighborhood and the black students who passed through each day on their way home from school. The men had come looking for signs of trouble; one saw them and the other did not.

"Clever little bastards," the lieutenant muttered. He told his companion to examine the building line across the street. What was previously invisible became immediately apparent —a double row of soda bottles neatly lined up along the length of the buildings. "We'll find twice as many in the playground. You better call a sector car to block the trolleys at Fulton Street until we get this cleared up. They got an ambush all set up. The Indians are jumpin' the Indians. Look at the wires." His partner glanced overhead and saw large, wet rags twisted around the trolley wires. These would dislodge the power pole of any passing trolley and make it a sitting duck for a bottle barrage. "Ask for a bus supervisor to be sent here to clear the lines, too," the lieutenant called after his retreating companion. He walked into the playground, his stick tucked in his armpit, toward a group of children. "If you want to stay here—play—otherwise get the hell out. I know what you got planned and it's off," he barked. Not a bottle was in sight, but as he walked along the fence line swinging his stick in the tall grass, the pop of exploding glass was clearly heard.

1 · Expectations and Suspicions

The rookie shares the widely held opinion that policemen have special skills to see things. If only he knew what these abilities were. At the academy he was encouraged to be suspicious of everything he sees. "When you go on the street, you will develop a sense about these things," one instructor said; another insisted that you develop "a nose for trouble." The mysterious skills hinted at by these phrases are not made explicit by the examples that the instructors offer—"Watch out for men sitting in cars around schools and playgrounds," "people walking late at night," or "people carrying large packages." Always illustrations of heroics and cleverness from a dimming past when acuity paid off.

Each policeman must teach himself to see what he is looking at, just as he must teach himself to patrol. Older men help him out occasionally with hints and tips, but the skills he acquires are discovered by accident, by example, and by making mistakes. It is not a painless learning process, either for the policeman or for the people he encounters.

Regardless of how busy he is learning his way around the district, figuring out how to use the radio properly, learning how to do his paper work, staying out of accidents, and handling his assignments, he cannot help noticing that people treat him differently than they did when he dressed like others. Everywhere he goes people watch him. When he enters a shop, customers check him out. He can rarely sit down at a lunch counter for a cup of coffee without someone commenting in a friendly fashion on his presence or his gun. He is never quite certain whether some people glance at him furtively and quickly or if his imagination and self-consciousness are tricking him. Often, he is as quick to look away from others as they are from him. He knows that his uniform makes him liable for almost anything, but he does not understand what people expect of him. The anxieties generated by this uncertainty encourage his appreciation of those places where he receives what appear to be undiluted welcomes. The greetings extended to him by some of the business people, hospital personnel, waitresses, and garage men he knows are more than just tokens offered to him in exchange for some future aid or favor. These are little acts of friendship, which not only provide him with moments of relaxation but also enable him to measure the reaction of others who see him only as a policeman.[1]

The policeman gets used to being approached by people he does not know; he accepts the fact that he is impersonally available to the public. When a person wants something, he does not approach and say, "Excuse me, Officer, my name is . . ." No matter how much time they have or how polite they are, no introductions are thought necessary. The patrolman comes to accept this as natural, and like everything people treat as "natural," he comes to depend on it. He is leery of people who do introduce themselves formally, unless they are recognized as local businessmen or "neighborhood nuts." He becomes equally leery of people who approach him without any request at all, because he learns that nobody approaches an unknown policeman just to pass the time of day.[2]

With the development of his expectations about the place he works and the requirements of his job, the patrolman comes to terms with his special place on the street. He ceases to be self-conscious about wearing a uniform, although he never forgets for a moment that he has one on. He knows that people are scrutinizing him as he passes, glancing quickly, averting their eyes when he glances back. When he enters a public place on a call, particularly a barroom or a store, the patrolman sees how careful others are to give the impression of not looking at him. At first he does not know what to make of these reactions. While he was at the academy, nobody told him about the "policeman's

[1] I have profited from a reading of Harvey Sacks's "Notes on Police Assessment of Moral Character" in David Sudnow, *Studies in Social Interaction* (New York, Free Press, 1972), pp. 280–93; and from Goffman, "Normal Appearances" in his *Relations in Public*, pp. 238–333. See also Nathan Joseph and Nicholas Alex, "The Uniform: A Sociological Perspective," *American Journal of Sociology*, Vol. LXXVII (1971/72), pp. 719–30.

[2] On public contacts among the unacquainted, see Goffman, *Behavior in Public Places*, pp. 124ff.

stare," but he quickly teaches himself what he can do. As one patrolman in another city notes:

> An officer has a habit of looking directly at a man when he is talking to him. As a civilian we are inclined to look past them. We don't want to get involved. As an officer you are already involved with them. So you look at them. And that very stare marks an officer, no matter whether he is in civilian clothes or police clothes. You look around them instead of at them as a civilian.[3]

Long before he learns how to evaluate these glances and eye aversions, to use them in arousing and quieting his suspicions, the patrolman learns that he has a right to stare at anyone for as long as he wants. Whatever others may think he is looking at or for, when he stares at someone he is expressing his special rights as a policeman. Like any other city dweller, he knows how careful people are about being caught staring overly long or, in some circumstances, at all. He knows that fights start over claims that one person has violated another's privacy by staring. He knows, too, that it is unsettling to be stared at; but he need fear no reprimand. If someone angrily asks him, "What are you looking at?" all he need reply is "You." It is his way of telling those people at whom he is looking of his claims on their behavior in public. Others may approach him unbidden and unannounced to make demands and requests, but he may intervene in their lives without even approaching them. It is a considerable power, which some patrolmen learn to use with subtlety; it is a tool that his trade allows him to acquire, but it is not a secret skill. The skill is in its application, but it rests on his power to violate the unwritten rights of others.

Even after he has familiarized himself with his working area and accustomed himself to the special demands of police

---

[3] "A Quiet Strip: Officer Schalbrack's Story," p. 72.

Another officer, from New York, recalls, "Paul studied the people on the street. He'd learned to hold their eyes. Many glanced at him and turned away quickly. Others held his eyes for a moment before turning away. Then there were the defiant ones, but eventually even they were stared down. As each one turned away there was a look of guilt on his face as though he'd revealed too much to the cop's prying eye." Radano, pp. 187–8.

cruising, the patrolman focuses his attention at eye level. He scans his surroundings in a flat plane, rarely checking out what is above him, because the things he is primarily interested in—people walking and driving—are not overhead. A man who works in an area where there are many tall buildings can hardly be expected to show interest in places he cannot reach or even see without some difficulty. Even in residential areas where buildings rarely go above several stories, the patrolman seldom systematically scans above street level. If he is assigned to work in a poor neighborhood where slum renewal has left numerous high-rise housing projects, the patrolman is conscious of the places above him and scans them when he gets out of his car, because his experience has demonstrated the wisdom of wariness. In many projects, screening has been installed to prevent people from throwing things on those below, but this has not kept a policeman from being hit, or just missed, by a falling bottle. But it is only in these places, where his vulnerability is demonstrable, that the officer exercises this caution. When he cruises through a project, protected by the steel roof of his car, he resumes his normal scanning habits and ignores the places above him.

Even when confronted with evidence of interesting actions going on above eye level, he is not encouraged to develop the habit of looking up. At the scene of a fire, a patrolman was commenting on his bad luck. He said the fire was in a house he was going to hit the next day for harboring a speakeasy. While standing on his school crossing, he said, he had noticed people ringing the doorbell. The lady whose apartment had just burned out would lean out the window and throw down the keys. The policeman admitted that he would not have noticed her if he had been driving past, but insisted that he would have found out about her sooner or later anyway.

When he begins to appreciate his special place on the street, the patrolman also realizes that he is seeing only a fraction of what is going on about him. The inexperienced officer is always looking in front of him or into the alleys and cross streets as he cruises his area. As his curiosity about people develops and he sees how diffierently they treat him from other people, he begins to follow them in his rear-view mirror. He starts casually, either to watch a passing girl to get a rounded picture of her, to see what car is behind him at a light, or to check a pedestrian whom he has noticed too late to look at from the front. However he begins, there slowly dawns in him the realization that his rear-view mirror and side-vent mirror are not just useful for safe driving but provide him with another dimension for observing his surroundings. He acquires the habit of indirect observation as part of his regular scanning pattern, and some men spend a good deal of time with their heads inclined to the left, watching people to see whether there has been any change in their manner after they think he has passed by.

Rear-view observation is particularly useful to the vice-wise policeman. The uniformed officer knows that only pure luck allows him to witness a vice transaction unless he has specific information and can conceal himself or observe from a distance with the aid of binoculars. Sometimes he can hide in a doorway or an alley, but his possibilities for successful concealment are limited. Everything about his appearance is designed to maximize his visibility. He must frequently rely on indirect observation as the only effective way of watching people who are alert to his presence. He may park his car and pretend to do paper work, while carefully scanning his mirror. If he has a partner or there is a friendly passer-by, he will pretend to engage in conversation, while he uses a convenient plate-glass window to see what is going on behind him.

Once the patrolman learns that he can see backward effectively, he integrates what is behind him into his active field of observation. He does not look back only when he sees something of interest; he looks back because what is there is as much a part of his surroundings as what is in front of him. Like his predecessors, who learned to walk with one eye cocked over their shoulders to see whether their sergeant was behind them, the cruising patrolman is particularly alert for any car that seems to be following him. If he has any reason to suspect that it is not coincidence when he does spot one, he undertakes measures to test his suspicion. He alters his patrol route to see if the other car follows, and if it does, he takes action.

One night a patrolman asked the dispatcher to send his sergeant to him. The sound of his voice added to the urgency that normally attends this request, but when the sergeant arrived, everything seemed normal. The officer approached and said that he had stopped the battered automobile that was parked in front of his patrol car. "I noticed them followin' me and I went up a one-way street the wrong way and they followed me. I pulled 'em over and the plates don't match the registration. You know who they are? They're ginks; those fuckin' cops have been following me for two days."[4]

"Well, they went up a one-way street the wrong way and it is your duty as an officer of the law to give them a summons. Just don't lock 'em up for driving with an improper registration. The plates are probably stolen," the sergeant said and returned to his car. The ginks were so embarrassed at having been caught that they sought to evade the humiliation of having to turn the ticket over to their commanding officer by asking the policeman to forget the entire matter. He was so angry at their crude efforts to plead for mercy that he gave them an additional ticket.[5]

During his training period, the recruit is encouraged to patrol with his window open, alert for any unusual sounds and smells. Under the common law he is considered a sight officer who may arrest for any crimes he sees being committed. The law interprets his sight to include all of his natural senses. If he smells something he feels reveals evidence of criminal activity—a still or drugs—it is sufficient cause for him to investigate without a warrant. He is regaled with tales of glory detailing old-timers' successes in nosing out stills, but he does not rely heavily on his sense of smell while patrolling. There are few stills left; the only thing he is alert

[4]Gink is the term used generally by patrolmen in Philadelphia to describe anyone who is considered a spy, although specifically in this instance it referred to members of the department's internal-security division. In New York these men are called "shooflies" and in London they are referred to as "rubber heels." The patrolman was being investigated on a morals complaint.

[5]The police keep license plates which they recover from abandoned cars for use in undercover operations because they know very well that information on car registrations in available to anyone for a price. By using plates registered to private citizens, they make it more difficult to expose their undercover operations.

for is any hint of smoke. All of the things that he listens for with interest—squealing tires, calls for aid, gunshots—can be heard through a closed window, and in winter few men open their car windows more than a crack. The advent of air conditioning keeps the cars sealed in summer, too.

Unusual sounds aid him so rarely in achieving success that they are highly prized, giving proof to colleagues of a man's sensitivity and alertness. The exposure of concealed criminal activity also allows the patrolman to assert his feelings of superiority, which are constantly undermined by criminals who evade his watchfulness. Even when his investigations reveal only the sounds of aging plumbing, he is not denigrated by others, because they appreciate the alertness he displays and they know how difficult it is to distinguish the meaning of what is heard. A lieutenant was called to the scene of a burglary early on a Sunday morning after one of his men had made an arrest. The officer, a man not well liked by the lieutenant, had captured a boy cutting a hole in a store roof. He told the lieutenant that he had heard a pounding noise and, since he could not see anything from the street, had decided to investigate. The lieutenant was suspicious of the claim, since he doubted the man's capacity, and he carefully checked whether the place could be seen from the street. When he was satisfied that it could not, he congratulated the man and ordered the sergeant to "put him in" for a commendation.

The patrolman uses his knowledge of the area he works to arouse or calm his suspicions of what he sees. Anything "out of place" interests him greatly. It can either be something commonplace but not in its usual place, such as an abandoned car on a street where these are usually not found, or just something unusual in his area. He is frequently not interested in parked cars unless looking for a specific one, but he quickly notices any he considers out of character. He is primarily concerned to recover stolen cars, and when he learns that a car he has noticed is not stolen, he usually loses interest unless he is vice-wise. If the patrolman spots an expensive car in a poor neighborhood or a fashionable sports car in an area where they are uncommon, he makes an effort to find out to whom it belongs. He checks out the license number or he may make a stop when he sees the car being driven. He considers expensive cars an indicator of someone who may be involved in the "rackets." Also, the appearance of *any* car in some places arouses his interest because it tells him that someone is doing something covert or possibly illegal. A patrolman drove into a cul-de-sac and, after scanning the place with the aid of his spotlight, said to his companion, "Always check for cars parked in here. There's no good reason to be here. Either they're abandoned or stolen. Otherwise somebody is gettin' laid or doesn't want anyone walkin' by to know they're in the bar at the corner."

Just as a car may be out of place, so may a person. Locations he identifies with certain activities momentarily taint everyone he sees there. When he sees people standing on a corner where he knows drugs are sold, he checks them as he goes by. Bars where fighting and robberies are common are scrutinized more carefully than other places as he cruises along. The people standing in these places may give no sign of illicit behavior, but the patrolman presumes they are up to no good. He may not stop and check them, but he does watch them more carefully as he passes than he would if they were standing in a place he did not associate with trouble and work.

Persons he knows to be connected with criminal activity are noted wherever they are. The policeman feels that all he needs to know about a person is what that person has told him by his behavior in their previous contacts. If he has arrested someone for being a drug user, that is sufficient to presume that the person continues to be one and should be stopped whenever and wherever he is seen. There is nothing that this person need do to arouse the officer's suspicion; he has only to appear. One afternoon a patrolman noticed a man carrying a car battery. The man had been arrested by the patrolman for possession of heroin, and he remembered the officer. He insisted the battery belonged to him and asked the policeman to accompany him home, where he would prove his ownership. When he had satisfied the officer that the battery was indeed his, he pressed his advantage to complain about being stopped. The policeman listened to him and then replied without rancor, "Listen, my man, I know you're a junkie. Any time I see you going down the street with a battery or whatever, I'm going to stop and check you out. It doesn't matter to me what color you are or where you are. All that matters is that I know you're a junkie."

2 · Mobilizations

When a crime is reported, the policeman has only a few minutes in which to make an arrest. If he does not capture a suspect at or near the scene, his chances of making an arrest are almost nil. The new policeman does not know what to look for, but he is introduced to the ways of looking by listening to the exchange of information over the radio, the questions asked by the dispatcher of men at the scene of crimes, the reading of holdup memos, and the announcements of flash information. He soon learns that the principal things he wants to know are whether the suspects are armed, how they made their escape, and, naturally, in which direction they went. If there is a make and color on the car, the patrolman cares about little else, because a car is the largest and most prominent thing he can look for. It may be exchanged for another, but it cannot be concealed in the vicinity of a crime.

Two patrolman were sitting in their car about noon, waiting for school recess. The alarm bell sounded and the dispatcher broadcast flash information on a bank robbery in another part of the city. "Can you imagine how dumb they are, using a white Caddy? If they don't ditch it, they'll be grabbed in a few minutes," one commented. "Shit, I wish our robbers were that stupid." Within moments the dispatcher returned to the air, announcing their capture. "Dumb! It's like rolling a sailboat down Market Street. Even if they'd been a little smart, like dropped a guy off or picked up a woman or a kid so there's a different group in the car than you're lookin' for, I'd still pull 'em over in a Caddy. Too much coincidence. But if they go by in some junker, who knows? If they were cool, they could go right by."

Even when he doubts the car he is looking over is the one he is seeking, the patrolman will stop it because he knows that he rarely has more than one chance to catch anyone fleeing an area in a car. If there is anything about the car that resembles the description he has received, he goes into action. This is especially true of newer cars or special models. The car he is looking at may have a different color or be an altogether different model from the one reported, but the appearance of the same "kind" of car in his area after the report of a crime is too much for him to overlook. However, if he is looking for a car that is like fifty thousand other cars, he is guided by the behavior of the occupants rather than the car itself. He has no way of adjusting for persons who have the good sense to change cars, to leave their car and walk, or to take a cab. He knows these possibilities exist, but since he cannot do anything to counteract them, he behaves as if they did not.

If the suspect has fled on foot, the experienced patrolman learns to look for two specific kinds of things—the person's physical characteristics and some distinctive article of clothing. Often, frightened onlookers or wounded victims are not notably reliable reporters under the stressful conditions of the moment. The veteran officer does not ask a witness how tall a suspect is but rather how he would compare to someone present. The only piece of information he gets that he treats as absolutely reliable is the person's race; he does not think anyone mistakes white and black people for each other. Everything else he treats as guidelines for action. Any matching characteristics arouse his suspicions sufficiently to make a stop. If he has two kinds of information, one matching trait is usually enough. For example, if he is looking for someone of a certain size with a particular kind of hat or coat, he stops anyone who is not the right height but whose clothing matches the suspect's. If the person is the right size, the kind of clothing he is wearing interests the officer less, because he knows clothing can be added or discarded. Frequently he will look to see whether a suspect has on several layers of clothing or, if he is wearing a coat, whether the shirt underneath is the color of the one announced over the air.

In these moments, the patrolman is attracted by the person's appearance. There are no behavioral signs that arouse him. He is making a stop on the odds, and his suspicion is low. Since he knows he has only a few minutes to capture a suspect, any hint of culpability is sufficient for him to make an inquiry. These stops usually last only a few moments, unless the officer has any reason to further his inquiry and return to the scene with the now-suspected person. It is common for the same person to be stopped successively by several patrolmen within a few minutes of a reported crime, each man being attracted by the same distinctive feature of the person's appearance.

Even when he is going on a non-emergency call, "investigate prowlers" for example, the patrolman tends to be suspicious of people he sees in the immediate area. These calls are rarely accompanied by any description, but this does not deter the patrolman from stopping a person he finds "loitering" in the area. He presumes that if someone has taken the trouble to call, there must be something to investigate, and any person he views as someone likely to be a troublemaker —a teenager for example—may be questioned. Even in places he regards as neutral, he looks the people over carefully. Although he knows that people sometimes try to use him for their own ends, he treats almost any call given to him by the dispatcher as legitimate.

Two patrolmen took a call to investigate males acting suspiciously in an alley. When they arrived, they found the alley empty and littered with wine bottles, which might have been there for weeks, so they did not bother to get out of the car. They spotted two teenage boys, who crossed the street a few houses up and walked past them on the other side. "That's probably them," one said and hailed them over without moving from the car. They came over, and after chatting for a few minutes, one of the boys asked the black patrolman why he was always being stopped. He claimed that he had been stopped fifty or sixty times and he was only nineteen. "You got some kinda quota?" The patrolman carefully explained to him why they had come to the street and his reasons for calling the boys to the car. They looked at him, shook their heads, and walked away. He finished writing his ped stop and drove on.

A call was given to investigate three males acting suspiciously in the 2900 block of Washington Street. Two cars pulled into the block, one at either end. The patrolmen parked and walked toward each other on the empty street. A man got out of a parked car and walked into a bar. The officers noted that there were two other men, apparently sleeping, on the back seat of the automobile. It was late morning. "That's gotta be them," one said, as he rapped on the window with his stick. The other officer went into the bar to ask the man he had seen enter to accompany him out to the street. Twelve patrons sat glued to their stools, not moving or looking as the men walked past.

On the pavement the two men were angrily questioning the policemen's right to order them out of the car. When he replied that there had been a call to investigate some people acting suspiciously, one retorted, "Bullshit, that's a lotta crap, man." The patrolman who had sought to ease the situation by explaining his actions shrugged. "O.K., let's talk about it inside the district," he said, jerking his head toward the patrol wagon, which had just pulled up. "But this better be your car, my man."

An examination of the men's papers and a phone call to the registry of motor vehicles established that the car belonged to one of them. The patrolman told them that they were free to go, but one man, familiar with police procedure, said that the police were obliged to drive them back to the place where they had been picked up. He was absolutely right, but the patrolman, angered by their resistance, did not want to comply. The corporal, who was listening to the exchange, nodded to the officer, and he told the men to get into his car. The brief ride back to the scene was very quiet.

The setting of every call to work is momentarily contaminated in the patrolman's view. Every person in that setting is tainted simply by being there. He does not have to do anything, give any of the signs that arouse a patrolman's suspicion of persons walking or riding down the street to attract his attention. Two officers took a call to "investigate juveniles around parked cars" in a parking lot. When they arrived, they saw no one about but noticed a car with an open trunk. One officer spotted two men sitting in a car parked farther along the same row. They were older and had not taken any particular notice of the police. He went over and talked to them. When he came back, he said, "I don't know about them. They might have seen us comin' and jumped in there to bluff. You don't know what they'll do when you get close to them."

Regardless of the circumstances in which he is looking for someone, the patrolman usually assumes that the person is leaving the site as he approaches. Sometimes this presumption is rooted in practical considerations, but more generally it is symptomatic of his own conception of his place on the street and his relationship to the people about him. Any crime committed adjacent to places that the patrolman believes are havens for fleeing criminals—freightyards, parks, public housing projects, subways—causes him to investigate these places first. But when he has no specific reason to assume that suspects have gone in any particular direction, the patrolman makes the presumption that they have gone in a direction other than the one he has taken to the scene. He assumes implicitly that anyone he is looking for is moving away from him, even if the suspect cannot know which direction he is coming from. He rarely thinks of searching an area he has already passed through, nor does he consider the possibility that the person he is seeking may be sitting around the corner having a soda or watching the action from a nearby roof. The suspect must be frightened and working as hard as the patrolman. These are rules the policeman invents for his work; they are not mutually agreed upon by the police and the people they pursue. Since people escape so often despite his best efforts, the patrolman must establish some conception of what he is doing that allows him the possibility of success. If he did not, he would soon give up mobilizing himself and would let calls go unheeded.

His suspicions are impersonal until he has a reason to take someone into the station. Even if he thinks the person guilty of something, he will charge him only if he can connect him to the specific call he is investigating or if a fight results from the stop. Two patrolmen took a call to "investigate boys playing on trucks." When they arrived, they discovered several trucks with broken windshields and slashed tires. They saw some boys scavenging in a nearby junkyard. They approached the fence, which had been breached, and ordered the boys to come out. One officer said to them, "Why did you break those trucks? Somebody saw you do it." They vociferously denied the claim and the patrolman believed them. Although he could have charged them with trespassing in the junkyard, he simply told them to leave. If they had not resisted his effort to implicate them, he might have taken them in, although he knew they could be charged only if he lied about where he had found them.

Two officers were driving past a liquor store that had been burglarized several times in the previous weeks. Earlier in the evening they had come by to check a ringing alarm, only to find nobody about. They saw two men walking slowly past the iron-grated windows. "Let's take them two," the driver said, slowing down when he has passed the men to look at them in his side mirror. When they were abreast of the car, the driver got out and ordered them to halt, while his recorder circled quickly around the rear of the car to cut off any possibility of flight. They were angry about being stopped and reluctantly complied with the orders to put their hands on the nearest wall for a frisk. One of the men said, as the officer was about to put his hands on him, "Hey, man, I got a blade in my right pocket." The white patrolman removed the switch knife, which was taped to impede the spring mechanism. It was the only weapon the men had. While the patrolman was writing up a ped stop, his partner explained the reason for it. The men shook their heads and said they were not burglars. One patrolman asked why the knife was taped, and the man said that if he carried a switchblade he could be jailed, but since it was taped, it was just a regular knife for protection and he would not be arrested.

"Shit, man, I can lock you up for this with the tape or not."

"Ya, I know."

"But I won't because you're all right. But I'm keeping the knife. You shouldn't carry these things around."

"Lissen, man, you don't live here. You got a gun. You think I'm gonna walk around here without some protection? You know what them fuckin' jitterbugs do to you for no reason at all? Even if you lock me up, man, I'm still gonna carry something. Else I gotta stay in the house."

The patrolman looked at him and shrugged. "Take it easy, fellas," he said, handing the knife back to the surprised man.

"Thanks, man," he replied, slipping the knife back into his pocket and renewing his interrupted journey.

The dispatcher's broadcasts of the characteristics of persons and cars offer the policeman his first solid clues to the kinds of things he should look for when he is cruising and scanning the people around him. The persons he stops during the brief flurries of action caused by his mobilization also give the rookie his first knowledge of hostility and acquiescence in the face of his power. In the beginning he does not know what to make of these responses, although he is not indifferent to them. They are very important in any assessment he makes of the person in his hands and how he should treat him. But since he does not see his own actions as a personal expression weighing against the character or the rights of the person stopped, he does not have much sympathy for their objections, which he usually treats as symptoms of guilt. When he has acquired more experience, his understanding of people's objections increases, because every patrolman knows that there are policemen who abuse their power. Sometimes a man will refuse to work with a colleague whose attitudes he regards as dangerous and compromising. The experienced policeman also knows that most of the people he stops are not guilty of violating the law (although he cannot know this until after he has stopped them) and regard his actions as a personal affront.

But his understanding does not lessen the difficulties he must face. The patrolman knows that he cannot allow the sentiments of the people he stops to affect his decision on whether to continue making stops. If he did, he could not stop anyone on the street, because every person stopped by the police has objections. Most patrolmen ease their task by avoiding the use of insulting language. Some may try to mollify people by explaining their actions, although there is no guarantee that they will be believed, or that the explanation will be acceptable. A stop is an exercise of pure power and nobody likes to be confronted with his powerlessness. But the patrolman's understanding of people's objections does encourage him to assess what he knows of behavior, what he learns of the character of the people in his area, to develop cues that suggest that one person is more likely than another to be doing something illegal. These cues vary from place to place, they certainly change from time to time, but they are the substantive things upon which the experienced patrolman bases his "reasonable suspicion" and which cause him to stop people who are making their way along public streets on their private business.[6]

No policeman is obliged to stop people on the street. If he sees someone whose manner he finds suspicious, he does not have to do anything. There is nobody watching him, forcing him to do his job. People around him may not even know he is watching someone, not to mention harboring thoughts about their manner. While he is required to produce some activity, he can use his traffic stops and his imagination to manufacture the evidence required by his sergeant. But he cannot conceal his true inclinations from his colleagues. The signals and cues he uses in deciphering people's purposes and characters are acquired while he is engaged in cooperative work with other members of his platoon. By the time he develops the knowledge and self-confidence necessary to make "suspicion stops" on his own, he has already displayed his commitment to hard and potentially dangerous work in the presence of his colleagues. They know whether he has "what it takes" to work on his own. If he produces little paper work, that will not change their opinion. The patrolman's understanding of this limits his inclinations to harass people or to push them around. It is also a spur encouraging him to produce what his department is demanding of him. If

[6] The right of the police to stop people and informally question them is rooted in English common law. While this right has been challenged in the courts as well as on the streets, the Supreme Court has consistently refused to abridge the right of the police to stop people. The courts have carefully regulated the rights of the police with regard to their searching persons with the intention of producing evidence that may be admitted in court, but no abridgment has been placed on their power to stop and frisk anyone suspected of harboring ill will toward an officer. The right of the person stopped to refuse to answer any questions put to him is not clearly settled. The law is summarized in Jerold H. Israel and Wayne R. LaFave, *Criminal Procedure in a Nutshell: Constitutional Limitations* (St. Paul, Minn., West Publishing, 1971), pp. 128ff., 171ff.; and discussed extensively in Wayne R. LaFave, *Arrest: The Decision to Take a Suspect into Custody* (Boston, Little, Brown, 1965), pp. 344ff. For a discussion of the rights of police to stop and frisk in a number of countries, see Claude R. Sowle, ed., *Police Power and Individual Freedom* (Chicago, Aldine, 1962).

he knows how to work and has the "heart" for it, he has no need to make fake work or to stop the first drunk he sees, just to make a ped stop.

3 • Pedestrian Stops

When the patrolman learns that he is a central figure in any street scene, he begins to assess the degrees of awareness people display and to note the kinds of adjustments they make to conceal and control their concern (if they have any) about his presence. A person who glances furtively is noticed. Anyone whose body is facing toward the street but whose head is averted to give the impression that he is looking elsewhere unwittingly signals his concern to the patrolman. A person whose body is facing away from the patrolman but whose head is inclined sideways to glance at the policeman is easily spotted. Persons standing on street corners, perusing newspapers or staring overhead, first make the young patrolman angry and then cause him to laugh when he discovers the transparency of these little ruses. These efforts to conceal concern, while not daring to convert it into motion, frequently cause the body to tense, giving the person a rigid appearance that is wholly "unnatural" and making him even more apparent.[7]

There are many persons on the street who successfully conceal and control their interest in the police and give no obvious signs to alert the patrolman. People who have been stopped frequently sometimes learn to control themselves sufficiently to limit the chances of attracting the patrolman's attention. While the patrolman knows there are a lot of cop-wise people, he cannot do anything to limit the development of their skills, except to refuse them any information on why he has stopped them.

In addition, there are people who are naturally skilled at avoiding the attention of the police. The patrolman is also not likely to stop women on suspicion and does not look at them carefully or in the same way as he does men. One reason is that he cannot frisk a woman on the street, and no patrolman willingly places himself in a potentially dangerous

[7]These adjustments are what Erving Goffman calls "orientation disjunctions." *Relations in Public*, pp. 261ff.

situation, where he is deprived of one of his fundamental rights of self-protection. If there were patrolwomen, the number of stops on women would undoubtedly increase.

The policeman does not think it unnatural or unwarranted for people to be aware of his presence on the street. He expects them to notice him, and implicitly he demands this attention. When he sees someone appear to ignore him, his suspicion is immediately aroused. Riding up a crowded street, an officer noted a large group of men standing in front of a bar in the next block. "As soon as they see the car, they'll start jiving around. I know they got a game going up there, you can see the way they're standing. Someone will scoop up the money and the dice and duck in the bar, and the others will stand around lookin' at each other." As the patrol car drew up to the bar, the crowd diminished slightly, and the six remaining men stood looking about, mostly at the sky. The patrolman rolled down his window and, without stopping, called out in a friendly fashion, "When did you guys get interested in stargazing?" He chuckled as he cruised along, commenting, "You don't want 'em to think you don't know that they spotted you. You let 'em know you know what's up, and it keeps 'em on their toes, always lookin' for you."

Anyone who indicates an intention of flight at the appearance of a patrolman immediately comes under suspicion. Obviously when a policeman turns a corner and suddenly someone begins running, he suspects them of fleeing from his presence. But even if he does not connect their flight with his appearance, he takes it as evidence that something is amiss in the area. Young boys are often stopped simply because the patrolman sees them running down the street, and often that is all they are doing. But the officer knows from his experience that running is also a sign of violence in places beyond his sight. It is a signal that causes doubt about the character of the person or raises questions generally about the place. The patrolman does not make this distinction in his reactions to it, since either interpretation causes him to do the same thing—stop the person who is running.

There are more subtle signals that the patrolman knows are indications of flight and usually cause him to make a stop. While cruising along a street, he is watching to see if anyone begins to move away. Anyone who is standing in place and starts suddenly is immediately suspect. If a man slips into a bar or even puts his head inside while the car rolls by, the patrolman assumes the person is either trying to avoid him or warning someone in the bar that the police are about. People who have their backs to the street and give no appearance of looking backward while they are moving away from him are also noticed; the patrolman does not assume that only he uses windows and mirrors for indirect observation.

The patrolman frequently engages in eye games with unknown persons who are standing on the pavement. He does this not only to create situations where he will be victorious (which he inevitably is) or to unsettle the people he polices but informally to test their character. People who return his stare are often passed because the officer assumes that their boldness indicates no fear of being stopped. "Look at that group. They wouldn't hurt you if they had the chance, would they?" an officer said, staring at six teenagers walking along. "Want to stop 'em?" his partner asked. He replied, "Not worth it. They're too bold. They want to be stopped. They must be clean."

If the same person who has calmly returned the patrolman's glance, and thereby lowered any suspicion of himself, turns a corner or disappears into an alley, the policeman is likely to have second thoughts and will go to the corner to see whether the person is running or still walking. In the early morning two policemen were standing in front of a bar reported to be the target of a burglary. A young, bearded black man wearing a dungaree suit walked past and looked coolly at them. The men looked back and nothing was said. The man continued down the street, and the two officers looked at each other and then followed his progress. The black policeman moved several steps in his direction and then stopped. He said to his partner, "If he goes around the corner, we're gonna take him." The man continued past the intersection and the patrolmen returned to their car.

Most people a policeman stops usually make some sudden movement that betrays their concern about his presence. These people are simply unable to contain their tensions and are compelled to release them physically. Two patrolmen were driving through a residential neighborhood late at night. They were nearing the end of their tour and were not paying much attention to the street. As they passed through a poorly lit intersection, the recorder yelled "Stop" and got quickly out of the car. By the time the driver had set the brake and joined him, his partner had three men at gunpoint. "Don't any of you move a muscle," he ordered. While his partner covered him, he approached one man and said, "What did you throw down in the gutter?" Although the man's companions urged silence on him, meeting with stern warnings from the police to keep still, he readily admitted that he had thrown down a gun and he walked back with the patrolman to retrieve it. The patrolman had seen the men approaching out of the corner of his eye and had noticed one man suddenly turn around and move his right arm. If he had continued toward the corner, the men would not have been stopped.

Two uniformed men, driving an unmarked car, were slowly cruising a street when they noticed two boys standing together at a street corner. As they approached the intersection, the driver saw one boy quickly hand something to the other and then put his hands in his pocket. The driver slammed on the brakes and both patrolmen bailed out of the car, which was left standing in the middle of the street. The boy who had passed something to his companion began running, with the driver in pursuit. The other boy started to move in the opposite direction; the recorder grabbed him by the shoulder and spun him around. The boy struggled, and the officer slammed him against the car, reaching into the boy's right-hand pocket in the same motion. His fingers felt the familiar sensation of iron. "You little prick," he muttered, pulling out a .32-caliber pistol. The boy stopped struggling immediately.

On another occasion two patrolmen were driving through an area where holdups were common. They looked at three men coming out of a bar across the road. They would have had to cut across oncoming traffic to stop and question them, which they were willing to do, but the effort required more than a passing interest. "What do you think?" "They're just standing there. Don't look like nothin' to me." They continued along, and a few moments later the alarm bell rang and the dispatcher announced, "Holdup in progress at the Hi-Ho Bar." "That's them, those pricks," the driver yelled, swinging the car around and rushing back to the scene as quickly as possible. After a fruitless search for the men, the patrolmen were chagrined by their failure. "I don't believe it. We were that close and let them go right by. They were just comin' out of the stickup and we let 'em slip."[8]

The sudden movements that the patrolman sees do not necessarily need to convey the impression of flight to arouse his interest. If he sees something he interprets as a caution or a warning signal to persons unseen or an effort to conceal something, he will make a stop, if for no other reason than to show the person that he has not succeeded in escaping notice. For example, in some parts of the city, heroin sales are so common that people stand on the corners to do their dealing. It is not uncommon for a patrolman cruising past to see someone suddenly put his hand to his mouth. He knows that he has seen the person swallow a couple of bags of heroin or try to make the patrolman think he has. There is little the policeman can do if he has swallowed them. If he makes an arrest, the person will not be charged, and the officer will have lost a few hours of patrol time. But he does not allow the act to pass unacknowledged He may not even get out of his car to frisk the man, but he lets him know that he has been seen. "Well, at least I gave you a good case of the shits, you rat," an officer muttered to a man who was grinning at him. "Don't think I won't get you yet."

A patrol car was parked at one end of a street. At the other end a young man emerged from a house and after walking a few steps, he paused and returned to the house. He leaned in the doorway, and after a few moments he resumed his walk with a big smile on his face. The police-men in the car had seen him the moment he had come out

---

[8]The patrolman, of course, was not quite accurate. He had not let them pass since he had taken notice of them, but they had done noth-ing to arouse his interest. Not only did they show no inclination to move away but also no particular interest in his car. For another example, see Erving Goffman, *Strategic Interaction* (Philadelphia, University of Pennsylvania Press, 1969), p. 52.

of the house. They had no reason to presume that his actions and demeanor had any relation to their presence. Until he turned back, they had only glanced at him. But as he approached the car, they got out and stopped him. He was questioned about where he lived and what he was doing. Throughout the conversation he continued to smile. One man asked him why he had returned to the house. He said he had forgotten to tell his brother something. He was frisked and nothing was found on him. The patrolmen did not expect to find anything. If they suspected the boy had turned about after spotting them, they also had to assume that he had disposed of anything incriminating. If he had not seen them, it was likely that he was telling the truth. Only by beating him or torturing him could they possibly find out whether he had spotted them. Since this kind of behavior is not tolerated in most places, they had no choice but to make a stop and let him know that in either case they had seen him and were keeping an eye out. They were indicating to him that he was not putting anything over on them, although it was quite possible that he had. This uncertainty is part of the price the patrolman pays for being the center of attention on city streets.

Some policemen use specialized forms of staring to test the flight and concealment intentions of suspects. These are all based on the notion that a person who is worried about the presence of the patrolman can be coerced or tricked into revealing his concern. When the patrolman sees someone who arouses his interest or curiosity, he has several options. He can simply stop him, without considering the matter any further, or he can ignore the person. Occasionally he chooses to do neither of these things, preferring to test the person's mettle. He can just stare at him until he gets a response, which influences him either to make a stop or to break off contact. If the man is standing, the patrolman may just stop his car and gaze at him passively. If the person under observation is moving, the policeman may drive along beside him as he walks down the street. In either case, the person is told in an unmistakable fashion that he is being watched, examined, and scrutinized. He has to decide what to do, while trying to figure out what the policeman is going to do. This kind of wordless, intense contact can go on

for minutes. The two of them may be the only persons on
the street who know they are engaged actively in exchanging
information about each other. But the patrolman does not
feel isolated or alone, while the man he is watching may never
have felt so entirely stripped of his privacy and self-assurance
as he does in these few moments. These contacts are
frequently broken off without a stop, and often not a single
word is spoken. The officer has not done anything to the
man, who may go home shaken and distressed. The patrolman may have had no intention to do the man any harm,
but if he has, that does not bother him, since he feels only
persons who have anything to conceal from the police are
upset by these intrusions.

After a patrolman lets a person know that he has been
seen, he may choose not to stare at him but to continue
along, casually observing the man in his mirror. He is looking
for any sign of quick movement or apparent relief oc-
casioned by the passing of the police. If the patrolman believes that he sees the person do anything that conveys a
changed attitude, he will make a stop. If the patrolman thinks
that a group of people are checking him as he approaches,
he may try to trap them into revelations rather than stop,
because if he is alone, he cannot stop them if they run away.
He seeks to exploit their intense interest in him by confusing their expectations of what he is likely to do. The cop-
wise think he will stare them down, stop them, or go on by
—but if he does none of these, there is a chance they will
be confused and trapped into revealing things he wants to
know without the risk of a chase, which must end in some
kind of failure for the officer.

Instead of stopping and staring or riding on past, he drives
the car toward the suspects, openly displaying his interest in
them. This move is familiar to any group of boys who have
ever stood on a corner regularly. As he comes even with
them, he turns his head to look at them, not concealing his
interest in any way. He does not halt nor does he stop
looking. If he is successful, they will be following his actions
intently. He is making a play and they are responding to it.
They are not in "contact" in any normal sense, but he is
directing their lives at this moment. When he has gone past
them, he suddenly hits the brake, causing the car's wheels to

screech, and shifts the gears into reverse. When he does this, he is watching closely for any movements in the group, someone throwing something to the ground or a person moving to block off his direct view. They may run and he will not chase them, but if he has been successful, he might find a knife, drugs, or even a gun in the gutter.

While responses to his presence are the most commonly used measurement of others' behavior, the patrolman does not confine his suspicions of unknown persons to these alone. He frequently checks people who appear to be doing nothing out of the ordinary because of the unusual hour he sees them or the place they are in. On a weekday afternoon a patrolman noticed a boy enter the cellar of a taproom and emerge a few moments later with a bicycle. He was the owner's son and kept his bike there. The patrolman did not know this until he made a stop. On another occasion he saw a boy standing by the gasoline pump of a closed filling station. He pulled into the yard and the boy scowled at him. He noticed the owner of the station inside the office, waving his greetings. He did not stop his car, returned the greeting, and noted the frozen scowl on the teenager's face.

Sometimes he stops people because of the manner in which they are standing together, even if he does not associate this with any response to his own presence. A patrolman in another city recalls sighting his first holdup. He writes:

It had all started around eleven p.m. Paul was on patrol. [He] passed an alley that connected two parallel streets. He noticed two men at the other end of the alley. . . . What attracted his attention was the way they were standing in relation to one another. It was an unnatural way for two people to stand if they were in a normal conversation.[9]

[9]Radano, p. 101. The policeman is also interested in noting people's actions for what they tell him about things going on elsewhere. As the officer quoted above recounts, "Whenever I walk down the street and there are a group of people in front of me, if they are not looking in different directions, that means they are looking in one direction. And if they are looking in one direction that means that there is something occurring over there worthy of attention. People are like bird dogs. They point out situations a block away." "A Quiet Strip: Officer Schalbrack's Story," p. 13.

He does not know any more than anyone else what is "natural," but if he has that feeling, he may allow his presence to become known and test for additional responses. These groupings are most frequent around barrooms and places where people who are partying come outside to take the air. At these moments the patrolman is as interested in the possibility of fighting among people as he is in their reactions to him. If he suspects that the peculiarities of their grouping indicate the preliminaries of a fight, he is likely to mobilize himself, as he would under circumstances when he thinks he is near evidence of crimes committed or contemplated.

These stops frequently reveal nothing more than private conversations or concealments inspired by modesty in responding to calls of nature, the most urgent signal of all. But frequently (and often enough to encourage the patrolman to continue responding to these signals), they reveal much more. An officer was patrolling his sector on last out when he noticed two boys standing close together with their backs to the street. They were on the edge of the sidewalk. He stopped his car and stepped into the street. As he approached, they turned toward him; he ordered them to stand back as he continued forward. On the ground at the lip of a sewer he found a small hacksaw. He frisked them and found another blade in the jacket pocket of one of the boys. He told them to walk across the street to the grocery store. While his partner watched them, he examined the door lock and found cut marks on the metal. He turned back to them and they stared at the ground. There was no basis for arrest, and he did not want to go into the station for the several hours it would take to process them and transfer their case to the juvenile authorities. He wrote up a curfew violation. "Now get the fuck out of here. If I see either of you around here again, I'll bust your ass." He threw the blade into the sewer and put the saw into his case to take home and add to his collection of tools confiscated from amateur burglars.

Two patrolmen were cruising along a major street on a wintry evening. They were driving slowly because snow squalls had iced the streets, making driving treacherous. They noticed four men standing very close together across the wide road.

"We'll come around and take 'em. You go uptown and I'll come around the downtown end," the driver said. The unmarked car eased to the curb and the officers quickly surrounded the group. The four men had not moved. After the recorder had frisked the men for weapons, which he did not find, one of the four, noticeably less well dressed than the others and slightly drunk, asked if he could speak privately to one of the patrolmen. The other three men began to move, until the patrolmen went forward, sticks ready; they froze in place. "Hey, Officer, these dudes stopped me while I was trying to go to Firth Street. They asked me for some money and I told 'em I didn't have none. They were gettin' ready to jump me when you pulled up. They told me to be cool and give me all that brother shit, but I gotta get outa here or they gonna get me when you leave." The patrolman questioned him briefly, looked at his identification, and then told him to "make tracks," while he and his partner kept the other three standing in place. "If I see any of you on the street again tonight, I'm gonna whip your asses so bad you won't walk for a week. Now get the fuck out of my sight, scum."

The patrolman is also alert to people who appear to be following someone down the street. He is alert for anyone shadowing a woman, although he must be careful not to misinterpret what he sees. "Hey, look at that guy following the broad," a man said to his partner. The older man glanced over and said, "Look again. They're talkin' to each other. He knows her. He just wants some and she won't give it to him." They watched the couple move down the street, the woman staying several paces ahead of the scurrying man.

Two policemen were chatting in their patrol car, which was parked at a dark corner late one summer night. They noticed three women walking toward them from a distance. As the women approached, the officers noticed two men trailing behind on the other side of the street. They seemed to be watching the women. The patrolmen focused their attenion on the men. The driver put the car in gear and kept his foot on the brake. When the men came closer, they noticed the patrol car, stopped, and turned around. The car moved forward quickly, and within seconds the patrolmen had seized a rifle and a knife from the men; the women disappeared.

Some patrolmen discreetly follow drunks down the street, using them as bait for muggers. While many car burglars pose as drunks and stagger into parked cars to check the doors and windows, many patrolmen hang back and do not stop them until they are certain the man is not a drunk. The policeman following a drunk carefully scans any passers-by or persons standing about for signs of interest in the drunk. He does not wait for someone to commit a robbery but checks any suspect for weapons or contraband. Some patrolmen park by all-night coffee shops and wait for a drunk to leave; then they convoy him down the street. (Occasionally a policeman waits outside a bar at closing time for a drunken man to emerge and get into his car. He then stops him and makes a drunk-driving arrest.) Frequently, while waiting, the officer will watch the young patrons of these places to see if they display any signs of interest in the older or drunk clientele. The patrolman believes he learns something about their inclinations by just watching them. He can always make a stop another day. He will be back and so will most of the people who loiter around these coffee shops.

These casual baitings are formalized by some plainclothes operations designed to trap-muggers. A patrolman told of following his partner, who was dressed up as an elderly woman, down a darkened street. He saw two boys trail "her" for a block, the younger approaching several times to snatch her dangling purse, only to withdraw at the last moment. He was being trained in purse-snatching. After his third failure, the older boy became angry and struck his pupil several times. Then they resumed their stalking of the intended victim. When they came to an appropriately dark spot, the older boy made the grab, and the pair was arrested.

4 · Concealed Weapons

In neighborhoods where street crime is common, the police believe there are many persons carrying illegal weapons. A patrolman who works these areas carefully scrutinizes the people he sees for signs of weapons or contraband. He is looking for any one of many signs that indicate to him that the person has what the officer is looking for. When the officer quickly scans the person as he approaches or passes, he is not just looking at the man generally but is actually searching his body from top to bottom, checking specific features that he believes offer good indications of concealments.

Contraband is often hidden in hats, but a policeman will not stop someone simply because he is wearing a peculiar hat. While some people believe that a policeman will stop a person whose manner of walking implies arrogance or audacity, the patrolman is more likely to stop someone whose hat is on straight than cocked a jaunty angle. The reason is simple: if there is a gun concealed in the hat, the weight of the weapon will dislodge any hat worn at an angle. Therefore, a hat that is sitting conventionally attracts the policeman's attention more readily, no matter what he thinks of any person walking down the street with his arms swinging out and his hat cocked over one eye.

When he is checking for a weapon, the first place the patrolman looks is around a person's midriff. Most people who carry guns illegally, and whose occupation does not involve their frequent use, learn to carry their guns the way people do in the movies and on television. They do not wear them in holsters belted at the side, where their arm will cover the bulge, or near the small of the back, where there is hardly any bulge at all, but stuck in their belt close to the front of their body. Frequently these people keep the gun on the side opposite their natural hand so they can cross-draw, believing this is quicker and sharper. Most of these people are in the ranks of the losers. During the winter the patrolman is particularly interested in anyone walking about with his coat open or slung over his arm. While many people remove their coats when they have had too much to drink, some keep them off to make their guns more readily available. The patrolman cannot assume that any bulge he sees at a person's midriff is a gun, although he must make that presumption if he intends to investigate. Most patrolmen have stopped persons only to discover a rolled-up newspaper in a waistband or back pocket. All they can do is apologize.

In warm weather the patrolman is alert for people who are wearing jackets, which may conceal a weapon. Any person walking about with one side of his shirttail out of his pants is very likely to be stopped because this is a ruse commonly used to conceal a weapon. If he incidentally notices that a person is walking with an open belt, the patrolman frequently will make a stop, because belts are often used as weapons. A sharpened buckle can be pulled quickly, the belt wrapped around a wrist and converted into a fierce weapon in a few moments. It has the added advantage of not being illegal.

Some people carry weapons in their jacket pockets. These are relatively easy to spot because the experienced officer notices whether one side of a jacket swings while the other hangs normally. He cannot know whether the person has a gun or a bunch of keys, nor can he find out until he has committed himself to making a stop. But he cannot make this commitment without acting as if the person had a gun. If he does act otherwise (and no policeman does), he assumes risks that may quickly terminate his career.

The patrolman believes that people who are not experienced in carrying a weapon—whether it be a gun or a knife—frequently touch themselves as they walk down the street. They do this to reassure themselves that what they are carrying is still there, to practice reaching for it so they will be ready when the time comes, and also to enjoy the feel of its presence. (New policemen who do not think they are being watched can be seen touching their gun or reaching back to see whether their blackjack is where it is supposed to be.) Patrolmen in high-crime areas look at people for signs of touching, particularly when possible suspects are approaching other people. The officer who sees some kind of touching has no substantive proof that he is being given evidence of weapons, but his experience indicates that this is a strong sign worthy of investigation.

The patrolman does not pay much attention to people's legs, because anything strapped on a leg is difficult to detect. Few people keep weapons on their legs because they are difficult to reach (unless the person is sitting). Therefore, the patrolman who is looking for weapons concentrates on the upper part of people's bodies. But if he sees a young person limping, he is encouraged to watch him more care-fully. In some neighborhoods where gang fighting is common, the "capmen," the boys who carry weapons into battle, con-ceal shotguns (even when they are sawed off) by strapping them to their legs. This requires walking stiff-legged and causes a limp. While some people have natural limps, many policemen believe it is better to check them physically than to assume they are limping by an act of God. During a meeting between some police recruits and youngsters from poor neighborhoods, one black boy questioned the intel-ligence of the police in the following terms: "In my neigh-borhood the cops are really dumb sometimes. I see a kid walkin' with a limp, I head for the nearest doorway, because I figure he's got a shotgun. And then you see the cops ride right past him like he don't exist. That's dumb."

Weapons are occasionally concealed in a sock or stuck into the side of a shoe. These are difficult to spot, but policemen are interested in people's shoes for what they tell about the character of the people standing in them. Ex-convicts and others who have been confined learn to walk with their toes curled and forgo the use of laces, which are denied them until they are released. The patrolman who sees a man with-out shoelaces presumes that he is looking at someone whose past history makes him worthy of closer examination.

The interest of the policeman in body cues is no more recent than his interest in people's appearance and response to his presence. The types of things he is looking for, how-ever, are changing constantly because of alterations in peo-ple's styles of clothing. An old police manual warns men who are watching for weapons that

> . . . extreme care should be taken. . . . A search of this kind should be thorough, as men have been known to carry pistols sticking in the sides of their shoes, in the seat of their trousers, on a spring fastened to the in-side of a derby hat, up a coat sleeve and fastened to the forearm by rubber bands, and suspended by a cord around the neck and concealed beneath the coat and vest.[1]

---

[1] William A. Dawkins and Cornelius F. Cahalane, *Police Reserve and Home Defense Guard Manual* (New York, Dutton, 1918), pp. 88–9.

The cues a patrolman seeks differ from place to place, from neighborhood to neighborhood. While it is possible that persons in all parts of the city carry weapons on the street, the police everywhere do not receive reports of fighting, wounding, and robbery that cause them to keep an alert eye for possible violators. The things a man looks for are greatly influenced by what he thinks goes on among the people he polices. But even in the neighborhoods where the patrolman is constantly looking, the cues and tips he looks for change imperceptibly but steadily. Five years ago a patrolman working in a black neighborhood probably stopped a man who had an afro haircut because he believed him to be a militant, a gang member, or someone who carried a weapon. Whether this was in itself a legitimate kind of cue or a prejudicial response to a cultural and political expression that the police-man (and many others) found reprehensible is open to ques-tion. Similarly, in white areas, persons with long hair were frequently suspected of being drug users and traffickers; they were stopped on sight just for having long hair. Few policemen are any longer attracted by these features alone. Many of the people the patrolman sees on his daily rounds have adopted these styles, including some of his colleagues. What was once suspect is now fashion. He may still dislike it, but he does not notice it any longer. Although there are shifts of clothing and style, there is no fundamental change in the efforts of persons made nervous by the presence of the police to control their concern, nor of the policeman to seek out cues and signals.[2]

5 · Car Stops

A policeman has an unqualified right to stop any car moving on a public street to check the operator's license and registra-tion. He may also stop any car whose operator has com-

[2]A 1950 directive of the Los Angeles Police Department urged its men to be suspicious of persons wearing sneakers at night. If a police-man today stopped everyone wearing sneakers, he would have little time for anything else. This may have been a legitimate cue at one time, although that is doubtful, but changes in the economy and in public fashion have made it appear utterly ridiculous. International Association of City Managers, *Municipal Police Administration* (Chicago, International Association, 1961), pp. 192–3.

mitted an infraction of the motor-vehicle code and issue a summons, which is a judgment of guilt that may be acknowledged by paying a fine in lieu of spending time in court. Most stops are made for violations of traffic regulations or to point out some fault in the car, and all of them are made under the umbrella of the patrolman's writ to check licensing, but often these reasons are incidental to his real interest. When a patrolman refers to a car stop, he usually means a stop he has made for suspicion. While these stops frequently reveal infractions of the codes regulating the ownership and use of cars, these violations are incidental to the officer's interest in finding stolen cars, cars carrying contraband, illegally armed people, and persons sought by the police. While cruising the streets, the patrolman is constantly scanning the cars in his vicinity, checking out the machine, the driver, its passengers, and the manner in which it is being driven. Each of these elements can produce numerous cues that arouse his suspicion and cause him to make a stop.

The patrolman carries with him a hot sheet, listing in numerical and alphabetical order the plate numbers of all recently stolen vehicles that have been reported to the police. Cars whose occupants are to be considered armed and dangerous, cars that must be guarded for fingerprints for investigations, and cars for which a reward has been offered are clearly marked. These sheets are continually updated and reissued, but they never contain more than a fraction of the stolen cars operating in the city. Even so, there are far too many listed for any patrolman haphazardly to check cars he sees against the plate numbers on his sheet. He does not look at the sheet unless he suspects something about a car or its occupants. But if he has some suspicion, he does not have to rely entirely on his intuition and knowledge to make an assessment of what he is seeing. The hot sheet gives him an initial check on his observations. If a plate is not listed on the sheet, this may deter him from a stop when his suspicion is not great, but if he finds only a "partial" listing, the first three or four digits matching, he is encouraged to make a stop. There are too many chances for errors in reporting and printing to allow the difference of a few digits to deter him from stopping a car he has come to suspect for other reasons.

When he discovers a listed car, his suspicion is great and

he exercises great caution in making the stop, but if the man is experienced, he does not assume that it is a stolen car. If the man is alone he will normally ask the dispatcher to send him another car as "back-up," but this precaution is not an indicator of his belief that the car is what it appears to be. Every policeman knows of stops and even fights in situations where the patrolman involved assumed he had a stolen car—stops that ended by having the outraged owner bring suit against him for false arrest. Often cars that have only been borrowed by a relative or a friend are reported stolen. When such a car is returned, the owner often fails to notify the police, who continue to list it as a stolen car. The policeman who places unreserved trust in the hot sheet is courting serious trouble.

The patrolman can use his radio to make a more thorough check on a car without directly intervening by asking his dispatcher for a "moving car stop." The radio is linked directly to the National Crime Information Center (N.C.I.C.) run by the F.B.I. in Washington. It is a computerized information bank, which is daily fed the latest listings for stolen cars, weapons, appliances, and credit cards by most of the police departments in the eastern part of the country. (The number of reporting departments increases each year and eventually the system will embrace the entire country. Many states have their own systems, which interconnect and overlap with the N.C.I.C.) The patrolman can ask for a check on a license plate without stopping a car, and within a minute (barring infrequent mechanical failures) he has an answer. Since a license plate is easy to change, this is only a limited investigation, but one the patrolman considers sufficient if he is not harboring strong suspicion. A more thorough search requires physically stopping the car and obtaining its serial number, which is stamped into the frame by the manufacturer. These are also listed with N.C.I.C. and are written on the owner's registration papers. With the serial number the policeman can cross-check information from several different sources and be fairly certain whether or not he has found a stolen car. If he is still not convinced, he can order the car off the road and have someone examine the car for the hidden serial numbers.

Professional car thieves alter numbers and forge papers for

the new numbers and fool many policemen, but there are hidden serial numbers on all cars whose location is changed from year to year and is known to relatively few people. If a patrolman's suspicions persist beyond an N.C.I.C. check (which rarely occurs), this is the final and foolproof test. Most patrolmen do not know where the hidden serial numbers are, and those colleagues who do generally will not disclose their knowledge. If they are called in, they insist on examining the car in private and then giving their opinion. No policeman takes affront at this since they all accept it as natural for a man to protect his information. But before any of this can happen, the patrolman has to have reasons to make a stop.

Most stops are made on cars that are observed from the rear or cars that have been allowed to pass the patrol car to enable the officer to see them from the rear. Many of the signs he is looking for are on the rear of a car, and this is where every policeman looks most closely. The first thing he checks is the license plate. Any unusual aspect immediately arouses his interest. A car with a paper tag or a temporary license is more likely to be stopped than one with a regular plate, because a person driving a stolen car frequently disposes of the original plate and replaces it with a paper tag, trying to get by on the claim that his tag has been stolen and he is waiting for a new one. A tag that is not properly attached, one fastened by wires or hanging on one bolt, is suspected because these are signs indicating that the plate may have been recently changed. Similarly, a dirty tag on a clean car or a clean one on a dirty car implies to the officer that the two have only lately been mated and their marriage not celebrated legally. In recent years many cars have had their gas caps moved to the rear, behind the plate; in consequence, gas spillage has caused many plates to fade. Patrolmen with detailed knowledge of cars occasionally stop a car whose plate has not faded, in the belief that its normal appearance raises the possibility that it has only recently been attached.

The quality of license-plate manufacturing varies from place to place. Some states have chronically poor plates, which frequently fade. This is sometime due to sabotage by the prison populations, who are obliged to manufacture most of the license plates used in the United States. The specific things that patrolmen look for on plates may vary from state to state, but there is no question that they all look for certain characteristics. Some states require two plates and this affects the way a policeman will look at a car. Volkswagen plates are attached at an angle that exposes them to the sun in a way that causes them to fade with some frequency. A patrolman spotting an unfaded tag might decide to stop the car for a check.

New license tags are issued in a certain numerical order throughout the year. Some officers often use their knowledge of this in relation to the age of a car or the amount of time the driver claims he has had it to judge the validity of his word. In many states it is possible to have personalized license plates issued upon payment of a supplementary fee. A patrolman sometimes will check a car he does not think is likely to have such a plate on it. This is obviously a subjective judgment but one the policeman feels is warranted if he senses anything else amiss with a car or its occupants.

There are many other features about the rear end of a car that may arouse the patrolman's suspicions. The most prominent is a missing trunk lock. While it is common for people to lose or misplace their car keys, obliging them to force open their trunk, a patrolman assumes that the owner will repair the damage. Similarly, any signs of pry marks around the rim of the trunk are noted and investigated. A car lacking a rear bumper is halted because it is operating without the required equipment, but the policeman's main reason for making the stop is to check the possibility that it has been stolen from an auto-repair shop. Any malfunctioning of the rear lights or the signal system causes the officer to make a stop. Policemen also use ruses about faulty lights to get unwary owners to open their trunks. While the unwitting person is checking his wiring, the policeman can look inside and check the contents. Bumper hitches used for hauling trailers are common in some neighborhoods. When he sees a car with hitches but lacking the crossbar attachment, a patrolman may make inquiry to determine whether the car has been taken from a garage, where the bar is often removed when repair work is being done.

There are certain features observable from the rear that make a patrolman suspect a car is carrying contraband. Many old cars ride low to the ground because their suspension and springing are worn out, but heavily loaded cars also tend to sag. When an officer sees a car riding low, he must decide whether he has a junker or possibly contraband cargo. Many bootleggers use old cars for this reason and also because, if they are captured, the state not only confiscates their cargo but the vehicle, too. "Continental kits" on the rear of cars are no longer common, but they once were frequently used as hiding places for weapons and contraband. When he spots a car with a kit, the patrolman who decides there is anything a little odd about the car is likely to stop it and look in the kit. Finally, if he notices that the rear window of the car is very dirty, he will make a stop. A common trick of contraband runners is to apply a blowtorch to the inside of a car's windows, as the heat causes permanent changes in the character of the safety glass, making it opaque. From the outside it appears to be simply dirty and grimy. Even if he does not know this trick, the patrolman is suspicious of any car he cannot see into easily, and this alone is sufficient to make him wary.

Any car that seems to have mechanical problems is likely to be stopped because the patrolman is suspicious of anyone who abuses his property. He knows that he would not drive his own car if it had the problems he detects in others, and therefore he feels justified in making an inquiry. If he hears a loud muffler, an engine making unusual noises (which may be caused by excessive weight in the car), or sees a defective tire, he will make a stop. Heavy damage also makes him look carefully at a car, but few patrolmen regularly stop cars for damage alone, unless it is on the front end and has no rust. In some neighborhoods people cannot afford to repair the damage to their cars and drive them as they are, since they need them for work. But new front-end damage can mean a drunken driver or a possible hit-and-run.

The lack of any discrediting characteristics on the rear end of a car is quickly overlooked if the patrolman discovers any sign that the driver is inexperienced or unfamiliar with the car he is operating. If he notices that a car is not keeping in the proper lane or moves back and forth without moving ahead rapidly, his interest is immediately aroused. Any car operating cautiously, traveling just below the posted speed limit, also attracts his attention. On streets where parking on both sides is allowed, new and inexperienced drivers tend to stay as far to the left as possible, because they are uncertain about where the right side of their car is in relation to the parked cars. If the patrolman spots a car straying to the left, he will give it more than a cursory glance. If a driver refuses to move out of his lane even when he has an opportunity to move forward or to avoid a stop, the patrolman takes notice. If the driver makes the wheels spin, indicating unfamiliarity with the car's power, or the car wobbles when making a turn, indicating the improper use of power steering, the patrolman may ride along a bit to observe more closely. All of these things are indicators of inexperience and nervousness, which can mean a stolen car or an operator without a proper license. While many patrolmen would not stop cars for these reasons alone, every man notices them and is encouraged to look more closely for other reasons to be suspicious. Some patrolmen claim they stop cars that fail to use their turn signals properly. This is a punishable offense of the motor-vehicle code, but relatively few tickets are written for it. It seems unlikely that many patrolmen are likely to stop anyone just for failing to give the proper turning signal, unless it is in a selective-enforcement area where the men are directed to look out for improper turns.

When he has noticed anything that arouses his suspicions, the patrolman checks the passengers before deciding whether to make a stop. It is very unusual for a patrolman to make a suspicion stop of a female driving alone or with other women. If he observes a woman driving a car in which men are also riding, he is more likely to check because this is seen as an unusual arrangement. Women are frequently used as drivers in holdups, and if he sees this combination in a high-crime area, he is likely to make a stop. A man driving with young children is frequently stopped if there is anything about the car or his manner that arouses concern. Any car with many people in it, especially teenagers, quickly excites the patrolman's interest. But he is particularly alert for cars being driven by young men, possibly with a companion or two. These are the people who usually steal cars and are most frequently stopped by the police.

Many of the things the officer is looking for are a product

of prior situations, a consequence of events about which he knows nothing, although he often makes assumptions about some of them. But there is evidence which he looks for that is produced (or he assumes is produced) by his presence. Any shift in the driving behavior of people around him is noticed and assumed to be the result of the driver having noticed the police. A man who suddenly becomes very cautious is as carefully watched as the person who suddenly makes a turn. If a car has a number of occupants and he does not observe them engaging in conversation, he assumes this is because they are focusing their energies on his presence and trying to act normal. The patrolman watches the driver carefully for any head or shoulder movements that indicate he is trying to check the police out in his rear-view mirror. A skillful driver, like a policeman, can use his mirror without much body movement, and some policemen move their cars right in behind a suspected car and look at the driver's face via the rear-view mirror. They try to catch the driver's glance, give him something to think about, and force him into making a move. The patrolman is also alert to any movement within the car that suggests something is being concealed in preparation for a stop.

If the patrolman is not sufficiently convinced by his observations from the rear (or notices a car only when it pulls alongside his own), he can move beside it or stop next to the car at a light and make additional observations. When he is beside a car, he checks for a broken vent window, which is the most common point of illegal entry into a car. He also examines the inspection sticker, which is usually in the lower-left-hand part of the windshield, to see if it is valid. (The license plate and the sticker are the first things a patrolman learns to look at, and the rookie officer begins to specialize his observation even before he fully realizes what he is doing.) He examines the clothing and appearance of the people in the car in relation to the type of car they are driving. If the car has any tourist stickers on it, he decides whether he thinks the persons in the car are likely to have been to the places indicated. He also watches carefully to see how the occupants react to his watching them. If he notes efforts to glance at him without directly looking over, he is likely to make a stop even if he has no other reason.

When he is stopped at a traffic signal, the patrolman is generally alert to all the cars around him. He notices any cars that appear to stop behind his line of vision. If he suspects a car is trying to avoid his direct observation, he hesitates when the light changes to see what the other driver will do. If the driver hangs back or jumps forward to pass quickly, the patrolman feels his curiosity confirmed and he may make a stop.

There are occasions when drivers are made so nervous by the presence of the policeman that they do things that rivet his attention. These actions are sometimes so bizarre that even the least aggressive officer is likely to intervene. One night a patrolman who was not highly regarded by his colleagues walked into the operations room, placed an elegant foreign-made .45-caliber automatic on the table, and asked the clerk to give him a property receipt. The other men in the room could hardly believe he had gotten a gun, let alone made a solo car stop. "He was real nice. He told me he paid 125 bucks for it in Baltimore last week. It's a real beauty," the triumphant officer commented. The lieutenant, not believing his eyes, asked him why he had stopped the car. "The guy was driving in front of me down Baylor Street. When we pulled up at the light, he drove out of his lane to go around the car in front of him. There was no room for him to get by, and he was stopped half on our side of the road and half on the other. It looked pretty strange and I thought he might be a 1037 [drunk driver], so when the light changed I waved him over," he said. "When I asked him for his cards, he asked me if I was gonna search the car."

"What did you say?" the lieutenant asked.

"Well, when I heard him, you know, I thought something was pretty funny and I told him to get out of the car with his hands in view. Then he told me that he was wearing the gun in the shoulder holster and didn't want any trouble. He was real nice about it. I just took it off him and called the wagon."

The lieutenant just looked at the officer, and unable to think of anything to say, he walked out of the room.

While the patrolman is looking for substantive cues indicating flight, fear, concealment, and illegal possession, he is also making judgments based on his perception of the people and places he polices. Many view his actions as punitive, but even a patrolman who admits to being prejudiced denies that he stops people simply because he dislikes "their kind." He may stop only people he dislikes, but then he usually stops only those people who give him cause, by their behavior or the state of their car, to question their "legitimacy." A white patrolman who does not like black people may be more inclined to look at blacks than at whites, but he is still looking for things that suggest evidence of crime.

Black people stopped while driving new cars sometimes accuse the policeman of stopping them simply because they are driving a new, expensive car. Patrolmen who do make these stops expect to hear this accusation and are pleasantly surprised when it does not come. This may be one reason why many patrolmen are reluctant to stop anyone driving an expensive car, although their sergeants and lieutenants often urge them to do so. At roll call one afternoon a lieutenant urged his men not to neglect Cadillacs and to stop looking at battered cars. "A good burglar is not going to drive some beat-up wreck. He wants the good life. Don't hesitate. If you treat 'em right, handle it the way you are supposed to, there will be no beef, and if there is, you know I'll back you." Big cars mean money, and money to most men means political connections and influence, which can hurt them and get them transferred to the subway or some other unpleasant place.

A patrolman stopped a car that was moving slowly and cautiously ahead of him. The driver, a young black man, was accompanied by two white teenagers, a male and a female. The driver handed over his license and registration without comment. When he was asked why he was driving so slowly, he replied evenly that one of his tires was bad and he feared an accident if he had to make a quick stop. The patrolman handed him his cards and told him he could go on. As the car drove off, the patrolman said, "I could talk to that kid all day and he would not believe why I stopped him. He thinks it's because he's black and there was a white cunt in the car with him. So what the fuck am I gonna do, stand here and have a human-relations course with him? I did my job right and proper, professional, and that's what counts."

When the patrolman sees a car moving quickly down a side street or hears the squeal of tires, he does not know who is driving. He may assume from the neighborhood something about the color or ethnicity of the person—which may be prejudice but is also fact—but his decision to pursue or to ignore is rooted in his notion of what is going on. If he goes after a car with broken lights, defective signals, or no lights at all, it is because he considers the car worthy of investigation. It is no different from pursuing some youth whom he sees running down the street on the "shoe-leather express." He wants to know what the boy is up to, so he pursues him. If a car ducks into a side street, or squeals its tires going away from the officer, he wants to find out whether the car is fleeing him or if it is fleeing for any reason which interests him.

The policeman's main interest in places and things is for what they tell him about the people he is looking at. A patrolman rarely pays attention to a parked car unless there are people around it. If he did pay more heed, there might be fewer car burglaries. But when he sees a car with its motor running or with an open door, he looks in, whether he sees anyone about or not. If he sees a man and a woman in the car, he is likely to pass along, but any deviation from this standard pattern is more likely to titillate him.

Two patrolmen were working late at night. They saw a car parked under a street light, a woman sitting in the front seat. One patrolman said, "That's odd. Look at that broad. She's sitting in the middle of the front seat. When they're alone, they usually crowd in the corner. Maybe there's a guy in there with her and we just can't see him because he's nice and cozy." They drove around the corner to get behind the car, and when they returned, the woman had been joined by a man.

The patrolman is not looking just for theft; he is also alert to catch a working prostitute or a male homosexual. Since these people do not work everywhere in the city, there are patrolmen whose knowledge instructs them that certain sectors, certain blocks are more likely to be productive than others, and they are always watchful when they cruise these streets.

A patrolman who sees someone standing on the street side of a parked car is not particularly interested because he knows that most breaking in is done from the curb side. If he sees someone wandering along the sidewalk, he checks him carefully. If he spots a man sitting behind the wheel of a car and another man standing in the street talking to him, he does not take much notice, but if the other man is on the sidewalk, the patrolman gives them his complete attention. This is the classic lookout pose—the man alert to the street, screened partially by the line of cars, while he watches for the police, ready to flee while his partner is working on the ignition with a wire. In areas where dope traffic is heavy, he is more likely to check people sitting in cars because transactions frequently are made in cars. But if he spots a sexually mixed group in a car, he is less likely to presume possible criminal intentions than if he sees only males.

6 · Privacy, Prejudice, and Public Order

There is absolutely nothing flattering or reassuring about receiving the unsolicited attention of the police. The stopping of pedestrians and motorists may be theoretically comforting to the people as a whole, insofar as it increases their general security (which cannot be demonstrated), but each individual action is personally unsettling and disrupting. Whenever a policeman stops someone, he is suggesting, no matter how delicately he conducts his inquiry or how much consideration he has for the feelings of the person stopped, that he sees something worthy of question. The person's sense of himself is placed in doubt, hints of inadmissible deeds are whispered, and a re-evaluation, even if only temporary, of what he thinks others are seeing when he passes in public is required.

The patrolman is not praised for all the persons he has not stopped, and he is only indirectly censured for failing to spot and stop people who have successfully concealed their illicit intentions from his watchful eye and escaped with the fruits of their criminal acts. He is damned each time he makes a stop. If he finds a gun or heroin, he is damned only by the person he has arrested and the suspect's circle of friends, while others praise him, or would if they knew of his actions. If he discovers nothing, he is privately cursed, and his actions become a topic of discussion not soon forgotten and easily recalled, among the suspect's friends and family. Many people argue that the police stop people for racial reasons (to "keep the niggers in their place," as once it was the Irish, the Italians, or whoever), to keep neighborhoods from becoming contaminated by unwanted persons, to harass the young, to suppress political dissidence, to exercise a private need to show their authority, or just to push people around. Undoubtedly each of these motives has inspired policemen in some places; occasionally one or another of these has explicitly been made public policy. But what about the policeman who is patrolling the street, genuinely concerned to fulfill his obligations by suppressing crime?

In some places at certain times a patrolman is likely to stop anyone he sees because everyone on the street at that time is suspect by his mere presence. This is not only a question of the character of the people who live there but also of the nature of the place. It is likely to happen as often in places where rich people live as it is in places occupied by the poor. The police chief in Beverly Hills, California, one of the wealthiest suburbs in the country, recounts the following incident:

I recall one incident involving a new officer who stopped a suspicious character and asked the man to identify himself. It was a former mayor of our city, out for a late evening stroll in his old clothes.[3]

Policemen are generally suspicious of people abroad at night. They have always been urged to look into the motives of persons they see late at night, although the definitions of "late" have changed. "The patrolman should closely scrutinize all persons whom they encounter after Midnight," one manual ordered; another suggested 10:00 P.M. as an ap-

[3]Clinton H. Anderson, *Beverly Hills Is My Beat* (Englewood Cliffs, N.J., Prentice-Hall, 1960), pp. 33–4. For other examples of police stops in well-to-do neighborhoods, see Charles Reich, "Police Questioning of Law-Abiding Citizens," *Yale Law Journal*, Vol. LXXV (1966), pp. 1161–77.

propriate time to begin questioning people's motives. When cities were still walled fortresses, the police began to watch people when the gates were locked and the evening curfew began.[4]

There are places where the policeman does not bother stopping people at night because he expects to see them there. Other places, possibly only several blocks away, elicit a very different response from him. These attitudes are rooted in his notions of what a place is used for. He does not see anything odd about questioning people at night whom he would not stop during the daytime. He knows that most street crime is committed during the evening; that burglaries of businesses, thefts of automobiles, street robberies, and muggings are crimes committed under the protective cover of darkness. Even if he recognizes that his attitude and manner restrict the rights of those people who like to walk about at night, there is little he can do about their objections. He sees himself as trying to protect their right to walk about unmolested. Since it is hard work, he expects people who are not guilty of anything to put up with any inconvenience and annoyance. He feels that if he did not do his work, crime would increase even more rapidly than it has, and the people who object to his stopping them would then attack him and the department for not protecting them.

Nobody likes having his property and person poked about, and that is precisely what a policeman does each time he makes a stop. The officer understands this but does not know of any way to appease people. If he is working in an area plagued by burglary and theft, he feels obliged to stop people who are carrying packages, particularly in the evening. He cannot know that the two men pushing a large carriage are brothers who are moving into a new apartment and are using their free evening time to do it, so they do not have to give up a day's wages. No matter how polite the officer is to them, he cannot disguise the fundamental fact that he has made a stop. They have no choice but to remain until he has finished with them. They cannot say to him, "Excuse me, Officer, but we really don't have the time for this right now,"

---

[4]George Hale, *Police and Prison Cyclopaedia* (Boston, 1893), p. 38; *Patrolman's Manual*, para. 35.

and walk off. If they tried it, he would probably arrest them. He knows they are angry at him; he sees the anger in their eyes. But he checks his temper, and when he is finished questioning them, he allows them to go without an apology. He feels they should thank him, although he knows this will never happen. He does not feel any guilt or sadness; he has done his job properly and correctly.

The great majority of suspicion stops occur in poor neighborhoods, because that is where street crime is the greatest, where the most drugs are sold in the streets, and where people are the least safe. In some of these neighborhoods policemen stop people for reasons many people might consider reprehensible. For example, when a patrolman sees a white person he does not know in a black neighborhood, he thinks the person is there to buy either drugs or sex. He knows that many people would think him prejudiced or cynical for harboring such thoughts, but he also knows that these people have not seen what he has seen. The patrolman stops a black man in a white neighborhood because he feels the person does not belong there. This may be an unwholesome perception, but the policeman's experience tells him it is by and large valid. The policeman making the stop is not questioning the person's right to walk there but the infrequency of its occurrence. For the policeman these judgments are rooted in the reality of city life. He is not making a moral judgment (regardless of what his private opinions are) but is responding to what he sees daily on the street.

The policeman rejects the notion that he stops people without reason. Even the most aggressive patrolman limits the number of stops he makes. There are no formal restrictions on his right to stop people. He has the authority and the power to stop anyone and to emasculate their objections with whatever force or argument he feels necessary. If someone declines to answer any questions put to him, which is his right, the policeman may take him to the station house for investigation. He does not think that the questions he puts to people are the kind an honest person would hesitate to answer. The patrolman knows that he does not go out and stop just anyone he sees. He assimilates his experiences, files away advice given and tested, accumulates information about people and places, and develops cues that suggest that one person in this place or another person elsewhere is a "good stop," a "quality" stop, as the contemporary police-training literature says.

The policeman does not stop people merely to fulfill a quota or to satisfy a personal whim. He often interferes in people's lives without their knowledge by taking their license number and investigating who they are through official sources. When he stops a person, it is because he has been given an indication that there is something worthy of questioning. Many of these people are law-abiding citizens; they may also be people who are contemplating criminal acts or have recently performed one. The policeman has no way of knowing except to stop them and ask.

He is obliged to rely on his own judgments because he cannot easily accept what he is told by a stranger who has been stopped because of some suspicion, no matter how slight. He knows that people do not like being stopped, and he limits, as much as possible, the amount of contact between himself and his suspect. Some people object to the surly manner of the policemen who stop them, their reluctance to explain the reasons for the stop, but the policeman knows that explanations frequently lead to arguments, complaints, or something worse. The patrolman is reluctant to reveal his reasons for stopping people because he sees his cues as private knowledge which, if it were generally known, would aid criminals and make his work even harder than it is. Also, he is instructed not to engage in lengthy conversations with motorists because these can be interpreted (or misinterpreted) as efforts to solicit money. Many men protect themselves by becoming "tough cops," who limit their conversation to the formalities of the investigation and offer no hint of their reasons for making a stop.

Many of the cues the police look for in assessing people are associated with poor people and people who are indifferent to the *mores* dominating our public life. Poor people drive the most battered cars, are least likely to keep them up or to have them insured against the damage that policemen question. (They also drive the cars with the highest rates of emission; strict enforcement of pollution laws will bear on them more than on others.) For these reasons they are the most frequently stopped. But they also commit the most street crimes, steal the most cars, and are most often the victims of their neighbors' depredations. Similarly, people who do not care to shave, who wear shabby clothes, and who walk about at night must put up with the possibility that they will be scrutinized and occasionally stopped by a patrolman.

The most widespread attitude of policemen toward stops in public, one which could be characterized as prejudicial, is also one viewed by most persons as entirely "natural." No policeman will stop a woman on the street without special cause. Although many policemen spend a good deal of their time looking at women, no policeman casually scrutinizes women for signs of suspicion, as he does the men about him. When a supervisor tells his men, he wants quality stops, he frequently will emphasize that they are not to stop any cars with women in them. When a patrolman sees a car peeling rubber, he may go after it, but one glance at the woman driving it is enough to cause him to slow down and turn his attention elsewhere. This is certainly prejudice of the most fundamental kind. But every policeman recalls with horror the times he or a collaegue has had to arrest a woman, the charges made against him, the screaming in the street, the cries of rape and assault that he thinks people will always believe and that he would be likely to believe if he were not the one accused.

The policeman is also confused and often angered by what he regards as the illogical attitude of the "public" toward stops and violations of people's privacy. He finds it inconsistent and baffling that people should object to his making suspicion stops, which are based on the substantive cues that he has developed during a career devoted to assessing the behavior and motives of people, while nobody seems to object to the methods he is obliged to use in order to make vice arrests. Indeed, he feels that he must make vice activity or he and his department will be accused of collusion and corruption. The policeman recognizes that he indulges in shameful and illegal practices to produce vice activity, pressuring people for information by threatening them with arrest on false charges, illegally searching persons for "gambling work"; but there is no public outcry. The patrolman knows only that he must get vice activity, and nobody seems to care a great deal about how he gets it. There are no complaints from the department when he follows people around, forces them to give him information, and takes out warrants illegally to search homes and cars. But if anyone alleges that in the course of a stop he was impolite or suggested he be given some money, he will have to give a written statement to his captain and he knows that he is being watched by his superiors.

The police use most of their plainclothesmen, undercover agents, and informants to gather information about gambling and other vices. There are no objections in the newspapers to this, only occasional demands that the police enforce the laws more vigorously and honestly. All of this is very confusing to the policeman who each day is doing his "straight eight," giving the city the full use of his body and mind. He is honorably following the knowledge of his trade which is rooted in the realities of city life. He makes a stop on a person for reasons he knows are valid and then receives a complaint, which is investigated by his superiors. At the same time he knows colleagues and co-workers, who never receive any complaints or are investigated by anyone, who are violating the law constantly in their quest for vice information; who take payoffs and gifts for not arresting people; who drive new cars and take nice vacations, which he will never be able to do. His hatred for these men is often intense and usually private; his feelings of isolation from the community he is hired to serve intensified. He does not understand how people can object to his doing what he considers real police work, although he recognizes it is unpleasant (and he knows that it is sometimes dangerous), when they want him to continue snooping into the private lives of the people he polices.

CHAPTER SEVEN

Cops' Rules

> **Son:** *You know, Dad, I think I'll be able to take you in a couple of years.*
>
> **Father:** *You think so, boy? Listen, when we fight, it ain't gonna be any of that stuff they teach you in the Boy Scouts. We fight cops' rules.*
>
> **Son:** *Hey, that ain't fair.*
>
> **Father:** *Why not?*
>
> **Son:** *Because policemen fight dirty, you told me that.*
>
> **Father:** *That's right, boy, and don't you forget it. Just remember, cops always win.*
>
> —A policeman and his son

The policeman's principal tool is his body. He shares with many persons the use of their bodies as a piece of equipment essential to the performance of their trades. He is similar to a mountain climber; to athletes whose success is rooted in physical prowess rather than the skillful use of equipment; to runners, circus acrobats, sexual performers, laborers, and peasants. He also has, in common with people in many trades, a set of skills that are needed for the effective use of tools expressly provided to expand the effectiveness of his body. For him a gun and a nightstick are not simply weapons that terrify some and intrigue others but extensions of himself whose use (and non-use) is linked to his notions about how he uses his body to do his work. But unlike anyone else

267

whose body is the tool of his trade, the policeman uses his to control other people.[1]

Despite careful restrictions designed to establish firmly the boundaries of his authority, the policeman is endowed with quite extraordinary power. Even in communities where there is intense conflict between policemen and citizens, there is little resistance to the notion that there ought to be people patrolling the streets, licensed to regulate public traffic and even forcibly to restrict and restrain people. The policeman's power and skills are not authorized and encouraged for the purpose of entertainment or production but for the maintenance of order and the preservation of authority. But regardless of whatever functions are assigned to him, whatever uses are made of him by the government, the policeman views his work in personal terms. Whether he works alone or in the company of a partner, everything he does is measured in terms of his individual capacity. The manner in which he works, the tactics and techniques he employs are greatly affected by the policies of his department and the attitudes of his city's government toward its citizens, but whatever style he uses, he is motivated by his need to keep whole his notion of himself as an effective and capable worker.

The policeman is a unique kind of user of the city streets. He develops an intimate knowledge of the places he works, a knowledge of his territory not matched by many of the people who live there. He knows it better than his own neighborhood, but he is not "at home" there. He does not know most of the people he sees or is called to assist, but everyone knows that he is a policeman. Every aspect of his appearance has been calculated to assure that there can be no mistake about his social identity. His uniform not only makes him visible to people who wish to find him but limits his snooping directly in the private lives of citizens; it also gives an unequivocal statement to everyone that the person intervening in their lives is not a private person but a cop.[2]

[1] I have benefited greatly by a reading of Erving Goffman's essay, "Where the Action Is," in *Interaction Ritual: Essays on Face-to-Face Behavior* (Garden City, N.Y., Anchor Books, 1967), pp. 149–270.

[2] It is reported that New York City patrolmen complain that they are sometimes mistaken for private guards because a number of private agencies have designed uniforms quite similar to the official police uniform. Nathan Joseph and Nicholas Alex, p. 723.

Out of uniform he betrays a self-consciousness on the streets he polices which expresses his own understanding of the special character of his place in public. When he's on patrol, people feel free to approach him for advice or help, but if he approaches them, there are inevitably tensions and unease that cannot be masked, even if the encounter is not marked by displays of incivility. The person approached cannot know what the policeman wants of him, and the policeman, if he is suspicious of someone, does not know whether his feelings are accurate. Every encounter the policeman has in public, except when he is called to aid someone, must begin with an abridgment of personal freedom. Regardless of how much experience he has accumulated in dealing with people, reading their demeanor and attitudes, he cannot know how they will respond to him. He is a public stranger whose authority allows him to do things that private persons normally avoid doing at all costs, but whose powers do not diminish the tensions created when strangers meet.

When a policeman stops someone on suspicion, their relationship closely parallels the contact between a common street criminal and his victim. While the person stopped may not be surprised by the intervention of the policeman—people in some neighborhoods are stopped frequently—he does not anticipate its occurrence. Once the policeman has committed himself to an investigation, he is also revealing the purpose and intent of his actions, although this is incidental to his main concern. A criminal tries to initiate his contact with a victim covertly, taking him by surprise, but at some point he must reveal his intentions to the intended victim (unless he is a pickpocket, who relies on skill and deception). While the policeman is legally empowered to make a stop (and in some places citizens are lawfully deprived of the right to resist even the unlawful actions of policemen) and the criminal's actions are sanctioned only by his willingness to risk his liberty and to use force to accomplish his purposes, both are strangers who suddenly intervene in another man's life, absolutely depriving him of his freedom, at least momentarily. The criminal naturally seeks to minimize the time between the initiation of contact and his departure from the scene, while the patrolman's purpose is to detain the person for as long as he feels necessary to conduct his investigation. Both must be prepared to honor any actions necessary to carry out their purposes, unless they are willing to fail. A policeman has no guarantee that after he has established contact with someone and even explained the purpose of his stop that the unease and tension created will decline. They may well increase. The person stopped may have something to conceal from the police, or he may object in principle to the restriction of his liberty. The policeman's knowledge of his legal powers encourages him to proceed with actions that he knows arouse considerable hostility, but he also recognizes that the law does not prevent people from objecting and even resisting him.

A suspicion stop is only the most extreme form of engagement which comprises most of the work a policeman does. When he is hailed on the street or summoned by the dispatcher, there exists between the policeman and the person requesting his aid a consensus regarding his function, but even in these instances, the bonds of agreement do not often run deep and are easily overturned. He assumes that what the dispatcher tells him is the truth as it is known to him, but the patrolman recognizes that he may have been misinformed or misled, or the situation may have changed between the time the call was made and he arrives at the scene. When he is stopped on the street, he is attentive to what people tell him, but he does not necessarily believe what they say. He has been lied to too often and has come to recognize that people are willing to use him in ways they would not use someone they knew personally. When he responds to a call, the action he takes may not be the one that those who summoned him want, and they are not unwilling to express their dissatisfaction to him. Even when he stops people for a traffic violation or some other minor matter, he cannot know whether the person he is approaching will treat the moment casually; he does not know whether he might be stumbling into a situation that is explosive for reasons he cannot anticipate. The policeman may think his actions are not to be regarded with great seriousness, but the other party to the encounter may feel wronged, may misjudge entirely what the officer's purposes are, or occasionally, when the patrolman's intentions are to advance his private interests under the cover of public law, may understand him too well.

The policeman brings to almost all of his encounters some degree of suspicion and uncertainty. The law formally recognizes that he must assume risks that citizens normally do not undertake and provides him with the means to protect himself. The potential danger that arises each time he places himself in contact with someone suspected of criminal acts or intentions can be reduced by exercising his defensive right to assure himself that the person is not armed. He may not only circumscribe a person's liberty by stopping him on the street, he may also completely violate the suspect's privacy and autonomy by running his hands over the man's entire body. The policeman knows that a frisk is a humiliation people usually accept from him because he can sustain his authority by almost any action he feels necessary. While he does not frisk people often just to humble them, he can do so; when he feels obliged to check someone for concealed weapons, he is not usually in a position to request their permission, even if this were desirable.

The policeman also carries powerful weapons that he may use only to defend himself, to defend others who are threatened physically, or to prevent the flight of persons known to be felons and impossible to halt in any other manner. These limitations on his right to use force are relaxed only in the most unusual circumstances. Only when martial law is decreed is the policeman authorized to exercise force without limitation, and these measures are generally accompanied by the introduction of soldiers, whose training and equipment prepare them to control people by brute force. But when a policeman shoots someone in a dirty, dark alley, no declarations are required. In some cities the entire matter is covered over, while in others there are careful investigations designed to probe the patrolman's motives and to remind his colleagues that the limitations are real and the boundaries of their authority are being patrolled. In either case, the policeman does not have to request permission to use his weapons. He is authorized by the community, theoretically, to carry them and to exercise judgment about their use. They are not only a protection and a comfort to him (as well as a heavy weight that strains his stomach muscles over the years) but also serve to remind him, if any reminder is required, that each time he knocks on a door, approaches a person, or answers a call, there is potential trouble. He does not go about his work in a constant state of anxiety, but he must be alert for signs of danger and threat.

A policeman has many responsibilities and opportunities to perform, but he measures his capacity to "do the job" (and is judged by his colleagues) by his success in policing people. He gets little comfort and pleasure from being a watchman patrolling empty streets, looking at rows of darkened buildings. That is why many patrolmen hate last out and go to sleep unless constantly prodded by their supervisors. Those who do not sleep may continue patrolling, but unless they are given a job and kept involved, they too become bleary-eyed and indifferent. However, a single call from the dispatcher awakens all but the soundest sleeper, mobilizing them for action. People interest him, or signs of mistreated or misappropriated property. An empty street offers him no challenge, nor is he comforted by the possibility that its being empty means there is nothing for him to be concerned about.

Although a policeman seldom becomes involved in fights, he carefully assesses the physical assets of all the people he approaches. He is always making appraisals of a man as he comes near, deciding whether he can "take him" if he must. This is not an expression of his lust for combat but a recognition of his place in the scheme of things. When he approaches an individual or a group, the patrolman is not only risking injury and pain, he is also placing on the line his capacity to do his job. Since his body is his principal tool, he cannot separate its protection and defense, which are instinctive, from his need to use it in the performance of his work. Each time he does a job of police work, he enters a situation where violent conflict is a possibility.

The moment he accepts the responsibility of being a policeman, he assumes the risks of physical combat. Regardless of his personal inclinations toward fighting, he takes it as a matter of course that he will be hit and in turn will hit back. If he has any doubts, they are quickly put to rest in his initial contacts with veterans. "None of you has been hired to go out and get yourselves killed, but you will take your lumps. If you aren't ready for that, stroll out now and get a job in a shoe store," a lieutenant suggested to a class of recruits on their first day at the academy. Several weeks later the same class was being lectured on testifying in court when one student asked whether a man who had been assaulted had to appear in court. The instructor sensed something inappropriate about the sentiment that prompted the question and, ignoring it, replied, "Listen, if you guys aren't ready to take your shots, you better quit right now. Because I'm tellin' you, somewhere along the line someone is gonna lay it to you. I don't care how tough you think you are. It happened to me, it's happened to everyone. With me it was my own fault, I was takin' a broad down a flight of stairs and I got a little careless. She jumped me and worked me over with a shoe before I punched her in the mouth. And dealing with a woman is the worst." Few policemen seek to hide the fact that they have been beaten. While many men conceal embarrassments, failures that resulted from their being outsmarted or from a personal lapse, they do not try to hide admissions of defeat from others or themselves. Perhaps it is a way of reminding themselves of errors made, of things learned and not to be forgotten, a reaffirmation of their mortality. "See that bar? My first night on the street they put me in the hospital. I was out for two weeks. The sergeant took me from roll call and drove me to that garage down the street and told me to stay put until he came for me. Shit, I wasn't gonna sit inside all night. So I started walkin', and right in front of this bar I got jumped by four guys. They really beat the shit out of me. I never been beat like that since. But I sticked a couple of them pretty good before I went out. I guess that old sergeant knew what he was talkin' about," the sergeant said, with a wry smile.

A patrolman approaches people in a variety of situations. He comes upon them driving and walking; he sees them in places where he has responded to calls for help; he is approached by strangers for advice and aid, goes with them into houses to break up fights and settle accounts. He enters crowded public places and deserted private ones, looking for the source of trouble that has brought him there. Since he must constantly confront people under widely differing circumstances, he cannot develop a single approach to all situations. He behaves differently when he is working alone than when he is with a partner who understands his manner. If he is a frightened man unwilling to take the easy way out of his dilemma by resigning or feigning work, he can allow the fears that assail even the bravest to control him. He may approach every situation with his holster unsnapped and his stick poised, but his colleagues will shun him and he cannot long remain on the job, although he may stay for enough time to cause pain and grief to himself, his colleagues, and whoever has the misfortune to cross his path.

He must learn to control his fears and anxiety by looking for signs of danger in the places and people he approaches; he must learn to examine people for signs of resistance, flight, and threat, to limit their chances of hurting him or creating situations he cannot control or can control only with the use of force, which is inappropriate to the circumstances. He must learn to use his body as a tool, positioning himself in an unobtrusive manner so that he is always able to retaliate with force if attacked, while not giving a threatening and provoking appearance. He must learn to use the powerful weapons he carries, so they will do what they are supposed to do and no more. He must learn when to hit people and when not to hit them. He must also learn how to establish and express his authority by cajoling, requesting, threatening, "bullshitting them," as patrolmen say, to avoid using force. He must learn to use his body to express with his whole self the authority represented by the appearance he presents; he must learn to use it as a weapon when the occasion demands. He must learn when to mobilize his physical resources and when to let them slumber, allowing his legal power to act for him. In all of his actions he must learn to acquire a quickness, resolution, and decisiveness that urge him forward when others withdraw. He must accept and welcome the fact that, as a policeman, he must be in control of the situation lest it be in control of him.[3]

[3]"If one examines moments when an individual undergoes . . . chances, whether as part of serious work or dangerous play, certain capacities, certain properties of his make-up, appear to be of intrinsic or 'primary' relevance: in high construction work, care and balance; in mountain climbing, timing and perceptual judgment; in game hunting, aim; in gambling, a knowledge of the odds; and in all cases, memory and experience." Goffman, "Where the Action Is," p. 216.

1 · Tools of the Trade

Although the police assume that force and violence are an inevitable part of their work, there is a noteworthy absence in their training of emphasis on the techniques and uses of force. There is no way of instilling in a man a set of sophisticated tricks without also encouraging him to use them. While many policemen consider the threat of force to be the most useful technique available to assure their success, the administrators of the police recognize that unless there is careful regulation of attitudes toward force, the men can easily get out of hand. Little time is devoted to physical training or contact exercises. The men are taught a few basic "come-alongs," handholds,[4] which are designed to move drunks, to walk an unsecured prisoner, and to disarm an assailant. There is no special judo training or suggestion that a policeman should develop sophisticated combat skills. The instructors warn the men that they are given only basic moves to be used in emergencies. "We don't teach anything fancy because if you don't practice you forget them, and when you get to the district there's no time for that. Just remember, if you're rolling around the street with someone and everything else fails, go for the guy's jewels, that's the basic rule," the instructor laconically explained. The essence of physical training is street fighting, and this basic form of urban combat depends almost entirely on a person's willingness to hit and to be hit.

"The last thing you want to do is to pull your gun, but you'll learn when to pull it and when to leave it alone," the instructor said, emphasizing the special character of the gun, a theme constantly stressed in police training. "If a guy comes at you with a knife, you must decide whether he is a drunk who can be knocked on his ass with your stick or someone who knows how to handle it. If he keeps shifting it, weaving the knife in front of you, putting it behind his back, you don't want to fuck with him. You pull your gun and aim for his chest. If he keeps coming, bury him. But you'll learn when to pull it and when to leave it alone."

[4] David H. Gilston and Lawrence Podell, *The Practical Patrolman* (Springfield, Ill., C. Thomas, 1959), pp. 13–15.

The lack of emphasis on combativeness and physical prowess suggests that the police presume that any man who wants to be a policeman has the physical assets necessary to do the job. The men are told bluntly and often, formally and informally, that they will find themselves in situations where the use of force is necessary, unavoidable, and occasionally desirable. But every time they are taught a technique or introduced to a new weapon, their instructors stress the limitations that the law imposes and remind everyone how easy it is to go over the fine edge between defense and terror. There is never a hint that violence is to be treated casually.

"We are trying to make this job into a profession, not some Irish goon with a stick like it used to be," the instructor said, with a grin. "You can hit a man who resists arrest and you can keep hitting him until he submits. But once he is subdued, you cannot hit him—then it's brutality. If you hit a man who is cuffed, if you beat someone in the station, even if you give a guy a shot after he gives up because he hurt you, it's illegal. You're not much of a man if you do. You'll see guys out there who do these things, fewer every year, but there are still some, and in this business I guess there will always be some. But don't you be one of them."

The department also wants everyone to go on the street confident of his ability to meet any challenges, able to stand up and learn the job. Nobody is discouraged from thinking that physical prowess and courage are not necessary elements in the patrolman's make-up. On the contrary, the men are warned that some of them will not be able to handle the strain of the job and will quit soon after they leave the academy. But they are discouraged from looking for a routine way of handling problems. They are urged to understand the difference between a man who is willing to use force and one who is eager to do so. It is this willingness that experienced policemen look for in new men, and every recruit is made to understand this.

One afternoon, a visiting psychologist gave a lengthy lecture on human relations. The supervising sergeant openly slumbered at the back of the room, displaying his contempt for the discussion. At one point the lecturer asked the recruits how they would react to being called certain kinds of names. When several responded correctly, saying they would ignore personal epithets designed to undermine their professional calm, the sergeant rose and began pacing about the room. He started to say something but caught himself and returned to his seat. A burly Puerto Rican recruit rose and in halting English expressed his feelings. He was well liked by all for his willingness to take part in any classroom demonstrations and for his bluff attitudes toward the academy, which most men despise by the end of the first month of training. "I don't care what anyone call me, spick or anything," he said, "just as long as they don't touch my body. They touch my body, I care, I care a lot." The sergeant bounded up from his seat, beaming. "That's a policeman talking. I want you in my platoon, boy. Keep your hands off my body, I like that. Oh boy, I just can't wait to see you guys on the street," he said, beaming.

A • NIGHTSTICK

While physical strength and will are necessary assets, the policeman is armed with weapons designed to multiply his power considerably and allow him, if he acts decisively, to control people who are stronger and bigger than himself. The nightstick is a modern version of a weapon whose origins can probably be traced to man's ancestors. It has long been the symbol of force and authority. When the police were royal servants, before they acquired their present name and organization, the stick was not only a weapon but a symbol of office. It was carved and emblazoned and often adorned with a crown of brass or of some precious metal if its wielder held high office, although beneath the adornment it was still a stick, an efficient weapon that could inflict considerable pain. In democratic societies the formal signs of a policeman's authority have been separated from the power he is given to support it. While this has probably had little effect on his behavior, it has greatly reduced the value of clubs as an object of antiquarian lust. The nightstick has been stripped of all adornment except for the groove marks on the handle which allow it to be firmly gripped. It is smooth all around to prevent cutting and gashing when applied to flesh. Nightsticks vary in weight and length, but generally are made of hard wood (oak, hickory, rosewood, mahogany) or a heavy composition (plastic or pressed paper) and are about twenty inches long.[5]

The recruit is given little training in the use of the nightstick, and what he is shown is of little direct value to him. His formal instruction is limited to the use of the stick in a riot formation, when it is crucial that each man coordinate his movements with the men on either side of him. The stick then is used in a thrusting motion, while the patrolman stands stationary, holding the ground assigned to him. This is a duty a patrolman rarely performs, but it aids the recruit by familiarizing him with the size and weight of the weapon. How to use it, however, is something each man must learn for himself, picking up hints and advice from colleagues.

His training with the stick begins the moment it is issued. As soon as he has it in his hand, he hefts its weight, slapping his open palm, tapping an available elbow left exposed by a neighbor. This is not just idle play or an expression of authoritarian lust but a naïve effort to discover the dimensions of the weapon. Instructors willingly discuss the use of the stick when asked, and their frankness is a welcome relief from the dreary homilies that permeate much of the training routine. "The most important thing is to always remember to take your stick with you when you get out of your car. A lot of guys forget them and it can cause you trouble. You don't always need it, but people really respect a stick. They see you coming with it and they think, Oh oh," an instructor said.[6] "Unless you are involved in a fight for your life, don't aim for a guy's head. You hit a guy in the head you can kill him. Sometimes you come across a guy with a skull so thick that you'll just bust the stick and he'll keep coming. Don't laugh, I've seen it. Down in the subway one morning, I was tryin' to move a drunk and he wouldn't go. He was really big, and I took my stick in both hands and whomp right on top of his head. I opened him right up and he just grunted,

[5] Erland Fenn Clark, *Truncheons: Their Romance and Reality* (London, n.p., 1935) tells the reader more than he needs to know about English police sticks, although nowhere in the volume is there the slightest suggestion that the object of study was used to hit people.

[6] "The baton has a great advantage in that when a subject sees you coming at him with it he can imagine that you are going to hit him with it." J. McCauslin Moynahan, Jr., *The Yarawa Stick and the Police Baton* (Springfield, Ill., C. Thomas, 1963), p. 59.

'Now I'm mad.' My stick was in two pieces and he was coming forward. I just backed up and pulled the iron, and he gave up. I'll tell ya, fellas, afterward I was ashamed of myself. Even if you do stop a guy with a head shot, he's gonna end up with a turban and you gotta stand him up in court. It's embarrassing."

The symbolic character of the stick is used traditionally to illustrate the policeman in a positive light by portraying the friendly beatman twirling it skillfully at the end of a leather thong and negatively by showing him with club overhead, swinging on someone's skull. While some policemen do both of these things, they are hardly characteristic of the manner in which a patrolman treats his stick. A stick held in the hand by a leather thong can be easily converted into a lever by someone else, severely damaging a man's arm or bringing him off balance. Most patrolmen carry their sticks in a belt loop, or if driving, they carry it under their arm when they leave the car. There is a tendency among men who work in cars to forget to take their sticks, and this is encouraging a trend among many patrolmen to carry a short billy, which they can hook onto their belt without discomfort. In some places policemen do use a leather thong, but it is rare to see a district policeman, a working cop, who allows himself this frill.

There are policemen who develop reputations among their colleagues as "headbeaters" or "headhunters," but they are relatively rare. The patrolman knows that the stick can be a lethal weapon if applied to the head, heart, throat, or groin. Unless he loses control of himself, which occurs rarely, feels that he is fighting for his life, or has become a vicious person, he avoids swinging his stick overhead. Often a man may inadvertently hit someone on the head and will little regret his error, since he feels that the injured man forced him to use the stick in the first place and he must bear the consequences. But the patrolman usually avoids the head because it is not only dangerous to the victim but it can be dangerous to him. When a man raises his stick to swing, he is telegraphing his intentions most clearly to the victim. He also opens his entire body to a counterblow. If he is involved in a melee, free swinging may cause him to "stick" a colleague inadvertently. "The first night I worked with him we got involved and I brought my stick back and broke his thumb," a patrolman reminisced. "Shit, the only one I sticked good in that whole fight was the fuckin' sergeant. I really gave him a good shot. But I don't think he noticed it was me," another man said, trying to repress a grin.[7]

The patrolman learns to use his stick as an extension of himself. He not only uses it as a weapon but as a prod to awaken and move people he does not want to touch. But when he uses it as a weapon it is a tool whose efficacy is greatest when he is in intimate contact with the person he is trying to control. When he uses it properly, he can inflict great pain without leaving a mark or causing lasting damage. He can control and subdue people much stronger than he, bringing tears to the eyes of the bravest, if he is inclined. Short, sharp raps on the shins, knees, elbows, and ankles can bring anyone to a standstill; a hard blow to the thigh can fell almost anyone. He can also terrorize a person by raising the possibility of a terrible beating, and naturally this is a threat he can make good if he wants to. He can use his stick to give someone a "good body thumping," avoiding the arms and legs, which can be easily broken, and he uses the grooved handle as the hitting end to ensure that his victim will be cut and will bleed. Few men ever use their sticks in these ways, but every man understands that a stick has this capacity.

The stick is also used as a probe to explore places where he does not want to put his hands. Sometimes he forgets to use it, and the experience can renew his respect for the tools he carries. Two men were patrolling a dark street late one evening. In the shadow of a building at a corner where muggings were common-place, they spotted three young men. "Let's check 'em out," the driver said, stopping the car and getting out quickly. While his partner covered the scene, left hand resting lightly on his gun butt, stick held down at his side in his right, the driver frisked the three men. At their

[7] "A disadvantage of the baton is that in a lot of situations you must pull the baton back in order to strike. This momentarily leaves you vulnerable to attack and also gives your opponent a forewarning that he will or may be struck." Moynahan, p. 59; Gilston, pp. 17–20.

feet was a crisp, unsoiled paper sack from a supermarket, sitting upright on the ground. The driver examined it while his partner moved closer to the three men, who were becoming edgy. He ordered them to stop moving about and to keep their hands on the wall. The driver said that he was finished with them, they could go. They did, quickly. "You drive, will ya," he said, holding his hand away from his body. Someone had defecated into the paper sack and the evidence was on his hand. "Listen, fella," his partner said, "just keep your hand out of the window. I sure hope it doesn't fall off. Been a cop all these years and you stick your hand in the bag. It's O.K., don't worry, I won't tell anyone."

B • BLACKJACK

While the most frequently used weapon a policeman carries is his stick, which is invoked far more often than it is used, he has with him another personal weapon that is rarely displayed without being employed. The blackjack is a terrifying weapon. Its history is not nearly so lengthy as that of the nightstick, but it possesses refinements that greatly multiply its capacity for inflicting pain and that indicate a process of development which was the consequence of much thought and observation on how best to injure people. The blackjack is derived from a commonly used weapon of the Middle Ages called the star, a studded metal ball attached to a chain. The star was gradually modified, made smaller and more compact, and eventually became the slungshot—a piece of lead on a thong or welded to a metal rod. It was a favorite weapon of street thieves in the eighteenth century, when pistols were scarce, expensive, and often unreliable. The blackjack is a refined version of this nasty bludgeon, but its improvements have not been purchased with the sacrifice of any of its power.

The "jack," as it is called, is basically a round or flat piece of lead encased in leather. The flat-leaded jack, slapjack, is preferred by many policemen who work in cars because it fits easily into their back pockets without causing discomfort. The round jack, called a convoy, is usually fitted with a spring handle that allows the weapon to be used with a whipping action, which greatly increases its force. The convoy is a lighter weapon and recruits are urged to use it because it is likely to cause less damage. The slapjack usually weighs more; it has a wider hitting surface and hard, thick edges which can cause terrible cuts, while the convoy will not cut a person if used properly. The instructors are frank to warn recruits of the dangers inherent in the blackjack, seeking to instill an understanding of its power and danger.

"A jack is a beautiful weapon, but it is very dangerous, fellas," the instructor said. "I remember once we were looking for a guy who had beaten up a policeman and escaped from a wagon. I found him hiding under a car. To this day I don't know if he was coming out to surrender or to attack me, but he was just coming out before I told him to move. He was a real big guy and I didn't wait. I had my jack ready, and as he came up I hit him as hard as I could. I thought I killed him. He was O.K., but since then I haven't carried a jack unless I was going on some dangerous job. I don't want to beat someone to death, and with a jack you can never be sure. You should get yourself a convoy and use it in your fist. If you punch for a guy's heart, the whipping action of the spring will snap it forward and break his collarbone. Then you've got him."

Warnings and pleas are all the recruit receives. How can he be trained to use a weapon designed to injure and incapacitate? The department wants him to think of the blackjack as an emergency weapon used to defend himself in extreme situations. "Listen, fellas, I'm not supposed to talk like this, but since you're going on the street in a couple of days, I'm gonna give you a little advice," a popular instructor told a group of recruits. "I see some of you are carrying the Big Texas slapjack. Get rid of it. You get worked up out there, lose your temper, maybe you hit someone with the seam. You might as well kill him. You'll break his face in two and give him a hundred stitches without meaning to. That kind of rough stuff is out, guys; they'll give you ten days for nothing now. Get a convoy, it rubs your ass but it's safer, and believe me it will do the job." Throughout the final week at the academy, the instructors urged those who had not changed their jacks to do so, although several men insisted on keeping their slapjacks.[8]

The patrolman learns the power of his jack in the same way that he learns the characteristics of his stick. One light tap on his palm or elbow informs him of its terrible power, and he treats it with the respect due an instrument that can casually inflict permanent damage. Whenever the jack is mentioned in discussion, its use as an emergency weapon is emphasized. He carries it in a special pocket at the rear of his trousers or tucked into the front of his jacket in winter, but he rarely walks about with it in his hand. It does not look imposing or give the impression of being awesome. It is not a symbolic weapon but a lever that multiplies several times the amount of force a man can deliver with his arm. He is told that the jack is a knockout weapon to be used only when he wants to subdue someone quickly without worrying about the injuries he inflicts. "If you gotta use your jack, give him your best shot first. I never used one, but I seen a lot of guys fuck around, tap, tap, tap. You do that, all you end up doing is cuttin' someone, you hurt them, make 'em angry, and you don't put 'em down. When you use your jack, you want to put them down and out, and the way to do that is with the first shot. But you're better off if you never use it," an experienced veteran told a small group of rapt listeners.[9]

Men who forget their sticks when going on a job often rely on their jacks if they must become involved. Even though the jack can inflict considerable injury, it is less dangerous than drawing a gun. But most men do not use their jacks except when they are involved in hand fighting. Some men who cannot fully control a suspect whom they are going to search or frisk place their jacks at the base of

[8]The blackjack is the only piece of equipment that the Philadelphia patrolman must buy out of his own pocket. He receives an annual equipment allowance for everything which is not issued that he is required to have. When the police were established, the patrolman had to buy his own equipment, just as mechanics still own their own tools. In some cities the men are still required to buy their own gear.

[9]On the use of the blackjack, see Rex Applegate, *Crowd and Riot Control*, 6th ed. (Harrisburg, Pa., Stackpole, 1964), pp. 155–7; Gilston, p. 21.

the man's skull as a warning of what he can expect unless he stops fidgeting about, or they give him a light tap on the elbow, telegraphing a hint of what can follow. A blackjack can easily be used to inflict terrible pain and punishment. A man is usually involved in a fight with someone when he reaches for his jack, and he can easily cross the line between defense and punishment, even accidentally. A policeman knows when he is "tuning someone up," giving him a "lamp job," when he is beating someone beyond the legal limit in order to indulge a personal hate, but when he has a blackjack in hand, he may inflict serious wounds without meaning to.

C • REVOLVER

"O.K., quiet down. As long as you remain in the police department, the revolver you have just been issued is yours, until either it or you is destroyed. Well, fellas, it happens, you know," the firearms instructor told the assembled class. "We are going to spend the entire week teaching you how to fire this gun, and when you leave here, you will not be able to claim any excuse for making a mistake. You make a good move and they will take you downtown and give you a ribbon and your picture in the paper. Make a mistake and you are it, boy. You may think it's rough, but that's the way it is. You got a badge and a gun, but you live under the same rules as everybody else. There are only two reasons for pulling your gun and shooting—self-preservation and shooting a fleeing felon. You must know he is a felon. You must have seen him commit the crime. You shoot some guy running down the street because he don't stop, you're it. What are you gonna do, put him in your car and take him home? You do not shoot from a moving car under any circumstances. You do not shoot at cars that refuse to stop on your order. You do not fire warning shots under any circumstances.[1] If you have a problem you can't handle and

_____

[1]"A policeman may NEVER fire warning shots. Each time [he] fires his weapon he risks the wounding or killing of an innocent bystander. A gun should never be fired over someone's head merely to frighten a suspect into submitting to arrest. The revolver is not to be considered a

you all will, you don't pull your gun—call an assist or ask for some help, that's what the radio is for. If you need security, carry a blanket, but leave that gun in your holster. In the old days we had police shoot innocent people and it got passed off as 'he meant well' or 'he was doing his best.' Today we have a different society. If you kill someone, they want your neck. You don't have to like it but that's the way it is and you can always quit."

The American police, like their British counterparts, were unarmed except for sticks when they were first organized. Even sticks were not regularly carried on patrol by all policemen. Some departments had stores of sabers for emergency situations which were issued to the men and then collected when the city returned to normal. Some detectives carried guns in the eighteenth century, and although they were not regularly used by the police in England, they were more common in the eighteenth than in the nineteenth century. In America the city police began to carry guns informally during the middle of the nineteenth century. Some men who worked in tough areas bought their own weapons and carried them for protection against a population that was already beginning to arm itself with the relatively inexpensive and reliable revolvers being developed in América. There was considerable public demand that the police be armed when a number of unarmed policemen were murdered, but no official action was taken until after the Civil War. Soldiers brought arms back from the wars, and many patrolmen carried guns for protection in cities made more violent by passionate war and immigration. The police were then officially armed in order to regulate the collection of weapons of varying types and calibers which were in use. The police have resisted every subsequent effort to disarm them, and it is simply fatuous to think they will contemplate

---

crutch or scare weapon. Once you have decided to fire the weapon, you must be prepared to take the ultimate responsibility of inflicting death." Philadelphia Police Department, *Criminal Law: Use of Firearms,* Pamphlet 10, n.d. Some departments permit the use of warning shots. In New York City during 1970 policemen fired 183 warning shots in 81 separate incidents without causing injury, according to official departmental records. *The New York Times* (July 25, 1971).

sacrificing their weapons at a time when the populations of
our cities are arming themselves at an unprecedented rate.[2]

A revolver differs from the other weapons a policeman
carries in two important ways. First, it is a machine that,
while requiring his will and decision to operate, does not
oblige his involvement in its functioning. It does not take
much effort to pull a trigger. Second, the revolver is designed to kill people, and the police take great care that every
man issued a gun knows this. Each patrolman is issued a
six-shot, four-and-one-half-inch-barreled, .38-caliber revolver. The standard police .38 is favored because it requires
relatively little servicing, is not easily damaged if dropped or
used as a club, as it occasionally is, and will rarely misfire
unless it is cocked. It is also deadly at short range. "Every
time you fire your gun, there will be an investigation," the
lieutenant said. "I am one of the investigators, so listen
carefully to what I am saying to you. This gun will not fire
accidentally unless there is a malfunction. It will be carefully
checked for damage or defects. Unless you cock this weapon,
it will not go off, even if you hit it with a hammer. So don't
lie. And please, don't ever cock it unless you are prepared
to shoot someone."[3]

Before the recruit is even allowed on the pistol range, the
instructors carefully and clearly explain why the policeman
must use great caution with his gun. "Boys, there is no bullshit here. Forget all that crap in the movies and on TV. We
don't go for any of that F.B.I. crap here, no wing shots at
fifty yards. Under perfect conditions, with no pressure and
no time limit, I can hit a man at one hundred yards with
this gun, but on the street, under pressure, facing threats,
when you pull your gun to shoot, you are not going to wing
anyone. Even if you were that good a shot, you'd have to

[2]On arming the American police, see Lane, pp. 103–4, 134, 203;
Richardson, p. 113.

[3]Many policemen prefer a .45-caliber pistol, which is used by
the military police becase it has greater stopping power. A larger
bullet has lower muzzle velocity and therefore hits a solid object
more slowly, causing a larger wound and heavier impact. The smaller
.38 often will seriously wound a person without knocking him down.
However, the .45 requires considerable servicing and is likely to jam
unless it is cared for regularly. Applegate, pp. 297–9.

practice every day to keep your edge. When you pull it, you are aiming for the largest part, the middle, and you are shooting to kill, whether you mean to or not. Every time you fire this gun, you run the risk of killing. That's why we don't permit warning shots. You have no idea where the bullet will go, you don't know whether it will bounce off something and hit an innocent person sitting in a car. When you fire your gun, it's in defense of your life or to stop a felon without endangering the lives of innocent people. If someone is escaping down a crowded street and you start shooting, God help you. Don't forget it."

Live-ammunition training is designed to stress the fatal character of the weapon and the intimate circumstances in which most police shootings occur. Most of the firing is done from seven, fifteen, and twenty-five yards at fixed targets, which are body silhouettes with one arm concealed behind the back. Each part of the silhouette has a point value determined by its importance to a person's survival and ability to resist. A shot in the right arm is more highly rewarded than a shot in the leg, with kill shots being the most highly rewarded. The fatal character of shooting is emphasized at every possible opportunity in an effort to discourage men from reaching for their guns. If a man thinks himself competent with a gun, he may be willing to risk an effort to incapacitate someone when his gun should not even be unholstered.

At the shortest ranges the men are taught point shooting—shooting to survive. Most police shootings occur at these distances, and the training emphasizes the suddenness of their occurrence. In point shooting there is no aiming, the gun is simply shoved in the direction of the target and fired. You are shooting to kill. The patrolman is instructed to bend forward slightly as he draws his gun, placing his free arm across his chest. This is done to make the target he offers smaller and to use the large bone in his forearm as a deflector of any bullets that may be coming in his direction. "This is the kind of firing you are most likely to get into, fellas. It's you or him, and it's very close. No aim. You draw your gun quickly and safely—don't shoot yourself in the leg—and make like you are putting the barrel into his stomach.

Then squeeze." The instructors realize that many men will be terrified when they draw their guns and tell them not to be worried if they are shaking. They are shown a two-handed grip which allows a man to steady his gun with his free hand, permitting him to shoot more accurately. "If you ain't scared, you're nuts, but you gotta shoot straight," an instructor said.

When he leaves the academy, the patrolman is given a revolver and twelve bullets. He may buy any kind of gun to keep in his home, but he may carry only a .38 caliber on or off duty. The men are issued a lead bullet, which flattens and falls when it hits a solid object, reducing the risk of ricochet. Some men carve the heads of these bullets, causing them to flatten when they hit flesh, increasing the size of the wounds. Also available in police supply stores is special ammunition —steel-jacketed bullets with hollow points which shatter on impact, causing terrible wounds that are frequently fatal. Most departments have strict regulations against carrying unauthorized ammunition, but supervisors rarely check their men's equipment.

Every large department has special sharpshooter and anti-sniper units whose members are trained to use all types of ammunition, are allowed to carry Magnum revolvers, high-powered .38's, and have available to them semiautomatic and automatic weapons. Some of these men carry shotguns in their cars loaded with rifled slugs called "pumpkin balls," which can blow open a heavy wooden door at close range. Some departments even acknowledge that their men are allowed to carry the hollow-pointed SuperVel bullet, and several federal police agencies have made this ammunition standard. These bullets are prohibited by international treaty because "dumdum" bullets, as they are commonly called, are considered too ghastly for international warfare. The use of these bullets and the deployment of shotguns and automatic weapons can be justified only when the purpose of the police is to kill. Even if a policeman is likely to kill when he shoots, he is still using his gun in a defensive manner. But when he uses these special kinds of equipment, the chances of his not killing are slight. The defensive character of his actions has been eliminated and he is engaged in actions inspired by an inclination to use terror as a policy.[4]

The patrolman is not allowed to carry any weapon other than his stick, blackjack, and revolver, although there are some esoteric tools for inflicting great damage on human flesh available at police-equipment shops. Most patrolmen do not violate the strict departmental regulations, but there are still men who carry and use prohibited weapons. Even though the department forbids men to carry more than one gun on duty, in times of tension some men will take their own shotguns with them for the security it gives them. (There are also men who keep unregistered, confiscated weapons in their possession, in violation of the law, to be used, if necessary, to provide evidence for false arrest.) Rarely seen any longer are brass knuckles, which are now made of aluminum, but they have been replaced by a much more efficient weapon. Lead-loaded sap gloves are proudly described in one equipment catalogue for their deceptive appearance. "You would never know that this handsome flexible dress glove made of genuine Deerskin is loaded with 6 oz. powdered lead saps, built in." The catalogue neglects to add that you would not know until you were hit with them. These gloves come with the lead in the palm or the knuckles, giving a man the option of slapping or punching a person. Either is devastating. The only purpose of this weapon is to inflict punishment and to terrorize. Some men hollow out their sticks and have them filled with lead, making them much heavier to carry but much more potent. This is not prohibited, but few do it because of the added weight. Some men dispense with regulation sticks and carry an ax handle, or purchase a stick fitted with a metal ball on the knob end which can inflict severe pain and injury. Most men believe that there is less "special" equipment about than there has been in the past, and they attribute this to the pressure applied by the department against those who are caught in violation of the rules. But unless there is constant vigilance, some people will always exploit their situation or seek to increase their chances of success by carrying equipment that

[4]On special ammunition, see *The New York Times* (July 5, 1970) and *Philadelphia Inquirer* (January 9, 1970).

is designed not to defend the patrolman but to terrorize the people he polices.[5]

The patrolman treats his weapons as tools of his trade, necessary for the performance of his work. He understands their characteristics and realizes that they can inflict damage far beyond anything reasonable or necessary to do his job or protect his well-being. Their effective and proper use is for him a technical issue that is a measure of his skill as a policeman. Many men go through an entire career without using either a gun or a blackjack. Some men resign the first time they are obliged to hit someone with a stick. There is a characteristic and unforgettable sound when the "wood is put to someone" that some men prefer not to hear. As he learns his trade, the policeman also learns to use his weapons as extensions of himself, to be employed only when his performance is threatened or his autonomy and safety are being undermined. He does not treat them as toys, objects of play. In the station house it is not uncommon to see a man hide another's stick or steal his hat; this horseplay is common and accepted. Nor is it rare to see a man reach back for his jack or place his hand on his gun butt in mock anger, but only rarely does he draw them. A man may tap a friend with his stick, but only someone with whom he has a clear and strong relationship and only in a situation where there is no possibility of misunderstanding. The use of force is something every policeman must make a part of himself, something he must always be prepared to employ effectively and whose consequences he clearly understands.

2 · Controlling Space

Signs of danger and trouble suggest withdrawal and flight to most people, but for the policeman they are signals of

[5]Special gear does not have to be purchased; it can also be devised, as the following indicates: " 'What's your best punch?' 'Right cross.' He nodded and took my right hand and began to tape it, the way a boxer's hands are taped. There was a difference however. After a couple of turns of the tape, he laid two half dollars across my knuckles and then taped them in place. When he was finished, he said, 'Now put on your kid gloves.' " These preparations were made for a raid on a bar where a gang of muggers had their headquarters. It was in New York City during the late 1920's. McAllister, p. 137.

obligation and opportunity. He must be prepared to advance when others withdraw and to advance quickly to limit the risks which he takes. The only way a policeman can neutralize a potential threat is to take the person physically in hand, to unman him in some sense. When he decides to make a stop on suspicion, he does not approach at a leisurely pace and politely introduce himself. If the person has a gun, lingering at a distance invites disaster. But any degree of suspicion suggests the person may want to evade him, and if the officer hails him from afar, there is the possibility of flight and chase. These are not simply signs of resistance that must be extinguished but evidences of failure which will cost him considerable exertion, at the very least.

Frequently the patrolman must enter places where his vision is limited and there is always a chance of his being surprised. He is confronted with the dilemma of having to proceed quickly, especially in an emergency, and at the same time having to slow down in order to limit the danger to himself. But most of the places he goes to are peaceful and orderly. While danger may be everywhere, the policeman seldom encounters it. If he gives the impression of being cautious and suspicious wherever he goes, he will create tensions and disorder. He does not want to reveal any hint of reluctance to himself and to those who watch him, because the slightest fear can grow and cripple a man's capacity to act. "I was lookin' for a couple of guys who had run as I came around the corner. I saw 'em come into that alley, so I got out and went in after them. I told radio before I got out of the car, but it was no emergency. So I went up and I didn't see nobody and figured they made it out the back. The next day an old guy stopped me on the street and told me he had seen the guys run into an abandoned house at the back of the alley. They both had guns. He was afraid to yell because he thought they might start shooting and I was a sitting duck. So you never know, do you, buddy?" a patrolman said to his partner.

Statistically, a police car is the most dangerous place for a patrolman to be. More men are injured in accidents than in any other way, but the policeman feels completely secure in his car. He sits in an enclosed space with the crackling radio at his side, his contact with hundreds of colleagues

willing to risk themselves for him, an insurance that under-
writes his willingness to take risks. Although he is cautious
about allowing men to approach his car while he is seated
(women and children are welcome), he does not conceive of
any danger when he is in his car. Even when he must put a
prisoner in the rear seat, taking the precaution of placing
him in the far corner if he is alone, he does not think the
car contains any danger for him. But it is common to find
razors, lengths of pipe, and knives on the floor of a car, left
there by a complacent policeman.[6] A policeman does not
search his car at the start of a tour, although he is required
by department directives to do so. His car is a place where
he sits many hours each day; it is his safe place. Danger is
outside, in the places he is looking at, and his sense of security departs the moment he emerges. Each time he gets
out of his car, he assures himself in some way that he is
ready for anything. Even if he is only going to lunch, the
patrolman hitches his gun, making sure that it has not fallen
out of the holster onto the front seat. There are numerous
occasions when he does not carry his stick with him, but
he always assures himself that his capacity to retaliate is not
impaired. Even under stress, when he must rush quickly from
his car, he slaps his back pocket to assure himself that his
jack is there or unhitches the leather safety strap holding
his gun in place.

Whatever his purpose, the patrolman carefully and casually checks the terrain as he advances. ("Remember, there is
nothing routine in this business. No such thing as a routine
car stop. When you go to sign a store log, look in the window
first to make sure that nobody is lying on the floor under a
gun," an instructor said.) When he enters a store to answer a
complaint or to buy a package of cigarettes, he glances
through the window before entering. In ghetto neighborhoods, where continuous vandalism and the lack of insurance
have forced many businessmen to operate behind boarded
windows, the patrolman does not stride in. He lingers at the

---

[6]The following is from an official division memo: "During a recent
inspection, the following items were found . . . 2 straight razors, 1 large
pocket knife. . . . This meant that [men] drove around with persons in
the rear seat armed [sic] with cutting implements capable of inflicting
grievous or even fatal injuries."

doorway for just a moment, monitoring the scene by reading the behavior of the people who are there. If he is going on a call where the possibility of violence exists, he checks the interior through a window before rushing in. This may be only a quick glance, but he takes the moment, and if he does not, there are colleagues who will tell him that he is stupid. If there is no way to monitor the interior, he knows that the safest course for him is to move forward quickly rather than to hang around outside.

Two patrolmen were searching for a man who had committed a robbery. The victim had told one officer that he had been followed from a bar after buying some beer and held up several doors from his house. The robber had fled on foot, back in the direction of the bar. After finding nothing on the street, the older officer suggested that the robber might have returned to the bar to brazen out the search for him. The bar had frosted windows, which made external observation of the interior impossible. "Ruby, you cover the door," he said, unsnapping his holster and pushing the door open. He stood still for a moment, carefully looking about, and then entered. With his hand near his holster, he walked slowly past the silent, staring patrons to the rear of the bar. Using his stick while standing aside, he pushed open the doors to both bathrooms, finding them empty. He retraced his steps and joined his partner at the door. They departed as silently as they arrived, backing out of the door.

On another occasion several officers were standing in a parking lot on a Friday evening when a woman excitedly approached and said there was a young boy with a rifle in a nearby restaurant. The officers ran toward the building from two directions and looked through the plate-glass windows for any sign of disorder. Although there was no evidence of a disturbance or of a rifle, the woman had sounded so sincere and frightened that they were inclined to believe her. Both men unholstered their guns, one placing it inside his coat, while his partner kept his down behind his left thigh. Most patrons in the crowded eatery had no idea that the policemen had their guns in hand, although whispers could be heard: "Shit, man, he's got an iron," "I'm gettin' the fuck out of here before he caps me." They found nothing and left the restaurant just as a car pulled up with a boy in the back seat. A patrolman had spotted him running down the street with the rifle in his hand.

A doorway or a corner represents a clear hazard to the patrolman because he cannot know what is on the other side. He must learn to take precautions without compromising his decisiveness and will. On the face of it, common sense suggests that a person should not run around a corner without checking, but in their haste to make a pinch, many young officers forget and fling themselves in harm's way. They must learn by accident or example to protect themselves without losing their effectiveness.[7]

Two patrolmen were investigating a report of a man with a gun. The bartender told them a patron had pulled a gun and then fled. He claimed he did not know the man. "You're a fuckin' liar, pal," one officer said. They were standing on the pavement and one officer noticed a man standing at the corner, staring at them. The man turned slightly and there was a glint of metal reflected from the street light. "There he is," the younger man yelled, running toward the corner where the man had been. The older officer raced along the inside of the sidewalk, while his rookie colleague, gun in hand, ran along the curb. When they arrived at the corner, the older man reached out without looking and barred the younger man's way. "We look first," he muttered, peering around the building. His holster was unsnapped and his hand rested on the gun butt. They saw a man throw something beneath a car, and the older man charged, had the suspect in hand and bent over the hood of the car before his partner arrived to aid him. He had had to stop and holster his gun. "Nice pinch," the older man said with a grin, as his colleague retrieved two guns from the gutter.

After the suspect was taken to the station, the young officer thanked his partner for warning him. "When I was in the academy, I never thought I would draw my gun. You

[7] An example of learning the hard way is given in Radano, pp. 98–105.

know, I didn't even know I had it in my hand." The older man nodded and said he would learn when to pull it out and when to leave it. "But do me a favor, next time you draw it, don't put your finger on the trigger. It's bad enough worrying about these motherfuckers without worrying about you shooting me." His tone was absolutely friendly, but he was giving his partner an order, not advice. He knew an important moment had passed in a new career. He knew that the rookie had shown courage in the face of potential danger. Nobody can predict how a man will react when confronted with the "real thing"; the new man had shown determination and willingness. But he had to learn about his errors, to be made to realize what potentially disastrous things he had done which should not be repeated.

Some of the precautions he takes may appear innocuous and superfluous, but the experienced policeman does not neglect them, even when he does not anticipate trouble. Even when going on a meet complainant, he will glance in a window, if there is one available by the door. When he knocks or rings the bell, he stands to the side of the door if there is room. If there are two doors, the outer one opening toward the street, he keeps it open to prevent the possibility of its being used as a weapon. He always tries to adjust his position so that his gun side is away from the person who opens the door. If there is ample room for him to move about outside the door, he is quite casual in his preparation, but if he is standing on a narrow stoop or is obliged to stand below the level of the door, he remains alert, keeping his feet planted, plus exploiting any kind of handhold available. When he arrives at a door, he usually listens for any noises from within, trying to assess the possibilities of disorder and nasty surprises when it swings open.

The space immediately around him is considered inviolate. If the policeman is not fully in control of his body, he cannot do anything. His constant scanning of territory as he moves forward is designed not only to protect himself physically but to preserve his capacity to do his job. His stick and blackjack are personal weapons that can be used only when he is in close physical contact with someone. A policeman does sometimes throw his stick at a fleeing suspect, with occasional success, but his gun is the only weapon he carries that is designed to control more territory than he can reach with the length of his arm or the tip of his shoe. If there is any hint of conflict—argument, fighting, reports of weapons—his readiness to strike is great and his willingness to draw his revolver apparent. This is particularly true when he enters places where concealment is possible. He may draw his gun when entering a bar or a store where there is some kind of conflict, but then he risks at least complaint or angry responses from the people. If he finds a robber in a store, nobody complains, but if he discovers only an angry dispute between a customer and a storekeeper, he will appear quite foolish. Similarly, even if he hears noise inside a house when called on a disturbance, he does not draw his pistol but keeps his stick ready and moves forward without waiting for an invitation. He keeps his gun in reserve for moments of peril and to control places where there is no possibility that normal transactions between people can be occurring.

The most difficult and dangerous work a patrolman must regularly do is to investigate buildings for prowlers. Each time he must enter a darkened building, whether it is an abandoned house, a residence temporarily vacated by its occupants, or a factory closed for the day, he is faced with a grave challenge. He enters an enclosed place, each step taking him farther from the relative security of the street, where he can call for aid. Each step leaves his radio farther away. Concealment is possible everywhere, each room renewing the possibility of nasty surprise. For these reasons, few policemen ever enter alone to search, and rarely do they neglect to unholster their guns. If it is nighttime and a man is obliged to use a flashlight, it is usually held well away from his body in the hope that a waiting assailant will attack the light source.

Two patrolmen took a call of males on the second floor of a vacant house. When they arrived, they found that the lock on the front door had been broken. They advanced into the foyer and listened for a moment for any noises. The older man told his partner to cover him, and with drawn pistols they advanced into the building. With guns held loose-ly ready, they advanced down the hall, standing well apart from one another. They examined each room on the ground floor, while the man who was covering kept an eye on the stairway to the second floor. They advanced quickly up the staircase of the once elegant house, guns ready.

All the doors on the second floor were closed. They paused again to listen. Nothing. The first handle was gently turned, but the door would not open. The patrolman stepped back and kicked it in. The room was empty—wine bottles, mattresses, condoms, and hypodermic needles indicating its recent use as a shooting gallery. They proceeded to the other end of the hallway, where a double door blocked entrance to the rear of the house. The two men stood facing the door, one officer, who was left-handed, on the left side of his part-ner, keeping his gun arm away from his colleague's shooting hand.

They paused again, listening intently for any sound. Sud-denly, together, they caught a smell of human fear—the fresh, strong odor of excrement—and simultaneously they kicked the doors in. Standing in the farthest corner of the room, cowering in terror before the two, was a boy of about eighteen. One officer covered the suspect while his partner holstered and quickly but gingerly frisked the fellow. The unarmed teenager claimed he had been chased from a near-by park by a gang and had broken into the building to escape them. He had been hiding when he heard the noises made by the police and mistook them for sounds of the gang searching for him. When he heard someone outside the room, he lost control of himself. The older patrolman checked his identification and questioned him regarding his purposes in a neighborhood far from where he lived. He was dissatisfied with the explanation, being sure the fellow had come in search of drugs but, having no reason to hold him, contented himself with a warning. He told him to stay away from the area and, to reinforce his warning, refused to give the fellow a lift to a bus stop. No report was made of the incident as nothing had happened. True, the police-men almost shot someone, but almost is not something to write about.

The policeman does not try to conceal nervousness from his colleagues in investigating hidden places. Having his gun in hand is sufficient evidence of his estimate of the situation, and colleagues only seek assurance that their partners will do nothing to endanger their own safety and autonomy. Men who do not keep their guns down while running, or who cock their guns while moving, are reprimanded without regard to courtesy or politeness. But a man who shows indecision or reveals fear in a situation where others do not feel it is warranted risks exclusion. Two men may disagree on whether a drawn gun is necessary on a car stop, and if they cannot agree, they will not continue to work together, but their disagreement is rooted in tactics rather than in a question of capacity. No policeman denies that car stops are dangerous. But if a patrolman reaches for his gun when someone swears at him or threatens him, it is a sign of fear that demonstrates the man cannot be relied on.

Every policeman works with fear, and his cautions are designed to calm them, to maximize his personal assurance that everything possible is done to limit the chance of a nasty surprise. But his attentions are directed exclusively to areas which he is potentially able to control. A policeman working a tough area knows that some people bombard the police from above, but rarely does he bother looking above the second floor, unless he is given a specific caution. He does not forget there is danger above him, but he does not bother to look because he cannot control it, and looking up wastes his time and slows his movements. Similarly, snipers represent an enormous threat to the policeman because they can attack from relative safety, beyond the range of his vision; but he does not worry about them because there is little he can do. If snipers could work in a city with any effect, they could entirely undermine the capacity of the police to operate in their traditional manner. It is not simply that they want to kill policemen—others are similarly determined and occasionally succeed without shaking the will of other policemen to continue. But by attacking from a distance, they can completely deprive the policeman of his sense of autonomy, his belief that he can control his surroundings. When this happens, he is no longer able to act within the bounds of civil decency. If he thinks those who wish him ill have superior weapons, he must approach strangers in a very different way, using his power to enforce his will to work rather than to enforce the decisions he makes while doing his job.

In our cities public-housing projects are the most disliked and feared places where a patrolman is obliged to work. Even before he has to do the work for which he has been summoned, he must pass beneath high roofs, which frequently are used as platforms for launching attacks. He does not bother to look up since he knows it will do him no good. If he is on an emergency call, he may run, but otherwise he cannot give the impression of haste or appearing frightened, lest he betray to watchful eyes, including his own, evidence that will make it more difficult to do an almost impossible job. He must enter a densely packed building and ascend in a slow elevator, which takes him away from the radio and the street. He enters a place filled with terror, and regardless of his feelings for the people who must live there, he considers it an act of courage to even walk in the main door. But that is only the beginning. There are other places where the patrolman is exposed to danger, streets where he does not linger to do his paper work, bars he does not walk into casually or alone. But these are places which can be discreetly avoided; the projects cannot, and they combine the characteristics the policeman most fears—uncontrollable space, arduous and restricted passage to the street, and hostile people.

Sunday morning and a meet-complainant call on the tenth floor of an all-black project did not excite the patrolmen who had just finished breakfast. It was overcast but very peaceful. They rode up on the elevator without talking and arrived at the door. Just as they were about to knock, a noise was heard from within. The older patrolman muttered, "Shit. Ruby, I forgot my jack, let me do the talkin' and you cover the door." The black patrolman knocked and the door opened. He stepped in quickly and his partner followed, closing the door. The call had been given to them as a meet complainant and the older man had left his stick in the car and forgotten his jack. From the looks of the room, the dispatcher had made a mistake.

The woman who opened the door had called the police.

She and her sister stood in the smoky room with four men. The patrolmen said nothing, just stared at the four men and waited. The woman said she and her sister were getting ready to make breakfast for their two friends and wanted the other two gentlemen to leave. They had refused. Two men stepped back, indicating they were with the women, while the other two men, a tall wiry man and a short stout fellow with a big bulge in one pocket, moved closer together. The patrolmen said nothing. The black officer took one step forward, and with a slight smile he patted the bulging pocket. He stepped back, looked at the men, unsnapped his holster, and said, "O.K., out." The two men looked at him and then at the white policeman by the door and didn't move. The patrolman repeated his demand: "Out. Now." "O.K., man, we don't want no shit or nothin', but we was invited and then we get this crap." The officer opened the door for them; both policemen circled back from them as they passed.

When they had completed taking the information from the woman who had called, they left and pushed the elevator button. The door opened; the two men who had just been ejected were standing inside, smiling. It was a slow ride down. "You sure got a nice leather belt on your jacket," the thin man said to the black officer. "Keep your motherfucking hands off o' me if you want to walk home." By the time they reached the ground floor, the white officer's hand ached from gripping his blackjack. "I wasn't worried about them dudes," the black policeman said. "We coulda taken 'em, but I didn't want no shootin'. It's the only time I ever forgot my jack—just when I needed it. You know what that dude had bulging in his pocket? Money. I knew they weren't gonna give us too much shit with that kinda dough. They musta had a game there last night, and the broads had enough of 'em just when they was gettin' ready to take a piece," he said. It was still a quiet Sunday, although it looked grayer. They drove to the station house to pick up a blackjack.

Occupationally obliged to search out signs of difficulty and danger in their surroundings, it is not surprising that policemen tend to seek out secure places to sit and stand when they are inside. It is not true that they refuse to sit with their backs to a door or a window (although some men do), but the policeman prefers to be in a position where he does not have to worry about his back or his gun side. When he enters houses and bars, he always tries to keep a path clear to the street. Even in places where he feels relatively secure, such as a courtroom, he prefers to sit along the walls or at the back of the hall.

His consciousness of security also makes the officer appreciative of places where he feels he can relax his attentiveness. While patrolmen are accosted and even occasionally assaulted in station houses, most men feel a security in their locker room or the operations room that they do not have anywhere else when they are in uniform. The actual danger may be as great there as on the street, but the officer does not perceive this. In one station where the operations room was on the ground floor facing the street, the windows were left wide open during pleasant weather. Even during crises, periods when policemen were shot and there were rumors of projected assaults on police stations, the windows were not screened or curtained. A lieutenant, who in public always insisted on sitting with his face toward the door, kept his chair positioned with its back toward the open windows. Either he did not recognize the window as an open space, or he discounted the possibility that anyone passing could possibly threaten him in his sanctuary. To have acknowledged the possibility of danger would have required his acceptance of the fact that the operations room was not a secure place where he could relax his vigilance. He would have had to find another haven. Patrolmen frequently visit a firehouse, hospital ward, or an especially favored coffee shop, not just to rest, to make time with the women, to evade work, or to drink coffee, but to be in a place where they can relax and are not obliged to constantly scan their surroundings.

Every policeman knows there are no foolproof precautions that guarantee security. He knows that there are times when he must accept risks that cannot be wholly calculated. He also knows there are men who are willing to do things he does not care to do, and if they are credited with heroics for bursting into a room to disarm a man with a shotgun, he does not consider them any less stupid or himself any less brave. But no man is too strong or too clever to avoid all situations that he cannot master. And one of the requirements of being a "good cop" in the opinion of co-workers is having the combination of skill and will to hold on while waiting for aid. There is no shame among policemen if a man is beaten or injured, unless it is attributable to a lack of courage or to an avoidable error. There is little praise for a man who displays great courage if he does so at the risk of his life and of others'. The patrolman who cuts off a colleague by driving over a sidewalk and through a stop sign to make a pinch will find himself working alone or transferred if he persists. The downcast rookie, crowned by a brick on his first day on the street, fearing his career had been terminated before it began, was told unmistakably what lay ahead. "Don't feel so bad, kid. You're one of us now. But when you come back to work, maybe you'll remember to wear your hat when you get out of the car," his sergeant said. His success is measured by his capability in controlling people, but his failure is not measured simply by defeat—although defeat is always humiliating—but by errors, failures to act when necessary, and an unwillingness to take the calculated risks that everyone who uses his body as a tool must finally accept as a way of life.

3 · Controlling People

A policeman's principal concern is to physically control the people he is policing. While he sometimes wants to hurt or humiliate them, that is not nearly so often his purpose as it is the consequence of his efforts to control them. When he intervenes in a person's life, his attitude is basically instrumental. He mainly wants to place himself as quickly as possible in a position that will allow him to control the person, if that is required, or hopefully to discourage any inclinations to resist him or his orders. That is why he ignores the risks he takes in driving and violates departmental regulations by refusing to use the safety belt provided for him. The idea of being confined and prevented from moving quickly out of his car terrifies him.

Policemen act as though all people are right-handed. If he has any choice in the matter, the patrolman tries to move in a leftward direction toward a person in order to control his fighting arm. This allows him to stand at the person's right, at a slight angle, when he is facing him, which keeps his gun away from the man he is seeking to dominate. He consistently violates the normal distances which people seek to maintain when they are engaged in friendly conversation, often causing discomfort and nervousness when he does not mean to. He is not formally trained to do this, nor does he do it consciously, but an understanding of his actions would not deter him, since his objective is the maintenance of his personal security and not the discomfort of others. By constantly crowding people, he reduces their opportunities for kicking and punching him effectively. When he can, the patrolman stands slightly at an angle to the person he is confronting to avoid a crippling blow to the groin. Naturally he can be grabbed and wrestled with; this is the main reason why most policemen wear clip-on ties and hate any gear that offers someone a handhold on them.

The first and sometimes the only thing a policeman looks at when approaching someone is his hands. Recruits are warned repeatedly to train themselves to check people's hands first ("If the guy's got a brick, he better be building a house"). But he must do more than just look—he must learn to expect to see things. A policeman is frequently called into the presence of people who are distressed, depressed, angry, or fearful. It is not surprising that many of them are holding some kind of weapon, which they do not necessarily intend for use against him. He must be prepared to disarm them swiftly without resorting to force. Often he sees boys walking down the street carrying sticks or boards; he usually disarms them and sends them on their way, unless there has been a specific call or an order to bring them in. Anyone who comes into his presence is unceremoniously disarmed. A boy carrying a bow and arrow has the toy taken from him, and given to his mother after the policeman finishes talking with them. A woman opens her door for an officer taking a meet complainant, and he quickly grabs a butcher knife and a pistol. He enters the house, unloads the gun, places the knife in a drawer, sits down for a cup of coffee and a little conversation, and leaves after the woman has had a good cry and he is reasonably sure she will not commit suicide. People often tell him of weapons in their houses and offer to get them, but the experienced patrolman will not let anyone handle a gun in his presence. People holding paper bags are looked at carefully, because every policeman knows that it is not an elegant manner of transporting a gun but it is one that is used often enough. He is not concerned about hurting the feelings of the people whom he handles unceremoniously in these moments. He only cares about disarming them, for there are occasions when the door opens and he is looking directly into the barrel of a shotgun, and then he is stripped of everything he is but his blue suit.[8]

Anyone whose hands are concealed, wittingly or not, risks serious injury or worse when he attracts the attention of a policeman. Hidden hands imply danger to a policeman, and he must decide in a few seconds what course of action to take. Whatever he decides to do, he must continue until he has succeeded or failed, because there is no possibility of mediation with a policeman intent on assuring his security, and he will be satisfied only by seeing empty hands.

A young white officer noticed a man standing near a street corner turn away as the patrol car approached. He stopped his car and rolled down the window to look at the elderly Negro man. Instead of getting out of the car, he yelled across the deserted street to him, "Take your hand out of your coat." The man had turned back toward the car when it stopped, and he had his right hand jammed inside. He did not react to the command. They were frozen for several seconds; then the patrolman repeated his demand. When the man remained silent, the officer drew his pistol, continuing to remain seated in his car. He placed his gun

---

[8]"A 26-year-old man armed with a Luger pistol and a rifle disarmed three policemen early today and held them at bay for nearly two hours. . . . The man finally gave up his weapons and surrendered after having a cup of coffee with two of the policemen. The drama started when police received a report of a 'disturbance.' . . . The first officer to respond was Policeman Robert Patrick . . . who said he saw Hansen standing at the front door, his back toward the street. 'Did you call, sir?' Patrick asked. Hansen turned around and according to Patrick, "The next thing I knew I had a rifle to my head.' " *Philadelphia Daily News* (July 27, 1971).

in plain view and again ordered the man to show his hand. The man was very agitated but he remained silent. Slowly he began to extract his hand, but he gave the appearance of concealing some intention which threatened the patrolman, who cocked his gun and pointed it directly at the man. Suddenly the old man drew out his hand and threw a pistol to the ground. He stood trembling. The patrolman uncocked his gun with a shaking hand and approached. He was on the verge of tears, and in a moment of confusion, fear, and anxiety, he struck the man with the butt of his pistol. "Why didn't you take your hand out when I told you? I almost shot you, you dumb bastard." The man protested the treatment he had received, complaining that there was no reason to hit him. He said he had had no intention of using the gun but was carrying it for self-protection. The patrolman recovered from his fright, but despite his regret for striking the man in anger, he refused to acknowledge any responsibility. "Are you wearing a sign? How the fuck am I supposed to know what you're gonna do?"

From a purely technical point of view, the patrolman had initially made an error by failing to close the distance between himself and the suspect, allowing himself no alternative but to leave or to use his gun. If he had charged the man immediately upon suspecting him of some misdeed, any passer-by might have "seen" an elderly black man being "assaulted" by a policeman, but the patrolman would have avoided the chance of a much more serious incident. The presumption here is that the policeman was behaving correctly in having suspicions about the man and stopping to make any kind of investigation. Nobody obliged him to stop the man, and if he had continued on his patrol, his superiors and colleagues would not have known. But the patrolman makes these stops because they are his job. He knows colleagues who do not make them, or seldom do so, to avoid moments like the ones he had passed through, but if his morale is high and if he treats his job in a serious way, he has little choice but to exercise the skills he has developed. Whether these stops should be allowed is a political issue. They have tactical value to the police, but the use of suspicion stops as a police tactic cannot be decided from a simple, technical viewpoint but must be made in terms of the political values of the people who pay the police.

The positioning and distance of a patrolman in relation to the person he is seeking to control are absolutely critical. When they are separated by many feet, the chances of the policeman drawing his gun are considerable. But even if he is in close proximity to the suspect, the policeman can still fail unless he positions his body to do what he wants to. He uses his gun infrequently when he is close to a suspect, relying instead on his hand weapons and his physical assets. When he commits himself to this kind of action and fails, he is in serious trouble.

Consider the predicament of the patrolman turning off his fifteenth hydrant on a hot, steamy day. He approached the gushing hydrant, wrench in hand, watching the children splashing and a young man washing his Irish setter. He asked them to stand back, but the man continued to wash his dog, splashing water freely about and entirely ignoring the presence of the officer. He was told again to move, this time forcefully but without insult. The fellow looked up and said, "Fuck you, pig!" In that split second the patrolman committed himself. He lunged in anger, but trying to avoid the water, he arched his body and limited his reach. The fellow leaped back into the middle of the street and taunted the policeman with obscene gestures and remarks. If the policeman gave chase, he might capture him, but the chances were not good. Every time he took a step forward, the fellow sprang back, yelling louder and attracting larger and larger numbers of onlookers. The policeman grew angrier by the moment and was very reluctant to withdraw; although he realized his situation was untenable. He concluded the incident by vowing to "get" the fellow.

The policeman had every intention of settling the "score" with the young man and mentioned him to his sergeant and several colleagues, who urged that he remain away. The policemen did not find the young man, although one night he found them. When they were answering a call at another house, the fellow allegedly dropped a jug of water out of a second-floor window, narrowly missing a patrolman. The officer called an assist, broke into the man's house, and arrested him after an altercation. A number of law suits erupted out of this event, and the fellow moved out of the district.

The policeman's intense concern with position, his ability to see a suspect's hands and to make some judgment about his physical capacity and inclinations combine to make all car stops potentially explosive moments. A policeman usually stops a car because he thinks that it is stolen, that the occupants are trying to avoid him, or that there has been some kind of traffic violation. He has used his power to stop the car. He can see the driver and the other occupants, but he cannot make any judgments about what they are doing. He cannot see their hands or how big they are, or determine what they might do. All the unknowns he fears are present as he proceeds to investigate.

The patrolman is under orders—often disregarded—not to make suspicion car stops when he is working alone. Each time he makes a car stop, he is supposed to inform his dispatcher and, before getting out of his car, give his location and the color, make, and license number of the car. If he is alone and his stop is on suspicion, he is supposed to await the arrival of a back-up before proceeding. If his suspicion is strong and the stop is made at night, the patrolman tries to blind the driver by shining his spotlight directly onto the car's rear-view mirror. He does not take his eyes off the car once he has signaled the stop. He counts the number of occupants he sees and makes sure that they all remain visible. If he is alone and waiting for another officer, he will stay in his car and order anyone trying to get out to remain seated.

If two men are making a suspicion stop, they use speed and position to overcome the deficiencies in their situation. Both patrolmen emerge quickly, stepping out with one leg so that their bodies do not turn away from the car they are going to approach. The recorder stations himself at the right rear of the car, looking through the back windows to make sure nobody is hiding on the floor or concealing something under a seat. The driver approaches the front of the car and positions himself to maximize his advantage over the occupants. He stands to the rear of the front door and well away from it, to avoid the possibility of someone opening the door and knocking him down. By standing back, he obliges the person to turn around to him, an awkward and uncomfortable position. Policemen are urged to adopt this posture whenever they stop a car, but when a patrolman is issuing a traffic ticket, he finds it difficult to maintain a hostile posture without seeming aggressive. Few policemen walk directly to a car window without first making some judgment about the driver.

There is no way for the policeman completely to settle his anxieties when making a car stop. The people he is seeking to control are right before him; he is close to them, but he cannot get near enough to place them under his physical control. His personal estimate of his own vulnerability greatly increases his tension. Many patrolmen not only unlatch the strap on their holsters before approaching a car but actually pull their guns. At night it is not uncommon to see policemen unholster their guns and conceal them behind a thigh as they approach a suspicious car. There is relatively little the occupants of a car can do to ease the situation. Occasionally people who have considerable experience with the police place their hands on top of the steering wheel to indicate their peaceful intentions. But this does not calm him; rather it tells the officer that he is approaching someone who is cop-wise and his wariness increases.

The policeman's unease does not result from the attitudes of the people but from the constraints of the situation. Even when he sees people who give every appearance of peace, he is unlikely to relax his wariness. Two patrolmen approached a parked car with a running motor. It was very early on a frosty Sunday morning. The white policeman walked directly toward the driver, but his black partner restrained him. "Sleeping like a baby, right? Made a load and can't get home, so he pulls over and parks. Well, you want to check 'em out, see he ain't dead. But before you open the door or knock on the window, look inside first. You gotta make sure the car is in park and the guy don't have a knife in his hand. A lot of these dudes have been rolled so many times they keep an open knife on their lap before they doze off, for protection, you know. That's O.K., you know, but you don't want no surprises when you wake him up. Some of 'em been rolled by guys in blue suits, too, and you can't forget that neither."

A car stop combines the anxieties of entry into an enclosed space where concealment is possible with the frustrations of being unable to control people who are visible and in some sense publicly available. The policeman must try to balance his need to give a stern and forceful appearance, his "I mean business" manner, with a recognition that most stops turn into nothing, that they are false alarms that can get out of hand if he acts too aggressively or, in his desire to control the people, is insulting. In moments of extreme tension, when the police are mobilized in search of "cop killers" or feel that the department is being besieged and threatened, some men cast caution to the wind and openly use their guns to control car stops. A faultlessly polite patrolman pointed his revolver directly at a person's head, saying, "Sir, would you please stand out of your car?" But even having a gun ready is not always a guarantee of success.

Two patrolmen stopped a car they knew to be stolen. The plate was listed on the hot sheet and they had checked it with the dispatcher before moving. They were on special patrol in search of some men who the day before had murdered a policeman. Both policemen had their revolvers out as they approached the car, which held two men. The driver had his hands on the steering wheel and was looking back over his shoulder at the advancing officer. According to the patrolman, the fellow smiled and said to him, "Shit, man, you don't need that." He suckered the officer, who hesitated and then holstered his gun. He later claimed that he knew he had made an error the moment he did it. The man dropped his hand and came up with a .45, shooting the policeman twice, while the other man wounded the second officer. The two men were captured a short while later. There is no point in a policeman having his gun out unless he is prepared to shoot someone, and the police cannot be allowed to think of shooting except in defense. Their assailant must be allowed the first move, however slight, but the police have to be able to protect themselves. If they are not allowed to approach people closely, carefully controlling their movements and even violating their bodies, the only way they can make suspicion stops is with their guns un-hooked and their sticks ready to hit.

A patrolman with twenty years' experience had recently arrested two robbery suspects on a car stop. He recalled that although he had drawn his gun several times, he had never shot anyone. "I don't know, they were just bad, the way they were acting. The detectives found a gun under the seat. I was real close to them, working alone. I had my gun pointed right at the driver's head. If one of them had bent down, I would have shot him. It would have been too bad for me if it had been a handkerchief under there, but I would have shot him."

The policeman knows that he does not have an unre-stricted right to interfere with people's privacy, but his de-cision to violate their bodies is not made with regard either to their feelings or to their rights. At the police academy the distinctions between a frisk and a search are carefully explained to him, and the limitations of his authority are defined as clearly as the law allows, but his instructors stress that he should not hesitate to frisk anyone if he feels it is necessary.[9] "Any judgment you make is gonna have to be

[9] A policeman may examine the outer clothing of any person he stops on suspicion if he feels the person means him harm or may be con-cealing a weapon. If he feels anything that might be a weapon, he may go into the person's clothing and extract the object for examination. If in the course of the frisk he discovers any contraband or evidence implicating the person in some crime, it is not considered to be legally seized since the policeman has conducted what amounts to a search without reasonable grounds. The distinctions between stop and frisk are discussed in Lawrence P. Tiffany, Donald M. McIntyre, Jr., and Daniel L. Rotenberg, *Detection of Crime* (Boston, Little, Brown, 1967), pp. 44–57. The general issue is still under intense legal review, and the recent Supreme Court and federal court decisions will be amended and refined in upcoming cases. The most recent decisions are *Terry* vs. *Ohio*, 88 S.Ct. 1868 (1968); *Sibron* vs. *New York*, 88 S.Ct. 1889 (1968); *United States* vs. *McMann*, 370 F. 2d 757 (2d Cir. 1967). The stop-and-frisk authority of the police in a number of other countries is dis-cussed in Sowle, *Police Power and Individual Freedom*. In no country do the police appear to have less formal power than they do in America, although the actual practices may differ. A cursory discussion of police frisking in London and the negative responses of people is in Peter Laurie, *Scotland Yard* (London, Bodley Head, 1970), pp. 62–5.

backed up in court, but if you think you should, do it."
Body control is treated as a technical issue; considerable
time is spent teaching recruits how to efficiently violate the
privacy of fellow citizens.

Several recruits at the academy were arbitrarily selected to
enact a stop and frisk in class. They were given a situation;
first one and then the other played the officer and the suspect. Almost everyone failed. They spoke in muffled tones,
asked politely for some identification, and muttered questions about why he was loitering in the alley at so late an
hour. "You just gonna stand there and ask him to put his
hand in his coat pocket? Hey, boy, you're up an alley, it's
dark, and we ain't here," the instructor piped in. Everyone,
including a few ex-policemen back for a refresher, failed
badly and knew it. How do you frisk someone? How do you
not violate him? He's your friend and buddy.

The instructor concealed several guns and knives on a
student collaborator and arranged to demonstrate frisking.
"O.K., it ain't so easy. Half you guys would be on your ass
by now, and this guy's gonna play football with your head,
remember that. So now, we learn how to frisk." The collaborator and another student were called to the front of
the room. Two others were called up to frisk them. "O.K.
Put 'em on the wall and frisk 'em down," the black instructor
ordered. The recruits mumbled their orders, and without using their hands or stepping in close to the men, they positioned the "suspects" on the wall. Both men used their feet
to kick at the subjects' legs, spreading them to keep the man
off balance. "Hey, wait a minute. Why all this kickin'? Everybody starts kickin' the guy's legs. Why all the rough
stuff?" The men finished their frisk and were followed by
two other recruits. Throughout the hour nobody found any
of the weapons, and each man commenced his frisking by
kicking or roughing up his classmate.

The instructor exhibited his mock displeasure (his students
rarely find any weapons the first time) and demonstrated a
proper frisk on his collaborator. "When you frisk someone,
it is for your own protection. You don't have to kick him.
You have to put him under your control and frisk him systematically." The instructor used his entire body, placing the

man in the position he wanted him, feet back and spread wide, every muscle tensed to keep his head, which was far forward, from slipping down and causing him to fall. "You want to stand right in there. Don't be afraid of him. You gonna be afraid when he ain't in this position. Now you got him. Put your leg inside his, and if he moves you can trip him up. If he takes a few bumps, that's resisting. Frisk him systematically. Don't use your fingertips. Use your palms. Start with the palms on his head and work one side of his body and then the other. Look at his hair, and don't be afraid to put your hands in his crotch, it won't bite. And if the guy gives you any shit, why you can give him a little shot to remember you while you're there."

The instructor showed them the concealed knives and guns and told them, "They were hardly hidden. But you are gonna learn. And listen, the rough stuff is for nothing. It doesn't help you find anything. If you're nervous, the guy out there is gonna know it. He may have more experience at this than you. You give him a chance, he'll take it. Don't talk to him or let him distract you, just frisk him. Then if he don't stand still, you make him, but don't get tough just because you're nervous or don't like the guy's color or looks or whatever."

After several weeks of practicing and discovering the many places a weapon can be concealed (one student sliced open his finger on a razor blade stuck behind a belt), the students' admiration for their instructor was unbounded and their efficiency at frisking vastly improved. Most of the kicking had disappeared, and the recruits were beginning to use their bodies to place people on the wall and to control them while they were there. But even using loaded guns (with blanks) and switchblades did not create the necessary ingredients to make it all real—fear and anger.

Most frisking is actually done casually and in an offhand manner. When a policeman is working alone, he is reluctant to bend down, which he must do in a full frisk from the rear, and he will forgo it unless he has strong reasons to believe the person is armed. A decision to frisk is also affected by the relative size of the people involved. Few policemen frisk youngsters (unless they are quite large), because an officer assumes that if he gets any trouble from a kid, he can put him down. He contents himself with casually feeling the outer pockets of his jacket and his waist area. But the experienced man does not waste these few motions. He is not delicate in poking his hands about while he is making conversation.

A frisk usually occurs after a stop is made and the patrolman has made some determination about his initial suspicions, but there are numerous occasions when the frisk and stop occur almost simultaneously.

Two patrolmen were searching an area for suspects in the shooting of a police officer. There was little information about the killers except that they were young. Driving slowly down an almost deserted street, they passed a young man walking in the opposite direction. "Did he turn away? Yeah, let's get him. Shit, I hate backin' up on these dudes," he muttered to his recorder, throwing the car into reverse. He jumped out, ran between two parked cars, grabbed the man, and turned him about. He was frisking his midriff when the man said, "Hey, Hank, what's the matter, man?" The patrolman, surprised at hearing his name, looked up and noticed that he had stopped the brother of a close friend. He stopped the frisk and apologized. They smoked a cigarette, chatted, and parted. He had been so intent on quickly approaching the suspect without losing sight of the man's hands that he did not even look at his face. He was not embarrassed but considered the action an excellent example of how to do his job properly. "He might have been a killer. When you go up on someone like that, you got no business lookin' at his face," he said.

If the policeman has not stopped a person on suspicion or encountered him under circumstances that suggest involvement in disorder or crime, he will not frisk him unless in the course of conversation something is said suggesting violence or resistance. He does not search everyone he meets or everyone he stands next to on a dark street. He is never relaxed in the presence of strangers, and he assumes that his alertness and readiness are sufficient to handle surprises, but if there is a hint of a weapon present, his entire manner changes abruptly.

Two patrolmen were interviewing a man who claimed that two acquaintances had robbed him of a thousand dollars. "Wow, that's like a million bucks in this neighborhood. You must be a number writer, pal," one officer said, with a grin. The alleged victim did not think it funny, and the more he talked of his loss, the angrier he became. He was quite vague in giving a description of the robbers, and the patrolmen began to think the man was just another drunk. "I'm gonna kill them motherfuckers!" he mumbled, and in a second one officer had grabbed him by the arm, twisted him about, and started frisking him. From inside the man's overcoat he extracted an ice pick. "I didn't like the way he said 'kill.' You hear that kinda shit all the time, but he really meant it. An ice pick is the worst, too, because there's no hole when you pull it out. All the bleeding is on the inside," he said to his inexperienced partner.

Whenever he is making a suspicion stop, the patrolman conducts some kind of frisk. How he proceeds depends on whether he is working alone or with a partner. If he is alone, he will not bother to back-frisk anyone he thinks has no chance of overpowering him. But if the person appears to be strongly built and willing to "give it a go," he will turn him about, often accompanying his commands with a few threats, but he will not bend down to do a thorough search. Instead he uses his stick to feel the man's legs or, if he has no stick, does not bother to do a complete job. If he bends down, the policeman is vulnerable, and while the man may not hurt him, he has a chance to "make it"; no policeman wants to give anyone the opportunity of involving him in a chase.

When patrolmen work in pairs, their approach alters completely. Two men who work together regularly come to understand each other's attitudes and routines. They divide responsibilities, and each knows what he is going to do when they make a stop or go into a place where there is some kind of trouble. Whether they are stopping one man or five, one officer conducts the interrogation and the frisk, and the other stands back and controls the scene. If they have stopped a group of men, the patrolman does not hesitate to unholster his gun in order to make them more responsive to his commands. Working in pairs, one man can focus his attention on the frisk and does not have to worry about the chances of assault or flight.

Working alone, the patrolman's control of the situation is slight and tenuous. If he is working one to one, only fear prevents the person he has stopped from proceeding. The degree of force the policeman must use to make him obey depends as much on his willingness to appear forceful as it does on the actual use of force. There are many policemen who rarely use force for the simple reason that they appear willing (and possibly are) to do almost anything to subdue resistance. Other patrolmen, who misjudge their power (or like to abuse it), often find themselves in situations where they are risking serious danger for little reward.

A young, aggressive patrolman told of a problem he had encountered when he stopped six men outside a bar. "I had all six on the wall, you know, and I was gonna search the one on the end when one guy said they should rush me. I cocked my gun and nobody moved, and I told him if they came, I'd burn him. What else could I do? I started to frisk the one guy when the guys at the other end started drifting around the corner. I lost two, but I finished the other four." If he had expected solace and comfort from his colleagues, he was disappointed. "Carl, you are a dumb motherfucker. You keep up that crazy shit, you are gonna be in the hospital or dead."

Even if the policeman is careful not to exceed the limits of his capacity to safely control suspects, he cannot focus his attention closely on what he is doing when he frisks someone. Most frisks are done quickly and informally to assure the officer that the suspect does not have anything on him which might be used against the policeman. Patrolmen who fancy themselves specialists in gun pinches frisk people very thoroughly, but they are exceptional. Every time a person is arrested he is usually frisked twice, first by the arresting officer and then by the wagon crew, before he is transported to the station, but weapons are still overlooked, concealed behind belt buckles, in armpits, and even in a folded wallet.

A patrolman recalled a time when he was working plain-clothes and was arrested during a raid on a speakeasy. The police missed the small revolver he had stuck behind his belt buckle. "I was sittin' on the bench in the station, waitin', you know, to tell 'em who I was when we was in private, but I was worried if they noticed the gun they'd kick the shit outta me. So I called a cop over and real quiet I told him I was still carryin'. He almost shit." On another occasion, a young man was sitting in a station, handcuffed, waiting for some detectives to come for him. He acted quite nervous, kept looking about and fidgeting. Finally a patrolman approached and told him to keep quiet. He apologized and said he was very nervous because he had a gun in his pocket that the policeman had not taken from him. The patrolman seized him by the lapels, twisted him about as he raised him from the bench, and grabbed the gun.

Frisking is much more common in some parts of the city than in others, and it is not an activity engaged in exclusively by the police. There are bars and restaurants where regular patrons "bump" into strangers, checking whether or not they are armed. Prostitutes who work out of bars frequently seek to protect themselves from entrapments by plainclothesmen by holding hands and pretending affection for a potential client while actually checking to see if the man's hands match what he claims to do for a living and if he is carrying a small gun or a jack somewhere about his middle. These people frisk for protection, as a policeman does. An officer is for-bidden by regulation to frisk a woman except in an extreme emergency; he must turn her over to a matron or a police-woman. Undoubtedly the number of complaints against the police would increase if this restriction were lifted, but so, too, would the number of stops and arrests. There are many reasons why a policeman does not look with suspicion on women in public places (except in areas where prostitutes work), but one of them certainly is his inability to protect himself. Not only can he not frisk a woman, a policeman is reluctant to hit a woman, and even when he has justification (from his point of view), he recalls doing so with regret and chagrin.

Although a policeman views frisking as a defensive act devoid of personal comment, those he stops cannot help but feel angered by their powerlessness, if for no other reason. Regardless of how the policeman behaves or what he says, he is compelling the person to submit to him and to turn his body over for examination. Younger men in some parts of the city are so familiar with the routine that when they are hailed by the police, they stop and spread their arms to the side before the officer has asked a question or even approached. They understand that this signal of submission will gain them more gentle and circumspect treatment. Sometimes a patrolman runs his hands absent-mindedly over a man's pockets while engaging in conversation, not really meaning to frisk him but just letting him know that he is in control, that for the moment the man belongs to the patrolman. It is not a consciously hostile or aggressive act. It is an expression of the policeman's belief that regardless of the momentary tone of the interaction, his place in that relationship is supported ultimately by his personal will and readiness to exercise all of the authority invested in him. There is no way he can make this point without causing discontent, because the authority given to him can be exercised only by restraining the liberty of some persons and violating their autonomy. A policeman does not enjoy frisking people. During a busy tour he may wash up several times because many of the people he stops are filthy. He constantly grumbles about the dirt and the odors, but they do not cause him to keep his distance or to avoid intimate contact. He knows that when he is on the street, it is only his readiness to demonstrate his power that maintains the edge necessary for him to do his work and come home safely each day.

4 · Force and Violence

A good cop in the opinion of a policeman is someone who is willing to go on the street each day and do his job—take people to the hospital, break up fights, make car stops, go to the aid of a colleague in trouble, accept injury, and return to do it all over again—without hesitating to do whatever he must to accomplish his purposes. A policeman does not admire another man simply because he makes a number pinch or because he locks up a bank robber. Anyone can get lucky or learn how to do dirty work. A good cop does not have to love to fight or hit people, but he must be willing to do both and even risk injury and pain rather than accept defeat. "When I first came on the street, I didn't know nothing. I thought you wear a uniform and a badge, you got a gun, stick, and jack—who is gonna give you any trouble? Who would want to fight with you? You learn quick," a patrolman said.

Every policeman learns to accept in silence much that he dislikes about some colleagues—their indifference, viciousness, dishonesty—but he does not have to keep quiet about someone he considers unreliable or dangerous. Even men who have been around for a long time who become "shaky" are not spared because of sentimental ties. "He's just no kind of cop. Take old Jack, he don't do much of anything any more, but at least he won't fuck you up. But Fred. He's a terrific guy, we were in high school together and went to the academy together. We worked in the same squad for five years. He just was never any kind of cop, then or now. I even killed a guy once because of him. His fault, but I did the shooting.

"He had a disturbance house and he goes in and there's some shad all drunked up, really tearin' up the place. Fred, he tries to talk to him, and before he knows what's up, the guy's got a butcher knife. What does he do? He backs off instead of smacking the shit out of him with his stick. The guy's chasing him all around the house and the old lady calls an assist. We get there, four or five guys all at once, they're out in back of the house. We run down an alley into the yard, and when he sees us, he charges. We must opened up on him. The coroner said he looked like a screen. He did, too. I guess his old lady'll never call the cops again. But it was Fred's fault. I never worked with him since. Guys'll tell you that nobody works with him because he won't take nothin' —it's true he don't, not even cunt—but that's not why. He's just not a street cop."

Since the use of force is generally linked to emergencies, patrolmen cannot allow the attitudes of their colleagues to be ambiguous, to await testing on the street. New men are openly questioned and opinions given frankly.

A rookie patrolman was sitting in the roll room waiting for his tour to begin when his wagon partner left a small group to come and sit next to him. It was the first time anyone had spoken to him before roll call in the two weeks he had been in the district. "Hey, Tony, I been meanin' to ask you, where'd you get that little stick you carry?" "It's what they issued us at the academy," the rookie replied. "No kiddin'. Take my advice and get rid of it. Go down to Coteman's and get yourself one of them new plastic sticks. They're good and solid, not a toothpick." The rookie fidgeted, kept his eyes on the floor, and quietly replied, "I don't want to hit anyone with a stick. I don't want to be that way."

His partner smiled and replied, "Listen, Tony, I ain't tellin' you to go out there and hit people. I know this squad's got a hot reputation, but I ain't tellin' you to do that. I just want you to have a stick that will do the job when you got to use it. You're working with me and I got to depend on you. I gotta know if you're gonna be there when the trouble starts. Nobody has to tell you to hit someone. You'll know when you have to use it, but you should have a stick that will do the job when you swing it." The next day the rookie arrived with a new plastic stick.

Any evidence of failure is treated with great seriousness, and veterans make sure that all their colleagues are informed. A man who is unwilling to use force is viewed as a danger to everyone who works with him, and he cannot be allowed to persist in his ways. A patrolman returned to his squad after a vacation and he was being filled in on recent developments over a cup of coffee. "Listen, we got a new kid, Jackson, working the wagon with me. Watch out for him, he's shaky. I had to call an assist last night because of him, and he just stood there. He was so fuckin' scared, he couldn't even call for help."

"What happened?"

"We had some bullshit over on Elm Street. You know that dippy broad. She thinks that just because she's fuckin' a cop, she can call up and get her old man locked up whenever she wants to go out. Anyway, we get over there and the old man is sitting in the living room watching TV. She says he hit her and she wants him locked up. He says, 'Good evening, Officer,' and keeps watchin' TV. I told her I ain't lockin' him up for nuthin'. Well, she starts gettin' rammy, hollerin' about her rights and the fuckin' cops, and then her son and daughter—you know the daughter, don't you, buddy?— come in and they're hollerin' too. Plus a couple of their friends. I told Jackson before we went in to stay by the door and he ain't doin' nothin'. Well, it's gettin' a little warm in there, and you know me, I'm starting to get pissed off, so I figure we'll just leave. Then she just jumps me, and her son come at me, but I give him a good shot. I yell to the kid to get us some help, and so help me God, he just stood there. I'm pushin' her off, and I almost tripped over the kid backin' out the door, the prick. So I had to call an assist and go back in there and cool 'em all. You know the old man never stopped watchin' TV. But that kid is murder. I told him if it ever happens again, I'll punch his head off."

A policeman understands the meaning of fear, the loosening of the muscles in the midriff and the visions of terrible things happening to your body, and he does not condemn men for being afraid, but he does not want them around him when he is working. They are only a danger and a burden. A patrolman recalled an incident when he went to the aid of a rookie in a bar. "It was a rough place. I walked in there and the kid was standing in the middle of a bunch of 'em. They were real goons, truckers, and the kid was terrified, you could see it on his face. I turned right around and went to the car to call for help. When I got back in there, they were shovin' him around, so I just rushed 'em and took two of 'em right through the side door. The bartender saved us, he clubbed two guys with a bottle. The kid just stood there, he was paralyzed. It seemed like forever until help arrived, but we settled them guys good. When it was over, I wanted to punch the kid in the mouth, you know, but when I walked up to him, I could see he was shakin' like a leaf and tryin' not to cry. So I walked away and left him to the sergeant. But he straightened out O.K. He just froze that one time."

The policeman's willingness to commit himself physically to the control of people who resist him is an affirmation of the limitations imposed on him for controlling people. He cannot threaten to shoot or maim everyone who resists or flouts him but is obliged to operate within the limitations established by the community that employs him. However, if he uses his body as a tool and a weapon, he must accept injury and damage as a natural part of his work, something to be avoided if at all possible but something that is always likely to occur. Publicly and officially, no policeman admits that inexperience or error was responsible for an injury he or a colleague sustained, but in private they are frank in their evaluations.

During the last darkness of a dreary Sunday morning, a young patrolman called an assist. Men mobilized themselves to go to his aid, some half asleep, some sitting in the operations room talking to pass the time, others sitting grimly in their cars sipping coffee and waiting for the first rays of the sun—the whole squad raced to the call for help. On another night not long before, in the same area, a rookie policeman had been murdered.

The men arrived to find the officer struggling with a man and a woman, who were quickly subdued without injury. The patrolman had a painfully twisted knee and lacerations on his legs. He had spotted the couple parked on a main street making love, and seeing a chance for a vice pinch he had moved right in. When he explained the situation, his colleagues were very amused. "My man, what you have got to learn. When you got to fight an old man, you better call an old man to do your fighting for you," one man said, laughing openly. Another advised him, "Listen, before you go to the hospital and milk this little bruise for a couple of weeks I.O.D. [injured-on-duty status, which gives the man full pay], take a word of advice. Next time you see a guy stretched, let him get his rocks off before you pull him out of the car. It's still a pinch. Then he'll go anywhere you want with a smile, like a lamb. How would you feel if some dude come and pulled you out in the middle of your sweetness and honey? You'd really have a hard-on for him." The gathering laughed as the patrolman hobbled to his car for the trip to the hospital.

While all policemen agree on the necessity for force in their work, there is no agreement among colleagues on how much force is required or exactly when it must be used. In every large department there are some conflicts between white and black policemen over the use of force in certain situations, just as once there were fights between Italians and Irish, and Irish and native-born Americans. Some of these conflicts go beyond verbal exchanges, and the threat they pose to the unity of the department is attested to by the secrecy under which they are buried. In some districts there are fistfights between black and white policemen and threats of even harsher conflict. There are also other tensions that are not inspired by racial feelings. A man may lose control of himself and prolong beating a prisoner to a point where colleagues intervene to prevent serious injury. Some refuse to work with a man who has a reputation for being "hot" or having a "short fuse," because he may get them in trouble.

Occasionally a patrolman will try to beat another man's prisoner; this can create an explosive situation. The beating of people in custody is not widely practiced but it persists. If a man approaches a person who is handcuffed and hits him, he is committing a crime that should cause his colleagues to arrest him. While this rarely occurs, it is one of the few instances when a policeman will even jokingly suggest that the solidarity that binds them is on the point of dissolution. "You put your hand on my prisoner, pal, and I'm gonna put you down and lock up your ass." On another occasion, a patrolman who hit the handcuffed prisoner of a colleague was thrown down a flight of stairs by the outraged officer. "Son-of-a-bitch, he hits my prisoner and I have to stand him up in court tomorrow."

Every policeman is faced at some point with the temptation to beat a prisoner. There is always someone who angers him or arouses a fear in him that he seeks to eradicate by punishing the person who caused him to quiver. If his supervisors do not object, nothing can stop him. Two patrolmen were sitting in the roll room with their lieutenant. They had just arrested a married couple after a fight that ended in an assist. Nobody was hurt, but there had been some anxious moments. The turnkey approached them and asked if they wanted to go back and "give the old man a shot." They declined, and he said, "You're pussies." The lieutenant told him to leave the prisoners alone. "If you want to hit someone, go out and lock one up," he said. A few moments later the turnkey reappeared and asked again if the men did not want to work the prisoners over before they went downtown. They just shook their heads. Their sergeant offered his support. "There's times when you really want to give it to them but you're always glad the next day you didn't, when you have to make up the paper work, go see the captain, explain yourself."

The use of force is not a philosophical issue for a policeman. It is not a question of should or whether, but when and how much. Therefore, the amount of force a policeman uses does not depend solely on himself but also on the character of the people he polices and the policies of his department. There have been times in American history when the police openly fought with the people they policed. There was little effort made to conceal the evidence of their battles. Nobody was arrested, charged with resisting or assault and battery, and the victims were left where they fell. The mayor of Philadelphia in the 1850's, Richard Vaux, who was credited with organizing the municipal police of that city, proudly recalled his record and performance with an unvarnished frankness that is quite astonishing:

> There was no formal arrest, there were few prisoners in the docks in the mornings; the justices of the peace were not much troubled, but the fellow who was caught never forgot until his dying day the time he fell into the hands of "Dick" Vaux's police. I remember one night three of the Rangers [river pirates] were surprised, and jumped into the river and swam to a tugboat in the middle of the stream. It was very cold, and they thought Dick (I was there) and his men would not follow. They were never so mistaken in all of their lives. We got a boat and overtook them. The interview was more muscular than intellectual.

The rascals were pretty well satisfied before it was over. So were we. They didn't trouble us again during the administration.[1]

Throughout the nineteenth century, there was little public objection to the police openly using force to quell not merely riot but any neighborhood dispute. The police constantly battled with volunteer firemen, who often were paid political strong-arm men serving local factions and machines. In certain neighborhoods there were men who acquired reputations as "cop fighters." They were often associated with a taproom or a street corner, and the beatman knew that he would have to settle accounts with the men before he had any peace on his rounds. One policeman recalls them from the time he was a rookie in New York City after the First World War. "There were the older toughs who hung out in Jordan's saloon at the corner of 98th Street and Columbus Avenue. Among these were the cop fighters, men who went hunting for a uniform the minute they got drunk."[2] These neighborhood conflicts persist, an expression of relationships between the police and the people of certain communities that are clearly defined and limited. One veteran officer fondly recalls how it was when he became a policeman just after the Korean War. "Before we had the radio and cars, a guy was really on his own. I remember when I was only a kid in the department, only the sergeant had a car. A guy would take a whipping somewhere, in a taproom. The sergeant would go around and collect all of us. We'd form up at the station and march down there and just fight it out. They'd be waiting for us, knew we would be coming, and knew we would win, too. We whipped plenty of ass but we took it, too. Nobody used any weapons and we never locked anyone up for that."

The public no longer supports the policeman's informal use of force to settle accounts, but policemen still resort to force when they are challenged and feel that they will not be "dimed" by the people involved. Two patrolmen returned to their car after eating lunch in their usual restaurant.

[1]Sprogle, p. 109.
[2]McAllister, p. 25.

They found that in their absence their sticks, riot helmets, and ticket books had been stolen. The restaurant was in a neighborhood where the teenagers had a reputation for challenging the police. Once an unattended car had been put in gear and rolled down a hill while the patrolman was on a call. The area was a remnant of one of those legendary neighborhoods where the kids grew up to be policemen, firemen, crooks, priests, politicians, and burglars. Most policemen locked their cars when they got out, but these men had forgotten. Either they had to account for their lost equipment (the department is very suspicious about lost ticket books) or retrieve it. The men did not object to the loss, however, as much as they did to the challenge issued them. How could they go back to the restaurant again? They would not know who was laughing at them and joking about how they had done in the cops.

They opted for an informal solution to the problem. They spotted a fellow across the street from them and he was quickly placed in custody. He denied any knowledge of the crime, but he was handcuffed and thrown into the back of the car. One officer went into the restaurant to tell the owner, who was a friend, about their problem. He offered to make a deal. If in an hour all the equipment was returned, they would release the boy without any questions. Otherwise he promised to arrest the boy for some serious crime before the night was over. The men knew that the message would spread from the restaurant through the entire neighborhood in a matter of minutes; they left the area. When they returned, they found all of their equipment piled on the sidewalk. They released the boy. It was a draw, and the policemen were confident that nobody would make any complaint against them.

The department does not condone such behavior, although informally there are few policemen who would object to the actions taken by the patrolmen to solve their problem. The department seeks earnestly to limit the use of force by its men without limiting in any way their resolve to use force. The men are lectured on their legal rights, told the difference between quelling resistance and brutality—"If they resist, you can knock 'em on their ass and keep knocking 'em until they give up, but that's it"—urged to be polite and honorable with everyone until they are shown reasons to behave otherwise. But the police do not want their men to be reluctant to swing in self-defense if they are also being asked to perform tasks that inevitably draw them into conflicts.

Nor is physical attack the only way in which a policeman may violate a person. He can take an insulting tone, talk down to someone, adopt a familiarity that is unwanted but cannot be stopped. Patrolmen can be ordered to avoid doing these things, but if they are denied the use of threatening gesture and warning, they must consider avoiding many engagements where these are used in place of force or using physical force to obtain compliance. There is no polite way to order someone off a corner if there has been a complaint about noise, nor is there a polite way of telling someone to move along if the department has ordered a street cleared of demonstrators. There may be less violent ways, less inflammatory ways than are sometimes used, but there are no polite ways. And the policeman sees all of the available techniques as aspects of the same thing—his authority.

Two patrolmen answered a disturbance house on a hot Friday evening. They were familiar with the area: a working-class neighborhood filled with hard-working people, friendly girls, good drinkers, and young burglars. A pregnant woman, almost hysterical, greeted them at the door with a tale of conflict familiar to any officer. Her story, sustained by her husband and her sister, told of people next door who were trying to drive them from the neighborhood. "They live in the five houses next to us, the whole clan, and they want this one, too." The woman claimed she had been beaten by the foul-mouthed "crone" who was the leader of the effort to drive her from her home. The patrolmen were sympathetic to the pregnant woman, who remained polite despite her agitation, but there was nothing they could do. They urged her to stay in the house for the remainder of the evening, and as they left they noticed a number of bystanders watching them.

An hour later they got a return call. The street was packed when they arrived. The pregnant lady claimed that someone had tried to break in the back door of her house. Her sister, whose face was scratched, said that when she had gone outside, one of the women from next door had beaten her.

She said that she had shot a gas gun in her assailant's face. One patrolman told her, "Lady, don't tell me that. You could go for assault." The patrolmen sat down, had a cup of coffee, and urged the women either to get a warrant from a judge to prevent recurrences or to move. The women were frightened because the husband, a plumber, had gone out on a job. The policemen told the women not to open the door and then went to the neighbors. They were met by a man who said that "those women are bad-mouthin' my wife . . ." His wife came outside and told the policemen they should stay out of it. They ignored her remarks and told the couple to get a warrant restraining the people from making remarks or causing trouble. They also warned them that if there was another call, they would come with a wagon.

They got into their car and had driven only fifty feet when a front tire blew out. "That's it for tonight," the driver muttered, as he informed his dispatcher. While they waited for the repair truck, they were besieged with offers of food, beer, advice, and information from friendly neighbors. "Officer, you married?" "Lady, don't you know better than to introduce your daughter to a policeman?" People stopped to chat, suggesting that the pregnant woman was the victim "of that terrible family that's ruining our street." The husband of the pregnant woman returned from his job and the patrolmen stopped him. He was friendly and they were frank. "Listen, pal, I know how you feel comin' home to all this bullshit. But do yourself a favor, go to court and get a warrant. But don't pull any shit. I'm tellin' ya real friendly, if it starts you're all goin' in." The man smiled and promised he would make no trouble.

The street remained crowded and the patrolmen watched the scene, standing by their car, sipping sodas provided by a pleasant girl who said she was nineteen. Suddenly it erupted. The sister of the pregnant woman came out of the house and was struck by someone—who could see for sure from a distance?—in the head. The policemen grabbed their sticks and raced down the street as people drew back. When they arrived, a man was wrestling with the bleeding victim. He may have been trying to maintain the peace, keeping her from responding to the attack, but nobody waited to find out. "You're locked up, pal," one officer said, spinning him around and snapping a cuff to one wrist. Someone said, "She did it," and a patrolman spotted the crone who earlier had warned him not to intervene. He moved toward her.

"No fuckin' skinny cop's gonna lock me up, prick," she muttered, withdrawing toward her house. The patrolman followed her through the scattering crowd, up the stairs into the hallway. His partner was holding their prisoner and watched him go into the house. When he saw three other men go up the steps, he dropped his hold on the man and raced to the aid of his partner. "Get some help," he yelled to someone as he jumped up the steps, pushing at people, banging at them with his stick to make them move. "Get the fuck out of my way," he muttered, trying to reach his partner. Inside, his partner was holding on to the woman with one hand, fending off the three men with his stick. "You ain't takin' my mother," one burly fellow said, taking a swipe at him. The policeman jabbed him in the breastbone with the point of his stick. "The fuck I ain't."

At that moment the house was overwhelmed by policemen responding to the call. A woman had reported that some men had dragged two policemen into a house. The conflict was immediately extinguished. The husband, wife, and two sons were handcuffed, while one patrolman went outside to retrieve his handcuffs and prisoner, who was waiting patiently where he had been deserted. His large dog wandered about, growling nervously. "You better get someone to leash him, pal, or I'm gonna shoot him," the policeman said, unsnapping his holster. As the prisoners were loaded into the wagon, the assembled neighbors cheered. "Good work, Officers!" "Give it to 'em good." "Give 'em a shot for me."

Although the patrolmen did everything they could to prevent trouble in this incident, advising the principals to go to court and settle their differences amicably, it cannot be said they used force reluctantly or that they did not exceed their rights. By what right did they approach the husband returning from work to warn him to do one thing or another? Just because it was a friendly warning received in the spirit with which it was offered does not make it any less an act of blatant authority.

Very few policemen use physical force gratuitously. A man will cajole, joke, advise, threaten, and counsel rather than hit, but once his right to act is questioned, once his autonomy is threatened, he is prepared to respond with whatever force is necessary. And once his power is contested, he can do no wrong. The legitimacy of his authority allows him to do whatever he must to preserve it. An attack on him is treated as an attack on the state. A man resisting a policeman is suddenly an alleged criminal, and although he has not been convicted, the policeman knows he can treat him in a manner in which he cannot treat others. The policeman who says, "If some bastard hurts me, I'm not gonna just win, I'm gonna get even and he's gonna know I hurt," is expressing a sentiment that violates the law but one that cannot be eliminated because the law allows policemen to treat alleged criminals differently from people who are not criminals.

When a person breaches the law, his moral character is transformed in the eyes of society. Adherence to the law is regarded as so vital that an effort to evade its judgment in a large number of cases is sufficient reason for a person's exclusion from the community, and even his legal execution. Policemen kill people for crimes that would earn them only small jail sentences, but nobody seems to view this as a situation worthy of remedy. Instead, the public and the press treat some of these scenes as public theater. A man hijacks a plane and the visible power of the state is mobilized to suppress the crime. To prevent the hijacker's successful departure, sharpshooters are allowed to risk the lives of everyone on the plane. An example is made to deter others who might be considering similar acts. The patrolman who comes in off the street, his clothing slashed by a knife, dragging his assailant, saying, "I could have burned you and nobody would have said a thing," is speaking only the blunt truth.

If men are sent onto the streets to do work that is often dangerous, they will defend themselves whether they have permission or not. But more important than the limitations imposed on their rights and the stringency with which these are enforced is the problem of divorcing from these rights the moral justifications that accompany them. These allow some men to beat people into submission and beyond; to smack a boy caught sniffing glue in the belief that it may deter him from continuing a practice that may cripple him; to threaten and terrorize a junkie found with a few bags of heroin and force him to tell the patrolman where he can find more. A policeman does not need a set of rules to know when he is exceeding what is allowed; a policeman who hits someone with his stick knows when he is using it in a technical fashion to control their behavior and when he is simply beating in their head. But few men who exceed their rights ever do so without a feeling of justification—what they do is somehow the right thing to do, even though it must be concealed. And this feeling is not simply the invention of the moment. There are too many occasions when the patrolman could hurt people he dislikes but does not to explain the times when he does commit violence simply as the consequence of a defective personality or as the behavior of a moral monster. Nor does he even have to hit people to cause them pain and injury.

Everyone who is arrested must be handcuffed. Many people fear handcuffs because they deprive a person of the use of his arms, stripping him of the ability to defend himself from attack and to maintain his balance (and dignity) as he walks. But the police see handcuffs as an instrument that prevents resistance by prisoners and reduces the likelihood of assault on them by angry policemen. However, a pair of handcuffs can easily be converted into an instrument of torture. They can be put on incorrectly, twisted, forcing the prisoner's arms to be unnaturally strained. The cuffs are adjustable to fit different-size wrists, and slight pressure causes them to be tightened over the wrist bones, creating excruciating pain. If the manacled person twists about, severe wrist cuts may result; but if the wrists are firmly held by an officer, there will be only pain and red welts, which quickly disappear. Handcuffs are supposed to be placed with their keyholes facing outward, making them easy to open. But if they are reversed, the person's arms must be twisted to make it possible to insert the key, and this, too, can be a painful experience.

Almost all prisoners are transported in wagons after they are placed under arrest. Most trips in the wagon are uneventful, but they can be a most unpleasant experience, difficult to protest against. A wagon is simply an enclosed truck with benches running the length of its sides. The prisoner sits handcuffed on a bench. He has no handholds, and if the wagon is not full, there is nothing against which he can brace himself. It is really quite a simple matter for the driver to toss him around the back like a sack of potatoes. All he need do is speed up and slow down, hit the brake hard a few times, or drive over roads he knows are especially bumpy. Rarely is a prisoner injured by any of these methods, but anyone who runs when told to halt, swears or spits at a policeman, threatens him in any way may find himself chastened by these techniques. And how does a person complain that the handcuffs were too tight or that the driver of the wagon was not competent?

Few policemen indulge in any of these acts frequently, and rarely do any of them occur for no apparent reason. But even when he is not angry with someone, the patrolman regularly does things that border on disregard for a person's rights. If someone he approaches is smoking, he may order him to put out the cigarette, and if there is no compliance, he will take it from the person's mouth. People who loiter nearby when he is interrogating someone are told to move on, abruptly and urgently. When he takes someone in for investigation the suspect's pockets are stripped of combs, pen knives, cigarette lighters, matches, all of the oddments people casually assemble and always cherish. He does all of these things to protect himself, to lessen the chances that he may have to hit the person or use his body unnecessarily, but they are nonetheless offensive acts. Yet how can the person complain?

And what of the people he shoots? They are mostly felons, petty criminals who are rarely mourned. Most policemen do not shoot even when they have a clear right to do so. At times when he feels entirely justified in killing someone, a policeman may not shoot. One patrolman recalled a moment in his life when he was disarmed by a man who shot at him and missed, then fled. The patrolman claimed that he followed the man and managed to wrestle his assailant to the ground. "We were rolling around, you know, and he still had the gun and I was holding on to his hand so he couldn't shoot me. I was biting him on the face and kicking, my mouth was filling up with his blood and he was screaming. When he gave up, I just stood there holding my gun and I really wanted to kill him, I did, but I couldn't shoot. I smashed him with the butt."

Most shootings occur suddenly, in moments of fear without calculation. "The first time I fired my gun, I'll never forget it. I went in on a holdup and these two guys come running out and they shot at me. I couldn't believe it, you know. I pulled my gun but, honest, my arm was shaking so bad that I couldn't hold it steady. Then I remembered the two-handed grip they teach you in the academy and started firing. I didn't hit nothing, but I musta been close because they stopped dead in their tracks and usually you shoot they just run faster," an experienced patrolman recalled.

Two patrolmen entered an abandoned schoolhouse to investigate a banging noise. They were searching the cellar, certain that the sounds had been made by someone cutting pipe, although they could not find any sign of the man. They had found lengths of pipe stacked and ready for removal, convincing them that their presumption was correct. The cellar was lighted only by their flashlights and light that filtered in from the street outside. Suddenly the man, who was hiding in the ceiling, dropped down to the ground with a piece of pipe in his hand. He rushed one of the officers, who drew his gun and, while backing away, shot him four times in the legs. But the man did not stop, finally smashed the gun from the officer's hand, and turned to rush for the exit, where the patrolman's partner suddenly appeared. When the man was only a few feet from him, the pipe raised above his head, the officer fired twice into his chest. The mortally wounded man was rushed to the hospital, cursing the policemen continuously. He died with these curses on his lips.

The patrolman who had fired the fatal shots wept silently in the dank cellar, overcome with fright and horror. His injured partner consoled him and helped him climb out of the cellar. When both men emerged, their lieutenant said to the injured officer, "We're gonna have to send you to the range to improve your shooting." "Those leg shots weren't no accident. I didn't want to kill the guy for cutting some pipe. I thought I could stop him, but I guess he just snapped out." The lieutenant looked at him for a moment and then said quietly, "Well, I guess everybody has his own way of working."

Another man recalled, "I was working alone on daywork. A call came out of a purse snatch. I go over and I'm checking out the area when the bus driver come by and said, 'That's the guy over there.' He's standing in front of a bar and I get out of the car and walk over toward him, and he starts moving. The street is full of people and I go after him, telling him to stop. He pulls a knife, and then I took my gun out and told him to drop it. Then we start a little dance down River Street. Finally another car shows up and the guys jump out because they can't make it through the traffic. He musta seen them coming, because he starts back toward me, and I told him to drop it or I was gonna shoot. He didn't say nothin', and he just kept moving, and I put one in him. He had this funny look in his eyes, he didn't stop moving but he had this funny look, and I gave him one more. He just sort of walked to the left and he was gone. He wasn't any more than a couple of feet away from me when he fell."

Policemen are reluctant to fire their guns because they know how grave the consequences are. A man involved in a shooting is carefully investigated and transferred from active duty while the probe continues; he usually is not allowed to return to the district where the shooting occurred. He knows that the detectives carefully gather the evidence, collect witnesses, and turn the case over to the district attorney's office. He does not treat this matter lightly, although there are many in the city who doubt the sincerity of the department's efforts to control these shootings. But if the policeman did not feel this pressure, he would be less reluctant to shoot. Some men do fire willfully and in violation of the law, either to kill or to terrify someone into confession. Others, more frequently, lose control of their judgment and fire after a fleeing car.

When a man is involved in a car chase, dangerous passions

are unleashed. It is difficult for any man to take the risks of a high-speed chase without becoming angry and determined. Some of them are willing even to kill. It is against the law *only* because most car thefts cannot be charged as felonies. Unless it can be proved that the person who took the car meant to deprive its owner of the permanent use of his property, the theft must be treated as a larceny, which is a misdemeanor, and not as a burglary, which is a felony. In a sense it seems like a minor quibble, but the only way to eliminate any chance of patrolmen firing at cars in chases is to punish the patrolmen rigorously, to enforce the department regulations to the limit. The department is often reluctant to do this because there are men who shoot people in similar circumstances and are praised. Why, then, should a patrolman be punished for stopping someone who willingly endangers the lives of many innocent people by driving recklessly through city streets? However, each time a man is allowed to flaunt the department's own regulations, the possibilities for containing his power within the established dimensions are made more difficult. The public, too, is given reasons to be skeptical of the commitment of the police to maintain the legal standards that have been established for them and that makes the task of policing the people more arduous.[3]

The policeman's power does not extend beyond the range of his body. When he takes his uniform off and goes home, he has no more power than any other head of a family. He is not like a wealthy man whose authority rests on something other than his position. Collectively, however, the police represent much more than the sum total of the authority delegated to the men who wear the uniform: they control and regulate the city. They can harass people and groups, restrict some activities to certain parts of town, close the streets to some and open them to others. At times, and in some places, our police have been used simply as instruments of terror to control and contain dissident political groups, racketeers who were out of favor, prostitutes whenever a city gets up in arms about vice, drunks when there are com-

[3]New York City police fired seventy-nine shots at fleeing cars in 1970, according to official departmental records. *The New York Times* (July 25, 1971).

plaints about panhandling. At other times our police have been used to aid the rise of ethnic groups and abet their escape from the control of entrenched political cliques. The police are an instrument for the manipulation of force; they are technicians, whether they be well or badly trained.

Every police force, regardless of its reputation, has within it the capacity to become an instrument of repression. Nowhere in America is there a police force that murders on command like the Brazilian death squads do or the French police did during the Algerian war, but there are some men in every department who would be willing to kill if ordered to do so. Each time a policeman is killed, the public gets a hint of the potential that is there.

Policemen take the death of colleagues seriously. While they are far from the brotherhood that some portray, they do maintain closer associations with one another than with any other group in the population. At roll calls the sergeants still read the death announcements of all department members, giving each man an opportunity to send condolences. Since he views his work as a very personal business, a policeman sees the murder of a colleague as an encouragement to others who may wish to try the same thing on another policeman, possibly on him. He wants killers of policemen caught, and the department makes extraordinary efforts to achieve their capture. The death of a patrolman is also an opportunity for the police to garner a little good publicity, and rarely is the chance squandered. But behind the newspaper talk is the police organization, squeezing its contacts for information.

When a captain stands before a roll call and orders the men to go out and "bring everyone walkin' around with a swinging pair" in for investigation, he is not giving the men license to break down doors, terrorize people, or beat them at will, but unless the department maintains very strict supervision, these things can happen. "There won't be many dudes walkin' around tonight after they hear about this shooting. They'll think we gonna go out there and whip some ass. And you know, some guys will, but most will just do the job." But doing the job is making fifteen or twenty car and ped stops in a few hours, each one with a hand on a gun butt, ready to reach for a jack if someone gives him "some shit." Patrolmen, detectives, special-unit officers, everyone is out doing the job, closing up the bars and clubs, hitting the speaks, pinching the junkies, the gamblers, the prostitutes, closing down the area, "squeezing them for information"; making it hard for them to work encourages cooperation. And if the department is not completely in control, this activity can get out of hand very easily. "I remember, it was a few years ago but the guys are still around, you know one of 'em but I won't mention his name. They were looking for some guys who killed a cop. They found 'em up on a roof. Who knows what happened, but those guys didn't come walkin' down. Either they threw 'em off or they were so fuckin' scared they jumped, but they came down." Most people who kill policemen are found, captured, and brought into custody because the department does not want its men to commit murder, but if that were not the policy . . .

Sometimes the city deliberately loosens the restraints on its men to accomplish some necessary purpose. When the task is completed, the department is hailed for preserving the peace or supporting the community, which may be no exaggeration, but the men who accomplish these deeds are the very men who the same newspapers urge in their editorials to be calm and restrained in handling their duties. "We don't whip much ass any more, not like it was when I came on or when my brother was on. The last time we really had a workout was the night Martin Luther King got killed. They ordered all the bars in the city closed and Roy and I got a large section in South. We just went from one place to the next, and it was mostly stick work. We'd go into one place, all dagos, and I'd do the talkin'. You walk in and tell 'em to close up, and if they said no, I just walked up to the bar and started smashing bottles. Then we'd just beat the piss out of 'em and leave. Next place they'd be real quiet and then someone would say, 'We'll close up but get that nigger cop outta here.' Well, you know Roy, he don't take that shit from nobody, so we'd whip their asses. Then we'd go to some nigger bar and it would be the same shit all over again. That night was really something, yes sir, and we closed every one of them bars. It was a hell of a night."

Two policemen stood on a corner talking, when their

sergeant pulled up. "Those little pricks. Someone hit my car with a rock. I'm going back there." He didn't ask anyone to come with him, but the two men got into their car and followed. He stopped his car at an intersection and got out; he was joined by the other two men. The three of them walked slowly around the intersection, challenging the neighborhood to a fight.

The same three men had just the night before cleared a nearby street of a hundred people during a small riot. "Sergeant, I want that street cleared." "Yes sir. Come on, you guys," he said in an offhand way to a bunch of policemen, but when they had advanced a few yards into the block, one of the men glanced about. "Sarge, there's just the three of us." The sergeant turned. "Fuck them, they ain't cops anyway, we'll do it ourselves. We stay together but not too close. Tell 'em all to go in the house. Be polite and don't swing unless I tell you. But if they don't go!" "Please go into your house and close the door unless you want to be arrested." "Please go in the house." "I said, Close the door. Close the door or I'm gonna put this fuckin' stick up your ass, pal. Thank you." When they had finished walking the length of the block, they slowly returned along the opposite side, the sergeant setting the pace. "Don't walk too fast, don't give 'em the wrong idea. Look at that beautiful clean street."

The policeman does not exist without force, and the disputes over how he uses it are essentially political disputes over his function and mission. But opposition poses critical problems for the police because they cannot do their job without the cooperation of the people. They can survive resistance, they can even suppress efforts to prevent them from controlling the streets, but they cannot do the work for which people willingly pay taxes without the active cooperation of the citizenry. The rising crime rates of our metropolitan areas are putting the police under increasing pressure to become even more active and aggressive than they presently are. The more policemen are put on the streets, the more work they do, the more calls they answer, the more criminals they capture, the more complaints and "incidents" will inevitably occur. And most of the pressure for more policing comes from the same sections of the population who react most strongly to the manner in which the police conduct their work. This poses a dilemma that cannot be resolved by human-relations courses, civilian review boards, minority recruiting, better training, and more rigorous supervision. Each of these may be desirable, but they leave untouched the problem of the individual patrolman who must continue to use force in a hundred different ways in a time when people who claim they object to force also call him to move someone's car from in front of their house. The "professional" policeman of tomorrow with his college degree will be the same kind of man who has always become a policeman, a person who enjoys the "security" of the job, is willing to work long hours, and is also prepared to take the risks and gather the simple pleasures that come from using his body to do his work. He will do whatever he must to maintain his place on the street, whatever is essential to preserve the police as an institution; but this does not make the streets safe, it does not preserve the security of people in their homes or prevent the destruction of thousands of people by drugs and alcohol. Whether the police can do any of these things is open to question, but unless there is evidence that they can, opposition to them will probably continue to increase. If their legitimacy is increasingly questioned, they will use force simply to preserve themselves. If this occurs, our police organizations will have become something very different from what they are, although the men who are the police remain unchanged.

Part Three

BETWEEN
LAW
AND
ORDER

CHAPTER EIGHT

Little Crimes

In theory the policeman is responsible for the prevention of all crime, but informally he distinguishes between those crimes that are seen as a direct challenge to his authority and place and others—no matter how terrible—that do not directly threaten him. He distinguishes crimes by the traditional legal categories used in charging and prosecuting suspected criminals, but these are not what he uses in judging the seriousness of a crime. He may, for example, be much more concerned with a burglary than with a murder or a rape, although the burglary will probably get little public attention and the others are sure to receive at least a paragraph or two in the newspapers. It is not indifference, callousness, or the elevation of property over life that leads him to this ordering of his concern but rather his notions about his place on the street.

For the policeman, the determining factor of any crime's importance is its setting. He defines the location of all crimes by the deceptively simple distinction between "inside" and "outside." These terms have nothing to do with his notion of privacy or with the legal definitions of private and public places, but derive from his conception of his work. A crime committed outside may actually occur inside a building, while a crime committed inside may take place on a public street. Outside means any location a patrolman can be reasonably expected to see while on patrol. If a burglar breaks into a building through a rear door or cuts a hole in a roof, his act is considered an inside crime, because the patrolman had no chance to notice anything amiss, even if he was patrolling alertly. If a person is assaulted in his back yard or mugged in an alley, it is an inside crime, despite its

occurrence in a place legally defined as public. But if a burglar breaks open a front door to gain entry, it is an outside
crime, because there is no reason why the patrolman should
have missed it as he passed. Any outside crime is an affront
to the patrolman's notion of himself as a guardian of his
territory, an occurrence which suggests to his superiors
that he was not doing his work properly.

One night shortly before the end of the tour, a sergeant
was given a call to meet a patrolman at a jewelry store.
"Oh, shit, if that fucker blew this one, I'll give it to him
good," the sergeant muttered. He knew it was a serious call
because many patrolmen, and particularly the one who had
called him, do not take assignments in the last fifteen minutes of their tours to avoid having to work overtime without
pay. If they receive an assignment from the dispatcher that
is not an emergency (and occasionally one that is), they
accept the assignment formally and then give it to their
relief man when he takes over the car. When the sergeant
arrived, he found the patrolman talking with the owner,
while the jeweler's wife sobbed, lamenting in Yiddish about
the failure of the police to protect them. The store had been
burglarized; the owners, who lived in an apartment above
the shop, had discovered the crime when they returned from
the movies. The area had been plagued by numerous burglaries
in recent weeks and the sector men had been given the specific
responsibility of checking the shops several times each evening.
The front of the store was a single, large, plate-glass window, which allowed a clear view of the entire store. The
burglars had cleaned out the showcases and removed several
watches that were on display in the window. The sergeant
surveyed the scene and glared at the officer. "Either they
were little kids or they were crawling on their knees, Sarge,"
the man said hopefully. The owner asked the policemen to
accompany him upstairs while he showed them what had
happened in his apartment. Several rooms had been ransacked and one of the thieves had defecated on the kitchen
table.[1] In a rear bedroom a television set was sitting on
the floor by a small window, which stood open, its screen

---

[1]Defecations are common occurrences in house burglaries. Many
burglars become excited during the commission of these crimes and
must relieve themselves. The act is also an expression of the contempt
they feel for the place they have violated.

ripped away. "It must have been kids who came through here. See, the TV was too large for the window so they left it," the sergeant said. The patrolman was relieved. "It better be on your log that you checked this place a couple of times tonight," the sergeant said to the patrolman while the victims were occupied elsewhere. The man nodded and left, leaving his sergeant to mollify the owners and to notify the detectives. He was in the clear because the burglars had entered at the back of the building, away from his normal range of view.

The majority of all murders and aggravated assaults occur inside and therefore they are not "on" the patrolman. Once he accustoms himself to being in the presence of the battered and gory remains of the victims, he does not display much concern about these crimes (unless the victim is a child), although he knows they arouse considerable public agitation. He understands that the department treats murder seriously, assigning its best men to the homicide squad and allowing them an almost unlimited budget to accomplish their work. He admires homicide detectives because they work in the unit that enjoys the highest prestige in the department, and he envies them the large amounts of money they reputedly earn by being allowed to work unlimited overtime. He is attentive to any demand they make on him at a murder scene, although he is perplexed by the department's decision to devote such a considerable part of its resources to the solution of crimes which he feels are mostly bullshit. Many patrolmen have arrested "killers" simply by arriving first at the scene and taking into custody the remorseful murderer, who frequently is waiting to confess his crime.[2]

[2]Marvin E. Wolfgang, *Patterns of Criminal Homicide* (Philadelphia, University of Pennsylvania Press, 1958). Until recently most police departments in Europe and in this country "cleared" about 90 percent of all murders. While the number of murders in our larger cities has been rising steadily in the last several years, some of the departments have not been able to make arrests in increasingly larger numbers of homicides. In New York City, for example, there has been an almost continual decline in the clearance rate since 1963. In 1964 the clearance rate for murder was 87.3 percent; in 1968, 77.9; in 1971, 56.8; and in the first six months of 1972 only 49.8. In Detroit in 1971, the clearance rate was only 68 percent. Marvin E. Wolfgang, Franco Ferracuti, *The Subculture of Violence* (London, Tavistock, 1967), pp. 290–6; F. H. McClintock, N. H. Avison, *Crime in England and Wales* (London, Heinemann, 1968), pp. 105–8, 142–3. I am grateful to Ms. Adrienne Cowles for providing me with the figures for New York and Detroit.

Despite the frequent voicing of disparaging remarks about some victims—"Well, that's one less rughead we got to worry about"; "That's one nigger who ain't gonna talk back to his momma no more"—a policeman rarely fails to make an effort to save a victim from death when he is presented with an opportunity to do so. The principal way a patrolman can directly prevent a murder is by getting a grievously wounded person to medical treatment as quickly as possible. Regardless of how he feels about a person, the patrolman does not hesitate to get himself covered with another person's blood and gore or to assume the risks involved in driving quickly through the crowded streets of the city. The patrolman does not receive accolades from anyone for doing these things (although his failure to do them might be noted and censured); it is part of the job.

Women were shouting hysterically and running out of a store. The rookie, his first week on the street, stood over the dying man, his eyes riveted on the huge, pulsating hole in the man's chest. The shotgun blast had shattered the victim's breastbone, and the man's heart and lungs were plainly visible. The officer was changing color, but he was brought back to action in time by the sure voice of his partner: "O.K., boy, don't look at his head. Take a deep breath, hold it, and grab his feet. We gotta get him moving." The two men lifted the man, who was probably beyond help by then, and quickly brought him to the waiting wagon, which sped off to the hospital with its lights flashing and siren whining.

Any crime that occurs outside is treated seriously by the patrolman. Even if he is indifferent personally to the plight of the people who are being victimized, any failure on his part to fulfill his obligations cannot be covered easily by an excuse, and at the least he will earn a black mark for stupidity in the minds of his supervisors. But his personal commitment to use his car and his body to go quickly to the aid of any person calling for help (either directly or through the radio dispatcher) is no guarantee that the patrolman will be very successful. Two studies of street robberies in the quite different environments of London and Philadelphia have shown that the police do not solve more than 30 percent of the crimes reported to them. Almost half of the apprehensions in both cities were made by patrolmen within ten minutes of the first report of the crime. Many of these unsuccessful criminals were captured as the result of their victim's resistance or with the aid of a passer-by. The arrival of the police only sealed a failure caused by ill luck, ineptitude, or possibly the criminal's unwillingness to use violence. In both robbery studies the percentage of apprehensions made at the scene by the police or by private intervention was the same, although the number of robberies reported in Philadelphia (a city less than one fourth the size of London) was nine times greater. Time appeared to be the critical factor in almost all apprehensions. The clearance rate dropped very rapidly as the time between the commission of the crime and the informing of the police rose. For crimes that were not reported for more than a half hour, success came only when the victim was robbed by a friend or an acquaintance. Then it was a relatively easy matter for detectives to track down the suspect.[3]

Every crime against a person or his property requires an intention, a victim, and a setting in which the intention becomes a criminal act.[4] The moment of greatest risk for the street criminal occurs when he reveals his intention to the victim, continues until he has completed his work, and then declines rapidly as he withdraws from the scene. The ideal street crime (from the criminal's point of view) occurs when the victim, because of either the criminal's skill (a pickpocket, for example) or the victim's absence (burglary or car theft), does not know he is being victimized, allowing the criminal to withdraw undetected and unrecognized. Since the greatest number of crimes are committed against unattended property—burglaries of businesses, houses and apartments, trucks and cars—most crimes are not detected until well after they have been committed and remain unsolved. There are hundreds of thousands of "perfect crimes" committed each year, although it cannot be said that they great-

[3]F. H. McClintock, *Robbery in London* (London, Macmillan, 1961), pp. 30–46; André Normandeau, "Trends and Patterns in Crimes of Robbery." Unpublished Ph.D. dissertation, University of Pennsylvania, 1968, pp. 133–44.
[4]A burglary is an illegal entry into an unoccupied building for the purpose of removing the property of others. A robbery is the taking of property from a person with the use of or the threat of the use of force.

ly benefit those who execute them. Crime is not lucrative for those who take the greatest risks, but the accumulation of little crimes which go unsolved (and frequently unreported)[5] adds to the unrest and insecurity of all city dwellers. But whatever the risks are, they are apparently not sufficient to deter people from taking them over and over again.

Although there is no evidence to demonstrate that the amount of patrol the police have on the street affects the chances of victimization, or that the response rate of the policeman actually increases his chances overall to capture criminals, these two assumptions have always been at the heart of every police tactic for suppressing crime. The administrators have always sought ways of maximizing the number of men on crime patrol and having them respond in the most efficient way possible to signals of distress. Since the police do not have unlimited manpower, they have developed formulas for calculating the best distribution of the available men for maximum effectiveness. These "hazard formulas" differentially weigh reported crimes, arrests, accidents, calls for service, numbers of business places and licensed drinking establishments, road mileage, stolen cars, the numbers of schools and fires to compute the number of men necessary to police a given area. These formulas are inspired by the notion that the protection of an area requires the presence of a certain number of men continually on patrol to ensure its well-being and to discourage the criminally inclined from putting thier intentions into action.[6] The

---

[5]It is now established that in many categories of serious crime the official statistics of the police reflect considerable underreporting. This is caused mainly by the failure of the victims to inform the police; the police also contribute by failing to record some crimes reported to them or recording them as lesser crimes. See Philip H. Ennis *et al.*, *Criminal Victimization in the United States*, Field Survey to the President's Commission on Law Enforcement (Washington, D. C., G.P.O., 1967); Marvin E. Wolfgang, "Urban Crime," in *The Metropolitan Enigma*, James Q. Wilson, ed. (Garden City, N.Y., Anchor Books, 1970), pp. 270–311; Albert D. Biderman, "Social Indicators and Goals," in *Social Indicators*, Raymond A. Bauer, ed. (Cambridge, Mass., M.I.T. Press, 1966), pp. 111–53.

[6]Hazard formulas were developed by Orlando W. Wilson, the most influential police administrator of this century. He developed his ideas while chief of police in Wichita, Kansas, where he supervised the introduction of cars into patrol service. He was one of the optimistic proponents of motorized patrol, and his work did much to popularize the use of the patrol car. O. W. Wilson, "Distribution of Police

police have never been able to demonstrate that this fundamental assumption is correct, nor has anyone proposed an alternative to their approach.

The search for the most efficient use of manpower has been coupled with a persistent effort in recent years to exploit any available technology to make the patrolman more efficient, quicker, and more completely supervised. The results have not been encouraging. According to a survey conducted by the Los Angeles Police Department in 1965—then the most mobile force in the country and widely regarded as the most professional—the entire department working at maximum efficiency had at most one hundred opportunities each week to discover a burglary in progress and only two chances of catching a robber in the act. The department's analysts thought these estimates to be inflated because no department ever works at peak efficiency. There are always men absent, others taken for special assignments, and even more who do not work precisely to the norms established by those who develop patrol schedules. In addition, these estimates represented only 12 percent of the burglaries and 2 percent of the robberies *known* to the police. Using these admittedly inaccurate and inflated figures, the chance of each patrolman capturing a burglar occurred once every three months and a robber once every fourteen years.[7]

Nobody knows how many crimes the police deter by their actions; nobody knows how many additional crimes would be committed if the police did not patrol the streets. But

---

Patrol Force," *Public Administration Service*, Publication #74 (Chicago, P. A. S., 1941), and his widely used text, *Police Administration*, 2d ed. (New York, McGraw-Hill, 1963). A critique of Wilson by systems analysts who are trying to develop a more sophisticated kind of hazard formula using predictive data (based on model simulations) rather than the historical data used in the traditional formulas is in James S. Kakalik and Sorrel Wildhorn, *Aids to Decisionmaking in Police Patrol*, #R-593/4-HUD/RC (Santa Monica, Cal., Rand Corporation, 1971), Chap. IV.

[7]On the police exploitation of technology, see *The Wall Street Journal* (August 9, 1971); Los Angeles survey, President's Commission on Law Enforcement and the Administration of Justice, *Task Force Reports: Science and Technology* (Washington, D.C., G.P.O., 1967), pp. 12–13. The figures were computed as averages for the entire department. Men working in districts where burglaries and robberies were frequent had greater opportunities to make apprehensions than men who worked districts where there were relatively fewer crimes.

everyone knows that no matter how much crime the police do prevent, it is not enough to make city people feel safe. No one can say with any assurance what the police must do to make their deterrent effect the awesome force it was optimistically predicted to be by the theoreticians of the New Police more than two centuries ago. Nobody knows what is an "acceptable" amount of crime in any area of the city. The police were meant to be men who patrol territories, and they have no choice but to develop tactics that complement the nature of the strategy that gives them their identity. Unfortunately, each of the tactics developed by the police has side effects that create additional problems. The more rigorously they seek to enforce their tactics, the more aggravated these unanticipated and unavoidable consequences become.

1 • Street Crime and Police Tactics

There is no way to assess accurately the overall impact of the policeman's work. It is probably true that few persons dare commit crimes in his presence, making him an effective guardian wherever he is. (Of course, the presence of *any* other individual often deters some crimes.) But the policeman has many obligations that take him away from the street. He can do only one thing at a time and there is no way of measuring the utility of his different services. For example, if he were not transporting a person to the hospital, he might prevent a purse snatching. The person he is taking to the hospital might die, however, if the patrolman were not transporting him. Also, there is no guarantee that the patrolman could prevent the purse snatch. But even if there were such a guarantee, who is to decide which is his more important obligation? What are the criteria to be used in establishing the relative utility of each of these apparently desirable services?

The patrolman is frequently called upon to take reports of crimes that are not likely to be solved, encouraging some administrators to argue that the men should not waste their time collecting useless information while their sectors remain unprotected. But do these visits not contribute something to the victims and to the police?

Two patrolmen were met at the front door by a young girl as they entered a newly renovated building in answer to a burglary call. She led them up the stairs through an open door into a room where a woman sat slumped in a chair, weeping. She had just returned from her work as a char-woman at a large hospital. It was 11 P.M. She had found her front door open and her new television set gone. Her oldest daughter said that some boys from a neighborhood gang had been in the hallway. The girl and her four younger brothers and sisters had been playing in the street until their mother returned from work. It was hot inside; there was no reason to stay in.

The woman was getting her papers when one officer asked her if she knew the serial number of the set. She did not. A working mother of five children, she would be obliged to con-tinue paying for someone else's pleasure for the next twenty-seven months. If she did not pay the installments, the finance company would come and take her refrigerator and any-thing else that the thieves found too large to move. She began to weep again as the policemen were about to leave and said, "I wish you would arrest me and stop me from doing what I am going to do to those jitterbugs. There's no point in being afraid of those boys. You work for your money to buy things and they come and steal what they want. I am gonna get them . . ." The policemen returned and talked with her for a few minutes until they were rea-sonably sure that she would not rush out and do something dangerous.

"Don't put your hands on that box, young man, or you'll spoil the fingerprints. These junkies are sumthin'. They know when the checks are comin' and grab 'em before you can get them out of the mailbox." The patrolman had come to investigate a burglarized mailbox. A terrified old woman had lost her pension check and she had no money to pay her rent or to buy her food. He took the report from her and was about to leave when she asked, "Ain't you gonna call the detectives down to take fingerprints? There must be some on there. He didn't have a key, you know." The lady was old, neat, well spoken. The officer was polite, but he knew that she would not believe him when he explained to her that the detectives would not come if he called, and if they did come would not find any prints that could be traced. She had seen the police taking fingerprints on television; she knew it was something they did. She just looked up at him and said softly, without reproach, merely stating a fact, "They'd come if I was white folks." He knew that she would not believe him; he knew that many of his colleagues would just turn around and walk out, but everyone has his own way of doing the job, at least patrolmen like to think so. He explained to her briefly that it was not possible to trace anonymous fingerprints without spending great amounts of time and money, but he had been right—she did not believe him.

The value of these service calls to the patrolman and to the people he visits is incalculable. Often he can do little more than listen to woeful tales of wayward mates and children ("Lady, look, I don't know where your old man is. Maybe he went to the ball game") or calm down momentarily angry persons. What would these people lose if the police no longer came to their homes? Who would the poor and the wayward talk to? Should their confusions and frustrations be ignored and allowed to accumulate? And what of the patrolman? The service calls he answers are his principal means of meeting some of the people he polices, increasing his knowledge and understanding of their customs and habits. What kind of person would he be if he did nothing but remain on crime patrol, answering only high-risk calls and looking for suspicious signs in everyone who passed?

When the policeman does have time to patrol, there is little he can do that does not arouse some anger and bitterness. Nobody objects when he cruises back alleys, checking doors and windows with the aid of his spotlight or getting out of the car to handcheck a door. Nobody objects when he searches darkened buildings for prowlers. But even when he passes a street corner without questioning the men standing there, they may be angered by his surveillance of them. He does not know most of the people he sees; he cannot know what they are doing unless he stops and questions them. If he works in a neighborhood where there are numerous reports of street crimes, shootings, and knifings, it is not surprising that he will be on the lookout for persons who are armed.

In some neighborhoods many people take the precaution of arming themselves. Some city people have always carried knives and razors, a consequence of political and cultural traditions which obliged people to make their own law. But now there are also people who carry weapons simply to defend themselves from attack—not on their honor but on their bodies. With increasing frequency women are buying gas guns, which shoot tear-gas pellets from a pistol that looks like a small automatic, a lady's gun. Nobody knows exactly how many real guns are owned illegally in this country, but the number is rapidly increasing. The number of legally owned guns is also rising quickly. In Philadelphia, for example, during 1965, when a new gun-registration ordinance was enacted, 3,540 people were given a permit to buy a gun to keep in their homes. In 1970 the number increased to 8,240, and during the first six months of 1971 there were an additional 4,514. During the entire period, 38,082 people registered to buy a handgun, in addition to the almost 75,000 guns of all types previously registered under older regulations. There is no way of knowing how many of these people are illegally carrying their guns with them when they go out of their houses. Philadelphia, like most big cities, is very reluctant to give people permission to carry weapons on the street. "Permits to carry," have been issued to 1,559 people; almost a thousand of these are private guards, who are licensed to have a gun on the premises they guard but may not have their guns with them when they are not working. The other permits are issued mainly to men who guard money and transport securities or other valuables.[8]

Between 1968 and 1970, policemen in Philadelphia arrested 3,269 persons for violations of firearm regulations. The majority of these arrests were made as the result of suspicion stops in public places. This might appear to be a large

[8]On knife-fighting traditions, see "Streetcorner Man" and "The Challenge" by Jorge Luis Borges in his collection, *The Aleph and Other Stories* (New York, Dutton, 1970). Philadelphia figures from official police sources. The most recent estimate of ownership of guns in the United States was 12,500 per 100,000 people. This is, for example, twenty-seven times greater than the ownership of guns in Great Britain. George D. Newton and Franklin L. Zimring, *Firearms and Violence in American Life* (Washington, D.C., G.P.O., 1970), p. 121.

number of arrests and a considerable number of illegal weapons removed from circulation, but the figure does not reflect the enormous number of pedestrian and car stops that did not produce any illegal weapons. It does not reflect the anger and frustration many of these stops produced. During the same period 6,163 robberies at the point of a gun were reported to the police. The great majority of these crimes were committed in poor neighborhoods, principally black, the same places where the police made the majority of their arrests for the carrying of unregistered weapons. The people who live in these neighborhoods are frequently terrified to walk on the streets for fear of being mugged, but they are also angered when a policeman, black or white, stops them and violates their autonomy and privacy by frisking them and asking them where they live and where they are going.[9]

Suspicion stops are the only way a patrolman has of discovering the intentions of persons not known to him. They are also a tactic the department can employ in places where there is a sharp rise in street crime. The men who work the area can be ordered to make numerous stops, forcing everyone who walks the streets to be alert to the presence of the police. But most of these stops do not produce any evidence of crime. Of what value are all the reports the patrolmen must file on their stops? They result in arrests only infrequently. A sample study in Milwaukee of 8,400 checks based on stops showed a single arrest. If this is an accurate measure of the efficiency of these procedures, their value is questionable. Also, it is only a matter of time until the police develop a computerized patrol report that will enable the department to process quickly all the stops and checks made each day. What right do the police have to collect and process information on the movements of private individuals who are just walking on the street? It is not only what the police might do with such information that is at issue but whether they have any right to make such collections. The patrolman's obligation to file reports undoubtedly gives the department a way of controlling his performance, but that is hardly a justification for collecting large amounts of information about citizens for no demonstrable purpose.[1]

[9]Figures from official police department sources.

[1]Milwaukee data in Lawrence P. Tiffany, et al., pp 74–5.

In neighborhoods where there is a high incidence of street crime, the efforts of the police to give reassurance and protection often produce anxiety and disorder. The neighborhoods seem to be overflowing with police cars, which give the police an enlarged presence as they pass. Cars are frequently seen whizzing down the street, their sirens blaring and their emergency lights flashing. It is common to see police cars streak through intersections, breaking red lights, running over sidewalks and into alleys. Every day, many times on some days, people walking on the sidewalk see the police converge, jump from their cars with guns drawn, abandoning their cars in the middle of the street, doors open. People coming out of subway stations are overwhelmed as armed policemen rush past them. ("Shit, man, I told you we shudda stayed on the train.") People sitting quietly in a bar having a drink are suddenly shocked by the appearance of policemen coming in the doors guns out and sticks obviously ready. How can the patrons know that a disgruntled customer decided to stir up some action and called in a false robbery report? There is no way for a policeman to respond politely to a robbery report.

"Shit, man, I'm gettin' outta here. They're getting ready to whip some black ass tonight," a fearful patron said to a companion as a patrolman "accidentally" brushed three patrons at the bar, frisking them with his forearm to see whether they had guns in their waistbands. Is the man right? Perhaps he recalls the days when some police did raid bars looking for weapons. No calls, they just descended, four men usually, two coming in each door. One patrolman carried a pump-action shotgun, and in the silence generated by their appearance he would pump a shell into the chamber. The rasping noise would cause a shiver among the patrons, old-timers recall, and often it was followed by the sound of metal hitting tile as patrons dropped knives and guns to the floor before the frisks began. Now the police come in answer to calls, they do not frisk everyone they see, nor do they normally carry shotguns. They risk their lives, and the people for whom they are taking the risks are often angry and terrified.

"This is a bad fuckin' bar because there's only one door. When we get inside, you stay right by the door and don't let

nobody get behind us. If anybody moves, you stick 'em."
There had been a report of a shooting in the barroom. It
was very dark, the only illumination in the crowded room
coming from the neon lights framing the large mirror behind
the bar. The noise that seemed to be shaking the place when
they entered stopped completely. What appeared to be some
kind of a fight also stopped. The sergeant went right into
the middle of the crowd, his back covered by his partner,
who stayed by the door. He talked briefly with the bartender,
and then suddenly the shouting began again. The bartender
leaned across the bar and hit a man who was yelling at the
sergeant; the shouting died down again. Several people
moved toward the door and the officer unsnapped his holster. "Just stay where you are, pal," he said, and, they
stopped. After a few moments of conversation, the sergeant
backed away and the officers retired from the barroom, the
conflict settled.[2]

Many of the emergency responses of the police are to
calls which prove to be unfounded. The patrolman has no
way of knowing until his arrival at the scene whether a signal
is valid or not. Burglar alarms, for example, are constantly
going off for all kinds of reasons, but the patrolman cannot
know whether it is a false alarm or one caused by a
burglar. Even though he knows that most alarms are
"tripped," he must respond to them as if they were all valid.
If he fails to show up and there has been a burglary, he will
get into serious trouble. There are many burglar alarms
that ring a bell only in the place where they are installed;
these are designed to attract the attention of passers-by and
the police. The sector men know which of these alarms are
inclined to short-circuit during a rainstorm, and when these
are heard, the men do not hurry, although they must go to
the scene and investigate. But there are other kinds of alarms
that signal the police directly, causing the patrolman to respond quickly. Between December 1969 and July 1970,
there were 18,879 alarms reported to the police in Philadel-

[2]Bars with only one door are disliked because the police are deprived
of the element of surprise when they enter. Also, a single entrance makes
it impossible to surround a group of people and contain them by coming
from two directions. "When you step out of a bar you make a quick
step to the left or right, so that if anybody throws a bottle out the
door after you, you got a better chance of missing it." "A Quiet
Strip: Officer Schalbrack's Story," p. 9.

BETWEEN LAW AND ORDER 355

phia; only 705 were valid. Some, 4,481, were taped alarms, which are simple devices that trigger a taped message to the police emergency number. Of these, only 107 were valid. The others, 14,398, were installed alarms that ring in an office and then are reported to the police by a clerk after he checks the alarm signals; despite this supervision, only 598 of these were valid. Both types of alarms produce excellent profits for the manufacturers, installers, and the telephone company, whose lines are used for the signals. This lucrative and rapidly growing business would wither, of course, if the police refused to honor these alarm calls and the public did not underwrite the costs of sustaining the policy.[3]

The very high rate of crime in impoverished black neighborhoods poses a severe dilemma for the police.[4] If their only way of reducing the crime rate is to respond with speed to any call for help and to place as many men as possible on alert for these calls, there is inevitably going to be a very considerable police presence on the streets of neighborhoods where there is resentment toward the police. The responses of the men to calls for aid can only exacerbate these feelings, although the absence of the police from the streets might make the situation much worse. But if they fail to reduce the dangers that exist in these places, their failure only serves to increase the problems. This produces fresh demands for protection and a call for more police. It is an endless, dangerous cycle.

The high rate of store robbery in the black ghettos, for

[3] In London in 1965 there were 897 valid alarms out of 39,767 reports. J. P. Martin and G. Wilson, *The Police: A Study in Manpower* (London, Heinemann, 1969), pp. 93–4. An excellent description of the chronic failure of alarm systems nationally is in Albert Reiss, Jr., "Crime Against Small Business," Report of the Small Business Administration transmitted to the Select Committee on Small Business, 91st Cong., 1st sess., S. Doc. 91–14 (1969), pp. 29–40, 160 ff.

[4] A national survey of crime against businesses showed that while nationally there were twenty-seven burglaries for every one hundred retail stores, the burglary rate in the black neighborhoods was an astounding ninety-seven out of one hundred. The burglary rate in non-ghetto areas of central cities was also higher than the national average but at thirty-seven out of one hundred it was almost two thirds less than the ghetto rate. The survey also showed similar results for robbery, revealing a national victimization rate of five per one hundred stores, six per one hundred in non-ghetto areas of the cities, and nineteen per one hundred in the black areas of the metropolitan regions. Reiss, p. 75.

example, has forced many small businesses to close and is encouraging the owners and employees of surviving establishments to arm themselves. Almost half of all ghetto shopkeepers admit to having guns with them at work. The great majority of store robberies are against businesses that do less than $100,000 gross sales annually: variety stores, dry-goods houses, small groceries that service the neighborhood streets where city people actually live; these "Mom and Pop" stores are closing down rapidly. This not only causes a decline in the services available to the people, forcing a rise in prices because of a reduction in competition and consuming more of their time in shopping because they must go greater distances to do their marketing; it also increases the dangers they must face. At night, large numbers of people do not go out of their houses. If a person must go to a store, an exact route is often followed that is calculated to avoid dangerous blocks and corners. Each time a store is closed, the people who depend on it must suffer the anxieties and dangers involved in testing and developing a relatively safe route to a new store.[5]

The very high rate of robbery against bus and cab drivers initially caused a general inconvenience by requiring everyone to have exact change for his fare; then it increasingly disadvantaged the poor, who are the least able to compensate for the steady decline of available public transportation which has been one of the principal results of crime in the streets. Cab drivers, white and black, often refuse to work in many areas of the city, and nobody can force them to run risks which are so evident. It is easy to attack the motives of a white cab driver who refuses to accept a fare going to some part of the city. The person refused, often black, has every reason to be chagrined and outraged, but the drivers know they are facing real dangers and their decisions are not the consequence of paranoid delusion. They may be guilty of incivility, but they are reacting to a close and accurate reading of their situation. Bus drivers, too, often do not stop at scheduled stops on some routes, and many lines have curtailed their services. The continual repetition of these encounters between cab drivers and thwarted riders, bus drivers and passengers left stranded, and store owners

[5]Reiss, pp. 56, 76–7.

and customers refused entry after dark has done more than corrupt social contacts in the city. The necessity to do business in the presence of increasing numbers of armed guards, private police, and armed citizens is doing more than deepening the distrust among people and increasing the levels of communal enmity. It has made it more difficult for the poor to get to where there is work, and it has made the streets more dangerous.

Robbers are people who seek money, and their preferences for cabbies, bus drivers, and bill collectors reflects a calculation that these victims offer the best chances for a large return. The removal of cash from buses, the disappearance of cabs from certain neighborhoods (and illegal cabs have not made up the deficiency), the closing of stores and the militant protection of those remaining have forced robbers to turn to less lucrative but more available targets. This shift has certainly contributed to the increasing number of street robberies in recent years. Since purse snatching and drunk rolling frequently produce little cash, the robbers must work more often, increasing their risk of capture but greatly enhancing the general feeling of danger on the streets.

People who dread the streets they are obliged to walk every day must take measures to increase their sense of security. Like the patrolman who develops techniques to give himself a feeling of control when he goes places that arouse his fears, other people, too, take protective actions. The first thing that happens is that people use the streets less; they are careful, not casual about going out of the house. This makes the streets more dangerous for the people who do use them. With fewer people on the streets, muggers are encouraged to act, because they have to worry less about eyewitnesses or possible interventions from public-spirited citizens. When people do go on the streets, they are careful about where they walk and how they proceed. Many walk along the curbing, avoiding the shadows of buildings but arousing the interest of passing policemen, who see them near the parked cars, which are frequent targets of burglars. Surroundings are carefully scanned, and approaching people are watched until they pass. Money is concealed in underwear, jewelry hidden in the house.

It is impossible to calculate how much human energy is

drained off daily in efforts to generate self-confidence. How much attention and time that could be devoted to other matters must be given over to self-protection? What is the value of the human capital invested in these efforts which, if successful, produce nothing more than what every citizen of the republic is presumably guaranteed?

The police are constantly producing elaborate statistical analyses of the ecology of city crime in order to distribute their manpower more effectively, but it is simply not sufficient to know the area in which a mugger may operate, even an area as small as a square block, or the time of day he prefers. To stop a thief it is necessary to be where he is stealing or he will escape. Policemen taste defeat frequently, just missing the capture of someone who leaps out of a rear window as they enter the front door, or races into an unseen passageway leading to another street. Thieves do not plan to be captured, no matter how frequently their hopes and calculations prove incorrect. The car and the radio have made the police more effective than they have ever been, but it has not made them efficient enough to reduce crime. They do not know what can make them more effective than they are now, except greater speed and more manpower.

"O.K., lady, calm down. Did you see 'em? How tall was the one? Big as me? Did he have a knife? Lady, did you see if he had a knife? You think it was a gun? What did it look like? Was it like this one or did it have a short barrel? You don't know." "O.K., pal, just relax, at least he didn't fuck you up." "Get me some towels over here, bartender. Son-of-a-bitch gonna let this guy just bleed. Come on. O.K., fella, I'm gonna press this towel on your back to hold down the bleeding. Listen, can you walk to the car or do you want to wait for the wagon? Did you see who did it? Hey, Joe, he said two guys knifed him. No description. They went north on Hawley Street." "No, I don't think you're gonna die, mister. Yes, I'll call your wife when we get you into the hospital. Now, you lean on my arm and we'll make it to the car. Don't worry about getting blood on me."

The majority of muggers confine their work to an area they know well, often picking one-way streets so they can work toward the oncoming traffic and watch for the police. (Some aggressive patrolmen willingly take the risks of driving the wrong way on back streets for this reason.) Frequently they carry no weapon, wandering about for a hit—a woman, a drunken man, anyone they think can be overpowered. They cannot plan their jobs since they know only moments before they act when and where it will be. But once they move they must be quick, since speed is their primary insurance against failure. If a mugger is after a handbag, he will frequently push a woman down on the run and grab the bag without stopping. Some muggers cut the straps, sweep the bag off the victim's arm, and are gone before she knows she has been robbed. They rarely intend to hurt, but frequently older women are injured in the falls they take.

A man always poses a greater problem because he may resist, and any money on him is likely to be in a pocket or a wallet. Unless the mugger has a gun or feels he has sufficient time, he must knock the victim over and rifle his pockets. If the man resists, he must be subdued before the money can be obtained. The most common forms of mugging are against men at night, usually by several males who attack from the rear, rarely with any prior warning. Using surprise, they frequently smash the victim on the head with whatever is available—a piece of lead pipe, a table leg, anything that will stun him. The chances of later recognition are nil.

There were a few people standing at the curb as the patrol car arrived. A man lay on the pavement, very still, his head a bloody mess, a table leg lying beside him. Both legs of his trousers had been slit open with a sharp blade. The people moved off as the police got out and, when stopped, said they did not know anything. They had been in the liquor store when it happened. "Do you think he's dead?" the new man asked his partner. The patrolman leaned over the prostrate form, whose face was entirely obscured by caking blood, stared intently, and said, "Yeah, dead drunk. He'll be O.K. if that fuckin' wagon ever gets here." "Hey, Mr. Cop, I saw the whole thing," a little boy said, tugging at the patrolman's jacket. "Do you know who did it?" "There was three boys, they sneaked up behind him and went pow." "Do you know who they were, boy?" "Nope." "Go on home.

You shouldn't be out walkin' around this late alone. Hey, wait a minute, where do you live? O.K., go right home because I'm gonna watch you go down the street."

Often the victim's pants are slit open and the pockets cut away to speed the process of robbery. A little man clutched his pants, which were beltless. The legs were fastened with pins where the blade had sliced them open. The patrolmen helped him into the rear seat of the car. He had been robbed of seventy dollars, and they were going to cruise the neighborhood in search of suspects. He had seen them. "I was comin' through that lot behind the liquor store when one young bug jumped out and knocked me down. Before I knew what was happening, they had my pants cut off. One of 'em had a piece of pipe in his hand and he wanted to hit me with it, but the others said not to. They was almost arguing, and that's when I jumped up and started runnin' like hell." The terrified man told the story over and over, reliving his fears and narrow escape, while they cruised the area in a fruitless search for the criminals. After a half hour the patrolmen were relieved to be rid of him. They had heard it all before.

Two patrolmen were sitting in their car drinking coffee, which they had just gotten from a restaurant they frequented. It was 1 A.M.; they had come in answer to a disturbance call that was unfounded. "It's too warm for February, too quiet —something's gonna pop," the driver said. They sipped their coffee, ignoring the first twinges of the fatigue which would soon be assaulting them. They watched as a car came across the parking lot toward them. A man leaned out of a window as the car pulled up and said, "Hey, man, two dudes are kickin' the shit out of an old guy on North Street, in front of the Gay Paree Bar." The driver threw his coffee out of the window and put the car into gear, while his partner paid the price of inexperience—he took a faceful of hot coffee, trying for a last sip, as the rapidly accelerating car lurched. "I told you about that, boy," the driver said with a laugh, without taking his eyes from the approaching road. Both front windows were down as the car rumbled onto the main road, rushing past a lone man, standing and gesturing westward after the car. Both patrolmen peered into the foggy gloom, looking for signs of action. The car's headlights had been extinguished to mask their approach. "There they are," the recorder said, spotting two men bending over a form in the middle of the street about one hundred yards ahead. Suddenly the two men began running south. As the patrol car approached the prone figure, the inexperienced policeman began to open his door. "Close it," the driver snapped, hurling the car, lights on, into the small street into which the two men had fled. He screeched to a halt, and the officers were out and running after the fleeing men, who were only a few yards ahead of them. The driver yelled to them to halt or he would shoot. His gun was snapped in its holster. One man stopped and the other slowed, allowing the other officer to overtake him, grab his elbow, and spin him into a brick wall. The men were handcuffed after a frisk revealed no weapon but five crumpled dollar bills. It had been just a minute since the officers had seen the car approach them. They could not recall what the witness had looked like.

The recorder returned to the main road to check on the victim. He was already on his feet, staggering homeward. A man leaned out of a second-story window and called down, "Hey, did you get them faggots who was beating up that ole nigger, honey?" The officer looked up and asked whether the man had called the police. He smiled and said no. "Fuck you," the policeman muttered and continued after the man, who was walking slowly, supporting himself by holding on to the buildings. He came alive quickly when told that the men who had robbed him were under arrest. "Shit, I cudda taken 'em if they hadn't jumped me and pulled my coat over my head. I just come outta the bar, had a few drinks, you know." He grinned with pain. His face was bruised, his lips and tongue split by a solid kick in the teeth. He had wet himself. He identified the men (trying to punch one of them) and his five dollars, and they were taken into custody.

The older officer said, as the wagon pulled away with the prisoners, "It's a good thing they stopped when I shouted because they were gonna outrun us and we couldn't shoot 'em. No complainant, no witness, they might have done nothing. But they stopped and we got 'em, boy, we got 'em. Wait till I tell my wife in the morning."

Inside the station house the handcuffs were removed from

the two suspects, and they were ordered to place their belongings on the counter. The little money they had in their possession was returned to them while the lieutenant examined their papers. One of the men had been discharged from the Marine Corps the previous week, and the lieutenant, an ex-marine, told him he was a disgrace. He ordered both men to roll up their sleeves, checking their forearms for needle marks. "There's a hundred-dollar arm," he said, tracing the scar tracks along one man's arm with his forefinger. The man objected, saying he had been picked up for no reason and wanted a lawyer. "Shut the fuck up, creep," the lieutenant muttered. The other man was half-turned, whispering something to the victim, who was standing nearby. "You turn the fuck around and keep your mouth shut or I'm gonna close it for you, pal," one of the arresting officers said. "You try and intimidate my witness and down you go." The men stood silently while the lieutenant continued to examine their papers. "O.K., slate 'em [write their names in the arrest book] and take 'em upstairs to the detectives." As he watched them go, the lieutenant said, "Give me these Part I's all the time. These people never talk back to you. They don't have nothin' to say."

The failure of the police to control street crime cannot be attributed to their indifference or lack of effort. Most policemen enjoy nothing better than making a felony arrest. All of the ambiguities and contradictions that shroud so much of his work disappear when the policeman is in pursuit of someone he believes has done something criminal. Also, he fails so frequently and sees the consequences of so many crimes that go unpunished that he has a feeling of accomplishment each time he captures a felon. Men in high-crime districts see so many arrests for serious crimes that these do not have high prestige, but they still bring a man a sense of satisfaction. After all, he is told that preventing crime is what he is hired to do and only infrequently does he have the opportunity to demonstrate personally that he can do it. The frequency of his failure, however, should not obscure the considerable personal effort involved in this work, the risks and gambles a man must take getting to the scene of a crime and taking charge of the situation. Unfortunately, the returns on his investment are very small.

The failure of the police to control street crime is even

more serious when it is recalled that their greatest success is in capturing street thieves. Despite the admiration people express for detectives, which is sustained by the considerable publicity they receive, the police are not very effective against professional criminals. The accomplished thief, whose work is marked by thoughtful planning and careful consideration, much more frequently escapes detection and capture than does the mugger and window smasher. In both London and Philadelphia, the robbery "clearance rate" declined directly in proportion to the increasing size of the haul. The six-year clearance rate for reported robberies under $10 in Philadelphia was 57 percent, while the clearance rate for robberies over $9,000 was 17 percent. One kind of criminal hits you on the head with a board and another kind enters a supermarket, knocks on the manager's office door, and says, "Pardon me, sir, I hit your car outside in the parking lot and I'd like you to check the damage for the insurance company." When the door is opened, the thieves know exactly what they must do, and they have planned their route of escape. The only way these men can be stopped is for the police to watch them constantly. Their capture requires some luck, but mostly it is a result of good information; it is evident from the clearance rate that this is not easy to acquire.[6]

In an effort to increase the number of men who patrol the streets in search of criminals, many departments have created special units that have no specific territorial obligations and use unique tactics in their efforts to eliminate street crime. Most of the crime that plagues cities occurs after dark and this is why policemen consider the four-to-twelve shift the "combat tour," but the department has difficulty assigning larger numbers of men to this shift than to the other two. There have been numerous efforts made to abolish the four-platoon, three-shift system, eliminating the last-out shift or cutting it back substantially and transferring the men to nightwork. None of these efforts has really worked because the men complain that steady nightwork prevents them from spending any time with their families. Also, when some men are switched out of their regular rotation and assigned to "swing shifts," they do not work with

[6]Quotation from the *Philadelphia Evening Bulletin* (August 24, 1971). Normandeau, pp. 142–3; McClintock, p. 37.

their regular supervisors. This hurts their morale and affects the quality of their performance. (Men who are assigned to work with another squad argue that the sergeants give them the worst assignments, freeing their own men for the good sectors and the most interesting work.) Most of the plans are allowed to die a quiet death after the front-page stories that heralded their introduction are long forgotten.

A • SPECIAL PATROL

Special patrol units are manned entirely by carefully screened volunteers. Most of the men in these units are patrolmen who disliked the obligations imposed on them when they worked in a district. They are men who want to do real police work without the confining requirements of service calls and the demeaning obligations of vice activity. When a district patrolman does a particularly outstanding piece of work, he may be rewarded with a transfer into one of these special units. Aggressive supervisors are always looking for district policemen who seem to be discontented and eager for action. They encourage any man who catches their attention to apply. The men in these special patrol units rarely work during daylight hours; normally they are assigned exclusively to night shifts—5 P.M. to 1 A.M., 6 to 2, 7 to 3—depending on the closing hours of the bars and clubs in their cities. Nobody has a regular assignment, although each man develops a preference for some part of the city he knows particularly well. It may be a district where he has worked or a part of the city in which he has lived. He will not always be assigned to work that place, but his sergeant understands that he works best in an area that he knows and every effort is made to keep him in familiar territory. Each day the men are assigned a different beat, calculated on the basis of the latest available crime information. The men, who almost always work in pairs and have regular partners, may be instructed to be alert for a particular kind of crime—purse snatching, car theft, burglary—but they have no other obligations but to remain on crime patrol. They are usually assigned to a city-wide radio band, which will give them all of the crime calls and screen out the routine police messages in the area they are working. They do not handle any service calls except to aid seriously injured persons. All they do is patrol the streets and make suspicion stops, looking for illegal weapons and felons.

Unlike the district men, they have few obligations, and their sergeants judge their activity solely by the number of arrests, ped stops, and car stops they make. They do not have a quota to fulfill, but every man in a special patrol unit understands that unless he produces pinches, he will be sent back to the districts. The district policemen do not disguise their hostility toward special patrolmen who are free to move at will without regard to boundaries and without obligations to do any shitwork. The district men deride them for being "stickmen" and "pinch crazy," pointing out that the distinctive riding boots and peaked hats they wear are a sign of their peculiar mentality.

The men on special patrol are in some ways the premier street policemen. They ride in unmarked cars, wearing their uniforms but with their hats off (some wear baseball caps), slouched low in their seats, so as to disguise their identities. They prowl the most dangerous neighborhoods, looking for cars and people to stop. Some of them specialize in gun pinches, others in stolen cars, and they develop a meticulous concern for all the little clues which suggest the possibility of what they are searching for. On a busy night a "team," as the working units are called, will stop as many as fifteen or twenty cars. In addition, they respond to any high-priority crime calls within a ten- or fifteen-block radius of their location. Any call offering them the possibility of a pinch is sufficient to mobilize them. Frequently men refuse to go off the street at the end of their regular tours, electing to give the city free time in an effort to make an arrest.

In the areas where these men are concentrated they are intensely disliked. Everyone knows them on sight and people are particularly cautious in dealing with them. "Here comes the fuckin' boot cops" is a commonly heard warning. While they are probably no more violent than any other group of policemen, their constant exposure to dangerous situations makes them more likely than a district patrolman to hit someone who resists them. Rarely do any of them gratuitously beat a person, but a patrolman who is looking for a felony pinch is more inclined to hit someone who refuses to give him information than is a patrolman who can enhance his status by making a vice arrest.

B • PLAINCLOTHES PATROLS

When mugging becomes particularly frequent in an area of the city, the police resort to a variety of plainclothes tactics to surprise the unsuspecting street criminal, who is always looking for a uniformed policeman. It is the purpose of all of these operations, not simply to capture criminals in the act, but to undermine the confidence of others and deter them from putting their intentions into action. These operations are usually given wide publicity to arouse public admiration for the policemen's audacity and bravery (which are considerable) and to show the public that the department is being innovative in its efforts to suppress crime.

Patrolmen dress up as cab drivers, drunks, drifters, shopkeepers, and even old ladies, called "grannies." They wander around areas where mugging is widespread, hoping to attract someone. They carry a small radio, which keeps them in touch with their concealed partners; when the mugger strikes, he can be taken into custody. The men who support these plainclothesmen often use specially trained dogs who can run down a fleeing suspect, enabling the supporting team to remain at a greater distance and reducing the chances of them "blowing their cover." (When the arrests that these teams make are publicized, the horrible wounds inflicted by the police dogs on the suspects are discreetly omitted.)

These plainclothes operations can be effective in stopping attacks in anonymous public places—parks, subway stations, business streets—and against some kinds of service personnel. Wherever people come together from different neighborhoods and are unable to place the people they see, plainclothesmen can usefully perform hidden patrol work. But they cannot be effective in the local neighborhoods, where much of the crime occurs, because they will be quickly spotted, and if they are not, their first arrest ends their local effectiveness. People are suspicious of undercover police operations. In poor neighborhoods there are policemen who are infiltrating to obtain information on gambling, prostitution, political movements, and drugs. When plainclothesmen arrive allegedly to protect people from muggers, there are many who view the claim with a jaundiced eye.[7]

[7]In London when the New Police first used plainclothesmen in anticrime patrols, there were magistrates who refused to prosecute people accused of assaulting the policemen. Reith, pp. 82, 102.

Plainclothes service is extremely dangerous and exposes the policemen and the people around them to the possibility of being shot. Two patrolmen were riding along a main road shortly before 11 P.M. on a Friday. It was a hot August night and the radio reported a constant stream of emergencies and crimes in progress. The road was heavily clogged with traffic. Although they were heading for a restaurant to eat lunch, the car was in the sidewalk lane, the men scanning the street as they moved. The driver braked and the recorder twisted his head as they both heard the same noise. A gunshot does not sound like a firecracker or a backfire— it is short, sharp, and flat. A policeman knows when he hears gunfire. "Shit, another one," the driver said, opening the car door. The traffic continued to move steadily, and as the recorder moved from his seat, a boy ran past the car. The officer made a vain grab for his sleeve, and both men gave chase as the boy ran directly into the traffic to avoid capture. The patrolmen ran through the traffic and chased him to ground in an alley, where he surrendered without a struggle. Holding him firmly by his belt, they walked him back to their patrol car, while he protested that he had done nothing and they had no right to stop him from running. Standing by the car was a man wearing a taxi driver's cap and a gun stuck in his belt. "You rotten little motherfucker," he muttered, smacking the boy across the face. When he was restrained, he said, "I'm a 369 [trade slang for a policeman] on stakeout duty. Him and his friend tried to stick me up back in the train station."

The patrolman, disguised as a cab driver, was parked when two teenagers approached his cab, one on either side. One of the boys had placed a knife at the cab driver's throat, making a slight cut on his Adam's apple. "I leaned away from that knife and went for my gun, which was in my shirt. But the fuckin' thing got caught on a buttonhole, and the one with the knife got away across Washington Street. By the time I got my gun out and got off a couple of shots, he was gone." The combination of fear, chagrin, and near disaster were too much for him and he began to shake. The patrolman urged him to sit in the car while they waited for the wagon to take the prisoner to the station. "If I had got my gun out in time, you'd be one dead little motherfucker," he said as he got into the car.

Nobody mentioned to him that he might have shot a policeman or a passing motorist.

Muggers who unwittingly attack a police officer in disguise run the risk of being shot. The policeman does not know whether the man who has attacked him is armed. If he shoots him, there is little likelihood that his superiors will complain, because the victim is almost certainly a felon. But there may be considerable resentment toward the police for shooting people in the streets. Even people who desperately need protection from street criminals resent the police coming into their neighborhoods, entrapping suspects, and then occasionally gunning them down. The most cool-headed policeman working in these conditions is likely to be edgy. He knows that other policemen might mistake him for a felon. He does not want to run down the street chasing someone if he can avoid it, so his inclination to shoot is increased.[8]

It might be possible to defend the use of these plainclothes operations, despite the tensions they create, if anyone could demonstrate their effectiveness. Unfortunately, it cannot be shown that they reduce crime. It is possible that plainclothesmen used in some places may drive criminals elsewhere. They may even temporarily deter some, but there is no evidence that the use of plainclothesmen actually reduces the amount of crime in the city. It is possible that the widespread use of plainclothesmen would redistribute crime over a wider area, making the risks that people must accept more evenly distributed. But if this could be demon-

---

[8] A plainclothes unit in Detroit called *STRESS* (stop the robbers— enjoy safe streets) aroused considerable public resentment after killing twelve persons in a year. Other departments have similar units, and while none of these has yet produced the public outcry caused in Detroit, they all create similar tensions. *The New York Times* (March 10, 1972).

After a plainclothes detective was killed in New York City by a patrolman, the department ordered all of its anticrime plainclothesmen to wear color-coded hatbands for quick identification. These are to be changed daily, said the announcement sent out on the teletype, to confuse criminals. While this technique may give the men some protection, it will also reveal them to the persons they are trying to catch. *The New York Times* (April 5, 1972).

In England plainclothesmen on anticrime patrol carry only a short billy club, which can be concealed under the coat. But they also wear extra-heavy shoes, so they can use their feet as weapons if they get into a fight.

strated, it would surely cause an intense public outcry from that part of the population whose risks of victimization were being increased.

The police can also protect specific business places by using specially armed and trained stakeout men to guard them. These men are usually armed with shotguns loaded with rifle slugs and powerful Magnum revolvers. They sit in the rear of shops, liquor stores, and banks. If there is a robbery attempt, they appear and make an arrest. Under the circumstances it is not surprising that a large number of shootings and killings result. This tactic might improve the overall security of the stores in an area, but it is far from clear that it does not actually increase the general level of danger in the city. If the robbers are deterred from attacking stores but not convinced to give up robbery altogether, they will look for "safer" targets. Inevitably, this means street robbery of unwary or weak passers-by. Since this is the least lucrative kind of robbery, anything that encourages it is probably also encouraging a net increase in the number of assaults, even if the amount of property lost declines.[9]

2 · Crime and the Police

The police have been given an impossible responsibility. They cannot prevent crime altogether, and whatever amount of crime they actually do prevent by their presence on the street cannot be demonstrated. The people who support wholeheartedly their efforts to control crime are by and large persons who do not have to experience at first hand the inconvenience, tension, and unpleasantness police tactics invariably produce. The people who desperately need their help and protection (and constantly call on the police for aid) are often angered by what they perceive to be the police-man's indifference and callousness toward them. Whenever the police respond to demands that they "do something" about crime, whatever they actually do is likely to increase tensions without their also being able to show conclusively that it is helpful.

[9]On stakeout tactics, see the rather bloodthirsty public-relations puff-piece by Robert Daley, then public-information officer of the New York City Police Department, "The Deadly Score of the Stakeout Squad," *New York Magazine* (April 24, 1972).

The police have no direct control over the sources of crime. Whatever causes persons to become street criminals, causes that are not any clearer to policemen than they are to social scientists, physicians, and theologians, it is evident that the police have little direct influence on them. If heroin addicts, for example, are responsible for what is now seen as the most recent of the many "crime waves" that have afflicted cities throughout their history, the police have only limited means of controlling them. They can seek to cut off their drug supplies, arrest them for buying and selling drugs, and harass them. These efforts to control addicts are not proving any more successful than have the efforts of the police over the last two centuries to deal with the problems created by liquor. If the failure of the police to control crime causes some people to attack them for being corrupt, ineffective, and indifferent, the police can respond only by counterattacking. They may advocate changes in the law to free themselves of obligations that undermine public confidence in them, but they cannot deny any obligation until it is withdrawn. All they can do is arrest people. If this does not accomplish the purpose, and it does not, they then must seek to place the responsibility for failure elsewhere.

The police control only a part of the entire system that seeks to regulate public conduct. When they are accused of failure, they may, with some justice, point out that all they can do is arrest suspects, not confine them and keep them away from the public. Ever since the police were established, their failure to control crime has opened them to attack from any quarter and they have always responded to these abuses by criticizing the courts and the penal system. This is not true only in the United States, nor is it true only in recent times. Almost two centuries ago Patrick Colquhoun, friend and pupil of Jeremy Bentham and hardly a person who could be described as an enemy of the rule of law, wrote:

As the Laws are at present administered, it is a melancholy truth, not to be contradicted, that the major part of the criminals who infest this Metropolis, although committed by magistrates for trial on very satisfactory proof, are returned upon the Public in vast numbers year after year; encouraged to renew their former practices, by the facility they experience in evading justice.[1]

Those who view the courts as the guardians of the law perceive these attacks by the police as an effort to subvert the law itself. But the police see them simply as an effort to distribute the blame. Also, policemen have an intimate relationship with the judicial system at its lowest levels. They tend to view the courts in personal terms. They know that most persons hold judges in high regard, but policemen, particularly men who have gained higher rank, have seen too many examples of questionable dealings to be in awe of the courts. The attacks on the courts by policemen may not have any jusitfication in fact, but it cannot be demonstrated, for example, that they are any less justified than are the attacks made on the police.

Capturing criminals is not the same thing as preventing crime. Before the police can possibly be expected to perform their duty effectively, fundamental decisions must be made about what they should do. As has been suggested frequently, some of their manpower could be freed for other duties by changing laws to make activities now treated as misdemeanors non-criminal. (How much time will actually be saved· by making the behavior of the street alcoholics non-criminal is far from clear. People will continue to complain about them and someone will have to pick them off the streets. If another agency is not established for this purpose, the police will have to continue to perform this duty.) The capture of any kind of criminal may prevent him from committing more crimes while he is in custody and opens the possibility of punishing him (and avenging his victim) as well as offering him "rehabilitation," but it does not follow that his capture will prevent others from committing crimes. The possibility of actually preventing crime by making arrests may be greater for one kind of crime than for others. If this can be shown to be true, perhaps the police ought to be directed to concentrate their attention on this type of crime. Unless it is a crime that society feels is sufficiently serious to warrant considerable police attention, the test would be meaningless.

[1]Colquhoun, p. 4.

A decision may be made that one kind of crime is more serious than all others and the police should devote their energies to its suppression. For example, if a decision were made that street robbery and mugging are the most serious threat to public order, the entire criminal-justice system could be geared to dealing with them. The police could devote their manpower to arresting suspects. Quick and sure prosecution could be guaranteed by establishing special courts that gave heavy penalties, lengthy confinements, and no parole. These tactics might convince many criminals to give up robbery and turn to burglary, which is viewed as a less serious crime. Of course, it cannot be known with certainty what the impact of such an effort would be, but if it is not possible to find a way of reducing crime, it may be necessary to equalize the risks of victimization among all members of the community. The police could probably play a role in achieving this democratization of risk, although any effort to implement such a policy would spark an intense controversy.[2]

Until the police are given another strategy, they will continue to do what they have always done. The department will seek to maintain the integrity of its organization, and the patrolman will seek to preserve himself and his place on the street. Their collective policies and individual performances will continue to treat people differentially, and conflict and argument will persist. Everyone is not alike to the police. There are law-abiding persons (and criminals, too) whom they never see. There are people who challenge their role in society and others who challenge policemen by making the streets they patrol unsafe. City police are defined by their territorial jurisdiction and any effort to dislodge them is seen as, at the very least, an affront. Unable to prevent crime, they seek to ensure that nobody else can claim control of the street, which they view as belonging to themselves. If this dominance requires that the police saturate some neighborhoods, they will do so. The police can no more control the consequences of these actions than they can predict the impact of their unending experiments to show people that they are "doing something" about crime.

[2]Lester Thurow, "Equity versus Efficiency in Law Enforcement," *Public Policy*, Vol. XVIII (1969/1970), pp. 451–62.

CHAPTER NINE

Taking

*"You know the man who is doing
the work is getting the least."*
—A policeman

At times in our history some city governments have systematically organized the liquor and gambling businesses (and prostitution, too, when it was an important feature of city life rather than a service trade for tourists and conventioneers) to provide themselves with income and money to finance their political operations. Patrolmen and higher officials were appointed to the police force with the understanding that they would carry out the policies of the city, and their positions depended upon adherence to the wishes of the political leadership. Many of these men made money for doing illegal things, but basically they were being paid commissions for performing political services, which were a condition of their employment. Many police captains were actually little more than gambling and liquor commissioners, whose primary responsibility was to enforce the illegal licenses which the political machines granted to favored operators. The police did not organize protection but carried out the orders established by the elected leaders of their city or state. Policemen were frequently employed to act as steerers, bouncers, and doormen for gambling houses and speakeasies. In addition to payoffs, brothels often paid policemen in free services for the protection they received. But more often than not, the patrolmen who performed this work were assigned informally by their captains to guard these places and protect the city's investment.[1]

[1] Lincoln Steffens, *The Shame of the Cities* (New York, McClure &

The blatant involvement of the police in these illegal activities had several unintended consequences. The commanding officers of the department, who received the largest payoffs for organizing protection, could not impose tight discipline over the men under their command. It was impossible to prevent men who were not receiving regular payoffs from exploiting their opportunities to emulate their superiors. No department wanted some of its men to become fences, burglars, and even robbers, but it was difficult to prevent this without risking the exposure of all the illegal activities in which the police were systematically involved. Everyone in these departments also learned to limit his curiosity about what others were doing. To assure the loyalty and good faith of the men, superiors sought to "get something" on their colleagues that would prevent them from considering betrayal. Conspiracy and secrecy became requirements of employment.[2]

There were men in many departments who were not on the take and who refused to become involved. These men were allowed to remain and could even advance, but silence and loyalty were the conditions on which their tenure rested. The profession learned to segregate its activities to accommodate the conflicting obligations imposed on it by political conditions. Vice work was concentrated in a few carefully selected squads of men whose loyalty and inclinations were known to the men who chose them. Captains in districts where vice activity was strong did not get appointed unless they were "involved." They allowed their patrolmen to hustle what they wanted in return for loyalty and silence. "Honest" policemen could operate under these conditions, but usually these men gravitated to commands where there were no graft and no obligations to perform illicit service. The training division and the planning bureaus of most departments became the bastions of reformers who were disgusted with "politics" and corruption. The tensions that exist in all organizations between staff planners and

---

Phillips, 1904), Chap. III; Lloyd Wendt and Herman Kogan, *Lords of the Levee* (Indianapolis, Bobbs-Merrill, 1943); Richardson, pp. 181ff.; Andy Logan, *Against the Evidence* (New York, McCalls, 1970), pp. 43–4, 58ff., 63ff., 80–7, 105ff.

[2]V. O. Key, "Police Graft," *American Journal of Sociology*, Vol. XL (1935), pp. 624ff.

"doers" were intensified by the moral conflicts built into police work.

The direct involvement of the police in the protection of illegal operations obliged them to become agents for men who often employed common criminals. While the gambling and liquor operators were considered to be businessmen who happened to be in an illegal business, they frequently employed people who had learned their skills as pimps, strong-arm men, and common gunmen. The police and the city government often had to go into court to protect these criminals from prosecution for crimes they had committed. It was only a short step from there to the practice of some policemen setting up robberies and protecting selected criminals, who paid them a cut to operate. The city administrations had to assure their control over the criminal-court judges, who handled many of the cases affecting their business interests and employees, the "fixer" and the "bagman" became established fixtures in the police stations and courthouses of most cities. The decade of Prohibition witnessed the climax of these relationships in American cities. The involvement of the police in illegal operations, which had previously been restricted to certain districts, became general. Every city government sustained, in one fashion or another, a beer and liquor trade, and was obliged to protect and then make alliances with professional gangsters and killers. The open collusion between politicians and known criminals outraged even tolerant city people, and the constant revelation that police officials had swollen bank balances angered even "wets" who supported their city governments against social policies they found mystifying.[3]

The repeal of Prohibition marked the end of the flamboyant era when the public connections between politicians, "racket men," and policemen were openly acknowledged. But there is

[3]John Landesco, "The Criminal Underworld of Chicago in the '80s and '90s," *Journal of Criminal Law and Criminology*, Vol. XXV (1934), pp. 341–57, 928–40; John Landesco, *Organized Crime in Chicago: Part III of the Illinois Crime Survey of 1929* (Chicago, University of Chicago Press, 1968). Mark Haller, "Urban Crime and Criminal Justice: The Chicago Case," *Journal of American History*, Vol. LVII (1970), pp. 619–35. Hank Messick, *The Silent Syndicate* (New York, Macmillan, 1967), describes the emergence of the new racketeer during Prohibition in his characterization of the Cleveland mob. See Tannenbaum, pp. 153–73, on police corruption during Prohibition.

probably still no city in the country where a person cannot find a drink after hours. Presumably, it is no longer possible to "make book" in the district police stations, as was the case a few decades ago, but nobody who wants to put a bet down is frustrated. There is not a single number player who must go home unsatisfied because he cannot find a writer to take his action. There is not a single metropolitan newspaper that does not have some employees taking action in the press room, drivers who are "pick-up men," or reporters who use their office phones daily to place bets with their bookies.[4]

1 · The Dilemmas of Vice Work

The obligation to enforce the vice laws presents the police with insoluble dilemmas. Regardless of what system a department uses—vice squads, district and divisional plainclothesmen, or the distribution of responsibility among undercover units and district patrolmen—or the degree of freedom a commissioner has from political interference, the department administrators must constantly struggle to control the inclinations of some to exploit their opportunities for graft (and extortion). At the same time, vigorous efforts to enforce these laws undermine the possibilities for strict supervision because the work obliges the men to engage in illegal and often degrading practices that must be concealed from the public. Although no department has entirely eliminated the systematic, regular payoff—the "steady note," as it is called in Philadelphia, and the "pad," in New York City—and in some it continues in entrenched form, its elimination would not resolve the basic problems vice enforcement imposes on the police.

The public measures the honesty of its police by the absence of evidence of graft and payoffs. The administra-

---

[4]Warren Moscow, *What Have You Done for Me Lately?* (Englewood Cliffs, N.J., Prentice-Hall, 1967), pp. 157ff. Harold Gosnell, *Machine Politics: Chicago Model,* 2d ed. (Chicago, University of Chicago Press, 1968), pp. 42–3; Daniel Bell, "Crime as an American Way of Life," *The End of Ideology* (New York, Free Press, 1959), pp. 115–36; Alexander Heard, *The Costs of Democracy* (Chapel Hill, N. C., University of North Carolina Press, 1960), pp. 154–63. "Better Bets," *The Wall Street Journal* (November 12, 1971), on the growth of sports wagering.

tors of the police know that even if they control the inclinations of their men to take money, they must continue to struggle to prevent the loosening of standards and the indifference toward lawful conduct that is produced by the constant application of illegal and illicit techniques to make "vice pinches." While many departments have greatly reduced the opportunities for graft which their men may safely take, none has found ways of fulfilling its obligations to regulate public morality without resorting to methods that constantly provide policemen with temptations and encourage ambiguous attitudes toward official standards of conduct. Every police official knows that some of his men are regularly indulging in practices whose legality is questionable at best but cannot be prevented as long as the department demands vice activity. This condition obliges the administrators to rely on ginks, department spies, to ferret out those who step over the line between enforcement and collusion. Every patrolman is guilty of violating some department rule, and whether he is honest or not, every man is on the watch for the ginks. This atmosphere makes it almost impossible for policemen to share their knowledge with each other or to welcome openly innovations that threaten their privacy and therefore their security.[5]

Many of the illegal things that policemen do are not designed to generate payoffs for them but to meet obligations established by the department. If the patrolman were freed from having to make vice arrests, only the corrupt, the money hungry, would continue to do the illegal things so many policemen do. There are no legal ways to enforce the drug laws on the streets, so any pressure on the police to make more drug arrests is an open encouragement to them to lie and violate their pledge to uphold the Constitution. But to force them to make arrests and then to release the addicts who will only be arrested again compounds a tragic situation and makes a mockery of the efforts the police are obliged to make. The same is true of gambling. If they made a systematic effort to crush gambling in the city, the networks would redistribute their headquarters outside the city and

[5]The New York City police department has recently announced that almost 10 percent of the men assigned to enforce gambling and narcotics laws have been secretly recruited to spy on their colleagues. *The New York Times* (March 23, 1972).

continue to operate, although their overhead costs might increase. But even before this happened, the objections raised by the methods the police would have to use would be so great that they would stop raiding places and closing up bars and neighborhood grocery stores. Instead, the police compromise and maintain high arrest quotas for gambling, pressuring the men to make pinches and limiting their inclinations to take payoffs. It also provides statistical evidence that the department is "doing something" about vice. This tactic has probably reduced gambling graft over the years, but it has involved every policeman in a conspiracy to violate the law and to protect himself and others from revelations of misconduct.

The district policeman is well aware of the department's "official" policy toward vice, but he also knows that its purpose certainly is not the eradication of gambling or illegal drinking. All vice activity is computed on the basis of arrests, a policy that is not designed to encourage men to make quality arrests. It also encourages an indifference to the method by which the arrests are made, although if policemen arrested only known gamblers, they would still have to violate the law to do it. At times in many cities "bad arrests" were encouraged for the purpose of getting cases dismissed. Policemen also make deals with defendants to give "bad testimony" in court to assure their acquittal or the dismissal of charges, although this is more a matter of personal initiative than any kind of policy. The indifference toward the quality of gambling arrests is encouraged partly by the leniency of the courts, even when convictions result. While the great majority of arrests result in acquittals, few convictions carry any jail terms and the fines are rarely more than nominal. Whether this is deliberate policy and represents some giant conspiracy coordinating the police and the courts, as implied by some who describe the power of the Mafia in terms usually reserved for sovereign states, or is the consequence of many accommodations representing different groups and interests in the city, is unclear. But the pattern of large numbers of arrests and few convictions is found throughout the country. The pattern is the same in cities like Chicago and Philadelphia, which continue to have traditional ethnic political organizations, and in New York City, which has been dominated for years by a liberal, reform government.

During 1970 in New York City, there were more than nine thousand arrests made for common gambling; only seventy people went to jail. An analysis made of raids on seventy-three numbers banks in Brooklyn during the late 1960's revealed that 356 persons were arrested. Of these, 198 people had their cases dismissed and sixty-three were acquitted; seventy-seven people were fined an average of $113 each, five went to jail for an average of seventeen days, twelve had their sentences suspended, and one person when to jail for a year. In the state of New York during 1969, there were 2,096 arrests for felonious gambling, the most serious charge, which led to 281 indictments, fifteen convictions, and one jail term. In Nassau County, New York, in 1965, after revelations of corruption had produced a reform, there was no appreciable change in the outcome of gambling cases brought before the county courts. Most defendants were freed or given minor fines. In Philadelphia during 1970, 517 of 4,720 people charged with gambling were convicted. Five people went to jail and the remainder paid fines averaging $100 each. In Chicago in 1963, 76 percent of the 11,158 people charged with gambling had their cases dismissed; 1,118 of the 2,678 who were prosecuted were convicted. Seventeen people went to jail. A study of Chicago gambling prosecutions in 1950 showed that 70 percent of the cases were dismissed without a trial. The author noted that "day after day the same police testify as to the nature of the raids and the same small clique of lawyers makes the motion to suppress. The routine becomes so common that there is now very little attention paid to the facts. . . ." During the month of November 1950, he noted that 408 of the 564 cases were dismissed on suppression of evidence motions and an additional 110 were thrown out for lack of evidence. Forty-six people were fined, but half of these fines were rescinded on appeal to a higher court. Similar patterns have been noted for Detroit and Cincinnati. This is not a new practice in American cities, and study of court records would probably reveal a consistency extending back into the nineteenth century, intermittently broken by periods when reform governments made a lot of arrests and pressed hard for convictions, much to the annoyance of the electorate, who voted these reformers out of office at the first opportunity. In New York City in 1912, there was a well-published police crackdown on gambling after a particularly spectacular scandal. There were 898 arrests and 103 convictions. Nobody went to jail, and the payment of a small fine did not then (nor does it today) deter anyone from continuing his business.[6]

The patrolman is dependent upon the people he polices for his knowledge of their habits and manners. He knows what they allow him to see on the streets and in places where his presence is requested. They tell him things indirectly through the radio dispatcher. But the actions they conceal from him can be learned about only by deception or compulsion. Most gambling activity is carried on discreetly. A patrolman may know there is gambling in his area without ever having directly seen any. Number writers are alert to his presence, and the sight of his well-marked car and self gives ample warning of his approach. The young officer may make a vice pinch with some luck or by telling a lie to provide the legal basis for some evidence he has acquired. He may catch a few men involved in a dice game in an alley, and he can charge that one of them is "cutting" the game, taking a percentage, which makes it a crime rather than a social affair. Even when gambling operations were officially protected, number writers and bookies, who were usually persons well established in their neighborhoods, did not flaunt themselves publicly. Today few gamblers take action from people they do not know. This makes it almost impossible for the honest patrolman to see gambling transactions, and if he does not see anything, he has no right to stop and search someone for evidence.[7]

---

[6]*The New York Times* (September 13, 1971, October 29, 1971, January 10, 1972, October 23, 1972); *Philadelphia Daily News* (June 14, 1971); Donald Cressey, *Theft of the Nation* (New York, Harper & Row, 1969), p. 268; Wilson, pp. 100–3; Samuel Dash, "Cracks in the Foundation of Criminal Justice," *Illinois Law Review* (Northwestern University), Vol. XLVI (1951/52), pp. 385–406; Dallin H. Oakes, "Studying the Exclusionary Rule in Search and Seizure," *University of Chicago Law Review*, Vol. XXXVII (1970), pp. 665–757; Andy Logan, p. 117; Virgil Petersen, "Obstacles to Enforcement of Gambling Laws" and Morris Ploscowe and Edwin Lucas, "Gambling," *Annals of the American Academy of Political and Social Science*, Vol. 269 (1950), pp. 9ff.

[7]A patrolman who admitted that he had accepted money from gamblers, and even on occasion picked up payoffs for his colleagues, told investigators that he had never personally witnessed any gambling. "Well, I never actually saw any of these vice characters engaged in any

If the patrolman has no information regarding gambling, the only evidence he can look for is an exchange of money on the street or a person jotting something on a slip of paper. These acts could represent anything; nobody would argue that even in neighborhoods where gambling is common are they practiced exclusively by bookies and number writers. But patrolmen are encouraged to act on such slender evidence. New policemen are often reluctant to conduct searches under these circumstances because the lectures and warnings against making illegal searches which they heard repeatedly at the police academy are still fresh and clear, but as they gradually learn how important vice activity is in their careers and how difficult it is to obtain good information legally, their reluctance crumbles. They learn to do things that were never taught to them in the academy, although their instructors know that what is withheld from them will eventually be learned and practiced by the majority of men who go on the street.

Vice information is a commodity, and the patrolman learns that he must buy it on a restricted market where the currency he needs is provided him by his power and authority. The policeman who is accused of extortion is rightly condemned for being a crook. But the same man who exploits the moments when people are temporarily dependent upon him for their well-being and liberty to compel them to give him information is praised and rewarded. When a policeman catches two homosexuals, for example, in a car parked on a dark street, he has an almost unrestricted license to act. He may arrest them or release them; he may take money (either as extortion or as a bribe) or compel them to give him information under the threat of pain, possibly even applying a little force to underline the sincerity of his demands. All these actions are illegal, and the policeman who takes money is no more careful than the man who extorts information to conceal his actions from his colleagues. Each time a patrolman does any of these things, he blurs the boundaries that restrict and regulate his power.

A new man may ask his sergeant or a veteran officer

---

illegal activity, although I knew they were so engaged, but I personally never arrested any of them." *Philadelphia Inquirer* (November 18, 1971). All quotations cited from this newspaper are from legal depositions reprinted for the public record.

for advice and counsel before doing something he knows is illegal and possibly dangerous; but as the man gains confidence and experience, he restricts the exposure of his actions to only a few trusted colleagues. The more information he produces, the greater is his value to his superiors, whose dependence on his work encourages them to keep him happy, to reward him, and to protect him when he "gets in the jackpot," when he is in trouble. Each time he extorts information and tastes the rewards and successes it brings, he becomes more and more dependent upon it. But he does not have a constant flow of information, he does not have people falling into his power every day, and when he discovers that the pressure for vice activity is relentless, any reluctance he has to manufacture evidence and to break the law openly is likely to crumble.

A patrolman got out of his car and approached a news dealer who was sitting on a pile of papers. The policeman hesitated until the few people at the stand moved away and then he approached. He was a new man on the sector. The dealer had been on the corner for almost forty-five years. "Hello, Jack." "Good morning, Officer," he replied formally, not moving from his bench but folding a newspaper that he was going to give the policeman as he had always given one to every sector man. "Say, Jack, a guy told me an interesting thing about you." The old man just looked at him, still seated, shielding his eyes from the sun while he looked up at the policeman. "Yes, he told me you were writin' a number." The news dealer rose from the bench, angry and nervous. "It's not true. I been here almost forty-six years and I never wrote no numbers in my life. Whoever told you is lyin'. You want to search my stand and me, go ahead, but it ain't true, Officer," he replied, retaining the dignity and formality of his generation. The patrolman did not move but answered evenly, "No, this guy told me for sure you were writin' and he's pretty reliable. I tell you what, Jack, if you ain't writin' and I think you are, maybe you can tell me about a few of the other newsies in the area who are. I'm gonna keep an eye on you when I go past, but maybe I won't look so hard." The old man was trembling as he bitterly replied, "I don't know nothin' about that."

At that moment the regular beatman, who had worked the block for almost ten years, approached the corner. He and the news dealer were friends, colleagues almost. The beatman watched his papers for him, and in return the news dealer kept the policeman's extra equipment—his rain-gear and patrol forms—stored in the stand. He also kept the officer informed about things. The new sector man looked on silently as the beatman asked, "What's up?" The news dealer responded that the patrolman had accused him of being a number writer. The beatman smiled. "Go on, get in your car and go on patrol. Jack's a friend of the inspector and he ain't writin' no numbers." The threat behind the smile was as bright as the sun. The patrolman withdrew, remarking again that he would keep an eye on the stand as he drove past.

"Jack, don't get so excited. You just call the captain and make a complaint. Tell him you don't like being harrassed. And mention to him you know the inspector. I'll talk to the sergeant myself. Now, don't worry. Did the kid try and hit you for a note?" "No—and I wouldn't give him nothing because I didn't do nothing. You know that." "Yes," O. K., Jack you got to relax, think about your health. He's green. I think he was just trying to hustle some information. Now, don't worry, we'll get him off your back right now." Not everyone is so lucky.

The patrolman is an important person locally, but in the scheme of things he is not very powerful. He does not have a lot of money to buy information, as do some detectives and federal agents. He cannot organize a wiretap. He works eight hours a day and then goes home, and if he is hanging around the district when his platoon is off, the men in the platoon that is working the street will make sure they know what he is doing. He cannot spy on people or entrap them into committing illegal acts, as do the plainclothesmen he knows.[8] He is dependent for what he knows on the people in his sector who need the streets to do their work and live their lives. His information is a form of rent that he collects from local prostitutes, junkies, bums, petty

[8]On the techniques used by honest and sincere plainclothesmen in vice enforcement, see Robert Daley, "Portrait of an Honest Cop," *New York Magazine* (May 3, 1971), and Skolnick, pp. 101-3.

thieves, and burglars. Anyone who uses the street knows that the policeman who is friendly one day is the same man who may cajole, threaten, and even beat him the next. And if the people do not come up with information, well, they must take their chances.

Sometimes the patrolman gets information voluntarily. A store owner or a bartender may do him a favor in exchange for some small consideration or as a testament to a growing friendship. But generally these people want to give their information to his sergeant or lieutenant. If he is well established in his district and knows something about the gambling operations, he can get information from people in the trade who want him to eliminate their competition. But voluntary offers of information are infrequent. Even when he makes a cash payment, these transactions do not have any commercial character to them. There is no hint of equality or freedom. Money is given not so much as a payment but rather as a fee designed to keep the person afloat and in a position to maintain access to what the policeman wants to know. Possibly he will give the man liquor if his informant needs drink, or drugs if that is what is required to keep him talking and listening and watching. He does not pay for information, he finances its acquisition. The policeman acknowledges the character of his methods of acquiring information; he does not conceal for himself what he is actually doing. People who do favors for him—the businessman who mentions in passing that a lot of liquor has been seen going into a club or a certain girl has been having a lot of visitors—are not referred to as rats, pigeons, or even simply informers, a word which once meant teachers but now suggests only one thing—betrayal.

"You want another drink? Go ahead. Bob, give us a couple more down here." An off-duty lieutenant had casually run into his informant in a barroom and they were having a friendly conversation. They had known each other for many years, having met when the lieutenant was only a patrolman and the informant the manager of a big after-hours club. The manager was down on his luck now, the palsy in his hands signaling that his slide was prolonged. "You used to really take care of the cops, never forgot the district men.

Always a drink or two, something to eat at four in the morning. Real good, it's true," the lieutenant reminisced. The situation had changed. "Honest, Joe, I need that job. If you could help me out with McKay, I'd appreciate it a lot, you know." "Well, sure, I'll talk to him. But I'm surprised you didn't let me know sooner about that game. You're sure they got a game going in there?" "I didn't go inside, but I was told good information." "Well, why the fuck didn't you go in there and let me know?" "You wouldn't hit that place, would you? You're only a district lieutenant, I mean . . ." "The fuck I won't. You go in there and tell me what they got going and I'll hit 'em next week. Now will you go in there?" "Listen, they'd treat me real rough if they found out . . ." "Hey, I know that. You just get me the information and I'll speak to Kim for you. Bob, give us a couple more."

Every police official knows how his men acquire their information. If people disapproved of gambling, they would come forward and protest, but they rarely do. Regardless of whether the commissioner is considered a "liberal" or a "conservative," he knows, condones, and encourages the fact that his men break the law to make vice arrests. He knows that if they do not make arrests, there will always be someone—a local group, a state politician, possibly a federal agency—to hint at corruption and immorality in the police department. No matter what he may say about improving the relations between the police and the community and introducing programs to open lines of communication with minority groups, he continues to encourage his men to do things that undermine the possibility of trust between the patrolman and many of the people he encounters daily. He also knows that once the patrolman has obtained his information, he must make a mockery of the law in order to get the pinches the department demands as evidence of its honesty and commitment to upholding the law.

The fourth amendment of the Constitution establishes clear guides for the protection of our most private places—our bodies and our homes. In clear language, it marks out the precise manner the state must follow whenever it seeks to violate the privacy of any individual. It guarantees the right of the people to be secure in their persons, houses, papers, and effects, against unreasonable searches and seizures, shall not be violated, and no Warrants shall issue, but upon probable cause, supported by Oath or affirmation, and particularly describing the place to be searched, and the persons or things to br seized.

Before a policeman may obtain a search warrant he must swear to a judge that he has "thoroughly investigated the information so as to convince a disinterested party [the judge] that reasonable cause or grounds exist to justify a search." The department formally exhorts its men to remember that "all information given by an informant must be checked. The policeman is duty-bound to investigate the information given him." The policeman does not have to inform the court who his informant is or how he obtained his information, a requirement that would effectively destroy the possibility of the police ever acquiring information legally; this spares him from having to tell the judge a verifiable lie. But a policeman rarely is able to check the information he obtains; and if he did, the chances of his being spotted are great. The honest policeman has no alternative but to rely solely on what he is told by people who will tell him anything to get loose of his grasp, and he presents this as carefully evaluated evidence to a judge in a court of law. Everybody involved—the policeman, his sergeant and lieutenant, the captain who approves the warrant application, the assistant district attorney who approves it, and the judge who grants him the warrant—knows that the policeman is perjuring himself. The patrolman has no choice, and if the department does not want this to happen, it must select a different strategy for enforcing vice laws. Unfortunately, experience has shown that exclusive reliance on plainclothesmen and vice squads results in systematic corruption and widespread payoffs, while general responsibility has at least a restraining influence on the cupidity of men who learn that there is a dollar to be made.[9]

The supervisor's evaluation of the warrant applications brought to him is based on the needs of his squad, not on the quality and legality of the information. Even if the

[9]On warrants, see Israel and LaFave, pp. 109–27.

sergeant and lieutenant are absolutely honest, refusing to take any of the money they know they can get if they relent, they do not care about the credibility of the informant or the manner in which the information was obtained. Usually the supervisor's decisions are based on his evaluation of the man making the request. Usually gambling warrants are taken out by the most experienced men in the platoon, and often they do not reveal to anyone exactly how they got their information. Even if the sergeant thinks the information is good but does not trust the man or have high regard for his competence, he may refuse him permission or suggest that another man take out the warrant. Since perjury is going to be committed, the sergeant wants someone whose proven skills will prevent any embarrassments or unintentional revelations under oath.

Once permission for a warrant is granted, the only concern of the men involved is to make certain that the application is written in a manner that will assure its approval. The department is very helpful in this matter, offering guidance that clearly outlines the criteria that must be satisfied. "Police are not required to disclose the identity of their confidential informants, but, it is important for the policeman to fully explain why he believes the facts related to him . . . are true. . . . [There] must be included the informant's record of accuracy. . . . An important piece of supporting datum which can be included in the warrants is 'surveillance.' Police officers should indicate in a warrant what they have observed concerning the premises or property that is to be searched."

The possibility of error and misunderstanding is minimized by providing a model example of a proper application. "On July 15, 1966, I received information from an informant who I know to be reliable because information supplied by said informant during the past year has resulted in six arrests and five convictions. . . . Informant personally told me . . . that he personally observed . . ." The comforting assurance this form offers men who are afraid to do illegal things is the principal reason why almost every search warrant is written in this manner. The need to lie under oath bothers many men; it frightens them and even forces some to forgo the rewards of vice work altogether. Some men take out warrants with the intention of never serving them. They are used to appease their sergeant, who can claim to his superiors that his men were trying but their information went sour before they had an opportunity to serve the warrants.

No effort is made to disguise the illegal character of the enterprise. Since every warrant application is a collective enterprise ratified by commanding officers, no policeman is afraid to reveal the false character of what he is doing. The patrolmen and the operations crews, who prepare the applications, openly discuss the mechanics of faking warrants, although they are careful not to reveal the details. It is taboo to look at a warrant application without invitation; to do so is one of the acts that guarantee a patrolman open rebuke and even threats. Every patrolman learns that he must be a liar and a conspirator if he wants to remain a district policeman. He must become an expert in telling untruths or transfer to a unit that has no vice-work obligations.

"You gotta put in there that he gave you information before, Hal, or the judge won't go for it," a corporal said. "Aw, fuck it, this is good information. The guy who give it to me is a number writer, he should know." "Listen, you just put in there that the information you got was given to the special squads and they made all the pinches," a patrolman said to his partner. "Not me, I ain't committin' perjury. I never made a vice pinch before. You do it if you're such a big man." "Shit, you think you're any better than anyone else. Everyone perjures himself in vice—the cops, the courts, and the defendants. Go on." "All right, but you better tell me just what to say."

"Listen, Sarge, this is good information. We got it off a faggot just an hour ago. He said he saw a lot of stuff in the house but we gotta hit it right away before they move it out." "O.K., I'll make up the application and you run it right down to the judge. You got any pinches for narcotics off a warrant?" "Yea, a couple—" "O.K. I'll write the usual stuff about a reliable informant. But I'll have to say that surveillance has not been possible because the informant told you the stuff is going to be moved immediately. That way he won't ask you why there's so much hurry. You're sure it's good?" "If it ain't, that faggot's not gonna be walkin' in this town any more."

The constant demand for vice arrests and the violations of the law that men must practice to get good arrests makes it nearly impossible for a sergeant to prevent some of his men from indulging in practices that are blatantly criminal. A man may justify to himself a lie to a judge if he believes that his information is good and that the person he is investigating is a gambler, but some policemen do not bother to limit themselves to this self-constructed zone of proper behavior. In every part of the city where vice activity is strong, there are people who are generally regarded as marginal members of society, whose instability and lack of place brings them different treatment from that received by solid citizens. The patrolman's constant exploitation of bums, drunks, junkies, and prostitutes for information completely erodes the legal restraints designed to prevent him from exercising his authority over them in ways that express disregard for them as persons. He does not hesitate to search them when he sees them, going through their pockets as if they were his own.

A policeman, under oath, recounted an investigation that he conducted:

I received information from a female who I know as Jean. . . . This female, Jean, told me that there was a colored female by the name of Mary, who she described, who was inside a bar . . . and that this female had heroin on her person. . . . I went into this bar, in uniform, and took into custody the female who had been described to me. I placed her in the rear of the wagon and Officer Frame drove to the area of 15th and Webster Sts. where I alone conducted a search of this person. I found approximately fifteen bags of heroin which this female, Mary, had concealed under her panties. At about that time Officer Frame called back to me and mentioned something about a radio call "man with a gun" or something like that and said, "Let's leave." I let this female go and Officer Frame and I proceeded to respond to the radio call.[1]

There are policemen who are not only willing to search suspects illegally for evidence in order to make an arrest or to obtain information but are also willing to manufacture

[1]*Philadelphia Inquirer* (November 17, 1971).

evidence in order to establish the basis for an arrest. "Farming," the planting of evidence, is practiced throughout the department. There are sergeants and lieutenants who take a very strong line against this practice. When a man takes over a new squad, one of the first things he does is to indicate to his men his position on farming. Some supervisors even insist on accompanying their men when warrants are served in order to prevent them from doing it. But even the most honorable sergeant knows he cannot stop his men from making illegal searches, planting evidence on people to compel them to talk, or fabricating evidence for warrants. If a man carries with him a numbers slip or a few bags of heroin he has confiscated and withheld, how can he be prevented from using them if he is willing to violate the law? Whenever a platoon is behind in its activity, the sergeant knows that any pressure he exerts on his men encourages them to behave illegally.

A patrolman approached a colleague who was filling out a warrant application in the operations room. The man had been waiting for him because he had information they were going to use to get a warrant for narcotics. "Sorry I'm late—we'll have to get the warrant tomorrow. I just got a couple more vice pinches on the way into the district. I seen this guy lyin' on the sidewalk over on Cony Street. I got out to look at him. Drunk as a fish, stinkin' nigger. So I went through his pockets the way you do before you call the wagon, you know, and I found a slip with numbers. I called the lieutenant and he said to put him on the books. The guy promised to give us a speak and maybe a still if we let him off the hook, so that's a couple more."

"The lieutenant let you put him on the books, huh? That new lieutenant, I guess he's never seen that dogshit numbers slip you got," the patrolman replied, with a small grin, concealing his displeasure over a practice he knew the man used regularly. "The guy was so drunk he didn't know whether it was his or not. He's got five pinches for illegal lottery anyway."

There are policemen who are willing to farm anyone they believe cannot resist them or whose protests will not be acknowledged because of their reputation or previous record.

There are many more men who hold these colleagues in contempt but are willing, nonetheless, to plant evidence on a person whom they regard as guilty. They defend their patently illegal behavior in terms of the need to get activity and the guilt of the suspect. They implicitly argue for the morality of their actions in comparison with the immorality of those who frame the innocent along with the guilty. This pathetic effort to maintain their dignity and honor is something only a policeman can understand.

There are many younger policemen who do not know how to get vice information and are not willing to extort it from people. They have few contacts that are likely to give them a line on a number writer. But they want to get vice activity and their only chance is to make a drug arrest. It is a common practice in many squads for some men to retain a part of the drugs they find on people; others are given some by their sergeant. These are mainly used to "buy" information, but there is no way that the officer's use of these drugs can be controlled. He may give it away for evidence, but he may also plant it on someone, sell it for profit, or use it himself. If he does any of these things, it is not likely that his colleagues are present, but even if they knew, what could they do? Every one of them has to some degree violated the law, and if they expose him, what is to prevent their own wrongdoings from being revealed?[2]

The inhibitions most policemen have about using any of these practices are weakened by what they see their colleagues doing when they make a "legitimate" narcotics arrest. How can a uniformed man actually witness a drug transaction? He sees many pushers on the corners, he knows them by sight, but few actually carry drugs on them. These are kept concealed nearby, and when a sale has been arranged, the buyer collects his drugs at another place. The patrolman cannot follow people around. Even if he were able to, it would require his ignoring the demands for service and the

[2]"I almost never had to buy anything—only one time. I always could get it from policemen. This is the way I got a large portion of my stuff —most of my drugs. They thought I was using it to plant on people," a patrolman who was an admitted user explained to investigators. When asked how the drugs were obtained, he replied, "I would say that in about eighty percent of the drug raids . . . when drugs are confiscated, that some is kept out . . . to be used for plants." *Philadelphia Inquirer* (September 5, 1971).

emergency calls he receives from the dispatcher. He may stop the pusher on the street and illegally search him. If he finds anything, the patrolman may decline to make an arrest because he does not want to lie in court, preferring to exploit the moment to get information from the man or to swell his supply of drugs. But there are men who have no inhibitions. Everyone in court, from the policeman to the judge, knows that most drug arrests are illegal. Every time a policeman tells of a "flying bag," the police description of a technique used to support court testimony, his words are greeted with open skepticism, but there are no grounds for a judge to presume that the man is lying. Often defendants do throw heroin to the ground upon the approach of a policeman in the mistaken belief that if the contraband is not on their person, it is not legally their goods. But many patrolmen use this claim to cover the planting of evidence or illegally seized contraband. If the officer is determined to make his arrest stick, he really has little choice but to tell a lie.

"Officer, you say the defendant was running ahead of you down an alley and you saw him throw the material to the ground?" "Yessir." "It was night and it was dark, correct?" "Yessir." "It was not well lighted in the alley?" "Yessir; no, sir, it was not." "Now this alley, was it clean or were there papers and debris scattered on the ground?" "Well, that is not a clean area of the city, sir, as you know, but this particular area was pretty clean." "I see, the unfortunate defendant chose the only clean alley in the city to run down and throw this material. Well, I shall have to send a letter to the Streets Department thanking them for their efforts, and tell them you have testified to their good work." Everybody in the courtroom, except the defendant, broke into laughter. He was convicted.

The honest patrolman who is determined to advance in his platoon cannot long resist involvement in these practices. They offer him the only substantial chance to make the arrests that bring him the credit he seeks. He learns that information does not come for nothing. He must get in and deal. If he has nothing to trade, if he is a "straight cop" who will not make deals or extort information, the only alternative he has is to beat information from people. This still happens, but it is not condoned. He sees that illegal searches and fake warrants are the only way to make vice arrests. He sees men he admires, good cops, men who take risks and arrive prepared to work, using heroin to buy information and even to frame people. He listens to them lying in court, hears them judge others by their ability to give false testimony; he wants to share their rewards, the favors granted them by their sergeant, the free time, the extra day off. He does not long resist, or he transfers.

A patrolman who testifies under oath in a manner that reveals he conducted an illegal search (or seizure) is not chastised or punished; if he confiscated drugs or a weapon, he may feel that he has served a useful purpose, although the suspect is freed. But if he is testifying about an arrest based on a search warrant, he must lie to protect himself and his colleagues. One reason most sergeants are very careful in selecting men to take out warrants is their need to be sure of the man's capacity to testify skillfully and with aplomb. A policeman can never be certain that a lawyer will not try to expose him. While most gambling cases are handled by relatively few lawyers whose only interest is to get the case dismissed or supressed and not to embarrass anyone, there always remains the possibility of unpleasant disclosures. An experienced vice man cannot possibly retain any respect for the rigid standards of law and evidence which, presumably, the society has an obligation to maintain. He has committed perjury so often and routinely that he sees the courtroom as just another element in a giant charade. There are many policemen who despise this state of affairs, but there is no alternative available to the policeman who wishes to continue in his job. He can simply refuse to get any vice, but if he wants to advance in his platoon, he must make vice arrests and this requires him to lie. He cannot tell the truth because the costs of doing so are grave personally and have no effect on the continuation of the system.

"Officer, how did you acquire the information which led to this raid?" "Well, sir, my partner and I were stopped on the street by this woman who said that she knew someone was a big number writer," the youthful patrolman said.

"She showed you the house and told you who the people involved were?" the defense lawyer asked. "Yes, sir." "What did you do then, Officer?" "We called for our sergeant, and he talked to her for a little while and said we should get a warrant and hit the place."

"So you got a warrant?" "Yes, sir." "Now, this warrant, how long after you talked to the woman did you get it?" The policemen in the courtroom waiting to testify in their own cases had been indifferent to the proceedings, but now they all sat alertly, watching the young policeman on the stand. He was in trouble and did not know it. "Well, we made up the warrant application and then went right back to the house and went in." "Did you know this woman or ever see her before?" "No, sir." "Now, Officer, on your application you state that the informant was well known to you and had previously given you good information." The room was silent; several policemen rose to leave. A sergeant sitting nearby put his head in his hands and swore softly and continually to himself. "Did you actually know her, Officer?" The patrolman was sweating, finally realizing what he had done. "Well, sir, uh, I did not know her but she was known to my partner and to the sergeant." "But you said on the warrant—it's in your name—that you knew her." "Yessir, but it was my partner who knew her." "Officer, you also swore in the warrant that you kept the house under surveillance. But you have testified here that you raided the house right away. What kind of surveillance did you make?" "Uh, sir, my partner and the sergeant maintained a watch on the place while I made the application and they . . ." "Your Honor, I think the policeman has indicated that this search was illegal and unwarranted." The sergeant had stopped swearing and looked as if he were preparing to murder the policeman, who was near tears. The judge excused him from the stand and dismissed the case. He asked the assistant district attorney to meet with him after the recess to discuss a matter in private. The officer walked from the courtroom, followed by his sergeant. "Oh shit, man, I never seen one so green before. That guy has got to be stupid or he's tryin' to fuck the sergeant real good," a patrolman commented.

BETWEEN LAW AND ORDER 395

The district policeman's involvement in gambling enforcement compels him to violate the law, degrade people, and disregard the established standards of honesty and truth that have been built into the legal codes over many centuries; it also undermines his ability to take pride in his work. In return for this he gets very little. He knows that enforcement is a sham that cannot prevent gambling and illegal drinking in the neighborhoods where they are entrenched. If he is shrewd, experienced, and willing, he can exploit occasional opportunities for payoffs, and if he works for a corrupted sergeant or lieutenant, he may have the chance to earn a steady note, but he will not get rich.

In every district where gambling goes on, there is money for those who want it and are willing to take the risks. "It's there, it's all over the place. All you need are these stripes and you know there's an envelope waiting for you. You know, guys come up to you on the street and ask you to stop here or there. If you want it, it's yours," a sergeant said. Regular payoffs are available to supervisors, but unless they are prepared to organize protection, their men cannot participate. If a sergeant will not allow (or is not allowed by his lieutenant and captain) a steady note, the men who want to exploit their vice knowledge for payoffs are limited to momentary chances. The patrolman who does this must be knowledgeable, because if he puts the squeeze on someone who is protected or connected, he can find himself under arrest and on the front page of the city's newspapers, an example to all other stupid cops. But the experienced men in the squad do know, they have seen who gets arrested, they know which places have not been raided, which number writers seem to operate freely and which do not. They can stop someone on the street and simply shake him down on the spot, threatening to take the man in "for investigation," which would ruin his business for the day and makes the payment of five or ten dollars well worthwhile. If a policeman discovers a card game or a crap game, he does not have to "take the game" but can call his sergeant and collect rent from the players. If he confiscates lottery or sweepstakes tickets from someone on the street or in a raid, it is not necessary to turn them in to the evidence clerk. "Hey, Frank, I want to talk to you. Did you get those lottery tickets?" "Yes, sir." "Well, hold on to them. I just checked with Pedro, they hold the drawing on Wednesday. Maybe we got a winner. So you keep them and if *we* don't hit it, then you can turn 'em in," the lieutenant said.

There are many policemen who are not knowledgeable about vice and do not dare to arrange a private deal for themselves or take something that is offered. However, many of these men are involved, whether they wish it or not, by their sergeants. A man does not have to take money from a gambler to become involved in criminal acts. If he brings someone in for investigation and his sergeant tells him to "let the guy walk," he must either comply and violate administrative regulations and the criminal law, or fight his sergeant. If he is willing to confront his superior, he must be prepared for an effort to drive him from the district and from the department. If he has done anything wrong, the sergeant will nail him; he will watch him like a hawk, pressuring him constantly for even the most trivial violation. Few men resist their bosses.

"I picked this guy up. I didn't know nothin' then. He was standing on the corner talkin' to someone and he had a big fuckin' roll in his hand, maybe two grand. And he had slips on him. I knew he must be a number writer or something, but I didn't know for sure. So I called the wagon, and he was offering me money and shit. Real friendly, no threats, and he wasn't nervous about bein' pinched. So the wagon comes and they took one look at him and smiled. You know Rollins, a good cop, right? He was the guy's fuckin' nephew, I found out later. So you know how he got on the wagon so quick. Anyway, he's gettin' in the wagon and slips the roll to the kid. I almost shit, but I didn't say nothin'. You think he made the books? We got into the yard and the sergeant was waiting. He never even got inside the building. He walked out of the wagon smiling and kept right on going. He even thanked me."

A sergeant may organize regular payoffs for himself and a few intimates without sharing or allowing his other men to share them with him, or he can allow steady notes to be distributed among all the men in the platoon. If this occurs, anyone who does not want to take may refuse, but he will not remain in the district very long. New men are sealed off from any contact with these payments, and even when a rookie works a wagon or a car with a veteran, he may not know that his partner is collecting for the platoon. Most steady notes are collected on the first day of day-work or four-to-twelve by a wagon crew or a car man. The veteran stops at a store or a house and tells his partner, "Kid, wait here and listen close, we don't want to blow any calls. I'll be back in a minute." The rookie does not know what is going on, and he is not told anything. Even if he suspects there are payoffs, he is not offered or allowed any concrete information until his colleagues are certain that he is "all right." One admitted grafter told investigators that he "started receiving these payments six to eight months after coming to the Seventeenth District." During these months the new man is tested informally to see whether he is willing to participate and involve himself. "It wasn't long before I learned about police corruption. Once when I was a rookie, my sergeant told me to close the club at 3 A.M. He told me there was a $5 note waiting for me and I told him if he wanted the place closed I'd close it, but if he wanted someone to leave it open and pick up a note to send someone else. He sent someone else . . . That's what they do. They test you. If you don't do it the first time, they usually leave you alone," a captain recounted in a sworn affidavit.[3]

Steady notes are strictly territorial. A fixed amount is paid to each sector wagon, and supervisor for the daywork or the four-to-twelve shift. One man may do the collections for the entire platoon, or different men may collect the notes on their sectors and, after taking their share, turn the rest over to someone, usually a wagon man, for distribution to others. From evidence given in sworn testimony, it appears that none of these amounts to much money. One officer in a district which had a reputation for being one of the most "active" in the city estimated that he earned about $90 a month in regular payoffs. He was a "bagman" for his sergeant, which meant that he was directly involved in the collection and distribution of notes, and therefore his knowledge of the economics was sound. In addition, this patrol-

[3] *Philadelphia Inquirer* (November 17, 1971, November 21, 1971).

man was a heroin addict, who dealt in narcotics with his sergeant's permission and encouragement. The trust presupposed by this mutual collusion suggests that the officer was intimately familiar with all the arrangements in his squad. If the policeman was making about $1,000 annually from regular payoffs, it can be safely assumed that his sergeant and lieutenant were earning at least double or triple his take. Most of the notes he collected were for $5 or $10, and his sergeant and lieutenant were usually paid multiples of his share. Also, they have opportunities to earn extra shares that the men do not know about.

There may be districts where steady notes do not exist, but there is no district where there is not a belief that someone is taking a regular payoff from gamblers or liquor men. When a man goes "into clothes," his relationship to former colleagues changes immediately. Without knowing for sure, they are all certain that he is making money. Everyone assumes that plainclothesmen take something. "They've been in clothes for some time now. You know how it is, everybody in the district knows who they are but they still make some pinches. And now Shoemaker's opening a store. You wonder where he got the paper? Who knows? The word is that they get paid $150 apiece on the first and the fifteenth. I guess you could open a store with that after a while, huh?" a policeman commented to his partner as they chatted, hidden in their hole during the murky hours of last out.

This attitude toward plainclothesmen is not disguised in their presence. They must accept the constant kidding of their friends or avoid contact with them. They are always being told how good they look, how fit, how nice their clothes are; they are kidded about all the "free tail" they must be getting and all the extra money they have in their pockets. "We had a ball last night. Hogan paid for everything, man: the broads and the booze; we had a ball." "Well, shit," someone replied, "he shudda paid, he's in clothes, ain't he? So he's got the paper, right?" There are policemen who bend every effort to get themselves into plainclothes, while others decline the offer because they do not want to become involved with prostitutes, undercover work, and graft. "There's no way it can't fuck up your home life. Your wife knows you're goin' out to sit in a barroom and make out with some broads. So what do you expect her to feel like? What do you think she's gonna think when you don't come home until the morning?" an experienced plainclothesman commented. "Three hundred? That's a poor district. I wouldn't go into that bullshit for less than double," a patrolman commented. He had declined an invitation to go into clothes for the simple reason that he feared what he would do. "I'm having a hard enough time staying clean in the district. I'm so bored you know, and now I know so much that I can make paper any time I want. That's why I'm going into the juvenile squad. There's no green there, just good, hard police work. There's no way you can go into clothes and be clean. The best you can do is avoid getting caught."[4]

Relatively few men are making money from gamblers regularly, and not even a majority are making money even occasionally, but every policeman who has dealings with vice is obliged to break the law and involve himself in a degrading sham. The policeman develops a set of attitudes that some people think cynical but that he sees as realistic in light of his knowledge of city life. "I don't make no more pinches unless the sergeant needs one real bad. It's bullshit. Look at that bar. You know who owns that place? Is he a big banker in the city? How many pinches has he got for numbers? Five or six. I locked him once. How much did he pay to get his record expunged? I don't know, but he ain't got no record any more and he's a fucking city councilman. So why should I make a number pinch for? I don't want to make any money off that stuff no more, it's gettin' too dangerous, and that's all those pinches are good for."

"O.K., Herbie, relax. You can see the captain in a minute." A wagon crew and their sergeant had brought an

---

[4] The systematic corruption of plainclothesmen and the organization of payoffs has been documented several times in recent years. The most dramatic and revealing revelations occurred in New York City during the "Harry Gross scandal" (1950) and in testimony before the Knapp Commission (1970). See Norton Mockridge and Robert H. Prall, *The Big Fix* (New York, Henry Holt, 1954), and Ted Poston, "The Numbers Racket," a newspaper series reprinted in *Organized Crime in America: A Reader*, Gus Tyler, ed. (Ann Arbor, University of Michigan Press, 1962), pp 260–74. A comment on lifestyles of plainclothesmen in New York is in Radano, pp. 143–51.

irate news vendor into the station. They had served a warrant for his newsstand but had found nothing. He had protested their actions and demanded to see the captain. After a few minutes the captain came to the door and greeted him in a friendly fashion. The news dealer was not mollified. "Look, this is the fourth ticket you guys took on me this year and you ain't found nothin'. Now I want this bullshit to stop. I am bein' harassed and I'm gonna make a complaint if it keeps up."

"Herbie," the captain said, "everybody knows you're a number · writer. I know it, you know it. Now, I'll make a deal with you. You take one pinch, just one, and I promise you there won't be any more warrants on you this year."

"No. I ain't goin' for it. You got nuthin' on me and I ain't takin' no pinches. But these guys gotta stop hittin' my business or I'm gonna see someone."

"O.K., Herbie, no hard feelings. They get information you know, they have to act," the captain said, with a smile, "but I will personally check it out next time, O.K.?"

"Well, you're O.K. You want *Playboy?* I'll send it up to you." The captain grinned and returned to his office. "Now, you guys leave me alone, right?" They smiled and he grinned. The sergeant offered to drive him back to his stand, but he decided to walk. No hard feelings, it was just a nice day. But the sergeant accompanied him to the door and, in view of anyone who cared to look, handed him a dollar to play a number. Later the sergeant said, "I was lookin' at the warrant while he was talkin' to the captain and noticed the last three digits of the serial number matched my kid's birthday, 914, so I decided to play it. That old Jew's been writin' numbers on the corner for almost thirty years. We just don't find the slips."

Driving past a taproom, a sergeant nodded. "You remember all the bullshit we had with that place? The roofers and the porkies were fightin' and they firebombed the place. The night when Thomas swung at that little prick and hit me in the head with his stick. Maybe you weren't workin' that night. We occupied the street for a couple of days and listened to all their horseshit. Can't blame 'em really, the roofers badmouthin' 'em all the time and not lettin' 'em use the bar. So they closed the place up and drove the roofers out. Now it's gonna reopen and the porkies have the bar. The shit they do. You know who's got the license? Pilz, the bookie over on Warner Street. That motherfucker got the license and he's puttin' a porkie in as front man. He can get a liquor ticket from the state, but I'm supposed to bust my ass locking him up for makin' book? Bullshit. Anyway, we'll get a good note out of the bar for watchin' the place."

The patrolman is obliged to violate the law, degrade people, lie, and even shame himself in his own eyes in order to make arrests he knows are meaningless and he suspects produce money for others. This not only tends to make him cynical about the law and the motives of many people he knows, it also makes him think of himself as a special kind of fool. He sees himself operating in a world where "notes" are constantly floating about, and only the stupid, the naïve, and the fainthearted are unwilling to allow some of them to stick to their fingers. Even in the most carefully regulated system, the patrolman's opportunities to break the law are considerable. If he is inclined, nobody can prevent him from tipping off somebody about an impending raid or pocketing drugs or money that he finds. Strict supervision is rarely possible. Even the many supervisors who do not take graft are involved in collusions with their men to cover up the illegal methods they use to acquire information, get warrants, and make arrests. These acts convert supervisors into colleagues, diminishing the distance between them and the men they command. If they oblige their men to adhere to all of the legal rules, they will only reduce the number of vice arrests that are being made and cause their captains, divisional inspectors, and the chief inspector to demand increases in the squads' activity, which will be accompanied with threats of transfer. They are trapped in a dilemma not of their own making. This is one reason why policemen deeply resent admonitions to be honest. They know that the editorials in newspapers are irrelevant to their situation. Policemen who know themselves to be honest invent distinctions between "good notes" and "bad notes" to rationalize their own misconducts. They compare the petty violations they commit against the acts of men who are really on the take, and secure for themselves a modicum of honor. They know that the only way a policeman can be honest in the exacting sense required by his oath of office is to resign. The policeman does not want to quit, so he makes little compromises, which bring him a few dollars and more importantly solidify his relationships with his colleagues, and he continues to do his job. He knows he does things that are illegal, but he has no choice. He knows that there are many dishonest policemen, but his rewards for doing work he considers "dirty"[5] are little more than the renewal of his right to continue in the job. He cannot prevent what he disapproves, nor can he explain to anyone without jeopardizing his career (and his life in some places), so he turns his face to the wind and does what he must.

2 · Bad Apples?

There is no way to prepare a policeman for the situation he discovers on the street. There are some open discussions at the police academy about the possibilities for graft, but most instructors restrict themselves to repeating the traditional homilies about "not selling your soul for a bowl of porridge." The men are told by some that they will be offered free food, which is the beginning of their slide into corruption. "They'll try to buy you with a ham sandwich; don't take it. Put your money on the counter, and if the guy won't take it, leave it for the waitress. You'll see when you go out on the beat. Maybe you don't have much money in your pocket, and when you finish your hamburger, the guy says to forget it. So you do it once, and then you go down the street and the next guy wants to put a little cheese on the burger for you. Now you're gettin' to like the job. Don't do it." From the back of the room another instructor called out, "Say, John, where is this beat you're talkin' about?" and the earnest moment dissolved in mirth.

[5]"Now every occupation is not one but several activities; some of them are the dirty part of that trade. It may be dirty in one of several ways. It may be simply physically disgusting. It may be a symbol of degradation, something that wounds one's dignity. Finally, it may be dirty work in that it in some way goes counter to the more heroic of our moral conceptions." E. C. Hughes, "Work and the Self," *Social Psychology at the Crossroads*, John H. Rohrer and Muzafer Sherif, eds. (New York, Harpers, 1951), p. 319.

The "bad apple" theory has been the traditional explanation of corruption and scandal in an organization that is required by its nature to appear honest and "neutral" in every possible way. This idea allows the career policeman to explain to himself as well as to the public the persistence of a problem whose solution is beyond his control. For the corrupt or the compromised, too, the idea of a few bad men having succumbed to the temptations of a wicked society is a comfort that allows them to conceal the political character of most scandals. Every revelation brings with it a flood of sermons, all with the same moral—a weak man is tempted by his position and gradually slides into the ranks of the dishonest. After the Knapp Commission revealed that some New York City policeman were involved in payoffs, the reporter who broke the story wrote of their corruption:.

> Police corruption begins with the notion that policemen by some peculiar divine right are entitled to free meals, free movies, and cut-rate prices on virtually everything they buy. This is known as "getting a break." "Even when I was in the Police Academy," a Tactical Patrol Force sergeant recalled, "I heard guys talking about getting a break." While almost all cops take free meals —it is so widely accepted it is impossible not to—the idea of getting a break is the platform, the launching pad, from which the bad guys spring.[6]

While this notion reaffirms our belief in the Christian idea of guilt and sin being personal and individual, it is a notion that offers the recruit no hope of coping with the real situation on the street. A policeman who becomes a thief does so for the same reasons that others are thieves—inclination and opportunity.

There are some instructors who try to give their students a more realistic picture of what to expect, but nobody can tell them how to avoid the web of collusions and compromises that makes everyone guilty. One day a lecturer was talking about the patrolman's freedom in issuing traffic tickets. "You

[6]David Burnham, "How Corruption Is Built into the System—and a Few Ideas for What to Do about It," *New York Magazine* (September 21, 1970).

mean we can give a guy a warning rather than give him a ticket if he makes a wrong turn?" someone asked. "That's right. Listen, fellas, let me tell you something you should know, since it's gonna come up as soon as you get on the street. We ain't supposed to talk this way, but it's important for you to know. Don't fuck with a motorist. Don't take a note from him. He's not like a prostitute or a number writer. If he complains, you are gonna be in real trouble. If you pull a guy over for something and he cops a plea about not knowin' the neighborhood, you can go with that. If he offers you a little something for a cup of coffee or lunch, well, that's your business. But don't go out there and pinch him for a note. That's a stupid fuckin' note and there's no sense blowin' a good job for a nickel or dime. You understand me?"

A few days later a lieutenant was discussing the policeman's obligation to remain honest and report all wrongdoings. "I know there are men out there in uniforms breaking the law. You will see some of them. If you refuse to take anything but do not report it, you are as guilty as they are, and you are not any better either. When I came into this department, I worked with the biggest bunch of crooks I ever saw. You have to refuse to go along. You have to . . ."

"Excuse me, sir, can I ask you something?" a recruit said. "I got a friend who's been on the street awhile. He told me that one night he went on a burglary call, and his partner and a few other guys stole some liquor from this place and offered him some. Now I ain't sayin' he wasn't wrong for takin' it and he's so fucked up about it he's thinkin' of quittin', but what do you expect a guy to do? It's like in the army. Everyone is checkin' out the new guy to see how he will act. O.K., there's no question you can refuse to take and they don't trust you no more. Well, you can handle that and still get along, but if you think that anyone is gonna drop a dime, you must be kiddin'. You do that once and you got a reputation that will follow you around. You're a rat and everyone will know it. Who's gonna work with you? Who will come to you if you call an assist?" Everyone in the room was noisily agreeing with their classmate.

"What's your name, son? Right. Listen, Jason, I ain't sayin' it's easy. I'm not telling you it don't take balls to do it. I was a lonely guy for a long time. Nobody to talk to, all the shit details, workin' the worst sectors in the district where there were no people around. They put me at the end of nowhere. But you see these bars? I made it. And now there are a lot of guys who dive for a fuckin' hole when they see me comin'. You gotta decide from the start in this job whether you're gonna be clean or whether you're gonna take. There are guys in this room, I know, who are comin' on the job with the idea of makin' a buck. I wish you would quit and save us the trouble of having to find you and lock you up. There are guys here who are already thinking about how they're gonna flash their tin and get this and that. Well, I'm tellin' you those days are gone in this department, and if you do it we'll get your ass."

The moralizing to which the recruit is subjected in the academy mercifully stops when he gets to the district, but he quickly discovers that even the frank advice of helpful teachers has not prepared him for what he finds. Although his experience depends greatly on the kind of district he is sent to, one thing he finds everywhere is bribery. Almost immediately people are trying to give him money, mostly motorists who are trying to get out of a ticket. He also hears rumors about things that suggest the involvement of some of his colleagues in obscure dealings, but since he is informally segregated from much of the squad's work, he does not know what is actually going on. All he is told in his first few weeks is where he can get his clothes cleaned for the "police price" and which restaurants will give him a break on his lunch check. These are gratuities the patrolman knows he receives only because he is a policeman, but he does not try to conceal them or disguise what they are since he is not doing anything illicit for them. He sees these as expressions of gratitude and friendship which mirror within his circle of influence the policies and attitudes that he sees operating at a higher level within the department and the city government.

In most American cities there are restaurant chains that feed policemen free or at a special rate. This is not the informal policy of some branch managers but a centrally organized decision. Cashiers keep a record of how many free meals they give away each day, and these tabulations are used to demonstrate the company's goodwill toward the department and the city. The patrolman does not know what kind of favors are given and received in return for this consideration, but he understands it is not done out of simple kindness. There are also restaurants and diners throughout the city known for their kindness to anyone in uniform. A radio call announced a holdup in a restaurant in a distant part of the city, causing a lieutenant to comment, "A lot of cars are gonna go in on that. They treat a cop real good in there. You can get a whole basket of chicken and they don't even give you a bill." The district patrolmen do not know where the "big bosses" dine, but they know that the considerations given to them differ only in the quality of the food and the accommodations offered to people in higher places.[7]

Every patrolman has one or two places on his sector or nearby where he is welcome to eat for a reduced price. There are very few men who regularly eat for nothing and probably no one ever pays a full price all the time. The district police are not welcome in all restaurants; those that insist on charging the full price usually do not get their trade. But since the policeman spends a great deal of his life at all hours on the streets of places he knows well but where he is not "at home," it is hardly a surprise that he should seek out places where he is welcomed in a friendly manner. He is not supposed to eat in places where beer or liquor are served (and he usually does not), limiting him mainly to diners and luncheonettes, which are small, personal businesses. Some of these places welcome any district policemen because their presence is viewed as a guarantee against trouble and disorder, while others have special arrangements with one or two men which reflect personal associations that extend be-

[7]Recently a high-ranking official of the New York City police department was suspended when it was revealed that he had failed to pay an $83 bill for a dinner he had eaten with three other people. The hotel picked up the bill and placed the tab in its records. *The New York Times* (October 17, 1971). This practice is not peculiarly American. A recent observer of the English police in London comments that "mumping," as they call it, is widely practiced and does not arouse any hostility toward the police or charges of corruption. Laurie, pp. 247–8. The word "mump" means, however, to cheat or to beg.

yond the obvious bond between the policeman and the businessman.

In one district there was a restaurant that gave patrolmen a small break on meals but reserved special consideration for the sector man, who had eaten there regularly for ten years. When he was late for lunch, the owner often called the station to see if he was all right. He never ordered his meals, since the cooks simply prepared whatever was best that day. He paid a flat price weekly. When he entered the restaurant, he gave the appearance of a man about to dine in his own house.

The personal connections that dominate police eating arrangements can lead to some curious accommodations between the district men and their hosts. In one restaurant the owner was known for his dislike of the men, and he insisted that his waitresses, who were known for quite the opposite sentiments, charge them full price. When he was not there, the girls gave them a police price. Some men would check the place out before entering and, if the owner was about, would go down the street to another place, where the food was not as good but the welcome warmer. The veteran men in the squad refused to eat in the better diner because of the owner's attitude, settling for the other place, where they were guaranteed a reduced price. But the younger men, who enjoyed the company of the waitresses along with their meals, were often willing to pay the full price for their pleasure.

In another district there was a sleazy diner that opened at 4 A.M. and was a welcome haven in the dreary hours of last out. The owner, who disliked and feared being alone, welcomed the patrolmen. The restaurant was located in a ghetto, and although the owner was white, his clientele was integrated; both white and black policemen frequented the place. All of the men first-named him, and he gave them free coffee and cheap breakfasts. They provided him with a sense of security and always kept an eye on his place when they drove past. His wife, however, refused to give anyone wholesale prices and whenever she worked the men did not stop by. At one point, she worked regularly during the afternoons and on daywork the men transferred their business to another place, where they also had to pay the full price but where the food was worth the money. However, they returned on last out.

There are restaurants and diners that encourage police patronage in an effort to assure special consideration. In one district a diner had serious problems with a teenage gang that constantly threatened to wreck the place. The owner offered free meals to the sergeant, the sector car, and the wagon only for stopping in. Any patrolman could get free coffee just by appearing. In almost every district there is one place that offers the sector man and the wagon special considerations that are not extended to anyone else. Often a patrolman off his sector will stop in at a place to get a soda and be taken aback when the owner asks him for the money. The policeman does not walk in and just take something, but he asks and allows the owner the opportunity to decline payment. If the person refuses, the patrolman is confronted with the choice of paying or putting back what he has taken. He rarely returns the item, since it is an embarrassment as well as a revelation of wrongful intent. "Shit, I ain't goin' back in that place no more. I had to pay for this soda. I'm stayin' on my sector," the patrolman muttered. The considerations given the sector man over others are well understood by all. One time, during riot duty, a captain stopped a sector car as it was passing and asked the man about places to eat in the district. The options did not sound promising, and he asked the man whether a certain sandwich shop was still operating. When he was told it was, the captain said jokingly, "It's on your sector, huh? Listen, why don't you go down there and tell the guy to give you some sandwiches for you and the other guys working the sector—all four hundred of us."

The patrolman understands that he is given consideration partly because of the security he represents to the small businessmen who run the places he frequents. He is not being paid off to overlook parking violations or given special consideration to protect something in the back room (although a hostile businessman might get a few more parking tickets than a friendly person). He is given a break just for his presence. But these regular associations arouse in the patrolman a preference for one over another and encourage him to do little favors for one person, requiring him to neglect some-one else. At closing time he may park his car while the owner counts his receipts and then accompany him to the bank. This is not an illegal favor, since any businessman in the city may request a money escort, but the department does not encourage the use of a service that it would have to discontinue if it were widely demanded. The sector man informally agrees to give consideration to a friend in exchange for kindnesses shown him throughout the year. He does not feel he is doing anything wrong since nobody can demonstrate to him that there is something else he might be doing that is socially more useful in these moments. If pressed to defend himself, he argues that he is only doing what the department does for big businessmen at a higher level.

There are some arrangements, however, between the police and businessmen that can be described only as organized protection. Whether these reflect departmental policy or secret arrangements within a district or a division is not clear, but since they require an illegal allocation of manpower and the faking of official departmental records, which no patrolman or sergeant can safely engineer alone, they must be conspiracies embracing commanding officers at least to the level of captain. In a number of districts some branches of a restaurant chain have a policeman assigned to sit inside during the four-to-twelve shift. This chain has an established policy of giving free food to patrolmen during certain times of the day and each branch keeps a careful record of what is given away. But the beatman's services are not offered in exchange for these favors; he is rented for a fee. It is against departmental policy to assign men fixed posts in commercial establishments; the men who do this work are officially listed as working on a sector car or a beat. In one district the man who handled the assignment on the four-to-twelve shift said that he was paid $20 a week for acting as a private guard. Since the arrangement required the permission of his sergeant and possibly his captain, it can be assumed that they, too, were being paid. The man had the additional responsibility of bringing extra food back to the station when he was picked up by the sector car at the end of his tour.

A new branch of this chain was opening in another district, and the manager, who was very concerned about the possibilities of being held up, was eager to negotiate an arrangement with the district police. A patrolman stopped by shortly before the place was to open and suggested to the manager that he speak with the sergeant, who could drop by if the man would call the district. Negotiations proceeded quickly and a bargain was struck. On the four-to-twelve shift a man would be stationed inside the restaurant, and every Saturday night the sergeant or his bagman would collect $100. The money was distributed among all the men who contributed to maintaining the arrangement. The beatman got $25, and lesser amounts were paid to the sector car, which was operated by the man's partner, and to the wagon crew that serviced the area. In addition, the sergeant, lieutenant, and captain were also given a cut. After about a month, the deal was suddenly canceled. Another restaurateur had complained about the special consideration being given to his competitor, and a phone call from downtown to the captain immediately terminated the agreement. The patrolman who initiated the negotiations regretted the passing of "a good, clean note with nothing on paper," but the police and the manager were able to salvage something. The manager continued to give out free food to patrolmen and supervisors whenever they stopped by to look the place over. This assured the restaurant of some additional protection and aided the manager's sense of security.

Although any arrangement that places a policeman in the role of a paid watchman is illegal and the payment of money for the granting of favors cannot be described as anything but bribery and graft, these transactions do not differ in character from others that are constantly forced on the police by direct political pressure. This goes on constantly in little ways —by assigning a patrolman to watch someone's house during a party, or giving a judge and his family special consideration in parking their family car—and also in more important matters. A large bakery in one district was having serious problems with gangs of teenagers, who were vandalizing trucks and terrorizing workers around the plant. The company was paying protection money to several gangs to police the area for them, but the disorders continued and culminated in the stabbing of one worker on the loading platform. The next day the district captain was ordered to assign a beatman to the plant on all tours; the sergeants were to instruct the sector cars and wagons to patrol the area intensively. The

BETWEEN LAW AND ORDER 411

captain claimed that the order from the commissioner's office had been initiated in the office of the governor. The owner of the bakery was known to be an important contributor to the governor's party. There was no special deal made that benefited the policemen performing the service, although after a few weeks on the job, they had made informal arrangements with workers to get free bread and they were also allowed to buy quantities at wholesale prices for squad parties and picnics. In many parts of the city major business streets have beatmen who act as informal watchmen for the important merchants of their areas. Most of these beats are established at the department level and are the consequence of political pressure of one kind or another being applied directly to the department through the mayor's office or the city council.

The police are also obliged to use their authority over street traffic to favor politically influential people and to punish those who are out of favor. "When I came to this district, I was really gonna do a job, you know," a captain said. "No favors and no deals. Well, I found out. You know that place over on Elm Street? All the trucks parked everywhere during the day. It's really dangerous during rush hour. Well, I told my supervisors that I wanted it cleaned up, to ticket all the trucks and force them off the street. Lieutenant Johnson just laughed at me; he said I was kidding. I told him I wasn't, and they started putting on the tickets. Well, it went on for a few days, and then I got a call from downtown, you know, and I was told to lay off. There's plenty of people who think I'm gettin' a note out of it, maybe you do, but it just ain't true. And those trucks are gonna be parked there until someone burns down the terminal."

"Goddamn it, the captain calls me at home last night and tells me that the heat is on Jason, you know, the beer distributor. He tells me to be sure to be here early in the morning and to go directly there and make sure everything is tagged." The place in question was that of a major beer distributor in the city whose facilities were centralized at one location. In addition to maintaining its own parking lots, the company routinely left its trucks on the streets while they were being loaded. This violation of city ordinance and state law was regularly ignored until the captain was called by his inspector and told the company had become involved in a political dispute with the mayor and the order was out to enforce every regulation to the letter.

"Shit, I know my men don't have anything to do with that guy. Sure a cop goes in now and again and gets a case of beer wholesale, but nobody is taking a note out of the place. Now they're asking me if I have anything to do with the guy. Sure, I know him; sure, I know he fronts for some racket guys, but I didn't give him a distributor's license. I met him at a couple of charity functions; he gives money to aid the kids in the district and stuff like that. I could get my ass kicked over this and I don't even know what the fuck it's about," a very nervous captain said.

The sergeant personally supervised the area, while his own men and a traffic officer put tickets on all trucks and private cars in the area. The company owner's private car was ticketed three times for different violations, while he stood silently on the pavement. By 9:30 A.M. every truck was off the street. The sergeant parked his car and looked at the empty street. A young woman approached the car and said, "Excuse me, Sergeant, I've been looking for a policeman all week to complain about the trucks that always park here and now I've found a policeman, but there are no more trucks." The sergeant smiled and told her that there would be no more illegal parking allowed and he was personally supervising the effort to clean up the streets. She thanked him and left. "Sure, lady. How long do you think it'll be before they get the trucks back on the street? We write maybe fifty or sixty tickets today and keep 'em off the street a week; you wanna bet they make up with the mayor?"

The influence of powerful business interests and merchants' associations on official police policy is mirrored at all levels in the department by semiformal and informal arrangements made by captains, street supervisors, and patrolmen. Many of these are illegal in a formal sense, but often they are no more than accommodations that would be imposed from above if they were not made by the district. They are essentially exchanges of services for favors, which are negotiated in a spirit of mutual advantage. Sometimes they are initiated by the police but more frequently by business people anxious to gain special favor. There is no evidence that the district police seek to compel favors by harassment or the withdrawal of services, although a decision to enforce parking regulations, for example, in an area where they had previously been neglected, might be viewed by some as an effort to extract a consideration. Many business men have no special contacts with the police, do not give them anything, do not offer them wholesale prices, and get the same level of service anyone else receives when he makes a request for a policeman or directs an inquiry to the district captain.

The granting of special considerations to influential business people at the departmental level and the slightly less formal adjustments made at the divisional and district level to fulfill the desires of powerful commanders make it very difficult for the department to control the initiatives of patrolmen in their sectors. If a captain and a sergeant receive some kind of consideration for extending a commercial beat or allowing people on some blocks to park illegally, how can they discourage their own men from exploiting a few opportunities? Even if the captain is unwilling to take a payoff, if he has the reputation among his men of being "clean," he will not decline little favors and Christmas gifts. One captain recalled, "Christmas time is when a lot of money comes to the police. Last Christmas I received $50 from a bank. I wish they had never sent it, but I didn't return it."

Christmas money is an almost universal practice in American cities. The police themselves honor the tradition. Patrolmen give gifts to their operations crews; squads that hold their supervisors in esteem frequently honor them with a present or with cash; and the radio crew is also given money. In their turn, the patrolmen make the rounds of the merchants and small businessmen who appreciate their efforts.

Nobody wants to be away from his district at Christmas, when "jingle bells" are in the air. Even if a man does not take money, there are bottles of whiskey and free food to be had. Some commanders warn their men that anyone who solicits gifts will be punished, but nobody is told that he cannot accept a consideration if it is freely offered. However, the line between the two is very thin and most policemen exploit the possibilities available to them. Each patrolman is responsible for his own sector, concentrating on the small stores and shops that he services regularly. Nobody gives him a lot, a "nickel" or a "dime" ($5 or $10) is considered a quite decent tip. Anything less than $5 is considered an insult. (The abolition of the $2 bill has probably benefited those policemen who seek money from motorists and tips from business people.) But there are many stores the patrolman does not go to, places where he knows that he is not welcome, places he does not frequent during the year. He is being paid for a service, just like the mailman and the newsboy. The most generous rewards come from the liquor stores, bars, and clubs that frequently require the services of the police. Usually the supervisors concentrate on these places, although some businesses do not wait for a policeman to come around but send money and bottles directly to the station.

In some places the patrolman does his own collecting, while in other squads the supervisors make the collections and split the money among their men. However, there is always some individual initiative being pursued, regardless of what kind of control the supervisors exert. Even if there were a ban on any kind of solicitation, it would not be possible to stop the men from getting something. They might take home less than they do now, but business people would stop them in the streets and give them packages of food and liquor, offers of wholesale prices on goods, and invitations to drop by, "to stop back," another time. These petty rewards—they rarely amount to $100, although a corrupted policeman who is on the take will make considerably more—are part of city life; to eliminate them would require a transformation of social relationships among city people. They are expressions of thanks for services rendered and claims on continuing service —some are extortions—made to men who are seen as useful servants, although the police do not like to think of themselves in this fashion. But how else can the gift of a few dollars to a man be described?

A problem with all of these arrangements, of course, is that they are illegitimate. If a sergeant chooses to make an arrangement with a garage owner or a shopkeeper allowing him to park cars without worrying about tickets, he is only doing what the department orders him to do on occasion for others. If he accepts money for doing this, he is committing a crime, but if he accepts a consideration only at Christmas or some special service—like free maintenance on his car—he is operating within the bounds of decorum. Nobody in the department can point a finger at him and say he is doing something wrong, although, of course, he is.

These arrangements exist in every district. Often they involve only a sergeant and the sector car, sometimes they extend to all squads; but they are informal arrangements that reflect the kinds of services policemen are constantly being urged to perform whether they receive a consideration or not. In one district, there was an auto-parts supply store that was losing money to vandals and shoplifters. The manager became friendly with a sergeant, who offered to drive him to the bank. The officer also encouraged his men to keep an eye on the place. The other squads did not share the sergeant's concern or his personal connection, but after months of urging, the other supervisors were convinced that it was desirable to give the store "some consideration." In return for this, the manager willingly sold the men goods at reduced prices and made even more favorable arrangements with the sergeants and the lieutenants.

Favors that require systematic attention or prompt responses can be guaranteed only by a sergeant or a lieutenant. A policeman can collect a few dollars from a construction site to keep an eye on the equipment, but if the builders want to work on Sunday, which is forbidden by law, they must see the sergeant. The extent to which a supervisor exploits his opportunities to make special arrangements depends on his personal style and the attitude of the captain toward him. There are some men who will not take anything for free, although they gladly accept wholesale prices. Some men have reputations in the department for being "good shoppers," and occasionally middle-ranking commanders show up in a district to ask a sergeant or lieutenant to have their cars repaired or their children outfitted for school. Many offers of favors and bargains come to a sergeant or a lieutenant without his asking, but there are men who do not leave to chance any opportunity to turn a dollar.

A lieutenant noticed that the front door of a closed supermarket was open and stopped his car to investigate. Inside he found the building filled with cartons and used restaurant equipment. A man was holding a clipboard and checking the numbers on a sheet of paper. He had a pistol stuck in his belt. The lieutenant said hello and commented that he had noticed the open door as he drove past and had stopped to investigate. The man nodded and told him that he had taken over the building to store his merchandise. The lieutenant asked him if there was anything he could do for him. "I don't think so." The officer stressed how dangerous the neighborhood was, and the man patted his gun and said he had just chased a bunch of kids away. "I guess you got it under control, then," the lieutenant replied, "but if you need anything, don't hesitate to call the district and ask for me." Before he left, the lieutenant had carefully examined every corner of the hall. The businessman smiled, invited the lieutenant to stop back and chat, and returned to his work. A few days later, driving past the building, the lieutenant said, "A real nice guy, that Jew; but he won't go for nothing—yet."

In departments where the police are openly involved in protecting illegal operations it is impossible to prevent the patrolmen from exploiting the opportunities available to them. But where payoffs are restricted and the department is known for vigorously investigating complaints, it is possible for the supervisors (if they are not on the take) to limit the patrolmen's activities to what are generally considered legitimate initiatives. A supervisor may get his groceries wholesale, but he does not have to let his men make the rounds, and if he is in control of them, he will limit their acquisitiveness to keep public attention away from their operations. But if a store owner expresses a willingness to sell at police prices to the men, he will not be discouraged, nor will an effort be made to disguise that it is happening, since it is a voluntary arrangement that does not involve any special considerations. In one district, for example, there was an egg wholesaler who was happy to sell at reduced prices to all policemen. On daywork, usually on Friday, one man would take all the orders and pick up several crates of eggs for distribution in the station house. Eggs were bought for the captain as well as the detectives, and each man came by and picked up his order.

Even if supervisors prevent their men from seeking considerations and favors, they cannot prevent businessmen from making offers of gifts to encourage good service. Most often a policeman does not have to ask for anything, all he has to do is wait to be offered. A patrolman who answers a call of vandalism at a factory is met by the foreman, who seeks advice on how to protect his windows. They have a brief and friendly conversation. After a few moments there is nothing more to talk about, but the patrolman does not leave. The foreman asks him if he is the regular sector man, and when he replies affirmatively, the officer is invited to stop back later and pick up a bottle. More often than not the patrolman is not offered anything, and if he suggests something be offered him, he risks a complaint and a reprimand. But if a patrolman does a favor for a garage owner, suggesting to a stranded motorist that he call one place rather than another, who is going to complain if the man returns the favor? Maybe he keeps a can of paint around, and if the officer has a minor accident with his patrol car, the damage can be quickly remedied without a lot of paper work having to be filed.

Many of these connections between policemen and business people are highly personal. Because a man is willing to do a favor for one person it does not follow that he is available to others for the same consideration. "You want to take a ride? I gotta go over and pick up some money from a florist," the sergeant said. "Hey, Sarge, not so loud, please," the corporal retorted. "No, it ain't like that." On the way over, the sergeant said he had asked his wagon crew to pick up some flowers for him and they had overpaid. In fact, as the sergeant discovered, they had not overpaid but had been obliged to pay the regular retail price. The florist, an ex-policeman, was no fool, and he was not taking any chances. "I'm sorry, Fred, but I wasn't sure they were really for you. I don't know them guys and I figured maybe it was just a private thing and I'm not gonna give 'em all a break. You know, if I start that, those guys'll put me right out of business." The sergeant nodded sympathetically, pocketing the five dollars. "I guess he should know. He was a big fuckin' crook when he was in the business," the sergeant said, as they drove away.

Many people are angered by the police exploiting their position to gain favors and special prices that are denied to others. There are police supervisors who personally refuse to indulge in these favors but allow their men to do it because they feel it prevents them from committing more serious violations. "Look, I'd rather they go in there and get the stuff wholesale from Thomas instead of him getting up a couple of bucks every week for their helping him out. They're still paying for what they get, and they ain't taking it out of his flesh," one sergeant said. Some businessmen have a real interest in encouraging the favor of the police and they will continue to exploit whatever opportunities are available to them. The police administrators cannot discourage the men, since few see anything wrong with accepting appreciations, and more importantly, they expect the men to provide informal services on occasion to members of the business community.

Objection to the police receiving special considerations should not rest on the argument that it makes them corrupt —which it does not—but rather on the effect these arrangements have on the manner in which police services are distributed in the community. The police, like every agency, have limited resources that must be deployed in response to the pressures and demands made upon them. They are under public pressures from the newspapers, city council, business and community organizations; they respond to internal pressures created by commanders who are interested in pursuing their own ideas about how the department should function, and pressures from special interests represented by city government, commercial and social organizations delivered privately and informally. Many of the things the police do for the city government are masked from public attention because they are either illegal or highly controversial.

The questionable character of many enforcement policies —gambling, liquor, traffic—requires that the elected politicians allow only the most loyal and tested men to rise to the top. They may be absolutely honest men, but they must be able to keep their mouths closed. Frequently they are given wide latitude in operating the department because many politicians do not want to know the details of some of the things they ask the police to do. The autonomy required to run the department is enlarged at the top by this discreet distancing; it also runs right down to the bottom. The collusive nature of so many administrative arrangements discourages constant and careful scrutiny of all decisions and actions in the district. Even the most ruthless administrator cannot control his commanders entirely. If he is ordering them to move against someone or to do a favor for another, he cannot expect them to ignore similar requests made directly to their offices. "I could make between $10,000 and $15,000 per year in addition to my salary and never leave my desk. Offers come in all the time in roundabout ways," one captain said. Each of these offers is a request for a favor, an appeal to prevent a policeman from doing something, or a bid for services that will deprive others in the district of a policeman's time and attention. All the captain's superiors can do is limit his inclinations to exploit opportunities by punishing those who are caught when they exceed the bounds of what is considered legitimate. It is the same attitude a patrolman expresses when he makes the distinction between good and bad notes.[8]

The exchange of favors for services is only one aspect of the private bargaining for police attention that goes on incessantly in every city. The local businessman who offers favors in exchange for some service he feels is necessary or desirable for the success of his enterprise is doing the same thing that the chamber of commerce does when it pressures the police, through the mayor's office, to stop them from ticketing cars in certain business areas. The objection to all these efforts, at whatever level they are conducted, is that they occur outside the formal political process. Frequently decisions are made for reasons that are more private than public, but this does not mean they were made for personal reasons. When a police official accedes to the requests of a large company, he is making a decision that is ratified within the complex political system that dominates city life, but it is not a decision reached by weighing the general interests of the people who finance the city. Even if the policeman "gets something" for his trouble, often enough whatever he gets is not the cause for his decision.

The petty rewards available to policemen probably add very little to the aggregate cost of operating the city. They do not affect the fundamental character of business or commerce in the city or the direction of their development. Their rewards are the *quid pro quo* allowed policemen and their supervisors for handling the dirty work of the social system. Policemen in some cities and a few policemen strategically located in almost every department have a chance to make considerably more money than the average patrolman is ever likely to see, even if he avidly exploited every opportunity available to him. But even the disclosure of payoffs to some New York City plainclothesmen of as much as $1,500 monthly cannot disguise the fact that in economic terms the total impact of police graft is insignificant. The real cost is the

---

[8]On political control of the city police, see Wilson, Chap. VIII, esp. pp. 233–4.

degradation of the job, the destruction of morale, the erosion of discipline and supervision, and the breakdown of clear standards of what constitutes "good work" which allows some policemen to become criminals in every sense of the word.

The dilemmas every city policeman faces are well understood by all of them, but they are in no position to explain them. How can a man explain to people that his is a job that obliges some men to break the law regularly, thereby allowing others to do so if they wish to take the risks? Much of what people call corruption among the police is supported actively by large sections of the population, while the things that are despised are most frequently directed against the part of the city population that is too weak to protest effectively (and when they protest are not believed or supported). This distinction was succinctly made by a former New York police commissioner in an interview he gave shortly before his resignation under fire. He commented:

> In the ghetto, the one who is hurt the most by police corruption is the ghetto resident; for the most part he is getting little or nothing. In fact, he's being hurt tremendously because of the corruption. The consideration, even the courtesy extended him is less. Now, when you move from the ghetto and you consider corruption in the middle class and the business community, they are only paying for some service or product and they're getting some worth, so it's really with the poor that corruption makes the greatest impact and hurts the most.[9]

3 · Regulation, Graft, and Crime

A policeman does not think of himself as an oppressor of the poor or as a guardian of the "haves" against the "have-nots," but by the time he has established himself in a district, he knows enough to realize that somehow he is involved in regulating important businesses among the poor and the working classes (liquor and gambling) for the profit of people he does not know personally and who frequently are unknown publicly. Even if he does not accept payoffs and refuses to degrade himself and others for information, he understands that the department is not enforcing the gambling

[9]*The New York Times* (June 8, 1970).

laws or the liquor laws. He may think that enforcement of these laws is not really possible or even desirable, since he knows how difficult it is to get good information legally, but he also realizes that non-enforcement is producing paydays and payoffs.

The state monopoly over liquor licensing has converted the right to drink into a source of political capital—cash and favors—which is exploited by state and city governments and their agents, the police, to assure compliance with their interests. Politicians extract enormous fees for selling and transferring lucrative licenses, and the police are obliged to maintain the efficacy of the system by harassing those who do not adhere and protecting those in favor. Not only are people denied the right to regulate their own drinking habits but they are frequently denied any control over who owns the bars and clubs they must drink in. Many licenses are held by dummy companies, whose owners are discreetly concealed. These licenses are moved around the city to exploit the most favorable locations, and politically weak neighborhoods are flooded in flagrant violation of the regulations that limit the number of bars allowed in any area. Local people have no say in the location of these places, nor do they benefit in any way from the other business that concentrations of drinking places encourage. In Philadelphia, for example, a city that, by state law, is supposed to have only 1,285 bars, there were 2,961 licensed barrooms in 1971. One section of the city, populated mainly by poor blacks, had more than 900 places operating, although there should not have been any more than 230, according to the law.[1]

The political character of the regulation of drinking has assured the indifference of the police to the letter of a law that, in any case, does not reflect the customs and attitudes of the people it most directly affects—those who go out to do their drinking. But a bar owner, unlike other businessmen, not

---

[1] The liquor business in America has not been studied nor has much attention been given to the licensing system, but an introduction to the legal history of the licensing system is provided by Frederick Johnson and Ruth Kessler, "The Liquor License System: Its Origin and Constitutional Development," *New York University Law Quarterly Review*, Vol. XV (1937/38), pp. 210–51, 380–424. *Philadelphia Inquirer* (October 12, 1970). On the operation of the licensing system in Detroit, see "Our Liquor Laws and How They Foster Corruption," *Detroit Scope Magazine* (September 7, 1968).

only needs the cooperation of the police to improve the operation of some aspect of his business, he is dependent upon them for his existence. If a license is not protected by someone who is politically influential in the city or the state, its owner must guarantee that the police will not harass him or rigidly enforce the law, which provides the opportunity for literally hundreds of violations. The city does not encourage the department to extort payoffs from taproom owners, nor does the department condone the practice, but it is practically impossible to prevent as long as the police are required to regulate the business.

There is hardly a bar in the city that does not voluntarily pay the police money at Christmas time. Even the neighborhood taprooms, which run a quiet trade and are rarely the scene of disorders, willingly give the district police a Christmas note, just to keep them friendly and responsive. From the bar owner's point of view, the few hundred dollars he invests are worthwhile if they cause the police to overlook a problem that might erupt or encourage them to respond quickly to a call for help. The owner gives a few dollars to the sector car and the wagon, as well as to the sergeant and lieutenant. He is also happy to offer the captain a bottle of whatever he likes. But these are only the respectable edge of what is available to the police from the liquor trade. In every district there are bars that encourage police patronage. No bartender hesitates to offer a policeman a drink every opportunity he has. The man may refuse, but the small credit gained by the offer can be helpful. (This is one reason alcoholism can be a very serious problem among policemen. A man who has a drinking problem has endless opportunities to drink while he is on patrol.) Some bars encourage police patronage, and sell beer and liquor to the men at special prices. Bars that are not protected politically but are the scene of trouble often encourage policemen to act as informal bouncers in exchange for drinks. Off-duty, a policeman does not have to carry his gun, but he may, and if he is in a taproom, sitting at the bar, who can protest if he takes police action when trouble arises? That is his duty. But, in fact, what often appears as innocent happenstance is actually the private work of a policeman using his public license to further his personal interests. Not infrequently, in some districts, a call will come out, "aid the off-duty 369 in a taproom" and working policemen respond, but with a reluctance they do not hesitate to express. In most instances they are going to the aid of someone who is working as an enforcer or bouncer, and they do not like taking risks for these reasons.

The district police must annually inspect each bar and approve the renewal of its license. Although this is the captain's responsibility, he usually assigns a lieutenant or a sergeant to carry out the inspection. This is done on daywork, and before entering the place, the supervisor informs the dispatcher that he is entering the taproom for an investigation. There is then a public record of his actions in case he is entering a place that harbors illicit action and someone complains about his being there. These inspections are usually cursory, since the police know that only refusals ordered or approved at the highest levels of the department will go through and have any chance of withstanding reversal before the state liquor board. If the supervisor is corrupt and the department lax, however, it provides a useful moment to extort a payoff. But even if the department is strict and the police reluctant to demand money, the opportunity to take what may be and frequently is offered is not restricted.

The lieutenant entered the dimly lit bar and stood at the door for a moment, looking at the go-go girl dancing in a cage before the disinterested stare of a few early-afternoon patrons. The owner approached quickly and greeted him in a friendly fashion. The lieutenant said he was there to inspect the place for a license renewal and asked the owner to sit with him for a few moments while he filled out the form. The man answered the perfunctory questions and kept interrupting to ask if the officer wanted anything to drink. Several times he commented on the dancing girls and asked the lieutenant whether he wanted to meet them. When the form had been completed, he asked the lieutenant if there was anything else. When he replied no, the owner asked to speak with him privately. After a few minutes the lieutenant returned with the glum-looking owner and left the bar.

"That dumb fuck. He was on his knees beggin' me to take a note. I don't know what he's got going, but he must want me real bad for some reason. Then he tells me I should drop back later and get it. Remember one thing—don't ever go back for a note. If it's there and you want it, take it, but don't ever go

for no comebacker! That's when they are going to set you up
for something. The guy drops a dime and you walk in and the
ginks have given him marked money and maybe they take
your picture. I told him that the license would be approved
anyway. Even if I turned him down, it would only make a
note for some guy on the state board," the lieutenant commented.[2]

A payoff for approving a license renewal is only a down
payment and not a guarantee of immunity. A bar owner does
not have to pay the police for the renewal, but if he is
operating illegally or has trouble in his place, he wants to pay
them. This payment is a signal to a supervisor to arrange a
steady note in return for continuous service and consideration. For the payment of $20 or $30 a week, the owner is
guaranteed that he will not be closed down or harassed by the
district police. He can call the station when he has a problem
with the assurance that he will get quick and decisive service.
On weekends a sector car is ordered to watch the place carefully and to respond quickly to any radio calls. When there is
a steady note from a bar or a club, it is usually collected on
the four-to-twelve shift on Friday or Saturday by the sector
man or the wagon. The money is divided among the men who
are directly involved. The car and wagon get a share, and the
sergeant and lieutenant, too. In addition, of course, the supervisors may arrange to collect additional notes from the
bars as premiums for continuing the service.

Although the existence of these arrangements is well known

[2] 'Never go back. Never, never! If he makes the offer straighten it out
then and there. Or lock him up. But never go back,' a policeman advised
a rookie." Radano, p. 132. The following account illustrates the practical wisdom of the advice: "A police sergeant with twenty years on the
force was accused of bribery yesterday after he allegedly tried to
shake down the operator of a social club. . . . He told the owner——
that he was the new sergeant and 'wanted to get things going' . . . and
told Mr. H. that he wanted $20 a week to insure that summonses
would not be issued against the club. Mr. H. notified the District Attorney's office and arrangements were made for a payoff. . . . Office
investigators . . . allegedly watched the sergeant accept three marked
$5 bills from Mr. H. [The District Attorney] said an electronic de-
vice worn by the operator recorded a statement from the sergeant:
'This is not the price we agreed upon,' he said, adding that he would
return next week for $20 plus the $5 balance. At this point, the
observer arrested the sergeant. . . . If convicted, he faces up to 7
years in prison." *The New York Times* (August 3, 1971).

to everyone involved in the trade, their initiation is approached with a certain diffidence in recognition of their illegality and the possibility that a rebuff could be followed by a complaint. A new owner had recently taken over a bar from a man who had been put out of business by continual fighting, which drove away many patrons and reduced a once prosperous business to a shambles. The lieutenant stopped in to see the owner, whom he had known years before in another part of town. Their greeting was cordial and cautious. The lieutenant wished him luck and mentioned that the previous owner had had many problems. The man acknowledged that this was the case but demurred at the lieutenant's opening offer. "You know, this ain't like the place you had in Center City," the lieutenant said. "The people up here are tough and they will really fuck you up if you don't keep 'em under control. So, if there's anything we can do for you, help out in any way, let us know." The owner thanked him carefully and said he could keep the place orderly. Several weeks later a brawl in the bar resulted in all the windows being broken, a good deal of the furniture smashed, and a few people ending up in the hospital. There was some speculation about the commitment of the police in hastening to the scene, and the lieutenant did not conceal his pleasure at the sight that greeted him. He took the owner into a corner and made an arrangement with him. "Remember, this ain't for nothing that happens in the future—this is only for the past."

Every time there is a brawl in a taproom, a policeman gets something. A patrolman who does not take money from motorists is often willing to accept $5 from a bartender for throwing someone out. The reticent and the innocent do not ask, but the experienced do not hesitate. Any sign of disorder suggests the concrete possibility of a "short note," $5 or $10.

A patrolman and a sergeant were driving past a taproom when they noticed several men on the sidewalk begin to shove each other. They parked and got out of the car, sticks in hand, and approached the group, which had crossed the street. Several more people had joined the group, including the bar owner, who was trying to settle the dispute. The policemen did not intervene and allowed the arguing to continue for some time. Since there was no actual fight, they had no reason to do anything. Anyway, they had not stopped to break up a fight. After a few minutes the argument withered, and the sergeant turned to the owner and said, "Another fight in your place." The owner, who had rushed out partly to prevent what was now happening to him, defended himself with a lack of will born of a detailed knowledge of the inevitable course of events. "Sarge, it started out here. It didn't have nothin' to do with my place." "They were drinking in your place, it's your fight. Get it up, now." The words were spoken entirely without heat, in a tone that suggested a player reminding a colleague of the rules they had mutually agreed upon when they commenced playing. "I don't have anything on me, could you . . ." "No, I can wait, go across the street and get it. I'll wait right here."

The owner returned to find the dispute, which was costing him $10, renewing itself. He was now in a hurry to pay the fee before the rate increased. Standing at the back of the small group of people, in the shadows provided by several illegally parked cars, he discreetly displayed his personal commitment to the maintenance of the relationships which bind the police and bartenders together by slipping the sergeant a bill neatly folded into a small square.

Many of these bar notes are not automatic and hinge on the initiative of the supervisor. A policeman cannot stop in and make a collection, although he may expect a few dollars if he is called. But a sharp supervisor does not have to have a reason. He may ride by a bar on four-to-twelve and just stop in. Driving past a bar on Saturday night, a lieutenant speculated on the whereabouts of a bar owner he had not seen for some time. "I don't see his car. He's always good for a note, too. I'll have to check on him." A short time later there was a call, man with a gun, at another bar in the same neighborhood. The lieutenant headed right over and was pleased to see several of his men already checking out the job. It was unfounded, although the patrons said a man had pulled a gun and left. The lieutenant took one man and went back into the bar. Everything was in order; then he turned his attention to the new owner, whom he had not met.

They withdrew to a corner and had a brief conversation, which concluded with the owner reaching for his wallet and the lieutenant gesturing to him to keep it and walk out onto the pavement with him. When they were outside, the man handed him a dime. The main reason the lieutenant wanted the man to go outside was not to disguise the payoff he was about to receive but to have the bar owner identify his car. "I'll keep an eye on it when I drive by," he said in a friendly manner. The owner pointed out his car, and then they shook hands. "Well, he's O.K.," the lieutenant said. "Now I know his car and don't have to go in the place when he ain't around. He told me that the other guy I was talkin' about is sick. That's why he ain't been around. I hope he recovers quick."

There are many opportunities for men with rank to make money that they do not have to split with their subordinates. "You know why that dumb-fuck sergeant has Smith drive him? Because he won't touch a note. That's right. I ain't kidding. He'll collect it for him but he won't take any. So if something comes along, he don't have to share it." Supervisors who willingly share with their men are appreciated, even if the patrolmen disdain the personal qualities needed to create the possibilities. "It's one thing if you're doing something for it, then it's only fair that you get a piece of it, but take Weber, he's an ace. Corrupt, but an ace. The other night, right, I see these guys puttin' up election posters and they shorted out the street lights by putting a nail through a cable. I called the lieutenant and he comes right over. He's talkin' to them, you know, and he tells them that they better make it because they could take a pinch for it. He tells 'em an inspector is coming and also someone from the electric company. So they ask if they can get going, and he just smiles. They got some paper all right and they came up with it, no squawks. He named a price and the one guy paid. He kept ten for himself and gave us seven-fifty apiece. That's damned good of him. He didn't have to do it because we couldn't'ta gotten it out of 'em," a patrolman said.

It is understood that any assignment that produces a note will be shared between the men who do the job. While these notes are not consistently available, they are prized because there is little likelihood of their causing any unpleasant reaction; they are cooperative, not coercive arrangements. A bar owner who is having a party, or a dance-hall operator who is expecting a large crowd, will ask the sergeant or lieutenant for a man to watch the cars parked out front or to keep an eye on the people. This produces a quick ten for the supervisor and a nickel for the sector car.

Experienced people are careful of the manner in which they make these payments because they know the police are perfectly willing to swindle them out of money if they see an opportunity. "That guy in the carnival is a shrewd bastard," the sergeant said. "He told me he ain't payin' for no invisible soldiers. Each guy gets it every night. I don't know what the captain and the inspector get, but they must be pullin' a note for approving this swindle." The carnival was ostensibly organized for some charitable purpose but was in reality a simple entertainment with a number of marginally legal games of chance, which had been rigged to protect the operators. The lieutenant was paid $20 a night, the sergeant $15, each of the four beatmen who actually policed the ground received $10 apiece, and the wagon crew and the sector car $5 each. A nice, tidy sum for six days and a cheap rental fee for the operators.

A patrolman cannot arrange a steady note without the approval and support of his sergeant. If he disapproves, it cannot exist, although the patrolman may take his chances to try for whatever comes his way. What he does depends a good deal on the inclinations and attitudes of his street supervisors. If a lieutenant or sergeant makes a practice of stopping off at bars, movie houses, and dance halls to "shake a note" from the manager, he is not likely to discourage his men from doing the same. These are payoffs that the supervisor does not share with anyone. They are tokens of his position, ratifications of claims to consideration in moments of need. When he walks into a theater lobby and after a brief, friendly conversation the manager hands him a copy of the program with a $10 bill folded into the crease, it is his. But his men know that he is doing it, and those who emulate him will try to do it wherever they can. There are some supervisors who refuse to share anything with their men, although they collect from people that the men arrest or threaten to arrest. This arouses great resentment, but the supervisors who do it often are trying to get their men to stop making vice pinches without authorization rather than cheating them out of money.

"When I first come to this district, I took a couple of bars. They were legitimate, not note pinches, but no more. The sergeant blew 'em out and that's all there was. I ain't workin' to make him rich. What's on the wall was true then and it's true now. Wiping it off don't make no difference," a patrolman said. He was referring to a scrawl on the locker-room wall that said, "Sergeant Norman still in the lead. The biggest crook in the 55th District." A sergeant who takes notes also seeks to regulate what the men do by offering certain things and making clear what can and cannot be done. When a man is given a sector, an "honest" sergeant tells him exactly what there is to be had, how much money from bars and stores. In exchange for this accounting, the supervisor expects the man to respect any rules he has regarding extortion of money from motorists, burglary, and theft. Some men take sectors with steady notes and decline the money. If the sergeant trusts the man's loyalty, he allows him to work, and the money is divided with the wagon or the notes die. But if a corrupt supervisor refuses to share with his men, he has little ability to control what some of them might do.

There are some policemen who become thoroughly corrupted by their experience. Everything they do, which is woefully little, is dictated by the possibility of private gain. They are constantly on the lookout for a way to shake someone; every infraction of the law they witness rings dollar signs, and they try for anything they think they can get away with. "Listen, kid, when I come on the department, I worked with an old nigger who gave me a good piece of advice, and I'm gonna give it to you. He used to say, 'Don't ever go home with nothing. Going home with nothing is wasting a day. Even if you don't need it, take it. Then when you retire, you gonna have a whole warehouse full of shit.' Good advice."

"I wanna talk to him," the patrolman said, as he spotted a man coming out of a store. "He's a beer distributor and I saw him selling it last night after nine o'clock. He could lose his license for that. What kinda beer you like?" he asked his partner, as he parked the car. "Hey, José, how you doing?"

"I'm O.K. Listen, I seen you last night watchin' me. I know I put some beer out after nine o'clock, but it was paid for before and they were just pickin' it up."

"Well, you know the law, you're supposed to be closed at nine. Right?" "Yeah, but, you know how it is here, some of these people they come to see me with no money, but they want some beer so I give it to them. They gonna get paid on

Friday and then they pay me. So who gets hurt?" the man replied, committing an indiscretion that was going to cost him more than a case of beer.

"José, you dumb fuck, selling beer on credit, too. That's a violation of your license. I want to talk to you about this inside." A few minutes later the patrolman returned. "We'll come back later and pick up some beer. That dumb fuck, he didn't think I knew he was sellin' beer to a speak. Well, he knows now."

Two patrolmen were driving down a quiet street and noticed several cars parked on a lot with a FOR SALE sign on their windshields. The driver smiled and stopped the car. He asked a man sitting on the steps of a house whether he knew who owned the cars. "I do," he replied. "Well, hello; I'm the tax collector," the officer said cheerily. It is against the law to sell cars in public without a license.

At one time, it was common practice in many departments for some policemen to extort money from motorists. Policemen even referred to places as "their corner," as if an intersection were a piece of private real estate. Often there was a certain justification in this attitude. Many sergeants treated sectors as franchises rented to patrolmen who had to produce a weekly commission for this boss. Although this practice has been eliminated in most cities, many policemen are willing to accept money from motorists and some are even willing to run the risks of extorting it. There are policemen who consider the offer of a gratuity or a payoff a personal insult; people have been beaten up by policemen angered at the affront implied by a bribe offer. But some men are willing to allow a driver the opportunity to propose a compromise. A few exploit their chances to extort bribes from people whose livelihoods are threatened by a ticket.

Poor people often do not register their cars properly or fail to obtain a license. When a license is revoked, they frequently accept the risks of driving without one because they need a car to go to work. A person stopped for being drunk also runs the risk of a serious fine or even a jail sentence. Any one of these offenses bears a money fine that is substantially in excess of a consideration a crooked cop is willing to accept. While it is illegal and wrong for the policeman to take his money, the offender is usually pleading with him to do so, sparing him the greater expense of a day in court and a fine. If his license is revoked or the revocation is made permanent by the additional violation, the person in all likelihood will continue to drive because economic necessity requires him to have a car.

Some patrolmen become specialists in enforcing the regulations controlling commercial trucks. An experienced man can look at a large trailer and estimate by the way it sits how much weight it is hauling. Many truckers ignore weight restrictions in an effort to make their runs more profitable, and they are quite willing to pay the police a consideration rather than take a ticket and have their trucks tied up. Some companies, which send heavy trucks, wide loads, or special equipment through the city, provide the drivers with money to pay off the police. The driver is given a specific route and he has money for each district through which he travels. If the driver can make it without being picked up by a patrol car, he can "go under" with the money. Policemen know the money is there and they keep an eye open for these trucks. But the few dollars a patrolman makes providing escort service is nothing compared to the money a man working an active truck sector can make if he wants to do it. "That bastard, when he gets twenty years in, he's gonna sell his sector," a patrolman said admiringly of a colleague who was a noted truck specialist.

Policemen who extort money from motorists or roll drunks for whatever they can find are far fewer than they once were, and they generally work alone. Most men in a squad know which of their colleagues are inclined to' commit crimes and they try to avoid working with them. But since everyone in the district is obliged to commit some kind of criminal act in order to do his job, men are not inclined to make any move against colleagues who can get them indicted. A man may "know" that a colleague is a thief and a disgrace, but if an alleged thief can reveal that his accuser has in turn committed some offense, then even the most indignant officer is likely to bite the bullet and continue working with the man, while trying to remain as far away from him as possible.

Every patrolman has opportunities to steal. Each time he answers a burglary call or discovers an open property, there is nothing to prevent him from helping himself if his supervisors do not care or are not present. If he is inclined to be a thief, he will be one. There are men who insist on calling their sergeant before entering a private house or require the owner to accompany them if they are present. Many patrolmen do not go in on jobs with some colleagues because they expect to find looting going on; they just drive right past. Some men even risk the ire of colleagues by refusing to handle the paper work for assignments which are theirs if they are not first on the scene. "I know it's my job, but you were the first car in and it's yours," a patrolman said to a colleague, who glared at him. "I been fucked before and once is enough. Take some advice. If you aren't there, don't make the paper. You don't know what happened before you got there, and if you make the 48, you're gonna get hung."

The continual involvement of the police in violations of the law and infractions of department regulations keeps open the possibility of an entire squad going sour. Individual theft and extortion can easily become conspiracy and organized crime. There have been occasions in many cities when people wisely refused to inform the police that they were leaving town because there was a good chance that policemen would rob them. These excesses have been eliminated from most big-city departments, but their reappearance is always possible in any police department where men are obliged to do work that makes them violate the law and conceal their work from public view.[8]

A district policeman who considers himself to be an honest cop knows that he cannot entirely escape involvement in illicit activity. He understands that he cannot explain to people who have never been on the street the difference between a good and a bad note, but having seen the opportunities available, he "knows" that there is nothing wrong with accepting a few dollars from someone who wishes to express gratitude to

---

[8]Several incidents of organized thievery are recounted in Ralph Smith, *The Tarnished Badge* (New York, Crowell, 1965). In New York City recently, eight policemen and six sergeants and lieutenants were suspended and arrested for burglarizing a meat-packing house. According to the newspaper account, the policemen and their supervisors were working together, loading meat into patrol cars and private automobiles. Other groups of policemen in New York City have been arrested recently for participation in stolen-car rings. *The New York Times* (January 24, April 13, 1971). A recent account of police burglars is in Gaeton Fonzi and Jim Riggio. "The Cops Who Wouldn't Shoot Straight," *Philadelphia Magazine* (April 1972).

him for getting his wife to the hospital or for finding his stolen car. If there are a few dollars coming for watching a bar or an offer of some consideration for capturing a burglar, no harm is done.

"He was a good fuckin' cop. You know I was the first guy to find him. He was slumped over the wheel with the phone still in his hand," a patrolman said to his friend. "It's a crazy, fuckin' job. He'd see something, you know, something not quite right, he'd look into it. And you know, he wasn't even supposed to be workin' that night. But it was Friday night and he had a note from a bar, you know, so he'd asked the sergeant if he could work because he wanted the few bucks. So he worked. But he was out there and he musta seen something, because nobody usually patrols down that road. But he seen something and he went lookin'. He found it, and now there are six kids with no father."

The policeman cannot escape the contradictions imposed upon him by his obligations. He knows that there are many people in the city who think him just a crook in a uniform. He knows that poor people who see gamblers, pushers, hookers on the streets of their neighborhoods think every cop is on the take. He cannot tell them it is not true. He cannot explain to them that even if every cop were as honest as the day is long, drug addiction would not stop, gambling would persist, and the bars would still operate after hours. He cannot explain to them that if he really were allowed to enforce the law, everyone would be screaming at the cops for invading their privacy and destroying their opportunities to do the things which they want to do and which middle-class people can do freely and openly. Tracks were allowed to operate because horse racing was the sporting pastime of the rich and powerful; today nobody questions the money politicians make by selling franchises to open new tracks to encourage the people to gamble. Private clubs are allowed to operate high-stake card games, while plainclothesmen are out hustling crap games for a few dollars; churches sponsor bingo nights and get the police to watch the front door, even when the game violates state law; and while some policemen are trying to lock up a clean-living number writer who always pays an honest count, the state is telling his clients to put their money into a lottery ticket. The state orders them to do their drinking in bars owned by people they do not know and possibly do not care to patronize, and forbids them to pay for a drink in someone's parlor. How can a policeman explain to the people who look at him a little funny that he isn't on the take when they see the evidence of corruption all about them? How can he explain to them that if he were to enforce the law, he would have to violate their rights and the laws which are supposed to protect them even more than he already does?

CHAPTER TEN

The Policeman's Lot

> *I've guarded a lot of dignitaries in*
> *my time. You give 'em a salute and*
> *you get a smile and a handshake.*
> *I've been called Bill, Jack, Frank,*
> *John, everything except my real name.*
> —A policeman

> *Whenever you need a cop you can't*
> *find one.*
> —A popular saying

The policeman is a solitary worker. The nature of his trade requires that he spend a good part of his work day alone; the nature of his obligation isolates him from most other people. ("Hey, fellas, sit down and have another beer. It's on me. Where are you guys goin' anyway? It's only eleven. Going to work? Who goes to work at eleven except a fireman and a cop?") He has little opportunity to maintain friendships with people who are not policemen. The policemen with whom he is personally friendly are men who work the same schedule he does. Inevitably, his close friends, if he has any, are some of the men from his platoon and squad. His relationships with people who are not policemen are limited by reticence on both sides. Many people feel constrained in the presence of a police officer. There are frequent jokes about the doing of illegal things. If he does become friendly with his neighbors, someone will eventually ask a favor of him which he cannot grant or make a complaint to him about the conduct of some policemen.

He is aware of the ambiguities in his work, but he cannot

435

discuss these openly with people who have not shared his burdens. "Death is a constant thing in the city. As police officers you'll be seeing plenty of it. You'll hear plenty of stories, but don't listen to them. I learned that dead bodies are easier to handle than live ones," the instructor told his recruit class on their first day of training. After a year on the street, none of those who remained on the job would deny the accuracy of the remark. But if a policeman expressed this sentiment to someone he knew casually (or even to his wife), they might think him a ghoul.

Policemen have always been required to, perform duties regarded as onerous and distasteful. That is one of the principal reasons they exist. City watchmen were obliged to serve at night during a time when fear of the dark, which all people share, was explained in religious terms. Watchmen were regarded as persons who enjoyed an unspecified but definitely unusual relationship with the Devil[1]. The fact that nobody who could afford to earn his living in a better way chose to be a watchman was an additional reason for the low opinion most people had of the watch. Today the police are obliged to do numerous things that they cannot publicly defend. They enforce many laws which are not and probably cannot be equitably administered. Everyone who gets a traffic summons for running a light knows there are times when he has not been punished for similar infractions and can easily recall instances when he has seen people escape punishment for violations that he regards as being "really serious." Many policemen do things that are illegal in order to fulfill obligations that are required of them; some men exploit their obligations and authority to steal and to take payoffs. There is a widespread belief that the police are corrupt, and any time an individual (or a group) feels resentment toward them, it can be most effectively expressed by calling into question the commitment of the police to honesty and the rule of law.[2] Every policeman knows there is corruption, but he cannot

[1] Werner Dankert, *Unehrliche Menschen: Die verfehmten Berufe* (Bern, Francke Verlag, 1963).

[2] The belief that the police are corrupt is not confined to the United States. For example, see D. Chappell and P. R. Wilson, *The Police and the Public in Australia and New Zealand* (St. Lucia, University of Queensland Press, 1969), pp. 42–3; and Bayley, pp. 116ff., 288–306.

explain its persistence without revealing the internal workings of his job; this can only get him into trouble. He cannot explain to people that he often lies in court, commits perjury, because the people he arrests, their lawyers, and the prosecutors also tell lies. He cannot explain to people how it is possible for him to work with men who steal and cheat without himself becoming tainted. (And after he has been in the "business" for a few years, he is not sure whether he has not been changed by what he has seen.) So he is obliged to live with the ambiguities generated by his trade.

The policeman is granted considerable authority, which people want him to exercise. Whether he wishes it or not, he is used as a symbol of authority and discipline. There is hardly a patrolman who has not stood at a school crossing and listened to a mother admonish her child to behave, lest it be turned over to the nice policeman for a trip to jail. Policemen despise this because they believe that if children are raised to fear and hate them, it will only make their work harder when the children become older. But the patrolman cannot express his sentiments to the offending lady without risking a complaint to his captain. Each time a person is victimized, he sees his loss as a product of the policeman's failure to do his duty. The officer cannot explain to people (or to himself) why he has so little success in preventing crime. He may complain about all the different kinds of work he must do, commenting silently to himself about some colleagues who do not carry their share, but he, too, is mystified by the failure of any measures to curb crime in the streets.

His work imposes so many burdens on his family that the policeman cannot seek its unequivocal support. There are many things he sees that he cannot tell his wife; other things he does not wish her to know. Any personal differences between them can be easily exacerbated. He is away from home a good deal of the time, and his wife knows that he has frequent opportunities to meet women. Even if he is happily married, his continuously changing schedule requires constant adjustment. If there are young children in the family, they must be kept quiet when he is working last out, so that he can sleep during the day. There are many family occasions and festive holidays he cannot celebrate with them. ("They seem to think we volunteer to work on Christmas.") Many patrolmen work a second job to supplement their incomes, further reducing the time that the men spend with their families.[3]

The presence of children at home creates an additional problem: where to keep your gun. Many policemen own a short-barreled .38-caliber revolver, which they carry when out of uniform, in addition to their long-barreled service revolver. Since the patrolman is away from home two nights out of three, it is not surprising that he wants his wife to have it if anyone threatens to break in. But if the gun is in an easily accessible place, there is the constant danger that a child might find it. Some policemen try to prevent their children from ever touching guns, not allowing them to have toy guns for fear of confusion with the real article. Others keep their guns in locked metal boxes, on the upper shelves of closets, or separate the bullets from the gun. When he comes home from work each day, the patrolman does not want to unload his gun, lest he forget one day to reload it before going to work. Some men disarm their guns by disengaging the cylinder, which contains the bullets, from the barrel, and locking their handcuffs through the opening, preventing any possibility of its firing.[4]

The only persons who can fully appreciate the policeman's situation are his colleagues. The solidarity policemen feel for each other is said by some observers to be a central feature of their personalities.[5] But the relationships among colleagues in a squad are anything but harmonious and trusting. No squad is a cohesive unit whose members openly discuss their work and experiences. While most men willingly acknowledge and

[3]Many policemen come to their job from another trade and are able to use their old skills doing part-time work. Few departments deny their men the right to work an extra job, requiring only that they do nothing that exploits the use of the uniform and the gun. The state also generates additional income for the men. In Massachusetts, for example, many cities and towns have an ordinance that requires the presence of an off-duty police officer at every construction site and public-works project. The pay rates are established by law, and any officer who wants to do this work need only sign up with his sergeant.

[4]One man purposely left his unloaded revolver on a table in his living room to see whether his three-year-old son would touch it. The boy went to his mother and told her that he had seen a gun in the living room and she should put it away.

[5]William A. Westley, "Secrecy and the Police," Social Forces, Vol. XXXIV (1956), pp. 254–7.

frequently stress their dependence on each other, no patrolman tries to disguise the secretive nature of much that he
knows. A policeman's information is his private stock, which
nobody else may presume to make claims on, unless invited
to share. What each man learns and does is not a subject for
discussion unless he chooses to initiate the talk or is asked by
his superiors. New men are continuously being integrated into
a squad, some permanently, some as temporary replacements
for men on vacation or sick leave. It is imperative that they
know nothing of the unit's work if the men are engaged in
any illegal practices. Even if they are not, it is not desirable to
give away information men have worked to acquire and
which is their proof of title to their territories. The only way
the need for secrecy and privacy can be met without compromising the squad's ability to fulfill its collective responsibilities is by the continuous formation and dissolution of
cliques and coalitions.[6]

The most intimate associations in any squad are those
formed between men who partner. A patrolman often works
with different colleagues, but his partner is the man who is
assigned to work regularly with him on the same car or
wagon. In departments where there is a policy of utilizing
one-man cars wherever possible, there are few partnerships,
except among the men who work the wagons. Partnerships
are founded on equality of responsibility and rewards. The
men share everything and must have confidence in each other.
They take turns driving, and a policeman will not work with
another man if he does not have confidence in his colleague's
driving skills. The men do not necessarily become close personal friends, but they must be compatible since they spend a
great deal of time together. Wherever possible, for example,
the department requires that wagon teams be racially integrated. Each sergeant tries out different combinations until
he finds two men who get along. These forced coalitions
rarely develop into friendships that extend outside of working

[6]Cliques and coalitions are common features of many work situations
and they are not linked exclusively to the needs of preserving secrecy
or disguising illicit behavior. See Whyte, *Social Relations in the Restaurant Industry*, pp. 311–51. For a discussion of cliques in industrial
settings among workers and at the management level, see Dalton,
pp. 52–68; and George C. Homans, *The Human Group* (New York,
Harcourt, Brace, 1950), pp. 70–2, 132–45.

hours, but the men manage, they discuss their family lives and their personal problems. It is understood that partners will not discuss with third parties any work in which they are mutually engaged. If the partnership is a voluntary coalition, the men often become close personal friends, exchanging family visits and spending a good deal of their free time doing things together. When this happens, they become the objects of continuing ridicule by their colleagues, who use any opportunity to question the true nature of the relationship.

If the sergeant is free to select his own wagon teams, these men usually become his closest associates in the platoon. They are the men he depends on to conduct surveillances for him, to develop sources of information, and to make the vice arrests which are necessary to preserve the platoon's stability and autonomy. Any information he has from a private source he shares only with these men, if he shares it with anyone. If he is taking money, his wagon crews usually pick it up for him. The bond between the wagon crew and their sergeant is strong and stable so long as they mutually support one another. The special relationship that exists between them is acknowledged by all platoon members. If the sergeant is absent, it is usually one of these men who makes out the assignment sheets and conducts the roll call.

Platoon members who do not have the knowledge and experience to qualify as a close associate of their sergeant frequently establish coalitions with colleagues who are in a similar situation. Even if they do not partner, these men often develop close personal connections. Their relationships frequently are dominated by strong personal loyalties, although they are also used to protect and improve the members' places in their unit. If one of them gets some information, he will ask his friend to share the rewards with him by going on the raid and participating in the arrests. The security and privacy of these relationships are also used to let the members freely express their frustrations, antagonisms, and opinions of others which, if spoken publicly, might result in difficulties with their colleagues.

There are men in every squad who do not develop any close connections to others. Rookies and men who are newly transferred have nothing to offer that can serve as the basis for any relationship. Some men are "loners" who do not want any friends, while others are viewed as being too dangerous in the way they work to be worth the risks of association. There are also veteran squad members who are widely admired but reject overtures to join coalitions or cliques. A man may have been a sergeant's intimate too often to any longer be interested in carrying the burdens close association requires. These men are usually approaching retirement age and are serving under sergeants who are much their junior in age and experience.

Most younger men actively seek out coalitions, however, in order to increase their usefulness to their sergeant. Some of these are short-lived agreements organized to exploit a temporary situation. An inexperienced man may accidentally obtain some vice information that he cannot verify or does not know how to use. He may give the information to his sergeant, hoping to be remembered for the effort, or he may seek out the aid of someone with experience who will share the credit and appreciation that may result from their mutual effort. Several platoon members may agree to handle collusively some matter that has come to their attention, developing the information before presenting it to their sergeant.

Nobody under the sergeant's command may make a vice arrest requiring a warrant without his permission. This gives him a veto over almost all gambling arrests. Some men will not approach their sergeant directly with a request but will first make informal inquiries among the men known to be close to the sergeant. The sergeant's authority allows him to screen the actions of his men before they can do anything potentially embarrassing. It also allows him to control whom they can arrest. This authority may be easily exploited for personal enrichment, but it also serves to protect the men from errors. If a sergeant feels, for example, that a patrolman is not sufficiently experienced to give proper testimony on cross examination in court, he will direct a more experienced man to take out the warrant and go to court.

The operations crew does not form a clique, although individual members may have close associations with some of the men on the street, doing them little favors whenever possible. Although the crew spends more time together than any other people in the police department, they have no interests that are served by such an association. They, too, may establish volatile coalitions for a short-lived specific purpose, but their central location in the squad and their extensive knowledge of its work obliges them to represent no one but their sergeant and lieutenant.

When a new man enters a squad, he is not ignored, but his access to what is going on is carefully regulated. There is no way to know what a rookie is like except to watch him work, to listen to him in court, and gradually to extract his opinions on the nature of the job and the district. He is rarely spoken to before roll calls, and if he enters a conversational circle unbidden, his presence reduces the men to silence. His colleagues are civil to him, they are willing to answer many of his questions, but they will not discuss with him anything about the work they do on the street. They do not dislike him, but they most certainly do not trust him. When all rookies walked beats, it was possible to isolate new men completely, but the radio patrol car has made this impossible. A rookie sees men working on the street, he goes on calls with them, and they come to his aid when he needs help. He must be sounded out quickly.

Several patrolmen stood by the open door of the expensive sedan that had been abandoned in the middle of the street. The ignition key was broken off in the lock, clothes were strewn all over the back seat of the car, and cassette tapes of popular music had fallen out of the open door onto the street. It was 3 A.M. A wagon pulled up. There had been no call for it, but it was the hour when any job attracted the attention of men who wanted to stay awake. The driver and his rookie partner approached. The officers talked for a few minutes, idly speculating about who might have left the car. The rookie stood slightly apart, listening. The wagon man bent down and picked up several tapes. "Here, kid, take a present home to your wife." The young man did not react immediately, but the wagon man did not take his smiling eyes from the rookie's face. He finally accepted them. "O.K., kid, let's go back to fighting crime," the veteran said, turning away without directly acknowledging the young policeman's acceptance of the stolen property. It was impossible to tell from the young man's look whether he realized that he had just committed a felony.

When a man is transferred from another district, it is possible to know something about him, and the squad loses no time in learning what they can. The lieutenant and the sergeants are informed by the captain of the reasons for the man's transfer, but unless they feel it is important to the well-being of the squad, the members are not informed. But the men have ways of finding out for themselves.[7]

During a coffee break in his second day in a district, a patrolman explained to several colleagues the reason for his transfer. He said that his sergeant had been after him and finally falsely accused him of having slept on duty. He admitted that he had been tired—it was last out; the others nodded sympathetically—and had parked his car at the curb on a main intersection to take a rest. He said that he had not gone to sleep or even put his head back on the seat. As the man got up to return to work, one of his new colleagues said to him, "Listen, fella, nobody sleeps in this district," a lie which the man who uttered it knew would be quickly discovered. After the man left, the other continued, "I don't give a fuck what he does but he ain't makin' a cunt out of us. The corporal spoke with a friend of his in the 65th [district] who told him that the kid went down three times after the sergeant warned him. The last time he caught him, he was stretched out. The guy said he's a dumb fuck and I agree."

Unless there is any reason to suspect that a new man is a gink, anything he might have done elsewhere will not be held against him by his new colleagues. But he must pass through a period when he knows little of what is going on around him. These men are anxious to pass through their period of trial because they know they are missing a great deal of action and are being denied access to the real life of their new squad. This period of adjustment and trial is not restricted only to patrolmen. A corporal was assigned to replace a man who had been severely injured, forcing his retirement. The injured man had been corporal for several years; his colleagues felt considerable affection for him. One night after the new cor-

[7] A patrolman had been transferred from another district because of an entanglement with a woman. It was his first day in the new district; a sergeant introduced him to his lieutenant. "I hear you think you're quite a lover," the lieutenant growled, glaring at the man. The man stammered. "Well, I got news for you, pal. You've got plenty of competition in this squad." They both laughed.

poral had been in the squad about a month, he stood up from his desk and stared at the other men in the operations room. He glanced down at the paper in his hand and then said to the crew, "You see these stripes? I'm the corporal—now why the fuck doesn't anyone tell me what's going on around here?" The men muffled their laughter until he had stalked from the room.

Cliques and coalitions are helpful in reducing personal antagonisms so that they do not develop into open conflicts that can disrupt the unity every platoon requires. Men are free to vent their opinions of others among close associates, but if they seek to enlarge their differences in direct confrontations with colleagues, they are inviting sanctions from their sergeant. The sergeant must actively work to prevent the development of factional disputes by muting personal antagonisms and distributing rewards and favors to all the men who earn them. He uses his opportunities, which arise daily, to move men around, to give them a different assignment as a breather (as well as a reprimand), or to move men out of each other's way. If this is not sufficient to stop disputes, he must choose between the two antagonists and rid himself of the man he considers less useful to him. The men understand this, and although fist fights and even shootings are not unknown among policemen, open hostility is infrequently expressed.

Colleagues actively seek to neutralize personal antagonisms and tensions arising from suspicion of each other by placing themselves in the debt of others through a continual disclosure of indiscretions, which could be damaging if revealed to persons outside the unit. Although a man's time is his own, his colleagues are frequently very well informed about his private life. Many men willingly discuss their personal affairs with others, knowing full well that what they say will become the common property of the platoon, if not the entire squad. There are outings, parties, and nights on the town that serve as occasions for marital infidelities and sexual performances. These moments are frequently recalled, each man reminding the others of what he knows about their doings, and also recalling to them his own vulnerability as evidence of his loyalty and faith.[8]

[8]For examples of mutual disclosure, see Radano, pp. 15–19, 167–81.

Colleagues must also exercise care not to violate each other's jurisdictional rights. Whenever men come together to do a piece of work that is not an emergency, they will defer to the man on whose sector the assignment is located. (If it is an emergency, the first man at the scene is in charge of the job.) If someone tries to take over an assignment which another man is doing, even if he is trying to be helpful, he will be rebuffed, unless he first obtains the man's permission. Poaching on another man's sector is forbidden, and unless it is checked when discovered, it can destroy a squad. A man found collecting information, taking activity, or hustling money on another man's sector, regardless of his status in the platoon, has no defense. He is open to a tongue-lashing and quite possibly a fist fight. If the sergeant does not punish poaching, he risks the complete disruption of his command.

The tensions that develop among men who are dependent upon persons from whom they are constantly withholding information and trying to keep secrets are also relieved by an almost continual joking. Prior to roll calls, in the locker room and in the roll room, practical joking and the trading of insults are normal features of squad life. Their absence is a good sign of serious problems in a unit, indicating considerable insecurity among the men. Anything is fair game for comment, ethnicity and race being the most common objects for humorous attacks, closely followed by personal appearance and sexual behavior.[9]

Mutual disclosures, jurisdictional etiquette, and humorous deprecations are usually sufficient to silence most antagonisms. In one squad, two men who had been colleagues for many years gradually developed an intense dislike for each other. They were in different platoons but both were important and valued members of the squad. They rarely spoke to each other directly, although they were in contact daily and continued to attend squad functions together. In private they did not miss an opportunity to denounce each other in the strongest terms—each implying serious doubts about the moral

[9]On the functions of humor in small groups, see Tom Burns, "Friends, Enemies, and the Polite Fiction," *American Sociological Review*, Vol. XVIII (1953), pp. 654–62; and Don Handelman, Bruce Kapferer, "Forms of Joking Activity: A Comparative Approach," *American Anthropologist*, Vol. 74 (1972), pp. 484–517. For examples, Radano, pp. 65–9, 151–6.

character of the other—but in their face-to-face dealings they remained absolutely correct. The lieutenant, who was a close friend of one of the men, did not allow the conflict to directly affect his relations with either man. Very few members of the squad knew of their dislike for each other. This situation persisted for many months without a single incident occurring between them. It was finally terminated when one of the men obtained a transfer to a special unit that he wanted to join. Men who openly express their dislike and contempt for colleagues run the risk of finding themselves at another time under the person's authority or command. Personal antagonisms are common among supervisors in the middle and upper ranks of the department. This is one reason why an intimate knowledge of personnel is important for any successful chief.

Most younger men in a platoon, established but eager for advancement and impatient with a system of achievement they do not fully understand and are not prepared for by their training, are always on edge with their senior colleagues. They consider the men who work in the operations room their inferiors because they are viewed as clerks who do not have to take the risks required of men who work the street. Whenever they give expression to their feelings, these men are careful not to relinquish their bantering tone. There are jokes about when was the last time any of the men have seen their guns, where they left their sticks, and whether rust has ruined their handcuffs. The patrolmen are careful not to reveal their real feelings (well known to the men in the operations room since they once had the same attitudes) and risk compromising their connections with the men who have the means of easing or increasing burdens in ways that do not require the sergeant's permission.

One night in a bar a drunk, off-duty policeman began to berate two patrolmen when he learned they were from a special unit which he disliked. Although they were angered by his remarks, they controlled their tempers, mainly because they were wearing their police trousers, having just finished work, which was a violation of department rules. (Policemen are forbidden to appear in public wearing only a portion of their uniform. This rule is designed to discourage a man from taking off his shirt or jacket and slipping into some place for drinks or some private business. This is also why some police trousers have wide stripes down the seams.) If they became involved in an incident that attracted official attention, they could get into serious trouble. After a minute one of them interrupted the drunken police officer. "Hey, Chief, how long you been working inside?" The startled drunk replied, "Two years. Hey, how'd you know I work inside?" and staggered away. The officer took his hand off the black-jack in his back pocket and grinned. "The guys who work the street in his district don't love us, but they don't say things like that about us."

The patrolman's obligations to respect his sergeant's arrangements conflict with his jealousy of men who have better assignments than he, despite the fact that he is possibly doing more work. Any feelings of resentment are usually kept concealed, because there is little that any man can do except to try and advance himself, get a transfer, or pass a civil-service test and be promoted. When the sergeant is absent, his arrangements continue unquestioned. Without any formal announcement, one of his close associates assumes the routine administrative duties that must be performed daily. Even if a replacement sergeant has been assigned, he will allow the regular sergeant's colleague to make up the daily assignment sheet and frequently even conduct the roll call. Sometimes the man will offer men who have no steady assignment a choice of what is available, testing them to see what they are interested in doing. Most men decline to commit themselves and allow their boss to give them what he wants. The men kid him about his role, occasionally calling him "sergeant," even saluting him, which is something they rarely do for their real boss. This is as much a reminder of his lack of formal authority as it is a modest acknowledgment of his informal but real power.

If a senior colleague seeks to exercise his authority, however, even in the interests of the platoon, the younger men may bridle and express the discontent that they constantly feel but dare not express to their sergeant. However, they must be careful not to demonstrate their disrespect in a way that is sufficiently strong to warrant a complaint against them and cause their sergeant to punish them for disrespect upon his return.

One afternoon an "acting sergeant" mentioned to his platoon that several men had left early the previous day without informing him. He did not mention any names. This is a violation that no policeman would commit against his sergeant unless he wanted to be punished. It is so fundamental a breach of courtesy and authority that it would normally be punished in a formal way. The acting sergeant passed over the insult to himself and said, "I don't mind personally, but if it happens someone were here checking on us, it might not look good for the platoon, so keep that in mind." Although he had patiently waited for the lieutenant to leave the room before admonishing them, his statement produced an open exchange of sneering among four younger men standing directly in front of him. Nothing more was said of the incident, but nobody called him sergeant again, nor did anyone leave early without permission.

The next afternoon one of the four men was assigned to walk a beat. He was one of the more important younger men in the platoon and was well thought of by his sergeant, who was waiting for him to settle down before giving him a permanent sector. As he entered the roll room, the acting sergeant called out to him, allowing everyone to hear, "Rawls, you're on beat one until the sergeant returns." Rawls had not been required to walk a beat for months. He nodded and said, "O.K.," and then, turning to a friend, mumbled his true sentiments, "Fuck him, I don't give a shit." The platoon was so short of men, however, that the beat was canceled and he did not have to walk. It is possible that the exchange was arranged as a warning to all of the younger men in the platoon, reminding them of their obligations and what awaited them along the path of rebellion, no matter how mild.

The sergeant's authority is not transferable because it is dependent on his personal relationships with his men. The men honor the rank and do not violate it, but they do not perform the work necessary for the platoon's overall success because he orders it. The patrolman refers to his sergeant and to all of the supervisors with whom he has direct contact, regardless of rank, as his boss. He sees his relationship to them in personal terms. Although recruits are taught how to salute while at the police academy (and most patrolmen have served in the military) and they are told that they should salute their superiors, it is uncommon in the districts to see a man's rank honored by this sign of formal recognition. There are some supervisors who demand to be "highballed" and their wish is grudgingly granted, but most supervisors forgo the privilege. It is unusual for anyone to salute at roll call. While the sergeant still uses some traditional military jargon to maintain parade order and discipline— "dress right dress" and "attention to orders"—these are not issued in the form of commands, the men are not expected to respond in a unified, formal manner, and at the conclusion of roll call they simply break ranks and walk out, rather than march from the station.

In the presence of his own men, a sergeant does not hesitate to first-name those with whom he is friendly. If he is angry at someone he usually first-names, he may emphasize his feelings by calling the man by his family name. The men who are allowed to first-name the sergeant in private do not do so at roll call, but all the men in a platoon know who these men are and that they are allowed to exercise this privilege. In the presence of his men, a sergeant will not first-name his lieutenant, although in private their relationship is maintained on a personal basis, unless they are enemies. The lieutenant, however, does not refrain from first-naming his sergeant, often in the presence of the men, and they rarely give each other salutes.

Only in the anticrime units is anything like formal military discipline maintained. At their roll calls there is never any first-naming; the men salute at the conclusion of orders. Equipment checks and pistol inspections are common, the sergeant following his lieutenant down the line in standard military fashion. The men do not disperse at the end of roll call but march from the roll room, in a single line. On the street these men give their supervisors a salute when they meet, and they do not refer to their sergeant as "Sarge." The district men are aware of this formal attentiveness, which they consider to be "chickenshit" and additional evidence of the peculiar mentality of the men in these units.

At the conclusion of every tour of duty, each man is required personally to turn over his patrol log and report forms to his sergeant. At this sign-off the men are supposed to salute their superior in a formal manner, ceremonially requesting permission to be dismissed. Many men still offer some kind of salute, often in a jocular, half-mocking manner, but it is rare that a sergeant even notices or returns the salute. He is usually too busy assembling the paper work being turned over to him, making sure that everything he is supposed to have from each man has been given to him.

The sergeant does not lead his men into their work, he supervises them. He needs their active cooperation or he will be a failure. Every sergeant understands this. If his men dislike him or feel that he is not competent, there is no way he can force them to do the work in a way that will satisfy the captain and the inspector. If the men are working well and doing the things that keep the captain and the lieutenant happy, he will let them get away with many things which he personally disapproves but does not consider worthwhile fighting over. One Sunday afternoon a sergeant pulled into a concealed area, where he found most of his platoon taking the sun and actively engaged in a card game. The cars were lined up, and one man was assigned to listen to the radio for any calls. The sergeant did not get out of his car but just looked at the scene. The men stopped playing for a moment, but nobody made any move to leave. "You fuckin' guys are nuts. If some captain finds you, I'm not takin' any responsibility for this." The men laughed and waved as he drove away. "He's the best. You do your job for him and do it right, he lets you alone," the dealer commented, shuffling the deck.

Perhaps supervisors would like to have the authority people attribute to their rank, but they do not. However, the public continues to believe that the police are organized in a formal hierarchy, each man responding to the authority of rank. "Hello, Lieutenant," the girl said, approaching the parked car. She was well known to the district men; she was a famous cop-fucker. They chatted for a few moments and then the girl asked, "Lieutenant, you're higher than a sergeant, right? That's what I thought. So if you gave a sergeant an order he would have to do what you tell him? Well, would you tell Sergeant Smith to let me blow him? If you told him, he would have to, right? And I really would like to."

The compromising and questionable character of some obligations increases the mutal dependence of the supervisors and their men, but it is not simply violations of the law and of administrative regulations that narrow the distance between them. Any supervisor who seeks to keep open the distance between himself and his men risks losing their esteem and affection. There are supervisors who oblige their subordinates to meet every formal obligation to the letter and do not allow any of the men to swear in their presence. These supervisors are obeyed, but if ever they get into any kind of trouble, they cannot depend on their men to aid them. Most sergeants and lieutenants constantly seek to minimize the distance between themselves and the patrolmen. They disdain formal respect, use dirty language, ignore petty violations, and even encourage some disregard for the law in minor matters in order to foster camaraderie and a feeling of solidarity. They feel uncomfortable if their men regard them as superiors. They just want to be treated as the boss, the source of favors and rewards.

The men must understand, however, that they are not the equals of their sergeant, and any failure to give him his due will be treated harshly. When a new sergeant takes over a platoon, there is a period of adjustment, which can be marked by conflicts while the men negotiate with their new boss and forget the habits and arrangements of their old boss, who may be mourned but is rapidly forgotten. The transition is usually eased by the transfer of the men who were intimately involved in the running of the platoon. It is during these periods that a sergeant is most likely to exercise his authority to take a man to the front. "The first day I had this platoon, two guys walked in late for roll call without calling up or nothin'. I told 'em right in front of everyone, 'You're goin'.' They almost shit. I wasn't kiddin' either. I made out the papers and took them into the captain. He knocked it down after callin' them in and talkin' to them. I didn't care, but I wanted them to know that they weren't gonna walk on me. They learned. I haven't had any trouble with them since," a sergeant said. These crises of adjustment pass quickly, but far more serious are the conflicts that erupt between supervisors who are struggling for control over a platoon or a squad. Then everyone is fearful because the unity of the squad is destroyed; all are aware that any infraction may be turned against them, used to force their loyalty in one direction or another.

A new lieutenant was appointed to head a squad that had fallen to last place among the four squads in a district in all activity categories. A new sergeant took command of one platoon, while the other remained under the direction of its veteran supervisor. The veteran saw that his position was threatened and began to pressure his men for activity. During the past months he had come into conflict with several of them, depriving them of their regular sectors and subjecting them to extra assignments and special duty. They were angry and demoralized, hopeful that the new lieutenant would eventually get the sergeant transferred and relieve them of what they saw as an onerous burden. The other men, loyal to the sergeant, viewed the lieutenant as a threat to their position; open hostility began to emerge. The men knew the sergeant was on weak ground and refused to produce activity for him. The less they did, the more pressure he exerted on the recalcitrants. On a Sunday morning he approached one of the men he most disliked and ordered him to take out a warrant for a lottery investigation. The man responded by going home sick and staying sick for the remainder of the daywork shift. He said he had plenty of work to do around the house.

The lieutenant sought to avoid open conflict with the sergeant and urged the men at roll calls to produce for him. The sergeant was rumored to be a good friend of the divisional inspector and the lieutenant did not want to be caught in the middle of a conflict which could end up with his being the villain; he tried to stay neutral. The sergeant and the inspector were both black and the lieutenant was white. The conflict was not racial, although this dimension could not be overlooked. After several months the inspector was retired and the sergeant transferred to another district. The lieutenant was quite pleased and reflected, "Sure he was no good any more, but I wasn't gonna try and push him out. Look, I'm white and he's a Negro. All I need is to get a reputation for being anti-Negro and I'm through in this department. I intend to be around for a lot more years and I don't want to be a lieutenant forever. So I took his shit and waited for someone else to push him out. They did."

Before his departure there were some remarkable fireworks that caused the platoon to cease functioning as a unit. One morning as the sergeant was finishing roll call, the lieutenant stalked into the room, his face flushed. The sergeant took one look at him and, without a word, moved aside. "Men," the lieutenant said, "anyone in the police department that puts his feelings on paper is going to get himself fucked. If you got a beef with someone, don't write a memo, go to the man and try and get it straightened out." The room was absolutely silent, the men staring straight ahead. "Maybe we haven't understood each other, but as long as I have been here, everybody has gotten what he wanted from me when I was able to get it. Nobody was ever denied anything and I have never threatened anyone with time for not making a vice pinch." He turned and headed for the door, paused, and said with a wan smile, "Remember, it's daywork—think vice," and walked out the door.

The sergeant dismissed the men without a comment. Everyone understood that one of them had written a memo to the captain, accusing the lieutenant of threatening to give him punishment work if he failed to make a vice arrest. The men walked from the station house without speaking to each other, barely exchanging glances, and got into their cars to spend the day finding out who was trying to undermine the lieutenant.

"Oh shit, man, it's days like today that I'm glad I'm clean. I don't know who did it, probably one of those guys close to the creep. I don't know, they aren't the kind to drop a dime in public. Maybe make a phone call or write a letter, but not a memo. As much as I hate that creep sergeant, all the shit I've seen him do, I couldn't drop a dime on him. I just couldn't live with myself. But think if a guy would fuck his lieutenant, what do you think he'd do to us, man? Baby, I am so glad we are clean. At Christmas I ain't so glad, but today I am," Raymond said to his partner.

There was hardly any contact among the men during that tour and nothing was said about the lieutenant's speech. Everyone waited for the disclosure they knew would come. The captain's clerk would see the memo and he would tell the corporal, who in turn would inform everyone else. The lieutenant also would not neglect to inform his allies in the platoon of the dangerous man in their midst.

The affair was not mentioned again publicly. The lieutenant and the sergeant privately confronted the man, urging a withdrawal of his charges. The man insisted on seeing the captain, who was reliably and widely reported to have told him to take his memo and "stick it." He then graciously accepted a clarifying memorandum from the officer explaining that his charges were the result of an unfortunate misunderstanding. The sergeant sought to keep the platoon together by rallying to the lieutenant's defense, supporting him before the men. He tried unsuccessfully to use the shock of betrayal to rally solidarity and regain mastery over the men before he lost control. "This used to be the best platoon in the district. Now it's getting the reputation as the shit squad, everyone wants to leave. If we all work together, we can make it number one again, but we gotta work together." The disaffected did not want to work with him or with a man who might betray them at any moment—and not just to their captain.

The lieutenant ranted in private against the man who had dimed him. "That little cocksucker, he doesn't know what it is to be a policeman. All he does is write tickets, nothin' but a fuckin' traffic cop. I know he never shows up first on calls. He's always takin' his time. He's nothin'. I know it's rough in this district. There isn't a white cop who wants to be here. But there's a job to be done and we are the ones who have to do it. If that prick thinks he's gonna get a transfer, he's nuts. He's gonna learn how to be a cop. I don't have anything to hide from him."

The accused was a loner and he remained isolated from the others. The sergeant's supporters were hopeful that the lieutenant would get in trouble, but they despised and feared the methods employed by their colleague. They shunned him as did the lieutenant's supporters. "He'll get all the shit in the world. Traffic post in the morning, all the details the prick used to give me. He'll get extra work and no breaks. If he calls in sick, they'll sick-check him twice a day. You think those guys have to use their sick time when they're off?" an angry and frightened man said.

This incident was not important. It did not leave the district. There had been no accusation of corruption, no complaint to the ginks, no investigation involving concealed surveillances, tapped telephones, interrogations, credit investigations, and threats. Yet every man in the squad was frightened, even the men who had never taken a note during their careers. Nobody was in danger of being arrested, yet each man behaved as if he might be sent to the wall at any minute.

The patrolman has no choice over who his colleagues are. If he gets into trouble, there is nobody to defend him, except his sergeant and lieutenant. If they dislike him, he is not likely to escape punishment. If he seeks to escape them because he disapproves of their conduct, his efforts will be noted, and wherever he goes, a reputation will precede him. If he complains officially of some misconduct, he will be known as a gink, feared by everyone, even the men who privately despise the doings he reported. Men who do not know him, do not know what "really" happened, will know that he dropped a dime and will avoid him.

The policeman needs the support of his colleagues. It is not only that he needs them to come to his aid when his safety and well-being are threatened; he needs their understanding. They are the only ones who have "been there"; they are the only ones who know the ambiguities of the trade and require no lengthy explanations and excuses in the recounting of his experiences. In exchange for this understanding, every man who chooses to remain a policeman will put up with a great deal.

The policeman also understands how little power he really has. The person he stops on the street may think him an awesome figure, but the patrolman knows that he is just an armed servant who can be easily dismissed and replaced. Few policemen have any knowledge of city politics, or even police politics beyond the boundaries of their own district; most men do not know whom to turn to for counsel and support when they are troubled by something they have witnessed. Those who do, the smart, the well connected, are generally not men inclined to take risks. Many politicians and journalists have advanced their careers by exposing police wrongdoings, but few of the policemen who have become enmeshed in these crusades have endured in the business. The reforms always seem to stagnate, the reformers go on to higher office or withdraw to powerless but prestigious positions, but the men who "betrayed" the department are not forgotten by their colleagues. Experienced policemen believe they understand the "score," and rather than risk a rash act that might strip them of their position and leave them with few possibilities other than a return to the kind of work they left, they prefer to live with the contradictions of their job.

INDEX

abandoned cars, 142–44, 225

absenteeism, produced by last out, 67

activity, in police work, 44–54

alcoholism, among policemen, 422

anticrime units, military discipline in, 449

anti-sniper unit, 288

arson, 201

assault, 45

assist-officer call, 81–82, 101

automatic weapons, 288

auto theft, *see* car theft

"bad apple" theory, 403

"bagman," 375, 397, 410

bank robberies, 65

bartenders, as source of information, 207

Bentham, Jeremy, 10, 370

blackjack, 281; policeman's use of, 281–84, 290, 295

bomb alert, 121

Boston, 12, 16

bribery of police, *see* taking

Brooklyn (N.Y.), 15, 379; police in, 12; roundsmen in, during nineteenth century, 15

brothels, 373

buildings: abandoned, 144–48; investigated for prowlers, 296

burglar alarms, 16–17, 354–55

burglary, 66, 144, 206–7, 334, 341, 342, 345, 347, 355n, 372; calls involving, 100–1, 349, 431; defined, 345n; as Part I crime, 45

Burnham, David, quoted, 403

businessmen: organized protection for, 409; as sources of information, 204, 205n

cab drivers: policeman's attitude toward, 196; robbery of, 356,

357; as sources of information, 204

call box, 15–18; telephone introduced into, 16, 17

"capmen," 248

captain of police, 29–32, 34, 44, 52, 53, 54, 56, 80, 415, 418, 443, 454; district directed by, 23–24

car accidents, 96–97

car stops, 44, 47–48, 49, 59, 66, 249–60, 264, 298, 307–10, 352, 365; damaged, 152–53

car theft, 45, 250, 251, 255, 262, 265, 334, 345; as Part I crime, 45

Chadwick, Edwin, 10

check-cashing agencies, 140

Chicago, 50n, 378; gambling arrests in, 379; police districts in, 24

Christmas money, 413, 414, 422

Cincinnati, 379

city ordinance, violation of, 45

clearance rates, 48, 343n, 363

collusions and obligations, 102–23

Colquhoun, Patrick, 10, 182n, quoted, 370–71

Commission on Law Enforcement and Administration of Justice, President's, 22n, 25n, 205n, 346n, 347n

common law, 213n, 224, 234n

concealed weapons, 245–49; frisking for, 271

console crew, 73–74, 77, 102

Constables, English, 3, 4, 7, 8, 9, 11

Constitution, U.S., 122, 377, 385–86

contraband, 245, 246, 250, 253, 254, 310n, 392

control: of people, 302–17 *passim*; of space, 290–302 *passim*

convoy (round jack), policeman's use of, 281–82

"coops," 18n

457